VISUAL QUICKSTART GUIDE

Photoshop 7

FOR WINDOWS AND MACINTOSH

Elaine Weinmann
Peter Lourekas

 **Peachpit Press**

For Theodora Lourekas, our brilliant, beloved yia-yia

Visual QuickStart Guide
Photoshop 7 for Windows and Macintosh
Elaine Weinmann and Peter Lourekas

Peachpit Press
1249 Eighth Street
Berkeley, CA 94710
510/524-2178
800/283-9444
510/524-2221 (fax)

Find us on the World Wide Web at: http://www.peachpit.com

Visual QuickStart Guide is a trademark of Peachpit Press, a division of Pearson Education

Cover design: The Visual Group
Interior design: Elaine Weinmann
Production: Elaine Weinmann and Peter Lourekas
Illustrations: Elaine Weinmann and Peter Lourekas, except as noted
Editor: Cary Norsworthy
Production Coordinator: Lisa Brazieal

Colophon
This book was created with QuarkXPress 5 on a Power Macintosh 8500 and a Power PowerTower Pro 200. The primary fonts used were New Baskerville, Franklin Gothic, Gill Sans, and CaflischScript from Adobe Systems Inc.

ISBN 0-201-88284-1

9 8 7 6 5 4

Printed and bound in the United States of America

Acknowledgements

"PIECE-A-CAKE," said Peter, after taking his first peek at the Photoshop 7 upgrade. "We'll get it done in time to have the whole summer off," he added, smiling and polishing his golf clubs.

"Hah!" said Elaine, with a sneer. "Don't kid yourself. Every single screen shot has to be redone for Mac OS X. Like, hello?"

"We'll get somebody to do that," said Peter.

"Good, glad you got that covered. Now, what about the gazillion nitpicky changes that nobody talks about? They add a word next to a check box here, expand the range in a palette there… Next thing you know, it's the end of September, your golf clubs are rusty, the distributors are tearing their hair out, and Nancy Ruenzel's had a cow."

"Victor will help us," said Peter.

"Glad Mr. Smarty will be on board," said Elaine. "One more minor detail. We need to cover new features: Brushes palette, File Browser, Pattern Maker, Match, 'boo-boo' brushes—blah, blah, blah, blah…"

"Jump to" end of July. Book's done. We worked hard—and we had help! Our sincere thanks to the following people:

Nancy Aldrich-Ruenzel, Publisher, Peachpit Press, for trusting that we'd get it done.

Marjorie Baer, Executive Editor, for pointing us to helpful resources.

Cary Norsworthy, Editor, for her competence, resourcefulness, and sense of humor under pressure.

Victor Gavenda, Technical Editor at Peachpit Press, for testing the book in Windows and revising several chapters, complete with witty remarks and great catches.

Lisa Brazieal, Production Coordinator, for getting our electronic files ready for the print shop.

Gary-Paul Prince, Publicist.

Keasley Jones, Associate Publisher.

Nathalie Valette, cover designer.

All the other *Peachpitters*. We know you're there.

Nolan Hester, Nathan Olson, and *Conrad Chavez,* freelance writers, for helping us revise various chapters.

Jeffy Milstead and *Steve Dampier,* for revising the keyboard shortcuts.

Haig MacGregor, Darren Meiss, and *William Rodarmor,* copy editors.

Steve Rath, indexer.

Lois Thompson and the crew at *Malloy Lithographing,* for a high-quality print job.

And the *Adobe Photoshop team,* for makin' Photoshop even better (keeps us busy).

The Artists

Jeff Brice
4510 171 Avenue S.E.
Snohomish, WA 98290
Voice 360-568-7924
jb@jeffbrice.com
www.jeffbrice.com
(color section)

Alicia Buelow
150a Mississippi Street
San Francisco, CA 94107
abuelow@sirius.com
www.aliciabuelow.com
(color section)

Stephanie Dalton Cowan
Toll free 877-792-7096
stephanie@daltoncowan.com
www.daltoncowan.com
(color section)

Wendy Grossman
355 West 51st Street
New York, NY 10019
Voice 949-362-1848
and 212-262-4497
wendygart@aol.com
www.rosebudstudios.com
(pages 70, 238, color section)

David Humphrey
448 West 16th Street, 5th fl.
New York, NY 10011
Voice 212-780-0512
aikenhump@aol.com
(page 131)

Alan Mazzetti
834 Moultrie Street
San Francisco, CA 94110
Voice 415-647-7677
maymaz@pacbell.net
www.amazzetti.com
(page 556, color section)

Walter Robertson
Walter Robertston Illustration
and Design
10 Tamarac Place
Aliso Viego, CA 92656
Voice 949-362-1848
info@walterrobertson.com
www.walterrobertson.com
(color section)

Naomi Shea
80 Montague Road
Shutesbury, MA 01073
Voice 413-268-3407
naomi@naomishea.com
www.naomishea.com
(page 520, color section)

Suling Wang
Voice 415-334-6273
Fax 801-751-4690
suling_wang@mindspring.com
www.sulingwang.com
(pages xxv, xxvi, color section)

WE STILL REMEMBER clearly how difficult it was to scrape a color gallery together for early editions of this book. We had to use overnight carriers to get artists' work. Then, once we got the files, they were incredibly cumbersome to store. We had to rely on the telephone for communication (so retro!), and to tell you the truth, there wasn't much great work being done yet in Photoshop. Electronic image editing was still in its infancy as an art form. Oh, what a difference a few years makes! The Internet has made viewing of artists' portfolios easy and it's a snap to transmit work as e-mail attachments or on itty bitty disks. Even more important, we have an awesome selection of artwork and artists to choose from! The hardest part was narrowing down the number of works to the 32 images we decided to showcase.

Directory of Artists

TABLE OF CONTENTS

Note: New or substantially changed features are listed in **boldface**.

Chapter 3: **Startup**

Chapter 4: **Pixel Basics**

Changing dimensions and resolution

Chapter 8: **History**

Using the History palette

Table of Contents

Chapter 12: **Paint**

Chapter 15: **Masks**

Table of Contents

Chapter 22: **Print**

Table of Contents

Table of Contents

Suling Wang, ©2000 Harper Collins Publishers

Suling Wang, ©2000 Harper Collins Publishers

THE BASICS 1

Tool tips

Rest the pointer on a tool icon—without clicking or pressing the mouse button—to learn that tool's name or shortcut **1**. Use the same method to learn the function of a palette or options bar feature **3**. (Check **Show Tool Tips** in Edit [Photoshop menu, in Mac OS X] > Preferences > General to enable this feature.)

Tool shortcuts

Hide/show the Toolbox and all open palettes	Tab
Cycle through hidden, related tools on the same pop-out menu	Shift and shortcut key *or* Alt-click/Option-click the currently visible tool icon
Cycle through blending modes for the current editing tool or layer	Shift + or Shift -

2 *To access the **Reset Tool** command for an individual tool or the **Reset All Tools** command for all tools, right-click/Control-click the tool thumbnail on the options bar.*

Using the Toolbox

To **choose** a tool whose icon is currently visible, click once on its icon. Click the tiny arrowhead next to a tool icon to choose a related tool from a pop-out palette.

Or even better, choose a tool using its shortcut (memorize the boldface letters on the next three pages). If you forget a tool's shortcut, just leave the cursor over the tool icon for a moment, and the tool tip will remind you **1**. To cycle through hidden, related tools on the same pop-out menu, press **Shift** and the same shortcut key or Alt-click/Option-click the currently visible tool.

Attributes are chosen for each tool (e.g., blending mode, opacity percentage) from the **options bar** at the top of your screen (read more about the options bar on page 5) **3**. Features on the bar change depending on which tool is selected.

Options bar settings remain in effect for an individual tool until they are changed or the tool is reset. You can save settings as presets in the new Tool Preset picker. To reset a tool to its defaults, right-click/Control-click the tool thumbnail on the options bar, then choose **Reset Tool** from the context menu **2**. To reset all tools, choose Reset All Tools from the same menu.

TIP Choose whether tool **pointers** look like their Toolbox icon or a crosshair in Edit (Photoshop, in OS X) > Preferences > Display & Cursors.

If you try to use a tool **incorrectly**, a cancel icon will appear. ⊘ Click in the image window to make an explanation appear.

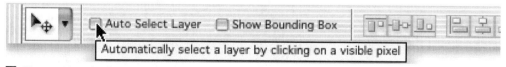

3 *Choose options for the current tool from the **options bar** at the top of your screen.*

Toolbox

*Use **Shift** to access related tools on the same pop-out menu. For example, to cycle through the Lasso, Polygonal Lasso, and Magnetic Lasso tools, hold down Shift and keep pressing "L".*

Click here to go to the Adobe Web site

Rectangular marquee M
Creates rectangular selections

Lasso L
Creates freehand selections

Crop C
Crops the canvas

7.0! **Healing Brush J**
Corrects flaws

Clone Stamp S
Clones imagery

Eraser E
Erases pixels

Blur R
Blurs edges

Path Selection A
Selects paths

Pen P
Draws curved or straight paths

Notes N
Creates non-printing annotations

Hand H
Moves the image in its window

V Move
Moves a layer, selection, or guide

W Magic Wand
Selects similarly colored pixels

K Slice
Slices images for the Web

B Brush
Applies brushstrokes

Y History Brush
Restores pixels from a designated state

G Gradient
Creates color blends

O Dodge
Lightens pixels

T Horizontal Type
Creates editable type on its own layer

U Rectangle
Draws rectangular shapes

I Eyedropper
Samples colors from the image

Z Zoom
Changes the zoom level

X Switch foreground/ background colors

Foreground color square

Background color square

Default colors D
Black and white

Standard mode Q

Q Quick Mask mode

Standard windows F

F Full screen with no menu bar

F Full screen with menu bar

Jump to ImageReady
(Ctrl-Shift-M/Cmd-Shift-M)

The Toolbox

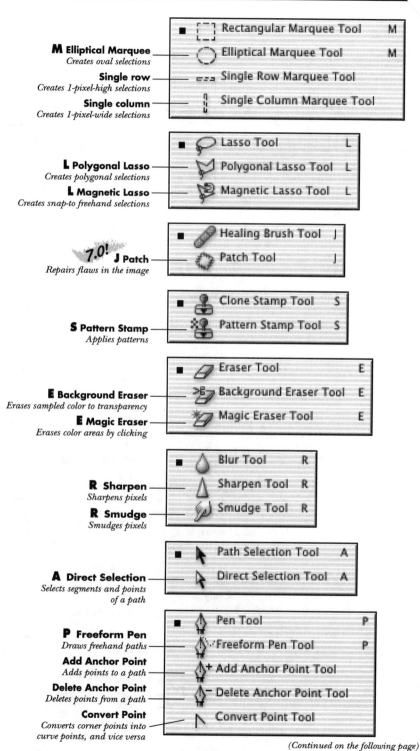

M Elliptical Marquee
Creates oval selections

Single row
Creates 1-pixel-high selections

Single column
Creates 1-pixel-wide selections

Rectangular Marquee Tool   M
Elliptical Marquee Tool   M
Single Row Marquee Tool
Single Column Marquee Tool

L Polygonal Lasso
Creates polygonal selections

L Magnetic Lasso
Creates snap-to freehand selections

Lasso Tool   L
Polygonal Lasso Tool   L
Magnetic Lasso Tool   L

7.0! **J Patch**
Repairs flaws in the image

Healing Brush Tool   J
Patch Tool   J

S Pattern Stamp
Applies patterns

Clone Stamp Tool   S
Pattern Stamp Tool   S

E Background Eraser
Erases sampled color to transparency

E Magic Eraser
Erases color areas by clicking

Eraser Tool   E
Background Eraser Tool   E
Magic Eraser Tool   E

R Sharpen
Sharpens pixels

R Smudge
Smudges pixels

Blur Tool   R
Sharpen Tool   R
Smudge Tool   R

A Direct Selection
Selects segments and points of a path

Path Selection Tool   A
Direct Selection Tool   A

P Freeform Pen
Draws freehand paths

Add Anchor Point
Adds points to a path

Delete Anchor Point
Deletes points from a path

Convert Point
Converts corner points into curve points, and vice versa

Pen Tool   P
Freeform Pen Tool   P
Add Anchor Point Tool
Delete Anchor Point Tool
Convert Point Tool

Tool Pop-Up Palettes

(Continued on the following page)

Annotate

The **Notes** tool creates non-printing Acrobat-compatible notes, which can be used for communicating with a client, output service, etc. **1** When you click a note icon, a note window containing the message opens. The **Audio Annotation** tool creates audio notes.

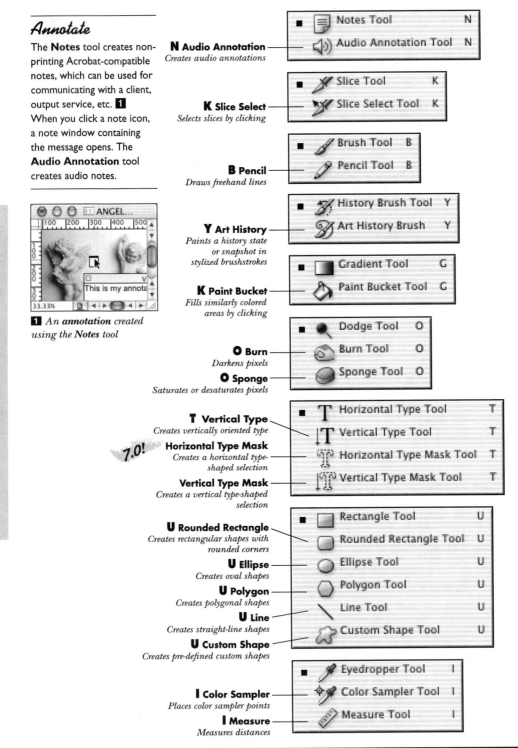

1 *An* **annotation** *created using the* **Notes** *tool*

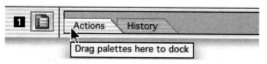

Palette well

On the right side of the options bar is an area called the **palette well** that you can dock (store) palettes in. To do this, drag the palette into the well or choose **Dock to Palette Well** from any palette menu.

If a tool is associated with a palette (e.g., the Brushes palette is used with the Pencil tool; the Character palette is used with the type tools), you can click the **Toggle palette** button **1** to show or hide that palette when that tool is selected.

Options bar

The options bar is used to choose settings for each tool (e.g., Opacity, Flow, blending Mode). Options on the bar change depending on which tool is currently chosen, and your choices will remain in effect until you change them. Like the palettes, the options bar can be dragged to a different part of your screen. Double-click the left edge of the options bar to collapse/expand it.

*Click the Brush arrowhead to open the **Brush preset picker** (a pop-up palette).*

*Press this arrowhead to open the pop-up palette **menu**.*

*Press this button to create a **new preset** from the current brush.*

*To **close** the Brush picker or any other pop-up palette, click anywhere outside it or click the arrowhead on the options bar.*

*The **options bar** for the **Brush** tool*

*The **options bar** for the **Rectangular Marquee** tool*

*The **options bar** for the **Gradient** tool*

*The **options bar** for the **Pen** tool*

*The **options bar** for the **Type** tool*

Options Bar

The Photoshop screen: Mac OS X

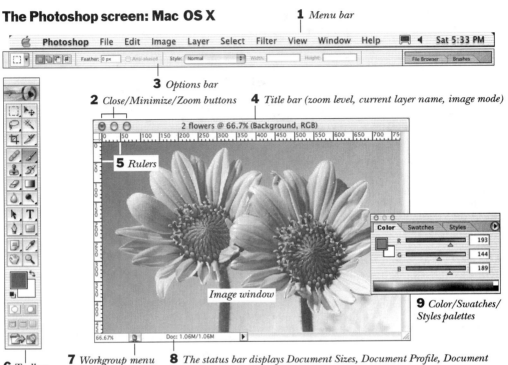

1 *Menu bar*

3 *Options bar*

2 *Close/Minimize/Zoom buttons* **4** *Title bar (zoom level, current layer name, image mode)*

5 *Rulers*

Image window

9 *Color/Swatches/ Styles palettes*

6 *Toolbox*

7 *Workgroup menu*

8 *The status bar displays Document Sizes, Document Profile, Document Dimensions, Scratch Sizes, Efficiency, Timing, or Current Tool information.*

Key to the Photoshop screen: Mac OS and Windows

1 *Menu bar*
Press any menu heading to access dialog boxes, submenus, and commands.

2 *Close/Minimize/Zoom buttons* (Mac OS X)
To close a file or a palette, click its close (red) button. Click the minimize (yellow) button to stow it in the dock. Click the zoom (green) button to enlarge a window to maximum size, or on a palette to show/hide extra options.

3 *Options bar*
Use to choose settings for the current tool.

4 *Title bar*
Displays the image's title, zoom level, current layer (or the Background), and image mode.

5 *Rulers*
Choose View > Show Rulers to display rulers. The position of the pointer is indicated by a mark on each ruler.

6 *Toolbox*
Press Tab to show/hide the Toolbox and all open palettes.

7 *Workgroup pop-up menu* 7.0!
Provides access to commands for checking files out from, or into, a WebDAV server. This menu is only available if Enable Workgroup Functionality is checked in Edit (Photoshop, in OS X) > Preferences > File Handling.

8 *Status bar*
The status bar displays Document Sizes, Document Profile, Document Dimensions, 7.0! Scratch Sizes (the amount of RAM currently available to Photoshop), Efficiency (the percentage of time Photoshop is working, as opposed to writing to the scratch disk), Timing, or Current Tool information. To reset the timer, choose Timing with Alt/Option held down.

9 *Palettes*
There are 17 moveable palettes. Click a tab (palette name) in a palette group to bring that palette to the front of its group.

The Photoshop screen: Windows

1 *Application Control menu box*

Menu bar

4 *Application close button*

3 *Application maximize button*

2 *Application minimize button*

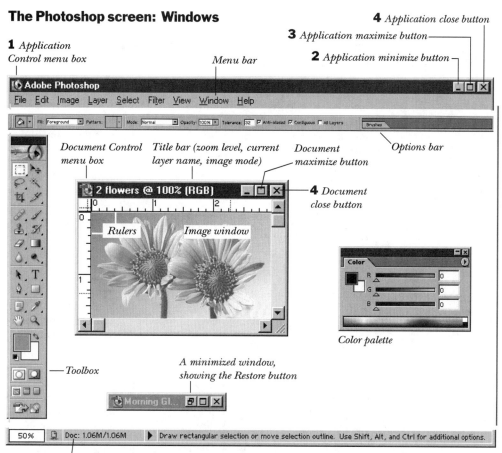

Document Control menu box

Title bar (zoom level, current layer name, image mode)

Document maximize button

Options bar

4 *Document close button*

Rulers

Image window

Color palette

Toolbox

A minimized window, showing the Restore button

The status bar displays Document Sizes, Document Profile, Document Dimensions, Scratch Sizes, Efficiency, or Timing information.

Key to the Photoshop screen: Windows only

1 *Application (or Document) Control menu box*
The Application Control menu box commands are Restore, Move, Size, Minimize, Maximize, and Close. The Document Control menu box commands are Restore, Move, Size, Minimize, Maximize, Close, and Next.

2 *Application (or Document) minimize button*
Click the Application Minimize button to shrink the document to an icon in the taskbar. Click the icon on the taskbar to restore the application window to its previous size.

Click the Document Minimize button to shrink the document to an icon at the lower-

left corner of the application window. Click the Restore button to restore the document window to its previous size.

3 *Application (or Document) maximize/restore button*
Click the Application or Document Maximize button to enlarge a window to its largest possible size. Click the Restore button to restore a window to its previous size. When a window is at the restored size, the Restore button turns into the Maximize button.

4 *Application (or Document) close button*
Closes the application (or image).

The menus **7.0!**

File

New...	Ctrl+N
Open...	Ctrl+O
Browse...	Shft+Ctrl+O
Open As...	Alt+Ctrl+O
Open Recent	▶
Close	Ctrl+W
Save	Ctrl+S
Save As...	Shft+Ctrl+S
Save for Web...	Alt+Shft+Ctrl+S
Revert	
Place...	
Import	▶
Export	▶
Workgroup	▶
Automate	▶
File Info...	
Page Setup...	Shft+Ctrl+P
Print with Preview...	Ctrl+P
Print...	Alt+Ctrl+P
Print One Copy	Alt+Shft+Ctrl+P
Jump To	▶
Exit	Ctrl+Q

File menu

File menu commands are used to create, open, close, save, place, scan, import, export, or print images; browse through images; manage workgroups; automate operations; and exit/quit Photoshop. Use the Jump To submenu to switch to a helper application, such as Adobe ImageReady or GoLive. In Mac OS X, the references and Color Settings commands are on this menu.

Edit

Undo Copy Pixels	⌘Z
Step Forward	⇧⌘Z
Step Backward	⌥⌘Z
Fade...	⇧⌘F
Cut	⌘X
Copy	⌘C
Copy Merged	⇧⌘C
Paste	⌘V
Paste Into	⇧⌘V
Clear	
Check Spelling...	
Find and Replace Text...	
Fill...	
Stroke...	
Free Transform	⌘T
Transform	▶
Define Brush...	
Define Pattern...	
Define Custom Shape...	
Purge	▶
Preset Manager...	

Edit menu

The Edit menu is a storehouse of image-editing commands that copy, transform, and paste imagery; apply fills and strokes; and create custom brushes, patterns, and shapes. Fade lessens the effect of the most recent edit. The Purge commands free up memory. Also found here are two word-processing commands, as well as the Preset Manager command, and in Windows and Mac OS 9, the Preferences and Color Settings commands.

Image

Mode	▶
Adjustments	▶
Duplicate...	
Apply Image...	
Calculations...	
Image Size...	
Canvas Size...	
Rotate Canvas	▶
Crop	
Trim...	
Reveal All	
Histogram...	
Trap...	

Image menu

An image can be converted to any of eight image (color) modes via the Mode submenu. The Adjustment commands modify an image's hue, saturation, brightness, or contrast. The Image Size command modifies an image's file size, dimensions, or resolution. The Canvas Size dialog box is used to add or subtract from an image's editable canvas area.

Layer

New	▶
Duplicate Layer...	
Delete	▶
Layer Properties...	
Layer Style	▶
New Fill Layer	▶
New Adjustment Layer	▶
Change Layer Content	▶
Layer Content Options...	
Type	▶
Rasterize	▶
New Layer Based Slice	
Add Layer Mask	▶
Enable Layer Mask	
Add Vector Mask	▶
Enable Vector Mask	
Group with Previous	⌘G
Ungroup	⇧⌘G
Arrange	▶
Align Linked	▶
Distribute Linked	▶
Lock All Layers In Set...	
Merge Layers	⌘E
Merge Visible	⇧⌘E
Flatten Image	
Matting	▶

Layer menu

Layer menu commands create, duplicate, delete, apply styles to, rasterize, add masks to, group, arrange, align, distribute, merge, and flatten layers. Some of these commands can also be chosen from the Layers palette menu.

The Menus

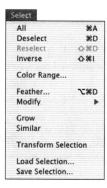

Select menu

The All command on the Select menu selects an entire layer. The Deselect command deselects all selections. The Reselect command restores the last deselected selection. The Color Range command creates a selection based on color. Other Select menu commands enlarge, contract, smooth, or feather selection edges, as well as save selections to and from channels.

View menu

Commands on the View menu control what's visible on screen. Use this menu to show/hide rulers, grids, guides, slices, selection edges, the currently selected (target) path, or annotations, or to change the current zoom level. The Proof Setup commands allow you to see how your image will look in different output color spaces, and the Gamut Warning highlights colors that won't print on a four-color press.

Filter menu

Filters, which perform a wide range of image-editing functions, are organized into submenu groups. Extract allows you to make complex silhouettes, Liquify pushes pixels around, and Pattern Maker creates seamless patterns from selections. The Digimarc filter embeds a copyright watermark.

Window menu

Window menu commands show and hide the palettes. Open images can be activated or arranged via the Documents submenu; Documents > New Window displays the same image in a second window. In Windows, you can choose Status Bar to show/hide the status bar.

Help menu

Use the Help menu commands to access the Photoshop manual onscreen, get the latest news from Adobe, connect to Adobe Online, or perform automated tasks via onscreen prompts.

The Menus

9

The palettes

How to use the palettes

Many of the operations that you will perform in Photoshop will be accomplished via moveable palettes. To save screen space, the palettes are joined into default **groups**, such as Navigator/Info and Color/Swatches/Styles.

To **open** a palette, choose its name from the Window menu. The palette will appear in front within its group.

Press Tab to **show/hide** all open palettes, including the Toolbox. Press Shift-Tab to show/hide all open palettes except the Toolbox.

To **display** an open palette at the front of its group, click its tab (palette name).

You can **separate** a palette from its group by dragging its tab **1**–**2**. You can **add** a palette to any group by dragging the tab over the group. Use the **resize** box (lower-right corner) to widen a palette if you need to make additional tabs visible. You can resize most of the palettes.

You can **dock** (store) palettes in the palette well on the right side of the options bar either by dragging the palette into the well or by choosing Dock to Palette Well from the palette menu.

If the current tool is associated with a palette, you can click the **Toggle** palette button on the options bar to show/hide that palette.

To **shrink/expand** a palette in Windows, double-click its tab or click the palette minimize/maximize button. In Mac OS 9, click the zoom button in the upper-right corner. In Mac OS X, click the zoom (green) button in the upper-left corner. If the palette isn't at its default size, click the minimize box/zoom button once to restore its default size, then click a second time to shrink the palette.

TIP Quick-change: Click in a field on a palette or in a dialog box, then press the up or down arrow on the keyboard to change that value incrementally.

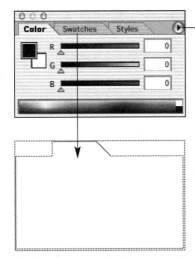

Press this arrowhead to choose commands from a palette menu.

1 *To **separate** a palette from its group, drag the tab (palette name) away from the palette group.*

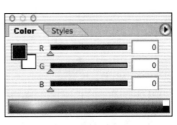

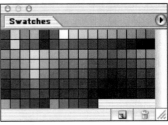

2 *The Swatches palette is now on its own.*

Pop-up sliders

There are two ways to use a pop-up slider : Either press an arrowhead and drag the slider in one movement, or click the arrowhead and then drag the slider. To close a slider, click anywhere outside it or press Enter/Return. If you click the arrowhead to open a slider, you can press Esc while the slider is open to restore its last setting.

2 *The **Workspace** commands are located under the Window menu.*

3 *In the **Delete Workspace** dialog box, choose an individual workspace name, or choose **All**.*

If **Save Palette Locations** is checked in Edit (Photoshop, in OS X) > Preferences > General, palettes that are open when you exit/quit Photoshop will reappear in their same location when you re-launch.

To really customize your onscreen working environment, you can set up special configurations of palettes and dialog boxes for different kinds of tasks and save them as **workspaces**. For example, you might want to keep the Character and Paragraph palettes open any time you're working on a text-intensive document, or create a workspace containing the Brushes, Color, and Swatches palettes for use when painting.

To create a custom workspace: **7.0!**

1. Open the palettes you intend to include, and arrange them on the screen as you like.

2. Choose Window > Workspace > Save Workspace **2**.

3. Enter a descriptive Name for the new workspace, then click OK.

To delete any or all custom **7.0!** workspaces:

1. Choose Window > Workspace > Delete Workspace.

2. Choose the name of the workspace you want to get rid of, or choose All **3**.

3. Click Delete, then click Yes.

TIP To restore the palettes' default groupings and locations at any time, choose Window > Workspace > Reset Palette Locations.

Workspaces

Color palette

The Color palette is used for mixing and choosing colors. Colors are applied with a painting or editing tool, or via a command such as Fill or Canvas Size. Choose a color model for the palette from the palette menu. Mix a color using the sliders, or quick-select a color by clicking on the color bar at the bottom of the Color palette.

To open the Color Picker, from which you can also choose a color, click once on the Foreground or Background color square if it's already active, or double-click the square if it's not active.

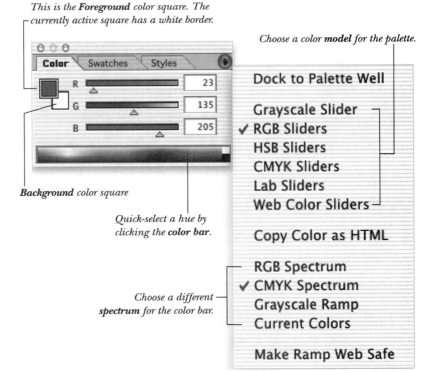

*This is the **Foreground** color square. The currently active square has a white border.*

*Choose a color **model** for the palette.*

Background color square

*Quick-select a hue by clicking the **color bar**.*

Choose a different spectrum for the color bar.

Color Palette

Swatches palette

The Swatches palette is used for choosing
already mixed colors. Individual swatches
can be added to or deleted from the palette.
Custom swatch libraries can also be loaded,
appended, and saved using Swatches palette
menu commands.

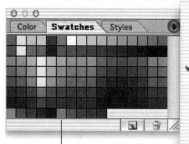

Color swatches

| Dock to Palette Well |
| New Swatch... |
| ✓ Small Thumbnail |
| Small List |
| Preset Manager... |
| Reset Swatches... |
| Load Swatches... |
| Save Swatches... |
| Replace Swatches... |
| ANPA Colors |
| DIC Color Guide |
| FOCOLTONE Colors |
| HKS E |
| HKS K |
| HKS N |
| HKS Z |
| Mac OS |
| PANTONE metallic coated |
| PANTONE pastel coated |
| PANTONE pastel uncoated |
| PANTONE process coated |
| PANTONE solid coated |
| PANTONE solid matte |
| PANTONE solid to process |
| PANTONE solid uncoated |
| TOYO Colors |
| TRUMATCH Colors |
| VisiBone |
| VisiBone2 |
| Web Hues |
| Web Safe Colors |
| Web Spectrum |
| Windows |

*Load swatches from
another swatch library by
choosing a library name.*

Swatches Palette

Styles palette

The Styles palette is used to apply previously
saved individual effects or combinations
of effects.

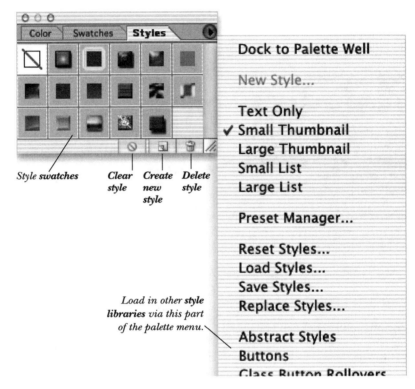

Style swatches **Clear** **Create** **Delete**
                  style   **new**   *style*
                            style

*Load in other **style**
libraries via this part
of the palette menu.*

Dock to Palette Well

New Style...

Text Only
✓ Small Thumbnail
Large Thumbnail
Small List
Large List

Preset Manager...

Reset Styles...
Load Styles...
Save Styles...
Replace Styles...

Abstract Styles
Buttons
Glass Button Rollovers

Navigator palette

The Navigator palette is used for moving
an image in its window or for changing the
zoom level of an image.

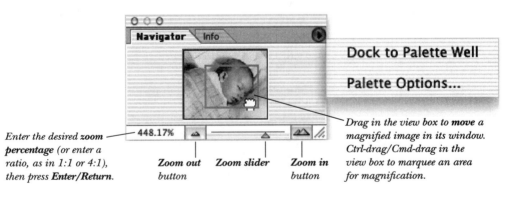

Dock to Palette Well

Palette Options...

*Drag in the view box to **move** a
magnified image in its window.
Ctrl-drag/Cmd-drag in the
view box to marquee an area
for magnification.*

*Enter the desired **zoom**
percentage (or enter a
ratio, as in 1:1 or 4:1),
then press **Enter/Return**.*

Zoom out **Zoom slider** **Zoom in**
button   button

Info palette

The Info palette displays a color breakdown of the pixel that's currently under the pointer ■. The palette will also show readouts for up to four color samplers, if they are placed on the image ■. If a color adjustment dialog box is open, the palette will display before and after color readouts. The Info palette also shows the x/y position of the pointer on the image.

Other information may display on the palette, depending on which tool is being used (such as the distance between points when a selection is moved, a shape is drawn, or the Measure tool is used; the dimensions of a selection or crop marquee; or the width, height, and angle of a selection as it's transformed ■).

Press one of the tiny arrowheads to choose a color mode for that readout (it can be different from the current image mode): Actual Color (the current image mode), Grayscale, RGB Color, Web Color, HSB Color, CMYK Color, Lab Color, Total Ink, or the current layer Opacity.

To do this via a dialog box, choose Palette Options from the Info palette menu, then change the mode for the First and Second Color Readouts. You can also change the unit of measurement for the palette (Mouse Coordinates) ■.

TIP If an exclamation point appears next to a color readout, it means that color is outside the printable, CMYK gamut.

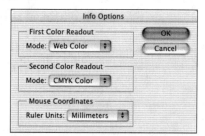

4 *You can choose options for different areas of the Info palette using the **Info Options** dialog box.*

■ *Color breakdown for the pixel that's currently under the pointer*

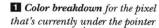

*Press this arrowhead to choose a different **unit of measurement** for the palette (and the rulers).* *The **Width** and **Height** of the current **selection***

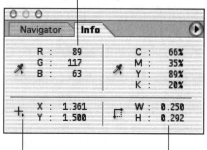

2 *#1, #2, #3, and #4 color readouts from four color samplers that were placed on the image*

3 *During a **transform** operation, the width (W), height (H), angle (A), and horizontal skew (H) or vertical skew (V) of the transformed layer, selection, or path are shown in this area.*

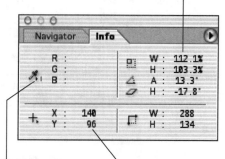

*Press an arrowhead to choose a different **color mode** for that readout.* *The x/y **location** of the pointer on the image*

Layers palette

Normally, when you create a new image, it has an opaque Background. Using the Layers palette, you can add layers on top of the Background, and then show/hide, duplicate, group, link, delete, and restack them. Each layer can be assigned its own blending mode, opacity, and fill opacity without affecting the other layers.

In addition to standard layers, you can also create two other kinds of layers: adjustment layers, which are used for applying temporary color or tonal adjustments to the layers below it, and editable type layers, which are created automatically when the Horizontal Type or Vertical Type tool is used. If you apply a layer effect to a layer (e.g., Inner Glow or Drop Shadow), a layer effect icon and pop-up menu will appear next to the layer name. You can also attach a mask to a layer.

Only the current (or "active") layer can be edited. To choose a layer, click its name or click its thumbnail on the Layers palette.

Starting out transparent

Click **Contents: Transparent** in the File > New dialog box to have the bottommost tier of a new image be a layer with transparency instead of an opaque Background.

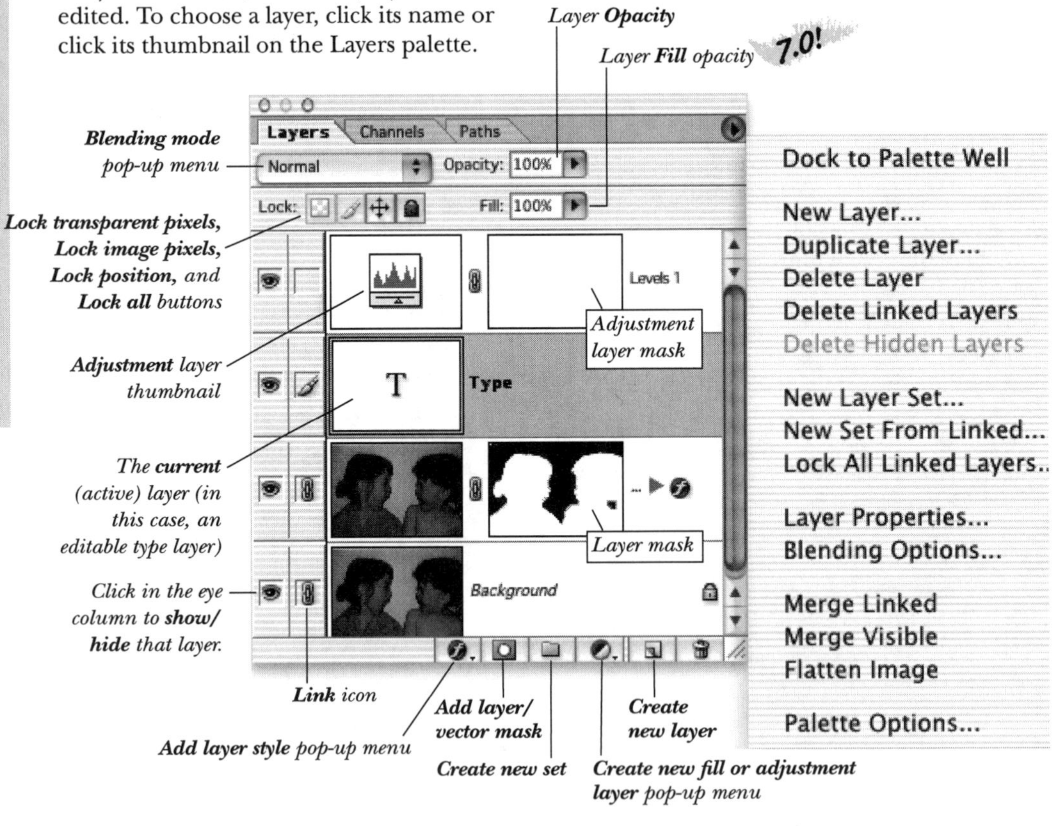

Layer Opacity
Layer Fill opacity
7.0!
Blending mode pop-up menu
Lock transparent pixels, Lock image pixels, Lock position, and Lock all buttons
Adjustment layer thumbnail
The current (active) layer (in this case, an editable type layer)
Click in the eye column to show/hide that layer.
Link icon
Add layer style pop-up menu
Add layer/vector mask
Create new set
Create new layer
Create new fill or adjustment layer pop-up menu
Adjustment layer mask
Layer mask
Layers
Channels
Paths
Normal
Opacity: 100%
Lock:
Fill: 100%
Levels 1
Type
Background
Dock to Palette Well
New Layer...
Duplicate Layer...
Delete Layer
Delete Linked Layers
Delete Hidden Layers
New Layer Set...
New Set From Linked...
Lock All Linked Layers...
Layer Properties...
Blending Options...
Merge Linked
Merge Visible
Flatten Image
Palette Options...

Channels palette

The Channels palette is used to display one or more of the color channels that make up an image. It is also used for creating and displaying alpha channels, which are used for saving selections, and spot color channels, which are used for producing spot color plates.

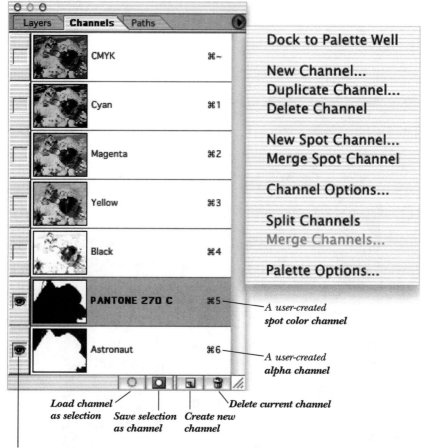

A user-created spot color channel

A user-created alpha channel

Load channel as selection

Save selection as channel

Create new channel

Delete current channel

*The **eye** icon means this channel is currently **displayed**. To display a channel, click its name or use the keystroke that's listed on the palette.*

Paths palette

A path is a shape that is composed of curved and straight line segments connected by anchor points. A path can be drawn directly with a shape tool or a pen tool, or you can start by creating a selection and then convert the selection into a path. A path can be filled or stroked. To create a precisely drawn selection, you can draw a path and then convert it into a selection. The Pen tool and its relatives—the Add Anchor Point, Delete Anchor Point, and Convert Point tools—can be used to reshape a path. Paths are saved and accessed via the Paths palette.

TIP While a shape layer or an image layer that has a vector mask is selected, the path for that vector mask will be listed on the Paths palette.

Paths Palette

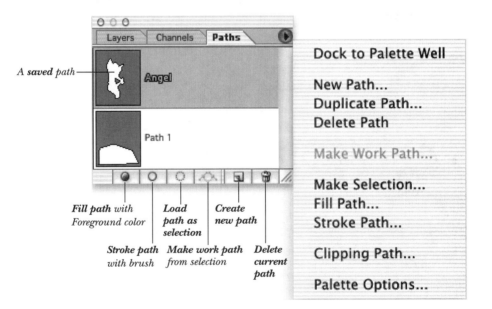

A saved path

Fill path *with* **Foreground** *color*

Load *path as* *selection*

Create *new path*

Stroke path *with brush*

Make work path *from selection*

Delete *current path*

Dock to Palette Well

New Path...
Duplicate Path...
Delete Path

Make Work Path...

Make Selection...
Fill Path...
Stroke Path...

Clipping Path...

Palette Options...

History palette

The History palette is used to selectively undo one or more previous steps in a work session. Each brushstroke, filter application, or other operation is listed as a separate state on the palette, with the bottommost state being the most recent. Clicking on a prior state restores the document to that stage of the editing process. What happens to the document when you click on a prior state depends on whether the palette is in linear or non-linear mode.

In linear mode, if you click back on and then delete a state, or resume image-editing from an earlier state, all subsequent states (dimmed, on the palette) will be deleted. In non-linear mode, you can click back on an earlier edit state or delete a state without losing subsequent states. This option is turned on or off via the Allow Non-Linear History check box in the History Options dialog box (choose History Options from the palette menu). You can switch between linear and non-linear modes at any time during editing.

The History Brush tool restores an image to a designated prior state where the brush is dragged in the image window. The Art History Brush does the same thing, but in stylized strokes.

Actions palette

You can record a series of commands in an action, and then replay that action on one image or a batch of images. The Actions palette is used for recording, storing, and replaying actions.

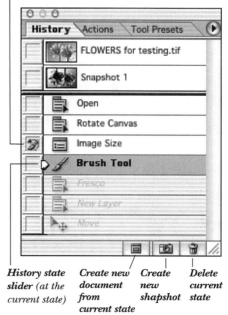

The current source for the History Brush

History state slider *(at the current state)*

Create new document from current state

Create new shapshot

Delete current state

*This is the **History** palette in **linear** mode. Note that some steps are grayed out.*

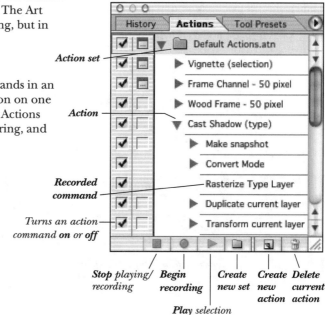

Action set

Action

Recorded command

Turns an action command **on** or **off**

Stop *playing/ recording*

Begin recording

Play *selection*

Create new set

Create new action

Delete current action

Character palette

When a type tool is chosen, type attributes can be chosen via the Character palette, illustrated below, or from the options bar.

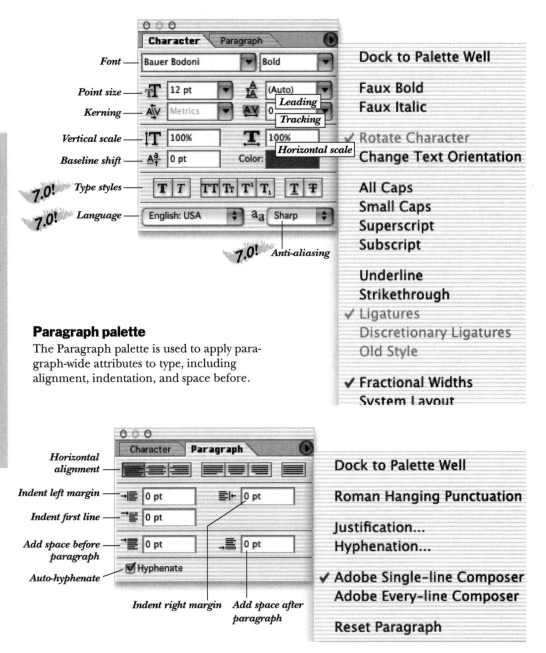

Paragraph palette

The Paragraph palette is used to apply paragraph-wide attributes to type, including alignment, indentation, and space before.

Tool Presets palette 7.0!

You can save and reuse tool settings, just like any other type of preset. Say, for example, you frequently resize and crop images to a particular set of dimensions. If you create a preset with the width, height, and resolution parameters you need, the next time you perform the cropping operation, you don't have to type in the numbers—you can just choose the tool preset from the Tool Presets palette or pop-up palette.

You can also save presets for type (complete with font, point size, and color attributes), and for selection tools, brushes, gradients, patterns, shapes, contours, and styles.

The Tool Presets palette is used for managing saved tool presets. By default, it only lists the presets for the currently active tool. To have the palette list the presets for all tools, uncheck Show Current Tool Presets.

Tool Presets are also accessible from a pop-up palette, which opens if you click the tool's thumbnail on the options bar.

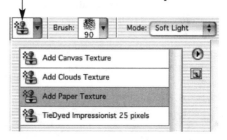

*Click a tool **preset** to make it the current tool, complete with its saved settings.*

Actions	**Tool Presets**	

Healing Brush 21 pixels
Magnetic Lasso 24 pixels
Crop 5 inch x 4 inch 300 dpi
Fill with Bubbles Pattern
Horizontal Type Myriad Roman 24 pt
Vertical Type Myriad Roman 24 pt
5 Point White Star
0.5 cm Black Arrow
Starburst Color Target
Art History Brush 20 pixels

Current Tool Only

*Click the **Create new tool preset** button to save the current tool settings as a preset.*

*Click the **Delete tool preset** button to delete the currently selected tool preset.*

Dock to Palette Well

New Tool Preset...

Rename Tool Preset...
Delete Tool Preset

✓ Sort By Tool
✓ Show All Tool Presets
Show Current Tool Presets

Text Only
✓ Small List
Large List

Reset Tool
Reset All Tools

Preset Manager...

Reset Tool Presets...
Load Tool Presets...
Save Tool Presets...
Replace Tool Presets...

Art History
Brushes

Brushes palette 7.0!

The Brushes palette is used for customizing brush tips for the Brush, Pencil, History Brush, Art History Brush, Clone Stamp, Pattern Stamp, Eraser, Background Eraser, Blur, Sharpen, Smudge, Dodge, Burn, and Sponge tools. The options are organized into categories, such as Shape Dynamics, Scattering, Texture, and Color Dynamics. You can also use the Brushes palette to choose options for a stylus or for an airbrush input device.

TIP The numeral under a brush tip icon is the diameter of the tip in pixels.

Picker or palette?

Brush tips for the painting and editing tools can be chosen either from the **Brushes palette** (illustrated below) or from the **Brush picker 1**, a pop-up palette that is opened from the options bar.

Commands for **loading**, **appending**, and **saving** brushes and brush libraries can be chosen from the Brushes palette menu or the Brush picker menu (click the palette menu button ▶ on the right side).

To **close** the pop-up palette (Brush picker), click outside it or click the Brush arrowhead again. To hide the Brushes palette (but keep it open), dock it into the palette well on the options bar; to redisplay it, click the palette tab in the well.

1 *Click here to open the **Brush picker**.*   *Brush tips*

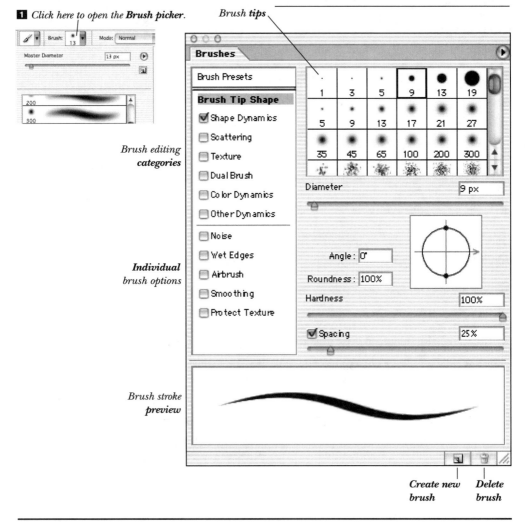

Brush editing categories

Individual brush options

Brush stroke preview

Create new brush   *Delete brush*

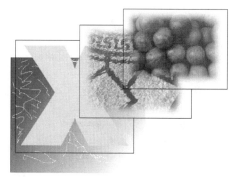

1 *Layers* *are like clear acetate sheets:* **opaque** *where there is imagery,* **transparent** *where there is no imagery.*

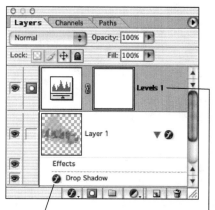

A **layer effect**   **2** *The Levels command, applied via an* **adjustment layer**

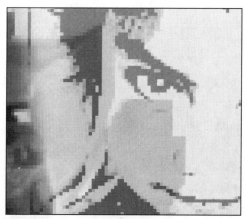

3 *Individual* **pixels** *are discernible in this image because it is shown at 500% view.*

Mini-glossary

Current layer and layer transparency

An image can have just a Background (no layers), or you can add multiple layers to it **1**. Only the layer that is currently highlighted on the Layers palette can be edited. Layers can contain special layer effects; they can be restacked and moved; and they are transparent where there are no pixels, so you can see through a whole stack of them. You can assign image components to separate layers and edit them individually without changing other layers.

Adjustment layer

Unlike a standard layer, modifications made to an adjustment layer don't alter actual pixels until the layer is merged with the layers below it **2**. Adjustment layers are ideal for experimenting with color or tonal adjustments.

Pixels (picture elements)

The dots used to display a bitmapped image in a rectangular grid on screen **3**.

Vector

In addition to pixel imagery, you can also create paths, shapes, and editable type. Each of these elements automatically appears on its own mathematically defined vector layer **4**. The overall file resolution can be kept at a level that's suitable for the pixel imagery, whereas the vector elements will print at the printer resolution.

(Continued on the following page)

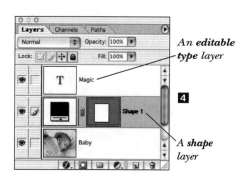

An **editable type** *layer*

4

A **shape** *layer*

Mini-Glossary

23

History

Every modification that's made to an image is saved on the History palette as a state, and the image can be restored to any prior state during the same work session.

Selection

A selection is an area of an image that is isolated via a "marching ants" marquee so that it can be modified while the rest of the image is protected . A selection can be created using a selection tool (such as the Lasso), using a command (such as Color Range), by converting a path into a selection, or by loading an alpha channel mask as a selection.

1 *A **selected** area of an image*

Effect

Photoshop includes ten effects (e.g., Drop Shadow, Outer Glow, Gradient Overlay) that can be applied to any layer and are fully editable. A style is a saved effect or combination of effects.

Image size

The Pixel Dimensions value is the number of pixels an image contains, whereas the Resolution is the density of pixels per unit of measure (usually per inch) **2**.

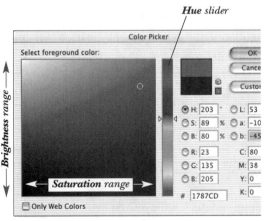

2 *The **Image Size** dialog box is used to change an image's **pixel dimensions** and/or **resolution**.*

Brightness/hue/saturation

Brightness is a color's lightness **3**; its hue is the wavelength of light that gives the color its name, such as red or blue; saturation is its degree of purity. The more gray a color contains, the lower its saturation.

Optimization

Optimization is the preparation of an image for Web output, and it involves choosing file format, color, and size parameters. Sometimes an image is also divided into slices in order to speed up its download time.

Rollover

A rollover is a change on a Web page (such as the appearance of text or a picture) that is triggered by the movement or clicking of the user's mouse over a specific area.

3 *The Photoshop **Color Picker***

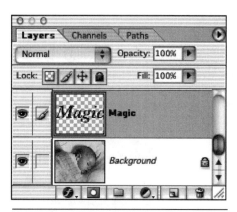

Build your image using layers

You can work on one layer at a time without affecting the other layers, and discard any layers you don't need. To conserve memory if you're working on a large image, merge two or more layers together periodically.

Using a **layer mask** or a **vector mask**, you can temporarily hide pixels on an individual layer so you can experiment with different compositions. When you're finished using the mask, you can either discard it or permanently apply the effect to the layer.

Quick on the redraw

To speed performance, choose Palette Options from the Layers, Channels, or Paths palette menu, then click either **Thumbnail Size**: None or the smallest thumbnail option.

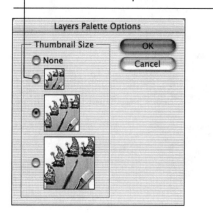

Production techniques

■ To undo the last modification, choose Edit > **Undo** (Ctrl-Z/Cmd-Z) (*Note:* Some commands can't be undone.) To undo multiple steps, click a prior state on the **History** palette or use the **History Brush** tool to restore selective areas.

■ Periodically click the "Create new snapshot" button at the bottom of the History palette to save temporary versions of the image. Click a **snapshot** thumbnail to revert to that version of the image.

■ Use an **adjustment layer** to try out tonal and color adjustments, and then later merge the adjustment layer downward to apply the effect, or discard the adjustment layer to remove that effect. Use the Layers palette Opacity slider to lessen the effect of an adjustment layer. Create a clipping group with the layer directly below an adjustment layer to limit the adjustment effect to just that layer.

■ Use Edit > **Fade** (Ctrl-Shift-F/Cmd-Shift-F) to lessen the last-applied filter, adjustment command, or tool edit without having to undo and redo—and choose an opacity and blending mode for the operation while you're at it.

■ **Interrupt screen redraw** after executing a command or applying a filter by choosing a different tool or command. (To cancel a command while a progress bar is displaying, press Esc.)

■ Choose the lowest possible **resolution** and **dimensions** for your image, given your output requirements. Vector layers (editable type, shapes, and vector masks) print at the printer resolution—not at the file resolution. Once you become proficient in Photoshop, you can create a practice image at a low resolution, saving the commands you use in an **action**, and then replay the action on a higher resolution version.

■ Display your image in **two windows** simultaneously, one in a larger view size than

(Continued on the following page)

the other, so you don't have to constantly change view sizes.

- Save a complex selection to a special grayscale channel, called an **alpha channel**, which can be loaded and reused on any image whenever you like. Or create a **path** or a **vector mask**, which occupies significantly less storage space than an alpha channel and can be converted into a selection at any time.

- Use **Quick Mask** mode to turn a selection into a mask, which will cover the protected areas of the image with transparent color and leave the unprotected area as a cutout, and then modify the mask contour using a painting tool. Turn off Quick Mask mode to convert the cutout area back into a selection.

- Since CMYK files process more slowly than RGB files, you can work in RGB Color mode, use View > Proof Setup > **Working CMYK** to preview your image as CMYK Color mode, and then convert it to the "real" CMYK Color mode when it's completed.

- Memorize as many **keyboard shortcuts** as you can. Start by learning the shortcuts for choosing tools. Use onscreen tool tips to refresh your memory, or refer to our shortcuts appendix. Shortcuts are included in most of the instructions in this book.

- Try to allot at least 50% of available **RAM** (at least 128 MB) to Photoshop, or four times an image's RAM document size.

- Choose the Edit > **Purge** submenu commands periodically to regain RAM that was used for the Clipboard, the Undo command, the History palette, or All (of the above) **1**. The Purge commands can't be undone.

*Use the **Purge** submenu commands to free up memory.*

Context menus save time

To choose from an onscreen **context menu**, right-click/Control-click a Layers, Channels, or Paths palette thumbnail, name, or feature **2**. Or choose and use a tool, then right-click/Control-click with the pointer over the image window to choose commands or options for that tool **3**–**4**.

2 *You can choose some **palette** commands via context menus.*

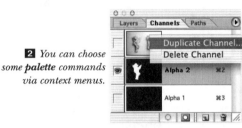

3 *Right-click/Control-click with a **type** tool to choose from a list of **type** commands.*

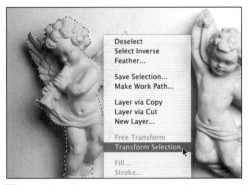

4 *Right-click/Control-click with a **selection** tool to choose from yet another list of **commands**.*

PHOTOSHOP COLOR 2

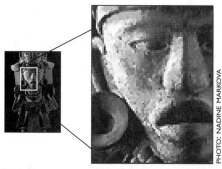

1 *A close-up of an image, showing individual **pixels***

PHOTO: NADINE MARKOVA

2 *The **additive primaries** on a computer monitor*

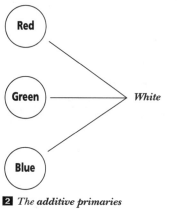

3 *The **subtractive primaries**—printing inks*

THIS CHAPTER consists of an introduction to color basics (color models, image modes, and blending modes), and also to Photoshop's color management features.

Color basics

Pixels

The screen image in Photoshop is a bitmap, which is a geometric arrangement (mapping) of a layer of dots of different shades or colors on a rectangular grid. Each dot, called a pixel, represents a color or shade. By magnifying an area of an image, you can edit pixels individually **1**. Every Photoshop image is a bitmap, whether it originates from a scan, from another application, or entirely within Photoshop using its painting and editing tools. (Don't confuse Bitmap image mode with the term "bitmap.") If you drag with a painting tool across an area of a layer, pixels under the pointer are recolored. Bitmap programs are ideal for producing painterly, photographic, or photorealistic images that contain subtle gradations of color.

RGB vs. CMYK color

Red, green, and blue (RGB) lights are used to display a color image on a monitor. When these additive primaries in their purest form are combined, they produce white light **2**.

The three subtractive primary inks used in four-color-process printing are cyan (C), magenta (M), and yellow (Y) **3**. When they are combined, a dark, muddy color is produced. To produce a rich black, printers usually mix black (K) ink with small quantities of cyan, magenta, and/or yellow ink.

The display of color on a computer monitor is highly variable and subject to the whims of ambient lighting, monitor temperature,

(Continued on the following page)

27

and room color. What's more, many colors that are seen in nature can't be printed, some colors that can be displayed onscreen can't be printed, and some printable colors can't be displayed onscreen. All monitors display color using the RGB model— CMYK colors are merely simulated. You don't need to bother with a RGB-to-CMYK conversion if your image is going to be output to the Web or to a film recorder.

TIP Most desktop ink-jet printers produce the best output if you allow the printer's driver to perform the conversion to CMYK. This is especially true of printers that use six (or more!) ink colors.

An exclamation point will appear on the Color palette if you choose a non-printable (out-of-gamut) color **1**. Exclamation points will also display on the Info palette if the color currently under the pointer is out-of-gamut **2**. Using Photoshop's Gamut Warning command, you can display non-printable colors in your image in gray, and then, using the Sponge tool, you can desaturate them to bring them into gamut.

You can use the grayscale, RGB (red-green-blue), HSB (hue-saturation-brightness), CMYK (cyan-magenta-yellow-black), or Lab (lightness-a, axis-b axis) color model when you choose colors in Photoshop via the Color Picker or Color palette.

Channels

Every Photoshop image is a composite of one or more semi-transparent, colored-light overlays called channels. For example, an image in RGB Color mode is composed of the red, green, and blue channels. To illustrate, open a color image, then click Red, Green, or Blue on the Channels palette to display only that channel. Click RGB (Ctrl-~/Cmd-~) to restore the full channel display. (If the channels don't display in color, check the Color Channels in Color box in Edit [Photoshop, in OS X] > Preferences > Display & Cursors.)

Color adjustments can be made to an individual channel, but normally modifications

Web graphics

If you're creating an image for a Web site, use the RGB color model. Bear in mind that RGB colors—or colors from any other color model, for that matter—may not match the color palette of your Web browser (see page 458). For the best results, load one of the Web or Visibone palettes onto the Swatches palette, and use the Web Color Sliders and Make Ramp Web Safe options on the Color palette.

Default channels per image mode

One	Three	Four
Bitmap	RGB	CMYK
Grayscale	Lab	
Duotone	Multichannel	
Indexed Color		

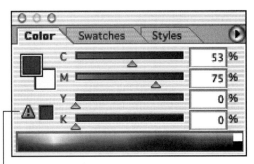

1 *Out-of-gamut indicator*

2 *Out-of-gamut indicator*

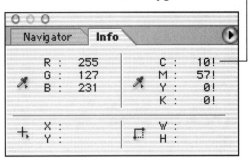

Channels (side tab)

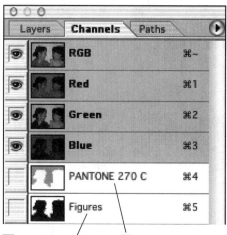

1 *An* ***alpha*** *channel*　　**2** *A* ***spot color*** *channel*

3 *The* ***Mode*** *submenu*

4 *The* ***Proof Setup*** *submenu*

are made and displayed in the multichannel, composite image (the topmost channel name on the Channels palette), and affect all of an image's channels at once. Special grayscale channels that are used for saving selections as masks, called alpha channels, can be added to an image **1**; you can also add spot color channels **2**. Only the currently highlighted channels can be edited.

The more channels an image contains, the larger its file storage size. The storage size of an image in RGB Color mode, which has three channels (Red, Green, and Blue), will be three times larger than the same image in Grayscale mode, which has one channel. The same image in CMYK Color mode will have four channels (Cyan, Magenta, Yellow, and Black), and will be even larger.

Image modes

An image can be converted to, displayed in, and edited in any one of eight image modes: Bitmap, Grayscale, Duotone, Indexed Color, RGB Color, CMYK Color, Lab Color, or Multichannel. Simply choose the mode you want from the Image menu > Mode submenu **3**. To access a mode that is unavailable (whose name is dimmed), you must first convert your image to a different mode as an intermediate step. For example, to convert an image to Indexed Color mode, it must be in RGB Color or Grayscale mode.

Some mode conversions cause noticeable color shifts. For example, dramatic changes may occur if an image is converted from RGB Color mode to CMYK Color mode because in this case, printable colors will be substituted for rich, glowing RGB colors. Color accuracy may diminish if an image is converted back and forth between RGB and CMYK Color modes too many times.

Medium- to low-end scanners usually produce RGB scans. If you're creating an image that's going to be printed, for faster editing and to access all the filters, edit it in RGB Color mode and then convert it to CMYK Color mode when you're ready to imageset it. You can use View > Proof Setup **4** in

(Continued on the following page)

Image Modes

conjunction with View > Proof Colors (Ctrl-Y/Cmd-Y) to preview an image in CMYK Color mode without actually changing its mode. You can CMYK-preview your image in one window and open a second window to display the same image without the CMYK preview.

Some conversions will cause layers to be flattened, such as a conversion to Indexed Color, Multichannel, or Bitmap mode. For other conversions, you'll have the option to click Don't Flatten if you want to preserve layers.

High-end scanners usually produce CMYK scans, and these images should be kept in CMYK Color mode to preserve their color data. If you find working on such large files to be cumbersome, you can work out your image-editing scheme on a low-resolution version of an image, save the commands using the Actions palette, and then apply the action to the high-resolution, CMYK version. You will still, however, have to perform some operations manually, like applying brush strokes with the Brush tool.

Some output devices require that an image be saved in a particular image mode. The availability of some commands and tool options in Photoshop may also vary depending on an image's current mode.

These are the image modes, in brief:

In **Bitmap** mode , pixels are 100% black or 100% white only, and layers, filters, and Adjustment commands are unavailable, except for the Invert command. An image must be in Grayscale mode before it can be converted to Bitmap mode.

In **Grayscale** mode **2**, pixels are black, white, or up to 254 shades of gray (for a total of 256). If an image is converted from a color mode to Grayscale mode and then saved and closed, its luminosity (light and dark) values will remain intact, but its color information will be deleted and can't be restored.

An image in **Indexed Color** mode has one channel and a color table containing a maximum of 256 colors or shades (8-bit color). It

1 *Bitmap mode, Method: Diffusion Dither*   **2** *Grayscale mode*

*The **Channels** palette for an image in various modes:*

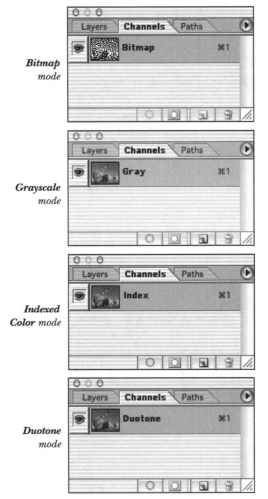

Bitmap mode

Grayscale mode

Indexed Color mode

Duotone mode

*The **Channels** palette for an image in various modes:*

RGB Color mode

CMYK Color mode

Lab Color mode

Multichannel mode

is often helpful to reduce images to 8-bit color for use in multimedia applications. You can also convert an image to Indexed Color mode to create arty color effects. If you're going to reduce an image to 8-bit color for the Web, though, you'll optimize it in the GIF format (see Chapter 23.)

RGB Color is the most versatile mode because it is the only mode in which all of Photoshop's tool options and filters are accessible. Some video and multimedia applications can import an RGB image in the Photoshop file format.

Photoshop is one of few programs in which images can be displayed and edited in **CMYK Color** mode. You can convert an image to CMYK Color mode when you're ready to color separate it or output it on a color printer.

Lab Color is a three-channel mode that was developed for the purpose of achieving consistency among various devices, such as printers and monitors. The channels represent lightness, the colors green to red, and the colors blue to yellow. Photo CD images can be converted to Lab Color mode or RGB Color mode in Photoshop. Sometimes files are saved in Lab Color mode for export to other operating systems.

A **Duotone** is a printing method in which two or more plates are used to add richness and tonal depth to a grayscale image.

A **Multichannel** image is composed of multiple, 256-level grayscale channels. This mode is used for certain grayscale printing situations. You could use multichannel mode to assemble individual channels from several images before converting the new image to a color mode. Spot color channels are preserved if you convert an image to Multichannel mode. If you convert an image from RGB Color to Multichannel mode, the Red, Green, and Blue channels will be converted to Cyan, Magenta, and Yellow. The image may become lighter as a result, but otherwise it won't change significantly.

Image Modes

The blending modes

You can select from an assortment of blending modes on the options bar, on the Layers palette, or in the Fill, Stroke, Fade, or Fill Path dialog box. The mode you choose for a tool or a layer affects how that tool or layer modifies underlying pixels (the "base color" in the descriptions below). The "blend layer" is the layer for which a mode is chosen.

TIP To cycle through blending modes for the currently selected tool, press Shift + or Shift -.

Note: If the "Lock transparent pixels" button is selected on the Layers palette for the target layer, only pixels—not transparent areas—can be recolored or otherwise edited.

Opacities add up

When you choose a mode and an opacity for a **tool**, be sure to factor in the mode and opacity of the current **layer** you're working on. For example, if you choose 60% opacity for the Paintbrush tool on a layer that has a 50% opacity, your resulting brush stroke will have an opacity of 30%.

NORMAL

All base colors are modified. *Note:* For an image in Bitmap or Indexed Color mode, Normal mode is called Threshold.

DISSOLVE

Creates a chalky, dry brush texture with the paint or blend layer color. The higher the pressure or opacity, the more solid the stroke.

DARKEN

Base colors that are lighter than the paint or blend layer color are modified; base colors that are darker than the paint or blend layer color are not. Use with a paint color that is darker than the base colors you want to modify.

MULTIPLY

A dark paint or blend layer color removes the lighter parts of the base color to produce a darker base color. A light paint or blend layer color darkens the base color less. Good for creating semi-transparent shadows.

COLOR BURN

A dark paint or blend layer color darkens the base color by increasing the layer's contrast. A light paint or blend layer color slightly tints the base color.

COLOR DODGE

Lightens the base color where the paint or blend layer color is light by decreasing the layer's contrast. A dark paint or blend layer color slightly tints the base color.

LINEAR BURN 7.0!

A dark paint or blend layer color darkens the base color by decreasing the layer's brightness. A light paint or blend layer color slightly tints the base color.

LINEAR DODGE 7.0!

Lightens the base color where the paint or blend layer color is light by increasing the layer's brightness. A dark paint or blend layer color slightly tints the base color.

LIGHTEN

Base colors that are darker than the paint or blend layer color are modified, base colors that are lighter than the paint or blend layer color are not. Use with a paint color that is lighter than the base colors you want to modify.

SCREEN

A light paint or blend layer color removes the darker parts of the base color to produce a lighter, bleached base color. A dark paint or blend layer lightens the base color less.

OVERLAY

Multiplies (darkens) dark areas and screens (lightens) light base colors. Preserves luminosity (light and dark) values. Black and white aren't changed, so detail is maintained.

PIN LIGHT

7.0!

The blend color (light color) will replace the colors in the base color, depending on their relative brightness. Pixels darker than the blend color will be replaced if the blend color is lighter than 50% gray. If the blend color is darker than 50% gray, then it will replace pixels lighter than the blend color. Can be used to create special effects.

SOFT LIGHT

Lightens the base color if the paint or blend layer color is light. Darkens the base color if the paint or blend layer color is dark. Preserves luminosity values in the base color. Creates a soft, subtle lighting effect.

HARD LIGHT

Screens (lightens) the base color if the paint or blend layer color is light. Multiplies (darkens) the base color if the paint or blend layer color is dark. Greater contrast is created in the base color and layer color. Good for painting glowing highlights and creating composite effects.

Blending Modes

LINEAR LIGHT

Burns (darkens) the base colors by decreasing brightness if the paint or blend layer color is dark. Dodges (lightens) the base color by increasing brightness if the paint or blend layer color is light.

VIVID LIGHT

Burns (darkens) the base colors by increasing contrast if the paint or blend layer color is dark. Dodges (lightens) the base color by decreasing contrast if the paint or blend layer color is light.

DIFFERENCE

Creates a color negative effect on the base color. When the paint or blend layer color is light, the negative (or invert) effect is more pronounced. Produces noticeable color shifts.

EXCLUSION

Grays out the base color where the paint or blend layer color is dark. Inverts the base color where the paint or blend layer color is light.

Blending Modes

HUE

The blend color's hue is applied. Saturation and luminosity values are not modified in the base color.

SATURATION

The blend color's saturation is applied. Hue and luminosity values are not modified in the base color.

COLOR

The blend color's saturation and hue are applied. The base color's light and dark (luminosity) values aren't changed, so detail is maintained. Good for tinting.

LUMINOSITY

The base color's luminosity values are replaced by luminosity values from the paint or blend layer color. Hue and saturation aren't affected in the base color.

BEHIND

Not available for layers. Only transparent areas are modified, not existing base color pixels (turn off "Lock transparent pixels"). The effect is like painting on the reverse side of clear acetate. Good for creating shadows. Can't be used on the Background.

CLEAR

Not available for layers. Makes the base color transparent where strokes are applied (turn off "Lock transparent pixels"). Available only for a multi-layer image when using the Paint Bucket tool, the Line tool (with the "Fill pixels" button clicked), or the Fill, Stroke, or Fill Path command. Can't be used on the Background.

*This Synchronize alert box may open when Photoshop is launched if the current color settings have been modified in another Adobe program (e.g., Illustrator 10). Click **Synchronize** to have Photoshop's color settings match (be synchronized with) the color settings from the other program. Note for Mac OS X users: Both Photoshop and the other program must have been installed at the same user level for the programs to be aware of each other's color settings.*

Color management

Problems with color can creep up on you when various hardware devices and software packages you use treat color differently. For example, if you open a graphic in several different imaging programs and in a Web browser, the colors in your image might look completely different in each case. And none of those programs may match the color of the picture you originally scanned in on your scanner. Print the image, and you will probably find that your results are different again. In some cases, you might find these differences slight and unobjectionable. But in other circumstances, such color changes can wreak havoc with your design and turn a project into a disaster.

A color management system can solve most of these problems by acting as a color interpreter. A good system knows how each device and program understands color, and it can help you move your graphics between them all by adjusting color so that it appears the same in every program and device. A color profile is a mathematical description of a device's color space. Both Illustrator 10 and Photoshop 7 use ICC (International Color Consortium) profiles to tell your color management system how specific devices use color.

You can find most of Photoshop's color management controls in the Color Settings dialog box, which is accessed from the Edit menu in Windows and Mac OS 9, and the Photoshop menu in OS X. This dialog box includes a list of predefined management settings for various publishing situations, including prepress output and Web output.

Photoshop also supports color management policies for RGB and CMYK color files, for files using spot colors, and for grayscale files. These color management policies govern how Photoshop deals with color when opening graphics that do or don't have an attached color profile.

TIP Consult with your prepress service provider, if you're using one, about color

(Continued on the following page)

Color Management

management. Make sure your color management workflows will work together.

TIP If you're planning to use the same graphics for different purposes, such as for the Web and for printed material, you may benefit from using color management.

Calibration

The first step toward achieving color consistency is to calibrate your monitor. Previous versions of Photoshop installed a utility program, the Adobe Gamma Control Panel, which was used to define the RGB color space your monitor could display. The Adobe Gamma utility is still installed with the Windows version of Photoshop 7, but the Macintosh version relies on the operating system-level monitor calibration utility that's part of the Monitors (in Mac OS 9) or Displays (Mac OS X) control panel **1**. You will adjust the contrast and brightness, gamma, color balance, and white point of your monitor.

Both the Adobe Gamma and Monitors/ Displays control panels create an ICC profile, which Photoshop can use as its working RGB space to display the colors in your artwork accurately.

Note: You have to calibrate your monitor and save the settings as an ICC profile only once; the profile will be available to all applications.

To calibrate your monitor (Mac OS):

1. Allow 30 minutes for the monitor to warm up and the display to stabilize, and establish a level of room lighting that will remain constant (paint your windows black, ha-ha). Make the desktop pattern light gray.

2. Mac OS 9: Choose Apple > Control Panels > Monitors and click the Color button.

Mac OS X: Choose Apple > System Preferences, click Displays, click the Color tab, then click Calibrate.

3. Click the right arrow to advance to the next options pane.

Pining for the Good ol' Days?

If you're a Mac OS 9 user, and you miss the old Adobe Gamma Control Panel, Adobe grudgingly provides it for you, but they don't make it easy. You'll find it tucked away in the Goodies folder on the Adobe Photoshop 7 CD-ROM, in Calibration/Mac Classic Only/Adobe Gamma.

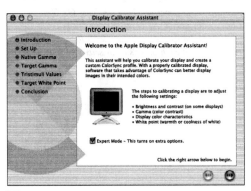

1 *This is the starting place for calibrating your monitor in Mac OS X. It has a different appearance in Mac OS 9, but the calibration steps are the same.*

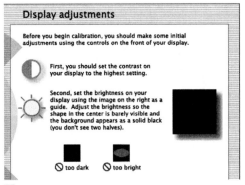

2 *The first step in calibrating your monitor is to set the* **contrast** *and* **brightness** *to the proper values.*

Determine your display's current gamma

Your display's actual gamma is affected by contrast and brightness settings and other characteristics of your display.

Move the slider until the grey shape in the middle blends in with the background as much as possible. It may help to squint or step back from the display.

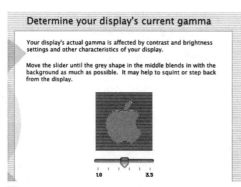

1.0   3.5

1 *Drag the slider to make the gray apple fade into the background.*

Select a target gamma

Select the gamma setting you want for your display. (Watch the picture on the right to see the effect as you click the different options.)

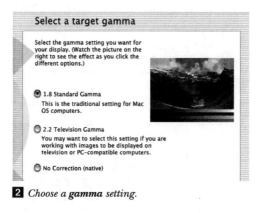

◉ 1.8 Standard Gamma
This is the traditional setting for Mac OS computers.

○ 2.2 Television Gamma
You may want to select this setting if you are working with images to be displayed on television or PC-compatible computers.

○ No Correction (native)

2 *Choose a* **gamma** *setting.*

Select a target white point

Select the white point setting you want for your display.

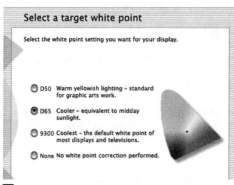

○ D50 Warm yellowish lighting – standard for graphic arts work.

◉ D65 Cooler – equivalent to midday sunlight.

○ 9300 Coolest – the default white point of most displays and televisions.

○ None No white point correction performed.

3 *Choose the* **target white point** *that's appropriate for the type of work you do.*

Note: In the following procedure, some options may not be available for LCD (flat-panel) monitors.

4. Turn up your monitor's brightness and contrast settings; leave the contrast at the maximum; and adjust the brightness to make the light gray oval barely visible and the background appear solid black (**2**, previous page).

5. The gray square represents a combined grayscale reading of your monitor **1**. Adjust the gamma using this slider until the solid gray apple shape matches the surrounding, stripey box. It helps to squint. If you checked the Expert mode box earlier, you'll have separate adjustments to make for Red, Green, and Blue.

6. Choose the gamma you want your display to use: 1.8 (Standard Mac OS) or 2.2 (Windows and TV), or No Correction to leave the display at its native gamma **2**. Again, if you chose Expert Mode, you'll be able to choose from a spectrum of gamma settings.

7. Tell the utility what kind of chemical phosphors your monitor uses by choosing the description that comes closest to matching your display.

8. Choose a target white point, based on the kind of work you'll be doing **3**. If you checked Expert Mode, you will have a continuous range of white point settings from which to choose.

9. Name your profile, then click Create to save it in:

Mac OS 9: System Folder > ColorSync > Profiles folder.

Mac OS X: Users/[CurrentUser]/ Library/ColorSync or Library/ ColorSync/Profiles/Profiles.

Photoshop can use this profile as its working RGB space in the Color Settings dialog box (see page 43).

Calibration: Mac OS

To calibrate your monitor (Windows):

1. Allow 30 minutes for the monitor to warm up and the display to stabilize, and establish a level of room lighting that will remain constant.

2. Make the desktop pattern light gray.

3. Choose Start menu > Settings > Control Panels, then open the Adobe Gamma utility.

4. Click Step by Step (Wizard), which will walk you through the process **1**.
or
Click Control Panel to choose settings from a single dialog box with no explanation. (If the Adobe Gamma dialog opens directly, you can skip this step.)

Note: Click Next. If you're using the Assistant, click Next between dialogs.

5. Leave the default monitor ICC profile.
or
Click Load and choose a profile that more closely matches your monitor **2**.

6. Turn up your monitor's brightness and contrast settings; leave the contrast at the maximum; and adjust the brightness to make the alternating gray squares in the top bar as dark as possible, but not black, while keeping the lower bar bright white.

7. For Phosphors, choose your monitor type, or choose Custom and enter the Red, Green, and Blue chromaticity coordinates specified by your monitor's manufacturer.

8. For Gamma, the gray square represents a combined grayscale reading of your monitor. Adjust the Gamma using this slider until the smaller, solid-color box matches the outer, stripey box. It helps to squint. You might find it easier to uncheck View Single Gamma Only and make separate adjustments based on the readings for Red, Green, and Blue.

9. For Desired, choose the default for your system: 1.8 (Mac OS)—or 2.2 (Windows), if this option is available.

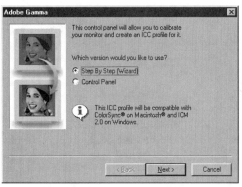

1 *This is the **Adobe Gamma** dialog box, set for the **Step by Step** calibration method.*

2 *This **Adobe Gamma dialog** box will open if you choose the Control Panel option. With **View Single Gamma Only** unchecked, adjustments can be made to the individual Red, Green, and Blue components.*

Finding the calibration utility

Macintosh

Mac OS X: Choose Apple > System Preferences, click Displays, then click the Color tab in the Displays pane.

Mac OS 9: Choose Apple > Control Panels > Monitors, then click the Color button.

Windows

Choose Start Menu > Settings > Control Panels > Adobe Gamma, or run the Adobe Gamma.cpl utility from C:\Program Files\Common Files\Adobe\ Calibration.

10. For White Point: Hardware, choose the white point the monitor manufacturer specifies, or click Measure and follow the instructions.

11. For Adjusted, choose Same as Hardware, or, if you know the color temperature at which your image will ultimately be viewed, you can either choose it from the pop-up menu or choose Custom and enter it here. *Note:* This option isn't available for all monitors.

12. Close the Adobe Gamma window and save the profile in Windows > System > Color (extension .icm). Photoshop can use this profile as its working RGB space in the Color Settings dialog box (see the next page).

Note: If you adjust your monitor's brightness and contrast settings or change the room lighting, you should recalibrate your monitor. Also, keep in mind that this method is just a start. Professional-level calibration requires more precise monitor measurement using expensive hardware devices, such as a colorimeter and a spectrophotometer (a what?).

Calibration: Windows

To choose a predefined color management setting

1. Choose Edit (Photoshop, in OS X) > Color Settings.

2. Choose a configuration option from the Settings pop-up menu:

Color Management Off emulates the behavior of applications that don't support color management. This is a good choice for projects destined for video or onscreen presentation.

ColorSync Workflow (Mac OS only) manages color using the ColorSync color management system. Profiles are based on those in the ColorSync control panel (including the monitor profile you may have created using the Apple Display Calibrator utility). Best used when you want to keep color consistent between Adobe and non-Adobe applications.

Emulate Photoshop 4 uses the same color workflow used by the Mac OS version of Photoshop 4 and earlier versions. This option doesn't recognize or save color profiles.

Photoshop 5 Default Spaces uses the same working spaces as the default settings in Photoshop 5.

U.S. Prepress Defaults manage the color using settings based on common press conditions in the U.S. In the European or Japanese Prepress setting, the CMYK Work Space is changed to a press standard for that region.

Web Graphics Defaults manage the color for content that will be published on the Web.

Point and learn

The **Description** area at the bottom of the Color Settings dialog box **1** provides valuable information on options that the pointer is currently over. Make use of this great feature!

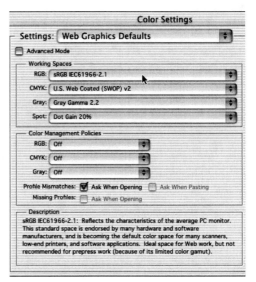

1 *The Color Settings dialog box, with the Web Graphics Defaults setting chosen*

Document-specific color

Photoshop 6 (and later) supports **document-specific color**, which means each open document keeps its own profile for controlling how the document previews and manages color on output. The current working space is used to create previews for documents that don't have an embedded profile.

Choose individual work space settings

You can choose color working spaces, which define how RGB and CMYK color will be treated in your document. For CMYK settings, you should check with your service provider. You can also specify dot gain for grayscale images and spot color or gamma for grayscale images. The following choices are available for RGB settings:

Adobe RGB (1998)

This color space produces a wide range of colors, and is useful if you will be converting RGB images to CMYK images. This isn't a good choice for Web work.

sRGB IEC61966-2.1

This is a good choice for Web work, as it reflects the settings on the average computer monitor. Many hardware and software manufacturers are using it as the default space for scanners, low-end printers, and software. sRGB IEC61966-2.1 should not be used for prepress work—Apple RGB or ColorMatch RGB should be used instead.

Apple RGB

This space is useful for files that you plan to display on Mac monitors, as it reflects the characteristics of the older standard Apple 13-inch monitors. It's also a good choice for working with older desktop publishing files, such as Adobe Photoshop 4.0 and earlier.

ColorMatch RGB

This space produces a smaller range of color than the Adobe RGB (1998) model, but it matches the color space of Radius Pressview monitors and is useful for print production work.

Monitor RGB

This choice sets the RGB working space to your monitor's profile. This is a useful setting if you know that other applications you will be using for your project don't support color management. Keep in mind that if you share this configuration with another

(Continued on the following page)

Work Space Settings

user, the configuration will use that user's
monitor profile as the RGB working space,
and color consistency may be lost.

ColorSync RGB (Mac only)

Use this color space to match Photoshop's
RGB space to the space specified in the
Apple ColorSync 3.0 (or later) control
panel. This can be the profile you created
using Adobe Gamma. If you share this configuration with another user, it will utilize
the ColorSync space specified by that user.

Work Space Settings

Color Settings

Settings: Custom

☐ Advanced Mode

Working Spaces
RGB: Adobe RGB (1998)
CMYK: U.S. Sheetfed Coated v2
Gray: Dot Gain 10%
Spot: Dot Gain 20%

Color Management Policies
RGB: Preserve Embedded Profiles
CMYK: Convert to Working CMYK
Gray: Preserve Embedded Profiles
Profile Mismatches: ☑ Ask When Opening ☑ Ask When Pasting
Missing Profiles: ☑ Ask When Opening

Description
Color Management Policies: Policies specify how you want colors in a particular color model managed. Policies handle the reading and embedding of color profiles, mismatches between embedded color profiles and the working space, and the moving of colors from one document to another.

1 *Color Management Policies options are chosen from the middle portion of the Color Settings dialog box.*

You can choose a customized color management policy that will tell Photoshop how to deal with artwork that doesn't match your current color settings.

To customize your color management policies:

1. Choose Edit (Photoshop, in OS X) > Color Settings (Ctrl-Shift-K/ Cmd-Shift-K).

2. Choose any predefined setting other than Emulate Photoshop 4 from the Settings pop-up menu.

3. For Color Management Policies **1**:

If you choose **Off**, Photoshop won't color-manage color files that are imported or opened.

Choose **Preserve Embedded Profiles** if you think you're going to be working with both color-managed and non-color-managed documents. This will tie each color file's profile to the individual file. Remember, in Photoshop, each open document can have its own profile.

Choose **Convert to Working…** if you want all your documents to reflect the same color working space. This is usually the best choice for Web work.

For Profile Mismatches, check **Ask When Opening** to have Photoshop display a message if the color profile in a file you're opening doesn't match your selected working space. If you choose this option, you can override your color management policy when opening documents.

Check **Ask When Pasting** to have Photoshop display a message when color profile mismatches occur as you paste color data into your document. If you choose this option, you can override your color management policy when pasting.

For files with Missing Profiles, check **Ask When Opening** to have Photoshop display a message offering you the opportunity to assign a profile.

4. Click OK.

To customize your conversion options:

1. Choose Edit (Photoshop, in OS X) > Color Settings (Ctrl-Shift-K/Cmd-Shift-K).

2. Check Advanced Mode **1**.

3. Under Conversion Options, choose a color management Engine to be used to convert colors between color spaces: Adobe (ACE) uses Adobe's color management system and color engine; Apple ColorSync or Apple CMM uses Apple's color management system; and Microsoft ICM uses the system provided in the Windows 98 and Windows 2000 systems. Other CMMs can be chosen to fit into color workflows that use specific output devices.

4. Choose a rendering Intent to determine how colors will be changed as they're moved from one color space to another:

Perceptual changes colors in a way that seems natural to the human eye, even though the color values actually do change; appropriate for continuous-tone images.

Saturation changes colors with the intent of preserving vivid colors, although it compromises the accuracy of the color; good for charts and business graphics.

Absolute Colorimetric keeps colors that are inside the destination color gamut unchanged, but the relationships between colors outside this gamut are changed in an attempt to preserve a color.

Relative Colorimetric, the default intent for all predefined settings options, is the same as Absolute Colorimetric, except it compares the white point, or extreme highlight, of the source color space to the destination color space and shifts all colors accordingly. The accuracy of this intent depends on the accuracy of white point information in an image's profile.

Save your settings

To save your custom settings for later use, click **Save** in the Color Settings dialog box. If you want your custom file to display on the Settings pop-up menu, in Windows, save it in the default location: Program Files/Common Files/Adobe/Color/Settings. In Mac OS 9, save it in System Folder > Application Support > Adobe > Color > Settings. In Mac OS X, save it in User/[CurrentUser]/Library/Application Support/Adobe/Color/Settings. When you're ready to reuse the saved settings, choose the file name from the Settings pop-up menu. To locate a settings file that isn't saved in the Settings folder (and thus isn't on the Settings menu), click **Load** in the Custom Settings dialog box.

1 *When* **Advanced Mode** *is checked in the* **Color Settings** *dialog box, the* **Conversion Options** *become available.*

Note: Differences between rendering intents are visible only on a printout or upon a conversion to a different working space.

Check **Use Black Point Compensation** if you want adjustments to be made for differences in black points between color spaces. When this option is chosen, the full dynamic range of the source color space is mapped into the full dynamic range of the destination color space. If you don't choose this option, your blacks may appear as grays. We recommend that you check this option for a RGB-to-CMYK conversion, but consult your print shop before checking it for a CMYK-to-CMYK conversion.

Check **Use Dither...** if you want Photoshop to dither colors when converting 8-bits-per-channel images between color spaces. Sometimes when an image is converted from one color space to another, colors that don't exist in the destination space are lost, resulting in banding or other color artifacts. With Use Dither... checked, Photoshop will mix blocks of similar colors to substitute for the missing color, thus achieving a smoother appearance. The file size may increase, however.

We recommend keeping Use Dither... checked when converting between RGB and CMYK spaces for print, but turning it off when preparing graphics for the Web. The Save for Web dialog box provides more precise controls for dithering images.

5. Click OK.

TIP When you save a file in a format that supports embedded profiles (e.g., the native Photoshop or PDF format), you can check the Embed ICC Profile option to save the profile in the document.

You may decide later that you want to change the color profile of a document or remove a profile from a document. For example, you may want to prepare a document for a specific output device, and you may need to adjust the profile accordingly. You also may want to use this option if you change your mind about your color management settings. The Assign Profile command reinterprets the color data directly in the color space of the new profile (or lack thereof), and visible shifting of colors can be the result. When you use the Convert Profile command, however, the color numbers are recalculated before the new profile is applied in an effort to preserve the document's appearance. In either case, keep Preview checked so you know what you're getting into.

To change or delete a document's color profile:

1. Choose Image > Mode > Assign Profile .

2. Click Don't Color Manage This Document to remove the color profile.
or
Click Working (plus the document color mode and name of the working space you're using) to assign that particular working space to a document that doesn't use a profile, or that uses a profile that is different from the working space.
or
Click Profile to reassign a different profile to a color-managed document. Choose a profile from the pop-up menu.

3. Click OK.

Note: If you save a file in (or export a file to) a format that supports embedded profiles, you will have the choice to select or deselect the Embed ICC Profile option. You should keep this option chosen (checked) unless you have a specific reason to uncheck it.

Where you'll see it

The assigned profile is listed as the **Source Space** in the File > Print with Preview dialog box if Show More Options is checked and Color Management is chosen from the pop-up menu. And if you choose Document Profile with Preview from the status bar pop-up menu at the bottom of the application/document window, the profile will also appear on the status bar.

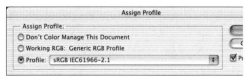

1 *The Assign Profile dialog box*

Preserve Color Numbers

The **Preserve Color Numbers** option in the Proof Setup dialog box is available only if the color mode of the current file is the same as that of the output device profile currently chosen in that dialog box. For example, if the document color mode is RGB and the chosen proofing profile is an RGB profile, then the Preserve Color Numbers option will be available.

1 *The **Convert to Profile** dialog box*

2 *The **Proof Setup** dialog box*

To convert a document's color profile:

1. Choose Image > Mode > Convert to Profile **1**.

2. Choose the space that you want to convert the document to from the Destination Space: Profile pop-up menu. It doesn't have to be the current working space.

For information on the Conversion Options, see "To customize your conversion options" on page 46.

Specifying a color management setup is all well and good, but sometimes all you want is to know how a document will look when it's printed out or viewed on a Windows or Mac monitor as part of a Web page. To do this, you can soft-proof your colors. While this method is less accurate than actually making a print or viewing your Web artwork on different monitors, it can give you a general idea of how your work will look with different settings.

To proof your colors:

1. From the View > Proof Setup submenu, choose which type of output display you want Photoshop to simulate.

Custom will allow you to create a proofing model for a specific output device using the Proof Setup dialog box **2**. To do this, choose the color profile for your desired output device from the Profile pop-up menu, then check or uncheck Preserve Color Numbers, if this option is available. If you check this option, Photoshop will simulate how the colors will appear if they're not converted to the proofing space. If you uncheck this option, Photoshop will simulate how the colors will appear if they are converted, and you will need to specify a rendering intent as described on page 46 ("To customize your conversion options").

(Continued on the following page)

Convert to Profile; Proof Setup

Check **Simulate: Paper White** to preview the shade of white of the print medium defined in the document's profile.

Check **Simulate: Ink Black** to preview the full range of gray values defined in the document's profile.

or

Choose **Working CMYK** to soft-proof colors using the CMYK working space as defined in the Color Settings dialog box.

or

Choose **Working Cyan Plate**, **Working Magenta Plate, Working Yellow Plate**, **Working Black Plate**, or **Working CMY Plates** to soft-proof various ink colors as defined in the current CMYK working space.

or

Choose **Macintosh RGB** or **Windows RGB** to soft-proof colors using a Mac or Windows monitor profile as the proofing space you want to simulate.

or

Choose **Monitor RGB** to use your monitor profile as the space for proofing.

2. View > Proof Colors will be checked automatically so the soft proof can be previewed. Uncheck this option to turn off proofing.

TIP To save a custom proof setup, click Save in the Proof Setup dialog box. Saved proof setups are listed at the bottom of the Proof Setup submenu.

TIP To learn how to use the color management features in the Print with Preview dialog box, see pages 412 and 413.

STARTUP 3

1 *Click Adobe Photoshop 7.0*

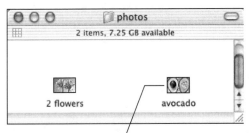

2 *Windows: Double-click the **Photoshop application** icon.*

3 *In Windows **Explorer**, double-click a Photoshop **file**.*

4 *In the Mac OS **Finder**, double-click a Photoshop **file**.*

IN THIS CHAPTER you will learn how to get started: launch the application, scan an image, create a new image, open an existing image, use the File Browser, and place an image into Photoshop. You'll also learn how to change an image's dimensions, resolution, or file storage size; apply the Unsharp Mask filter to resharpen an image after resampling; enlarge an image's canvas size; and crop, flip, rotate, save, copy, and close an image. And finally, you will learn how to change the zoom level of an image, move an image in its window, and switch screen display modes.

To launch Photoshop (Windows):

In Windows 95, 98, or NT, click the Start button on the taskbar, choose Programs, then click Adobe Photoshop 7.0 **1**. (If you don't yet have an icon for Photoshop on your desktop, open the Photoshop 7.0 folder, then drag the Photoshop application icon to the desktop.)

or

Open the Adobe\Photoshop 7.0 folder in My Computer, then double-click the Photoshop application icon **2**.

or

Double-click a Photoshop file icon **3**.

To launch Photoshop (Mac OS):

In OS X, click once on the Photoshop icon in the Dock. (To make an icon for Photoshop in the Dock, open the Adobe Photoshop 7 folder in the Finder, then drag the Photoshop application icon into the Dock.)

or

Open the Adobe Photoshop 7 folder in the Finder, then double-click the Photoshop application icon.

or

Double-click any Photoshop file icon **4**.

Launch Photoshop

Where images come from

An image can be created, opened, edited, and saved in over a dozen different file formats in Photoshop **1**. Of these, you might use only a handful, such as TIFF, GIF, JPEG, EPS, and the native Photoshop file format. Because Photoshop accepts so many formats, an image can be gathered from any number of sources, such as scanners, drawing applications, PhotoCDs, still images, video captures, or even other operating systems. An image can also be created entirely within Photoshop.

Scanning

Using a scanning device and scanning software, a slide, flat artwork, or a photograph can be digitized (translated into numbers) so it can be read, displayed, edited, and printed by a computer. You can scan directly into Photoshop, or you can use other scanning software and save the scan in a file format that Photoshop opens.

To produce a high-quality scan for print output, start with the highest-quality original possible. Some scanners will compress an image's dynamic range and increase its contrast, so choose a photograph with good tonal balance. If you're going to scan it yourself, set the scanning parameters carefully.

The quality of a scan will partially depend on the type of scanner you use. If you're going to dramatically transform the image in Photoshop (e.g., apply filters or add a lot of brushstrokes), you can use an inexpensive flat-bed scanner, which will produce an RGB scan. For more accurate color and crisper details, scan a transparency using a slide scanner.

For professional-quality output, have your artwork scanned by a service bureau on a high-resolution CCD scanner, such as a Scitex Smart-Scanner, or on a drum scanner. A high-end scanner can capture a wide, dynamic range of color and shade and can optically distinguish subtle differences in luminosity, even in shadow areas. High-end scanners usually produce CMYK scans, which usually have large file sizes.

| ✓ Photoshop |
| BMP |
| CompuServe GIF |
| Photoshop EPS |
| JPEG |
| PCX |
| Photoshop PDF |
| Photoshop 2.0 |
| PICT File |
| PICT Resource |
| Pixar |
| PNG |
| Raw |
| Scitex CT |
| Splat! Frame File |
| Splat! Stamp File |
| Targa |
| TIFF |
| Photoshop DCS 1.0 |
| Photoshop DCS 2.0 |

1 *These **formats** are available in Photoshop in the Mac OS.*

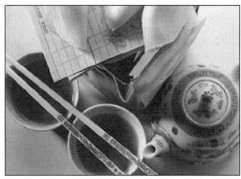

1 *72 ppi*

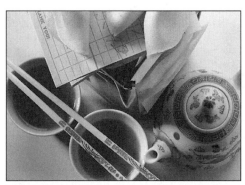

2 *150 ppi*

3 *300 ppi*

Desktop scanning software basics

Scanning software usually offers most of the options that are discussed below, although the terms may vary. The quality and file storage size of a scan are partially determined by the mode, resolution, and scale you specify, and whether you crop the image.

Preview: Place the art in the scanner, then click Preview or PreScan.

Scan mode: Choose Black-and-White Line Art (no grays), Grayscale, or Color (choose millions of colors, if available). An image scanned in Color will be approximately three times larger in file size than the same image scanned in Grayscale.

Resolution: Scan resolution is measured in pixels per inch (ppi) **1**–**3**. A high-resolution image will contain more pixels, and thus greater detail, but it will also have a larger file size. Choose the minimum resolution necessary to obtain the desired output quality from your final output device. But don't choose a higher resolution than you really need—the image will be larger in storage size than necessary; it will take longer to render onscreen, display on the Web, or print; and there will be no improvement in output quality. On the other hand, too low a resolution will cause a printed image to look coarse and jagged, and its details will be lost.

Before selecting a resolution for print output, ask your print shop what printer or imagesetter resolution and halftone screen frequency they plan to use. (The scan resolution is different from the resolution of the output device.)

As a general rule, for a grayscale image, you should choose a resolution that is one-and-a-half times the halftone-screen frequency (lines per inch) of your final output device, or twice the halftone-screen frequency for a color image. Use a high scanning resolution (600 ppi or higher) for line art. For example, if your print shop is going to use a 133-line screen for black-and-white printing,

(Continued on the following page)

Scanning

you should use 200 ppi as your scan resolution. If your prepress shop is going to use an imagesetter that doesn't have halftoning technology, ask them to recommend an appropriate scan resolution. To calculate the appropriate file size for a scan, see the instructions on page 57.

Cropping: If you're planning to use only part of an image, reposition the handles of the box in the preview area to reduce the scan area. Cropping can significantly reduce the storage size of a scan.

Scale: To enlarge an image's dimensions, choose a scale percentage above 100%. Enlarging an image or increasing its resolution in Photoshop or any other software program may cause it to blur because the program uses mathematical "guesswork" (interpolation) to fill in additional information. An image's original information is only recorded at the time of scanning!

Scan: Click Scan and choose a location in which to save the file.

16-bits-per-channel mode

An average-quality scanner can capture 10 bits of accurate data per channel from an image. A high-end scanner can capture up to 16 bits of accurate data per channel. If the 16-bit scanner also has a wide dynamic color range and good optical density (at least 3.3), then those extra pixels of data will capture even finer details of color and shade—even in shadow areas. Photoshop can open a CMYK file containing 16 bits per channel (a 64-bit total for four channels). All the image's original pixel information is preserved, and the image can be edited and adjusted.

There are some restrictions to keep in mind. First, a 16-bit image can only have one layer. Second, not all of Photoshop's editing commands can be used on it. And third, you have to convert a 16-bit image down to an 8-bit one before printing (Image > Mode > 8 Bits/Channel).

Available in 16-bits-per-channel mode

Tools	Adjustments submenu commands	Other
Marquee tools	Levels	Canvas Size
Lasso	Auto Levels	Histogram
Polygonal Lasso	Auto Contrast	Duplicate
Measure	Auto Color	Image Size
Zoom	Curves	Rotate Canvas
Hand	Color Balance	some filters
Eyedropper	Brightness/ Contrast	
Slice	Hue/Saturation	
Color Sampler	Channel Mixer	
Crop	Gradient Map	
Clone Stamp	Invert	
History Brush	Equalize	
Pen tools		
Healing Brush		
Patch		
Path Selection		
Direct Selection		
Type Mask tools		
Shape tools (paths only)		

16-Bit Mode

Scanning into ImageReady

The first time you choose a scanning module from the File > Import submenu in ImageReady, choose Twain_32 Source (Win) or Twain Select (Mac OS), choose a Twain device (the scanner), then choose Twain_32 (Win) or Twain Acquire (Mac OS).

Thereafter, to access the scanning software, just choose File > Import > Twain_32 (Win) or Twain Acquire (Mac OS). (See the Photoshop documentation for information about scanning modules.)

Note: To scan into Photoshop, the scanner's plug-in or Twain module must be in the Import-Export folder inside the Adobe Photoshop 7 > Plug-Ins folder.

If your scanner doesn't have a Photoshop-compatible scanner driver, scan your image outside Photoshop, save it as a TIFF, then open it in Photoshop as you would any other image.

To calculate the proper resolution for a scan, follow the instructions on the next page.

To scan into Photoshop:

1. Choose File > Import, then choose a scanning module or a Twain scanning device.

2. Click Prescan or Preview **1**.

3. Following the guidelines outlined on the previous two pages, choose a Scan Mode and a Resolution. Other options may be available, depending on the scanning software you're using.

4. *Optional:* Choose a different Scaling or Magnification percentage and/or manually crop the image preview.

5. Click Scan. The scanned image will appear in a new, untitled window.

6. Save the image (see pages 71–73). If it requires color correction, see pages 428–432. If it needs to be straightened out, see the tip on page 92.

1 *The dialog box for a scanning device.*

The resolution of a Photoshop image, like any bitmapped image, is independent of the monitor's resolution, so it can be customized for a particular output device, with or without modifying its file storage size.

TIP An image whose resolution is greater than the monitor's resolution will appear larger than its print size when displayed in Photoshop at 100% view.

Note: It's always best to scan an image at the outset at or very close to the final size and resolution that are required for your final output device.

To calculate the proper resolution for a scan or for an existing image:

1. Create a new RGB Color document (File > New), enter the final Width and Height dimensions, choose 72 ppi for the image Resolution, then click OK. (The resolution will be readjusted in step 5).

2. Choose Image > Image Size.

3. Click Auto on the right side of the dialog box.

4. Enter the Screen frequency of your final output device (the lpi, or lines per inch setting that your print shop will be using) **1**.

5. Click Quality: Draft (1x screen frequency), Good (1½ x screen frequency), or Best (2 x screen frequency).

6. Click OK.

7. Jot down the Document Size: Resolution value, which is the proper value to enter when you scan your image.

Note: If you're going to scale the final image up or down in Photoshop, you should multiply the resolution by that scale factor to arrive at the proper resolution for the scan. You don't need to multiply the resolution if you're going to scale the original image when you scan it.

8. Click Cancel.

Resolution for Web graphics

When creating an image for Web output, you'll need to estimate how large your user's browser's window is likely to be, and then figure out how much of the window you want your image to cover. Begin by determining what monitor resolution your viewers are most likely to use. These days, according to Web sites like websnapshot.com, which track such things, more than half of all browsers are running on monitors set to a 800×600-pixel size. When you subtract the space taken up by menu bars, scroll bars, and other controls that are part of the browser interface, you're left with a "canvas" of about 740×460 pixels, at the most. Given that for most viewers the browser window doesn't fill the entire screen, you shouldn't count on much more room than 660×420 pixels.

You might find it useful to create a blank document at a 660×420-pixel size (and a resolution of 72 pixels per inch) to use as a template. Keep it in the background while you work, so as you create the actual images for your Web page, you can see what portion of the screen they'll cover. (Don't fret over the inch equivalent for pixels. Onscreen imagery is measured in pixels.)

1 *Use the* **Auto Resolution** *dialog box to have Photoshop calculate the appropriate resolution for an image based on your chosen output parameters.*

File storage sizes of scanned images

Size (In inches)	PPI (Resolution)	Black/White 1-Bit	Grayscale 8-Bit	RGB Color 24-Bit
2 x 3	150	17 KB	132 KB	436 KB
	300	67 KB	528 KB	1.66 MB
4 x 5	150	56 KB	440 KB	1.39 MB
	300	221 KB	1.72 MB	5.44 MB
8 x 10	150	220 KB	1.72 MB	5.44 MB
	300	879 KB	6.87 MB	21.64 MB

Note: These file storage sizes are for a one-layer TIFF file with no alpha channels.

Potential gray levels at various output resolutions and screen frequencies

Output Resolution (DPI)	Screen Frequency (LPI)				
	60	85	100	133	150
300	26	13			
600	101	51	37	21	
1270	256*	224	162	92	72
2540		256*	256*	256*	256*

Note: Ask your print shop what screen frequency (lpi) you will need to specify when image-setting your file. Also ask your prepress shop what resolution (dpi) to use for imagesetting. Some imagesetters can achieve resolutions above 2540 dpi. Note that as the line screen frequency (lpi) goes up at a constant dpi, the number of gray levels goes down.

*PostScript Level 2 printers produce a maximum of 256 gray levels. PostScript Level 3 printers can produce a greater number of gray levels.

File Storage Sizes; Potential Gray Levels

Using the status bar

Windows: Choose Window > Show Status Bar to display the status bar, or choose Hide Status Bar to hide it.

Windows and Mac OS:

When **Document Sizes** is chosen from the status bar pop-up menu at the bottom of the application/image window, the status bar displays the file storage size for a flattened file (the first amount) and the file storage size for a layered file (the second amount) **1**.

When **Document Profile** is chosen, the embedded color profile is listed; the words "Untagged RGB" appear when there is no profile.

When **Document Dimensions** is chosen, the dimensions of the image are displayed, in the currently selected units.

When **Scratch Sizes** is chosen, the bar displays the amount of storage space Photoshop is using for all currently open pictures (on the left) and the amount of RAM currently available to Photoshop (on the right). When the first amount is greater than the second amount, Photoshop is using virtual memory on the scratch disk.

When **Efficiency** is chosen, the bar displays the percentage of processing time devoted to actual program operations in RAM. A percentage below 100 indicates the scratch disk is being used.

When **Current Tool** is chosen, the name of the current tool displays.

And finally, press and hold on the status bar to display the page **preview**, which is a thumbnail of the image relative to the paper size (including custom printing marks, if any).

To find out an image's storage size:

Windows: Use Windows Explorer to locate the file you're interested in, and look in the Size column **2**. Or for a more accurate figure, right-click the file icon and click Properties.

Mac OS: Look at the file information in the Finder. Or for an even more accurate figure, click once on the file icon in the Finder, then choose File > Show Info (Cmd-I) **3**.

Do this any time

Regardless of which option is chosen from the status bar pop-up menu, you can always Alt-press/Option-press on the status bar to display the image's **dimensions**, number of **channels**, **mode**, and **resolution**.

1 *The status bar with* **Document Sizes** *chosen. The figure on the left is the* **RAM** *required for the* **flattened** *image with no extra channels; the figure on the right is the* **RAM** *required for the image with* **layers** *and* **extra channels,** *if any. Note: If the status bar isn't visible, make the image window wider.*

2 *Windows: The storage size of an image is listed in the* **Size** *column.*

3 *Mac OS: For the actual* **storage size** *of an image, use* **Show Info** *(Cmd-I).*

Status Bar; Storage Size

7.0!

1 *In the* **New** *dialog box, enter a* **Name** *and enter* **Width, Height,** *and* **Resolution** *values. Also choose an image* **Mode** *and click a* **Contents** *type for the Background.*

2 *A* **new,** *untitled image window (Windows)*

To create a new image:

1. Choose File > New (Ctrl-N/Cmd-N).
2. Enter a name in the Name field **1**.
3. Choose a unit of measure from the pop-up menus next to the Width and Height fields.
4. Enter Width and Height values.
5. Enter the Resolution required for your final output device—whether it's an imagesetter or the Web (resolution issues are discussed on pages 53–56).
6. Choose an image mode from the Mode pop-up menu. You can convert the image to a different mode later (see "Image modes," starting on page 29).
7. Click Contents: White or Background Color for the Background. To choose a Background color, see pages 179–182. Or click the Transparent option if you want the bottommost tier of the document to be a layer.

   Note: An image that contains one or more layers can only be saved in the Photoshop, Photoshop PDF, or TIFF file format. If you're going to export the file to another application, though, you'll need to save a flattened copy of it in another format, since few applications can read Photoshop's layer transparency. (More about layers and transparency in Chapters 7 and 14.)
8. Click OK. An untitled image window will appear (Win) **2**/(Mac OS) **3**.

TIP If you want the New dialog box settings to match those of another open document, with the New dialog box open, choose the name of the image that has the desired dimensions from the bottom of the Window > Documents submenu.

TIP If there is an image on the Clipboard from Photoshop or from Illustrator, the New dialog box will automatically display its dimensions. To prevent those dimensions from displaying, hold down Alt/Option as you choose File > New.

3 *A* **new,** *untitled image window (Mac OS)*

Create a New Image

Opening files

To open an image within Photoshop:

1. Choose File > Open (Ctrl-O/Cmd-O).

2. Locate the file you want to open (Win)**1**/(Mac OS) **2**. Choose a specific format from the Files of type/Show drop-down menu, or choose All Formats/All Documents.

Once it's opened, an image can be saved in any format that Photoshop reads.

Mac OS: To search for a file, click Find, type the file name, then click Find again.

Note: If the name of the file you want to open doesn't appear on the scroll list, it may be because the plug-in module for its format isn't installed in the Photoshop Plug-Ins folder. Install the plug-in, then try again.

3. Click the file name, then click Open.
or
Double-click the file name.

Got a Profile Mismatch? See page 45.

For some file formats, a further dialog box will open. For example, if you open an EPS, Adobe Illustrator, or PDF file that hasn't yet been rasterized (converted from vector to bitmap), the Rasterize Generic...Format dialog box will open. Follow steps 4–9 on pages 68–69.

TIP To open an Adobe Illustrator file in Photoshop, follow the instructions on page 68 or 70.

TIP Special plug-in modules must be used to open images in some file formats, such as Scitex CT or PICT Resource (access them via File > Import).

Pick-n-choose

To specify a particular **file format** when opening a file in Windows, choose File > Open As, choose the necessary format from the "Open as" drop-down menu, then click Open. This is useful for opening Mac OS files that lack extensions. In the Mac OS, choose File > Open, choose Show: All Documents, choose a file name, choose a format, then click Open. To identify a file using its thumbnail, see the next page.

Quick switcheroo

To cycle between open image windows, press **Ctrl-Tab/Control-Tab**.

1 *Windows: Double-click a file name.*

2 *Mac OS: Double-click a file name.*

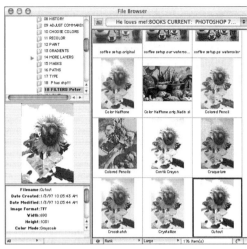

1 *The **File Browser** makes locating and opening files much easier.*

The File Browser is a palette that enables **7.0!** you to search for, view, sort, and open your Photoshop files using thumbnails, rather than just file names. Information about each file is also displayed in one or two panes in the palette. Images can be sorted by various criteria, and files can be moved, renamed, and deleted from the browser.

To open the File Browser:
Choose Window > File Browser **1**.
or
Choose File > Browse (Ctrl-Shift-O/ Cmd-Shift-O).
or
Click the File Browser palette tab in the palette well.

The File Browser panes
The File Browser is made up of four panes. Three panes display on the left side of the Browser **2**:

The **Tree** pane displays a scroll window with a hierarchical listing of the top-level folders and nested folders on your hard drive.

The **Preview** pane displays a preview of the selected file thumbnail.

The **Metadata** pane displays a scroll window with individual information about the currently selected file thumbnail, such as the file name, image size, color mode, resolution, etc., as well as any data that was entered in the File > File Info dialog box. If EXIF (EXchangeable Image File) is chosen from the pop-up menu in the lower-left corner of the palette, then information relating to images created with a digital camera may also be listed in the Metadata pane.

TIP You can resize any individual pane vertically by dragging its horizontal dividing bar (or bars). You can also drag the vertical bar to the left or right.

The **Thumbnail** pane on the right side of the Browser displays the image thumbnails and any nested folders within the currently

Thumbnail ⌐

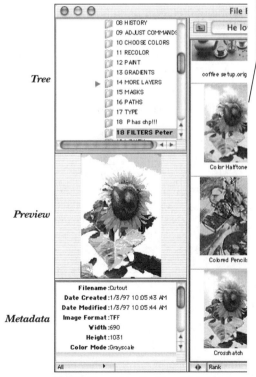

Tree

Preview

Metadata

2 *The **Tree View**, **Preview**, **Metadata**, and **Thumbnail** panes of the File Browser*

(Continued on the following page)

selected folder. Choose a thumbnail size from the options listed in the View By pop-up menu (below the Thumbnail pane) 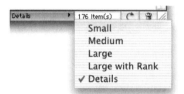. Details view displays a thumbnail and some of the Metadata information for each image in the selected folder.

TIP To have the Thumbnail pane take over the entire palette, click the Toggle Expanded View button. ◀▶ Click the button again to redisplay the left panes (Expanded view).

7.0!

To view files in the File Browser:

In the **Tree** pane, you can do any of the following:

■ Scroll upward or downward.

■ Expand or contract any folder using the arrowheads or by double-clicking.

■ Open a folder by clicking its icon.

In the **Thumbnail** pane, you can do any of the following:

■ Rest the pointer over a thumbnail to bring up a tool-tip information box for that image **2**.

■ Click a thumbnail to have its preview appear in the Preview pane, and to have information about it appear in the Metadata pane.

■ Double-click the thumbnail for a nested folder to reveal its contents. *Note:* In order to view nested folders in the Thumbnail pane, the Show Folders option on the File Browser palette menu must have a checkmark.

■ Drag a file from the Thumbnail pane into the Tree pane to move it to another folder, or Option/Alt drag a thumbnail to add a copy of that file to another folder.

■ To move back up the folder hierarchy, use the Tree pane; or use the pop-up menu at the top of the Thumbnail pane; or click the Up One Level button **3**.

The "real" file

To locate an actual file in the Finder/Explorer, click a thumbnail in the File Browser, then choose **Reveal Location in Finder/Explorer** from the palette menu. The file's folder will open as a window, and in the Mac OS, the icon will be highlighted.

1 *Choose a* ***thumbnail size*** *from the* ***View By*** *pop-up menu.*

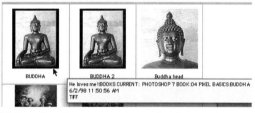

2 *Rest the pointer over an image thumbnail to learn more about the image, such as its path.*

3 *Up One Level button*

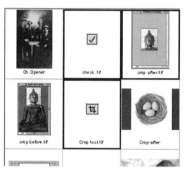

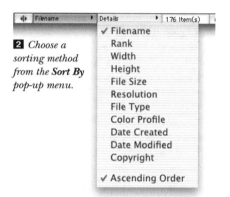

1 *Ctrl-click/Cmd-click to select multiple thumbnails if they aren't consecutive.*

2 *Choose a sorting method from the Sort By pop-up menu.*

3 *Enter a number (or a word) in the Rank field for each thumbnail.*

To open a file or files: 7.0!

1. Display the File Browser.

2. Click a thumbnail.

or

Ctrl-click/Cmd-click multiple thumbnails that aren't consecutive **1**.

or

To select a series of thumbnails, click the first thumbnail in the series, then Shift-click the last thumbnail in the series.

3. Double-click a thumbnail (or one of the selected thumbnails).

or

Drag a selected thumbnail (or one of the selected thumbnails) out of the File Browser.

or

Choose Open from the File Browser palette menu.

There are several ways that thumbnails can be arranged and rearranged in the Thumbnail pane.

To choose a sorting method for 7.0! thumbnails:

1. Use the File Browser to open a folder of images.

2. Choose an option from the Sort By pop-up menu below the Thumbnail pane **2**.

You can create your own rank (series of numbers) or categories (words, such as 7.0! roughs, finals, print, web) for sorting and displaying image thumbnails. Ranking categories will display in alphanumeric order.

To create a rank for sorting images:

1. Choose Large with Rank from the View By pop-up menu at the bottom of the File Browser.

2. Click next to the term "Rank:" below a thumbnail, then type a number or word **3**. Press Return/Enter or click elsewhere in the File Browser to accept the entry.

3. Choose Rank from the Sort By pop-up menu to use your ranking method.

File Browser

7.0! ## To rename a file:

1. Click a file name below a thumbnail.

2. Highlight the text to the left of the period, then enter a new name . Don't try to delete the extension (it won't go away). Press Return/Enter or click away from the name field to accept the entry.

TIP To quickly move to the next file name field, press Tab.

7.0! ## To delete a file:

1. Drag a thumbnail to the Delete file (Trash) button on the File Browser palette.
or
Click a thumbnail, then choose Delete from the palette menu. (To delete multiple files, first Ctrl-click/Cmd-click individual thumbnails, or click the first in a series of consecutive thumbnails, then Shift-click the last in the series.)

2. Click Yes.

7.0! ## To create a new folder:

1. Open the desired drive or folder.

2. Choose New Folder from the File Browser palette menu, type a name, then press Return/Enter.

TIP You can't delete a folder using the File Browser. *Très* annoying.

7.0! If you rotate a thumbnail in the File Browser, then when that file is opened, Photoshop will rotate the actual image!

To rotate a thumbnail:

1. Click a thumbnail.

2. Click the Rotate button **2** to rotate the thumbnail 90° clockwise, or Alt-click/ Option-click the button to rotate the thumbnail 90° counter-clockwise.
or
Choose Rotate 180°, Rotate 90° CW, or Rotate 90° CCW from the palette menu.

Caching out

The File Browser creates a cache file that stores thumbnail information (rank, rotation info, etc.) in order to speed up thumbnail display when returning to a previously displayed folder. The cache is linked to the current folder name. In Mac OS X, Photoshop automatically stores cache files in the hard drive's Library folder (System Folder in Mac OS 9), in this folder arrangement: Application Support > Adobe > File Browser > Photoshop7. In Windows, the cache is in \Program Files\Common Files\Adobe\ FileBrowser\Photoshop7.

To export the file browser cache, open the desired folder of images in the File Browser, set up all the thumbnail information, then choose **Export Cache** from the File Browser palette menu. The two cache files, named **AdobePS7.md0** and **AdobePS7.tb0**, will be placed into the folder currently displayed in the File Browser. These files can be used to copy the current File Browser display info to removable disks, or to a shared folder on a network. The presence of a cache in a folder will speed up the display of thumbnails. The cache files only display in Explorer/Finder.

TIP Use Edit > Purge to remove all but the current folder cache from the System or Library folder.

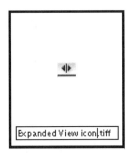

Expanded View icon.tiff

1 *You can change the **file name**, but not its extension.*

Rotate 90 CW or hold down option for Rotate 90 CCW

2 *Click the **Rotate** button to have Photoshop rotate the image when it's **opened**.*

Do it again

To reopen a file that was closed recently, choose that file name from the File > **Open Recent** submenu.

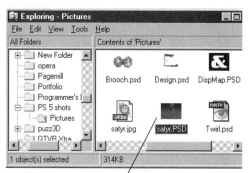

1 *Windows: **Double-click** a Photoshop file icon.*

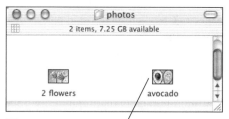

2 *Mac OS: **Double-click** a Photoshop file icon.*

3 *In **Windows**, choose Image Previews: **Always Save** in Preferences > **File Handling**.*

Preferences

File Handling

Image Previews: Always Save

☑ Icon ☐ Full Size
☑ Macintosh Thumbnail
☑ Windows Thumbnail

4 *In **Mac OS X**, choose Image Previews: **Always Save** or **Ask When Saving** in Preferences > **File Handling**.*

To open a Photoshop image from Windows Explorer:

Double-click a Photoshop image file icon in Windows Explorer **1**. Photoshop will launch if it hasn't already been launched.

To open a Photoshop image from the Finder (Mac OS):

Double-click a Photoshop image file icon in the Finder **2**. Photoshop will launch if it hasn't already been launched.

Thumbnails

Windows: To create image icons for Windows Explorer that will show when the Views menu is set to Large Icon, click the Save Thumbnail check box for individual files as you save them. To create thumbnails of all subsequently saved images for display in the Open dialog box, choose Edit > Preferences > File Handling, then choose Image Previews: Always Save **3**. A thumbnail icon will only appear for an image that has a .psd, .jpg, .pdf, or .tif file extension.

Mac OS: To create image icons for the Finder, choose Edit (Photoshop, in OS X) > Preferences > File Handling, choose Image Previews: Always Save, then check Icon **4**. To choose icons for individual files as you save them instead, choose Image Previews: Ask When Saving. Saving a multi-megabyte image with a preview could increase its file storage size. To create thumbnail icons of all subsequently saved images for display in the Open dialog box, check Macintosh Thumbnail and/or Windows Thumbnail. To access this feature in OS 9, the Apple QuickTime extension must be in the System Folder > Extensions folder (it's usually installed as part of the OS 9 System software).

Open File in Explorer/From Finder

You can open Kodak Photo CD files in Photoshop via the Kodak PCD Format dialog box. An image in the Photo CD format ("PCD," for short) can be converted to Photoshop's RGB Color or Lab Color mode.

To open a Kodak Photo CD file:

1. Choose File > Open (Ctrl-O/Cmd-O).

2. Locate and double-click a Photo CD file name.

or

Click a Photo CD file name, then click Open.

3. Under Source Image **1** (and **1**, next page):

Choose a Pixel Size. A size of 512-by-768 pixels will produce an image that is approximately 7 by 10.5 inches. The image height, followed by the width, will appear on the Pixel Size pop-up menu.

Choose a device profile (film and scanner type) from the Profile pop-up menu

(see the sidebar on the next page). Use the Image Info area on the left side of the dialog box to see the source image's film and scanner type.

4. Under Destination Image:

Choose a Resolution for the opened image. This choice, combined with the Pixel Size, will determine the onscreen size of the image.

Choose a Color Space (RGB... or Lab...) for the opened image.

Click Orientation: Landscape or Portrait.

5. Click OK. The image will open in Photoshop.

1 *The Kodak PCD Format dialog box in the Mac OS*

Kodak profiles

Kodak uses the 4045 and 4050 model film scanners and has also upgraded its PhotoCD transform profiles to version 3.4. The Photo CD device profiles are as follows:

Photo CD 4050E-6 V3.4	Ektachrome scanned on 4050 model
Photo CD 4050K-14 V3.4	Kodachrome scanned on 4050 model
Photo CD Color Negative V3.0	Color negative scanned on older or unspecified scanner
Photo CD Universal E-6 V3.2	Universal Ektachrome scanned on older or unspecified scanner
Photo CD Universal K-14 V3.2	Universal Kodachrome scanned on older or unspecified scanner

1 *The Kodak PCD Format dialog box in Windows*

When an EPS or Adobe Illustrator file is opened or placed in Photoshop, it is rasterized, which means it's converted from its native vector format into Photoshop's pixel format. Follow these instructions to open an EPS or Illustrator file as a new file. Or follow the instructions on page 70 to place an EPS file into an existing Photoshop file.

Note: To open a single-page PDF file in Photoshop, you can use the Open command (this page) or the Place command (page 70). To open a multi-page PDF as multiple images in Photoshop format, choose File > Automate > Multi-Page PDF to PSD (see page 390).

In Photoshop 7, Illustrator 9 and 10 files are listed as Generic PDF format, not as EPS.

To open an EPS, PDF, or Illustrator file as a new image:

1. Choose File > Open (Ctrl-O/Cmd-O).

2. If the file name isn't listed, in Windows, choose All Formats from the Files of type drop-down menu; in the Mac OS, choose Show: All Documents.

3. Locate and highlight the file to be opened, then click Open.
   or
   Double-click a file name.

   Note: If you're opening a PDF that contains more than one page, the PDF Page Selector will open 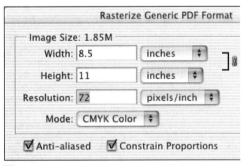. Use the scroll bar or arrows to locate the page that you want to open, then click OK. Or click Go to Page, enter a page number **2**, then click OK twice.

4. *Optional:* In the Rasterize Generic EPS (or PDF) Format dialog box, check Constrain Proportions to preserve the file's width-to-height ratio **3**.

5. *Optional:* Choose a unit of measure from the drop-down menus next to the Height and Width fields, and enter new dimensions.

6. In the Resolution field, enter the final resolution required for your image.

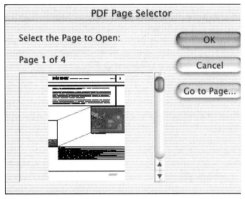

1 *For a **PDF** file, click the up or down arrow on the scroll bar to locate the page you want to open, or click* **Go to Page**...

2 *...then in the **Go to Page** dialog box, enter the number of the page that you want opened.*

3 *Check **Constrain Proportions** in the **Rasterize Generic PDF Format** dialog box to preserve the file's width-to-height ratio.*

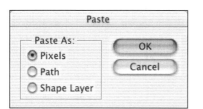

1 *When you paste an object from* **Illustrator** *into* **Photoshop,** *the* **Paste** *dialog box opens automatically.*

Entering the correct final resolution before rasterizing will produce the best rendering of the image.

7. Choose an image mode from the Mode pop-up menu. (See "Image modes" on pages 29–31.)

8. Check Anti-aliased to reduce jaggies and soften edge transitions.

9. Click OK.

TIP If the PDF contains security settings, those settings must be disabled via Acrobat Exchange before the file can be opened.

TIP PDF and EPS files open with a transparent background. To create a white background, create a new layer, choose white (or another color) for the Background color, then choose Layer > New > Background From Layer.

Pixel paste

You can copy an object in Illustrator and then paste it into a Photoshop image; the Paste dialog box will open automatically. Click Paste As: Pixels, Path, or Shape Layer **1** (shapes are discussed in Chapter 16). If you choose the Shape Layer option, the resulting vector shape will be editable in Photoshop. Not so if you use the Open or Place command to get the object into Photoshop.

Pixel Paste

When you place an object-oriented (vector) image into a Photoshop image, it becomes bitmapped, and it's rendered in the resolution of the Photoshop image. The higher the resolution of the Photoshop image, the better the rendering.

Note: You can also drag a path from an Illustrator image window into a Photoshop image window—it will appear on a new layer.

To place an EPS, PDF, or Adobe Illustrator image into an existing Photoshop image:

1. Open a Photoshop image.

2. Choose File > Place.

3. Locate and click the file that you want to open . To place a PDF that contains multiple pages, choose a page, then click OK (see page 68).

1 *Click a file name, then click **Place**.*

4. Click Place. A box will appear in the image window. Pause, if necessary, to allow the image to draw inside it **2**.

5. *Perform any of these optional steps (use the Undo command to undo any of them):*

   To resize the placed image, drag a handle of the bounding box. Shift-drag to preserve the proportions of the placed image as you resize it.

   To move the placed image, drag inside the bounding box.

   To rotate the placed image, position the pointer outside the bounding box (curved pointer), then drag. You can move the center point to rotate from a different axis.

6. To accept the placed image, press Enter/ Return or double-click inside the bounding box. The placed image will appear on a new layer.

TIP To remove the placed image, press Esc before or while it's rendering. If the image is already rendered, drag its layer into the trash on the Layers palette.

2 *The word "Delphi" was created in Adobe Illustrator, and then placed into a Photoshop file.*

*To produce this image, artist **Wendy Grossman** created the musical notes and other shapes in Illustrator and then imported them into Photoshop.*

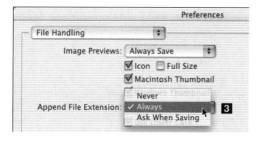

1 *Windows:* **Save As** *dialog box*

2 *Mac OS:* **Save As** *dialog box*

Saving files

You'll find specific instructions for saving in the EPS, DCS, PICT, and TIFF file formats in Chapter 22, and information about the GIF and JPEG formats in Chapter 23.

To save a new image:

1. Choose File > Save (Ctrl-S/Cmd-S).

2. Type a name in the File name (Win) **1** / Save As (Mac OS) **2** field.

3. Choose a location for the file.

   Windows: To locate another folder or drive, click the drop-down menu at the top of the dialog box.

   Mac OS X: To locate a drive, scroll as far left as possible in the browser window, then click a drive. (*OS 9:* Choose from the pointing-hand menu.) Double-click a folder to save the file in, or click New Folder to create a new folder.

4. Choose a file format from the Save As (Win)/Format (Mac OS) pop-up menu. Only the native Photoshop, TIFF, and Photoshop PDF formats can save files that contain multiple layers.

5. Check any options in the Save area of the dialog box (except the As a Copy option, which is discussed on page 73). You can also check Color: Embed Color Profile... if the file contains an embedded profile and the format you are saving to supports embedded profiles (see page 48).

6. Click Save.

TIP *Mac OS:* In Edit (Photoshop, in OS X) > Preferences > File Handling, choose Append File Extension: Always or Ask When Saving if you want a three-character file extension to be appended automatically to your files. This is essential for Windows export **3**.

Also check Always Maximize Compatibility for Photoshop (PSD) Files to have a non-layered version of every image save automatically with each layered version. This is useful if the image will be exported to another application.

Saving layers, vectors, and effects

Photoshop, TIFF, and **Photoshop PDF** are the only formats in which the following image elements are preserved:

- multiple layers and layer transparency
- adjustment layers
- editable type layers
- layer effects
- grids and guides
- ICC color management profiles (actually, the PICT, JPEG, Photoshop DCS, and Photoshop EPS formats also preserve these profiles)
- Lab Color image mode (the Photoshop EPS and Photoshop DCS formats also preserve this mode)

Note: An image in Duotone color mode can only be saved in the native Photoshop, Photoshop EPS, or Photoshop PDF format.

TIP Flatten a copy of any layered image instead of the original so you'll have the option of reworking it later (see page 154).

The prior version of a file is overwritten when the Save command is chosen.

To save an existing image:

Choose File > Save (Ctrl-S/Cmd-S).

The simple Revert command (instructions here) restores a document to its last-saved version. The History palette, which we discuss in Chapter 8, is a full-service, multiple-undo feature. Its partner, the History Brush tool, is used to selectively revert a portion of an image. Revert does show up as a state on the History palette, so you can undo it, if need be, by clicking an earlier history state.

To revert to the last-saved version:

Choose File > Revert.

What is the Duplicate command?

The Image > **Duplicate** command copies an image and all its layers, layer masks, and channels into currently available memory. A permanent copy of the file is **not** saved to disk unless you then choose File > Save. An advantage of the Duplicate command is that you can use the duplicate to try out variations without altering the original file. However, Duplicate should be used with caution because if an application freeze or a system crash occurs, you'll lose whatever's currently in memory, including your duplicate image!

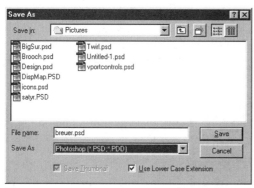

1 *In the Windows* **Save As** *dialog box, check* **Use Lower Case Extension** *to have the file's extension appear in lowercase style.*

2 *The* **Save As** *dialog box in Mac OS X*

Using the Save As command, you can save a copy of an image in a different image mode (save a copy in CMYK Color mode, for example, and keep the original version in RGB Color mode). Or you could use this command to spawn off a design (or any other kind of) variation.

To save a new version of an image:

1. Choose File > Save As (Ctrl-Shift-S/ Cmd-Shift-S).

2. Enter a new name or modify the existing name in the File name field (Win) **1**/ Save As (Mac OS) **2** field.

3. Choose a location in which to save the new version using the Save in drop-down menu in Windows; the Where pop-up menu in Mac OSX.

4. Choose a different file format from the Save As (Win)/Format (Mac) pop-up menu. Only those formats that are available for the current image (color) mode will be available.

Beware! If the chosen format doesn't support multiple layers, the Layers option will automatically become unavailable and the saved file will be flattened.

5. Check any available options in the Save area, as desired, and also check Embed Color Profile…, if that option is available (see page 48).

TIP Check As a Copy to have the copy remain closed and the original stay open. Leave this option unchecked to do the opposite: have the original close and the new version stay open.

6. Click Save. For an EPS file, follow the instructions on pages 421–422. For a TIFF or PICT file, follow the instructions on pages 424–425. Consult the Adobe Photoshop 7.0 User Guide for other formats.

TIP If you don't change the file name and you click Save, a warning prompt will appear. Click Replace to save over the original file, or click Cancel to return to the Save As dialog box.

Navigating

In this section you'll learn how to change the zoom level of an image, move an image in its window, switch screen display modes, display an image in two windows simultaneously, and recolor the work canvas.

*A portion of an image is **magnified**.*

You can display an entire image in its window or magnify part of an image to work on a small detail. The zoom level is indicated as a percentage in three locations: on the image window title bar, in the lower-left corner of the application/image window, and in the lower-left corner of the Navigator palette. The zoom level of an image has no affect on its printout size.

*If the image is magnified, you can drag the view box on the thumbnail to **move** the image in its window. Ctrl-drag/ Cmd-drag across part of the thumbnail (as in this illustration) to marquee the area you want to **magnify**.*

To change the zoom level using the Navigator palette:

*Enter the desired **zoom percentage** (or ratio, as in 1:1 or 4:1), then press Enter/Return. To zoom to the percentage and keep the field highlighted, press Shift-Enter/Shift-Return.*

Thumbnail

View box

*Click the **Zoom out** button to zoom out.*   *Move the **Zoom slider** to change the zoom level.*   *Click the **Zoom in** button to zoom in.*

TIP You can also change the zoom level by double-clicking the zoom percentage box in the lower-left corner of the application/image window, typing the desired zoom percentage, and then pressing Enter/Return.

TIP To change the outline color of the view box on the Navigator palette, choose Palette Options from the palette menu, then choose a preset color from the Color pop-up menu, or click the color swatch and choose a color from the Color Picker.

Zoom shortcuts

WINDOWS

Zoom in (window doesn't resize)	Ctrl +
Zoom out (window doesn't resize)	Ctrl –
Zoom in (window resizes)	Ctrl Alt +
Zoom Out (window resizes)	Ctrl Alt –
Actual pixels/100% view	Ctrl Alt 0
Fit onscreen	Ctrl 0 (zero)

MACINTOSH

Zoom in (window resizes)	Cmd +
Zoom Out (window resizes)	Cmd –
Zoom in (window doesn't resize)	Cmd Option +
Zoom out (window doesn't resize)	Cmd Option –
Actual pixels/100% view	Cmd Option 0
Fit on screen	Cmd 0 (zero)

1 *Click* on the image with the Zoom tool to *zoom in*. Note the plus sign in the pointer.

2 *Alt-click/Option-click* on the image with the Zoom tool to *zoom out*. Note the minus sign in the pointer.

To change the zoom level using the Zoom tool:

1. Choose the Zoom tool (Z).

2. *Optional:* On the Zoom tool options bar **3**, uncheck Resize Windows To Fit to prevent the image window from resizing as you zoom in or out. Check Ignore Palettes to allow the image window to be enlarged all the way to the edge of your screen.

3. To **zoom in**, click in the image window **1**, or drag a marquee across an area to magnify that area.
or
To **zoom out**, Alt-click/Option-click in the image window **2**.
or
To view the image at actual pixel size, click **Actual Pixels** on the options bar. *Note:* The zoom level will equal the actual print size only when the display ratio is 100% and the image resolution is the same as the monitor resolution.
or
To display the entire image in the largest possible size that can fit on your screen/application window, click **Fit On Screen** on the options bar (Ctrl-0/Cmd-0).
or
Click **Print Size** on the options bar to display the image at its print size.

TIP Ctrl-Spacebar/Cmd-Spacebar-click or drag to zoom in when another tool is chosen, or if a dialog box with a Preview option is open. Alt-Spacebar-click/Option-Spacebar-click to zoom out. To have the window resize automatically whenever the zoom level is changed using a keyboard shortcut, check Keyboard Zoom Resizes Windows in Photoshop (Edit in OS 9) > Preferences > General.

TIP For a slow, leisurely approach, you can also change the zoom level by choosing View > Zoom In or Zoom Out.

Zoom in or Out

3 *Choose settings on the* **Zoom** *tool options bar.*

Note: If the scroll bars aren't active, the entire image is displayed, and there is no need to move it.

To move an image in its window:

Click outside, or drag, the view box on the Navigator palette **1**.
or
Click the up or down scroll arrow on the image window. Or drag a scroll box to move the image more quickly.
or
Choose the Hand tool (H),  then drag in the image window **2**.

TIP Other shortcuts for moving an image in its window are listed on page 509.

To change the screen display mode:

Click the "Standard screen mode" button in the lower-left corner of the Toolbox (F) **3** to display the image, menu bar, and palettes, and the scroll bars on the image window.
or
Click the "Full screen mode with menu bar" (middle) button (F) **4**, **6** to display the image at full size without scroll bars, with the menu bar and palettes visible. The area around the image will be gray. This mode shows off an image in its full glory.
or
Click the "Full screen mode" (rightmost) button (F) **5** to display the full size image, palettes, and options bar (and rulers, if showing) but not the menu bar or scroll bars. The area around the image will be black (very dramatic).

TIP Press Tab to show/hide the Toolbox and any open palettes. Or press Shift-Tab to show/hide just the palettes, leaving the Toolbox open.

TIP Use the Hand tool (H) to move the image in its window when the scroll bars are hidden and the image is magnified, or use the Navigator palette. Hold down the spacebar to use a temporary Hand tool while another tool is selected.

1 *Click outside, or drag, the view box on the* **Navigator** *palette to move an image in its window.*

2 *Or move an image in its window using the* **Hand** *tool.*

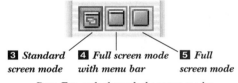

3 *Standard screen mode*   **4** *Full screen mode with menu bar*   **5** *Full screen mode*

Press **F** *to cycle through the screen modes.*

6 *Full screen mode with menu bar*

1 *An image displayed in **two windows** simultaneously: one in a low zoom level for previewing, the other in a higher zoom level for editing.*

2 *To **recolor** the **work canvas**, choose the Paint Bucket tool and a Foreground color, then Shift-click the work canvas.*

The number of images that can be open at a time depends on available RAM and scratch disk space. You can also open the same image in two windows simultaneously. For one you could choose a high zoom level, such as 400%, to edit a small detail, and for the other choose a lower zoom level, such as 100%, in order to view the overall image. Or you could leave the image in RGB Color mode in one image window and choose View > Proof Setup > Working CMYK for the same image in the second window. The History palette will be identical for both windows.

To display one image in two windows:

1. With an image open, choose Window > Documents > New Window. The same image will appear in a second window **1**.

2. *Optional:* Move either window by dragging its title bar, and/or resize either window.

Note: The work canvas color will be the same for all open images.

To recolor the work canvas:

1. Enlarge the image window, if necessary, so at least some portion of the work canvas is visible.

2. Choose a Foreground color (see pages 179–182).

3. Choose the Paint Bucket tool (G or Shift-G).

4. Shift-click the work canvas **2**. You can't undo this. To restore the default gray, choose 20% gray as the Foreground color from the Color palette, then Shift-click the work canvas again.

7.0!

Ending a work session

To close an image:

Click the Close button in the upper-right corner of the image window (Win) /upper-left corner of the image window **2** (Mac OS).
or
Choose File > Close (Ctrl-W/Cmd-W).

If you attempt to close an image that was modified since it was last saved, a warning prompt will appear **3**. Click Don't Save to close the file without saving; or click Save to save the file before closing; or click Cancel to cancel the close operation.

To exit/quit Photoshop:

Windows: Choose File > Exit (Ctrl-Q) or click the application windows's close box.

Mac OS X: Choose Photoshop > Quit Photoshop (File > Quit in OS 9) (Cmd-Q).

All open Photoshop files will close. If any changes were made to an open file since it was last saved, a prompt will appear **4**. Click Don't Save (or press D) to close the file without saving; or click Save to save the file before exiting/quitting; or click Cancel to cancel the exit/quit operation altogether.

Victor's tip

Mac OS X users are familiar with the traffic light buttons in the title bar of every window: Red means close, yellow means minimize (to the Dock), and green means zoom (to full size). One of the more obscure features of OS X is a little **dot** that appears in the Close button of an image window if the file has been **modified** since it was **last saved**. (From Victor Gavenda, our eagle-eyed technical editor.)

1 *Windows: Click the* **Close** *button in the* ***upper-right*** *corner of the image window.*

2 *Mac OS X: Click the* **close** *button in the* ***upper-left*** *corner of the image window.*

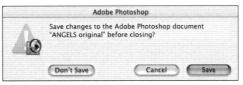

3 *If you attempt to close an image that was modified since it was last saved, this prompt will appear.*

4 *If changes were made to an open file since it was saved, this prompt will appear.*

PIXEL BASICS 4

Image Size

Pixel Dimensions: 307K (was 2.31M)

Width:	360	pixels
Height:	291	pixels

Document Size:

Width:	5	inches
Height:	4.04	inches
Resolution:	72	pixels/inch

☑ Constrain Proportions
☑ Resample Image: Bicubic
Interpolate the pixel information

1 *Check **Resample Image** and enter a Document Size: **Resolution** of **72 pixels/inch** in the **Image Size** dialog box.*

IN THIS CHAPTER you'll learn how to change an image's overall dimensions or resolution; sharpen the image afterward; change an image's canvas size; crop an image; flip an image; and rotate an image.

Note: Changing an image's dimensions in Photoshop while preserving its current resolution (leaving the Resample Image box checked) causes resampling, which degrades image quality. That's why it's always best to scan or create an image at or close to the desired output size. If you have to resample, apply the Unsharp Mask filter afterward to resharpen (see pages 84–85).

Changing dimensions and resolution

To change an image's pixel dimensions for onscreen output:

1. Choose Image > Image Size.

2. Make sure Resample Image is checked **1**, and choose an interpolation method from the pop-up menu. Bicubic degrades the image the least but also takes the longest.

3. To preserve the image's width-to-height ratio, leave Constrain Proportions checked.

4. Set the Resolution to 72 pixels/inch (or "ppi," for short).

5. Enter new Pixel Dimensions: Width and/or Height values.

6. Click OK.

To change an image's dimensions for print output:

1. Choose Image > Image Size.

2. To preserve the image's width-to-height ratio, check Constrain Proportions.
To modify the image's width independently of its height, uncheck Constrain Proportions.

3. *Optional:* To preserve the image's resolution, check Resample Image and choose Nearest Neighbor, Bilinear, or Bicubic as the interpolation method. Bicubic causes the least degradation in image quality.

4. Choose a unit of measure from the pop-up menu next to the Document Size: Width and Height fields.

5. Enter new Width and/or Height values, corresponding to the physical dimensions you've chosen for the printed image.
The Resolution will change if Resample Image is unchecked.

6. Click OK.

TIP To restore the original Image Size dialog box settings, Alt-click/Option-click Reset.

TIP File > Print with Preview can also be used to resize or rescale print dimensions, but it doesn't preserve the image resolution.

7.0!

Previewing the print

To see the image size relative to the paper size, press and hold on the status bar at the bottom of the image window **1** or choose File > **Print with Preview**.

To display the image onscreen at the size it will print, choose View > **Print Size**. The screen (display) size of an image is determined by the image's pixel dimensions and the monitor size and setting, whereas the display of the print size of an image is determined by the image's pixel dimensions and resolution—the number of pixels viewed per unit of printed length (usually inches). So for a high-resolution image at a 100% zoom level, choosing View > Print Size will display the image at an approximation of its actual printout size—not necessarily the physical printout size.

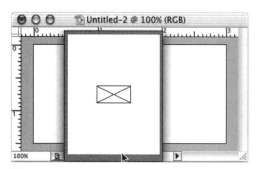

1 *To see the **image** size relative to the **paper** size, press and hold on the **status** bar at the bottom of the image window.*

Cash in on a high resolution

An image contains a given number of pixels after scanning, and its print dimensions and resolution are interdependent. If an image's resolution or dimensions are changed with **Resample Image** unchecked in Image > Image Size, the file's total pixel count is preserved. Increasing an image's pixels-per-inch resolution will shrink its print (physical) dimensions; lowering an image's pixels-per-inch resolution will enlarge its print dimensions.

If your file has a higher resolution than needed (more than twice the screen frequency), you can allocate the extra resolution to the print size dimensions by unchecking Resample Image (the Width, Height, and Resolution are now interdependent), and then lowering the Resolution to twice the screen frequency. The width and height values will automatically increase, and the file storage size and pixel dimensions will remain constant—no pixels will be added or deleted from the image.

If you must further enlarge the image's dimensions, click in the Width field, check Resample Image, then enter a new Width value. The Height value will change proportionally, and the file storage size and pixel dimensions will increase. The image will be resampled, though, so after clicking OK, apply the Unsharp Mask filter to resharpen.

Note: If you increase an image's resolution (resample up) with Resample Image checked, pixels will be added and the image's file storage size will increase, but its sharpness will diminish. If you decrease an image's resolution (downsample), information will be deleted from the file, and it can only be retrieved using the History palette before the image is closed. Blurriness caused by resampling may only be evident when the image is printed; it may not be discernible onscreen. That's why it's always best to scan or create an image at the proper resolution. Follow the instructions on pages 84–85 to resharpen a resampled image. (See also pages 53 and 56.)

To change an image's resolution:

1. Choose Image > Image Size.

2. To preserve the image's dimensions (Width and Height), check Resample Image **1**, and choose an interpolation method from the pop-up menu.
or
To preserve the image's total pixel count, uncheck Resample Image. The Width and Height dimensions will change to preserve the current pixel count.

3. Enter a Resolution value.

4. Click OK.

TIP The History Brush tool won't work on a resampled image. You'll only be able to set the source for the History Brush tool from the current state forward.

1 Check **Resample Image**, and the image will be resampled, or uncheck Resample Image to prevent resampling.

Image Size

Pixel Dimensions: 243K

Width: 286 pixels
Height: 290 pixels

OK
Cancel
Auto…

Document Size:

Width: 3.972 inches
Height: 4.028 inches
Resolution: 72 pixels/inch

☑ Constrain Proportions
☑ Resample Image: Bicubic

The Fit Image command has no effect on an image's resolution—it only changes its physical dimensions. Use it to make an image smaller.

To resize an image to fit a specific width or height:

1. Choose File > Automate > Fit Image ▉.

2. Enter a Width or Height value in pixels. The other field will automatically adjust *after* you click OK, so the width-to-height ratio will stay the same.

3. Click OK.

Fit Image
┌─ Constrain Within ───────
Width: `1199` pixels
Height: `970` pixels
OK
Cancel

▉ *Use the* **Fit Image** *command to change an image's* **dimensions** *without changing its resolution.*

Fit Image

Resize Image Assistant

This assistant will help you to resize your image using the appropriate resolution.

What will this image be used for?

◉ Print
○ Online

Cancel | Back | Next

1 *Click **Print** or **Online**.*

Resize Image Assistant

What is the desired print size of the image?

Width: 7 | inches
Height: 3.5 | inches

Cancel | Back | Next

2 *Enter the desired **print size**.*

Resize Image Assistant

Which halftone screen (LPI) will be used to print your image?

○ 65
○ 85
◉ 133
○ 150
○ 200
○ Other:

Description
Appropriate for web printing, weekly magazine, etc.

Cancel | Back | Next

3 *Click or enter the **LPI** that your print shop specifies.*

Resize Image Assistant

What level of image quality would you like?

Lower Quality Smaller File — 1x — 1.5x — 2x — Higher Quality Larger File

Results
Original Image Size: 132k
New Image Size: 2877k
Pixels Per Inch: 200

⚠ The new file is larger than the original which will result in a lower quality image. For best results, rescan at a higher resolution.

Cancel | Back | Next

4 *Move the slider to the desired image **quality**.*

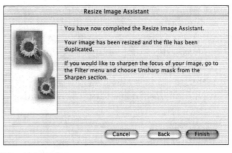

Resize Image Assistant

You have now completed the Resize Image Assistant.

Your image has been resized and the file has been duplicated.

If you would like to sharpen the focus of your image, go to the Filter menu and choose Unsharp mask from the Sharpen section.

Cancel | Back | Finish

5 *Click **Finish**.*

The Resize Image command duplicates an image and resizes the duplicate automatically. All you have to do is respond to a sequence of dialog boxes—Photoshop will figure out the math for you.

To resize an image automatically:

1. Choose Help > Resize Image.

2. Click Print or Online **1**, then click Next.

3. Enter the desired output dimensions **2**, then click Next. If you chose Online in the previous step, click Finish now. For print output, follow the remaining steps.

4. Click or enter the LPI as per your print shop's instructions **3**, then click Next.

5. Move the Quality slider **4**, then note the final image size in the Results area. If there's a message below the Results area, read that as well. If you want to proceed, click Next.

6. Click Finish **5**, and then save the resized image. (Or click Cancel.)

Resize Image

If you change an image's dimensions or resolution with Resample Image checked, convert it to CMYK Color mode, or transform it, blurring may occur due to the resampling process. To help correct this, you can apply the Unsharp Mask filter, which despite its name has a focusing effect. The filter increases contrast between adjacent pixels that already have some contrast. You can specify the amount of contrast to be added (Amount), the number of surrounding pixels that will be modified around each pixel that requires more contrast (Radius), and determine which pixels the filter affects or ignores by specifying the minimum contrast (Threshold).

Note: The Unsharp Mask effect may be more noticeable onscreen than on high-resolution print output.

To apply the Unsharp Mask filter:

1. Choose Filter > Sharpen > Unsharp Mask **1**.

2. Choose an Amount for the percentage increase in contrast between pixels **2** (and **1**, next page). Use a low setting (below 50) for figures or natural objects; use a higher setting if the image contains sharp-edged objects. Too high a setting will produce obvious halos around high-contrast areas. The larger the image, the less sharpening may be required. For a high-resolution image, use an Amount between 150 and 200 percent.

3. To choose an appropriate Radius value, which is a little trickier, you need to factor in the final size, the resolution, and the subject matter of the image. The Radius value (0.1–250) controls the number of pixels surrounding high-contrast edges that will be modified (**2**, next page). Try between 1 and 2 pixels. A higher value could produce too much contrast in areas that are already high-contrast.

The higher the resolution of the image, the more pixels there are on the border

1 *The original image, which is a bit blurry*

If you click on the image, that area will display here in the preview window.

2 *When using the **Unsharp Mask** dialog box, start with conservative **Amount**, **Radius**, and **Threshold** settings.*

1 *After Unsharp Masking with a **high Amount** (160), Radius 1.5, and Threshold 0: Note the halos around the edges and centers of the flowers.*

2 *After Unsharp Masking with a **high Radius** (6.0), Amount 130, and Threshold 0: The soft gradations have become choppy and the image has an unnatural contrast and sharpness.*

3 *After Unsharp Masking with a **high Threshold** (15), Amount 160, and Radius 1.5: Even with the same Amount setting as in the top image, the soft gradations in the petals and the background are preserved.*

between high-contrast areas, and thus the higher the Radius setting is required. Try a high Radius setting for a low-contrast image, and a lower Radius setting for an intricate, high-contrast image.

Note: The higher the Radius setting, the lower the Amount setting can be, and vice versa.

4. Choose a Threshold value (0–255) for the minimum amount of contrast an area must have before it will be modified **3**. At a Threshold of 0, the filter will be applied to the entire image. A Threshold value above 0 will cause sharpening along already high-contrast edges, less so in low-contrast areas. If you raise the Threshold, you can then increase the Amount and Radius values to sharpen the edges without oversharpening areas that don't require it. To prevent noise from distorting skin tones, specify a Threshold between 8 and 20.

5. Click OK.

TIP To soften a grainy scan, apply Filter > Blur > Gaussian Blur at a low setting (below 1), and then apply Filter > Sharpen > Sharpen Edges once or twice afterward to resharpen.

TIP To avoid waiting for the full screen Unsharp Mask preview on a large image, first get close to the desired settings using just the preview window with Preview unchecked; then check Preview to preview the results on the full screen; and finally, readjust the settings, if needed.

TIP Try applying the Unsharp Mask filter to one or two individual color channels (for example, just the Red or Green channel in an RGB image). If you sharpen two separate channels, use the same Radius value for both. You can also convert an image to Lab Color mode and then apply the filter to the L channel to sharpen luminosity without affecting any color pixels.

Unsharp Mask

Changing the canvas

The Canvas Size command changes the live, editable image area.

Note: If you want to enlarge the canvas area manually, right on the image, use the Crop tool instead (see page 89). You can also use the Crop command to reduce the image size.

To change the canvas size:

1. If the image contains a Background (you can look for it on the Layers palette), choose a Background color (see pages 179–182) **1**.

2. Choose Image > Canvas Size **2**.

3. *Optional:* Choose a different unit of measure from the pop-up menus. If you choose "columns," the current Column Size: Width setting in Edit (Photoshop, in OS X) > Preferences > Units & Rulers will be used as the increment.

4. Enter new Width and/or Height values. Changing one dimension has no effect on the other dimension.
or
Check Relative, then enter the amount by which you want to increase each dimension. Enter a negative value to decrease a dimension.

5. *Optional:* To reposition the image on its new canvas, click an unoccupied Anchor square (a square that has an arrow). The dark gray square represents the existing image area.

6. Click OK. Any added areas will automatically be filled with the current Background color (unless the background is a layer with transparency, in which case the added canvas areas will be transparent) **3**.

1 *The original image*

2 *Compare the **Current Size** with the **New Size** as you change the Width and Height values.*

3 *The same image with **added** canvas pixels*

1 *Marquee the portion of the image you want to keep.*

A whole image can be cropped using the Crop tool, the Crop command, or the Trim command. First, the Crop tool.

To crop an image using a marquee:

1. Choose the Crop tool (C).

2. Drag a marquee over the portion of the image that you want to keep **1**.

3. Do any of the following on the Crop tool options bar:

Check **Shield** if you want the area outside the crop marquee to be darkened by a cropping shield (it helps you see what will be left) **2**. Click the **Color** swatch if you want to change the color for the darkened area, and choose an **Opacity** for the shield color.

If you're cropping a layer, click **Cropped Area: Delete** to have Photoshop delete the cropped-out areas. Or click **Hide** to have them save with the file and extend beyond the edge of the current image area. Use the Move tool to reposition any hidden layer pixels that extend off the edge. This option is available for a layer, but not for the Background.

For the Perspective option, see online Help.

4. *Do any of these optional steps:*

To resize the marquee, drag any handle (double-arrow pointer). Shift-drag to preserve the marquee's proportions. Alt-drag/Option-drag to resize the marquee from its center.

To reposition the marquee, position the pointer inside the marquee, then drag.

To rotate the marquee, position the cursor outside it (curved arrow pointer), then drag in a circular direction. To change the axis point around which the marquee rotates, drag the circle away

(Continued on the following page)

Crop Tool

2 *The **Crop** tool options bar **after** drawing a marquee with the tool*

from the center of the marquee before rotating. (The crop marquee can't be rotated for an image in Bitmap mode.)

5. Press Enter/Return .
or
Double-click inside the marquee.
or
Click the ☑ on the options bar.

If you rotated the marquee, the rotated image will be squared off in the image window.

TIP To cancel the cropping process before accepting it, press Esc, or click the ⊘ on the options bar.

TIP To resharpen an image after cropping, apply the Unsharp Mask filter (see pages 84–85).

To specify dimensions and resolution as you crop an image:

1. Choose the Crop tool (C). 🔲

2. On the Crop options bar, enter **Width** and/or **Height** values **2**.
or
Click **Front Image** to insert the current image's Width, Height, and Resolution values into those fields. Use this option if you want to crop one open image to the dimensions of another open image.

The crop marquee will match this width-to-height ratio.

3. *Optional:* Modify the **Resolution**. If, after clicking Front Image, you raise the current resolution and then crop, the print size will decrease. If you lower the current resolution and then crop, the print size will increase. In both cases, the pixel count will remain unchanged.

(To empty the Width, Height, and Resolution fields, click Clear.)

4. Drag a crop marquee on the image, then double-click inside the marquee, or press Enter/Return, or click the ☑ on the options bar.

Unsnap

Normally, when resizing a crop marquee, if View > Snap To > **Document Bounds** is on, the crop edges will snap to the edge of the image. To override this snap function (let's say you want to crop slightly inside the edge of the image), turn the Snap To > Document Bounds feature off, or start dragging a marquee handle, then hold down **Ctrl-Shift-/Cmd-Shift** as you drag the handle near the edge of the image.

1 *The cropped image*

| 🔲 ▾ | Width: 500 px | Height: 400 px | Resolution: 144 | pixels/inch ⬍ | Front Image | Clear |

2 *The options bar before drawing a marquee with the Crop tool*

Crop an image to fit inside another

Open both images, activate the destination image, choose the Crop tool (C), click **Front Image** on the Crop options bar, activate the image you want to crop, then draw a marquee. After cropping, Shift-drag-and-drop the layer from the Layers palette or copy and paste the layer onto the destination image. The resolution will adjust automatically.

1 *Drag any of the crop marquee handles **outside** the canvas area into the work canvas.*

2 *The newly **cropped** image has different proportions. In our example, the added pixels filled automatically with black, our current Background color, because the default Background wasn't changed (Layers palette).*

Cropping with a marquee that's larger than the image effectively increases the image's canvas size.

To enlarge an image's canvas area using the Crop tool:

1. Enlarge the image window so the work canvas (gray area) around the image is showing.

2. Choose the Crop tool (C). ⌖

3. Draw a crop marquee within the image.

4. Drag any of the handles of the marquee into the work canvas **1**–**2**. If areas of the image originally extended outside the canvas border, those areas can now be included.

5. Double-click inside the marquee, or press Enter/Return, or click the ✓ on the options bar. If there were no hidden pixels, and if the bottommost layer is the Background, the added canvas area will fill with the current Background color. If the bottommost layer is a layer, the added canvas area will fill with transparency.

The Crop command is simple and straight-forward, but it's only useful if you don't need any of the options that the Crop tool provides. You start by drawing a selection marquee.

To crop an image using the Crop command:

1. Choose the Rectangular Marquee tool (M or Shift-M).

2. Draw a marquee over the part of the image you want to keep.
or
To control the size of the marquee, use the Style: Fixed Aspect Ratio or Fixed Size options on the Rectangular Marquee tool options bar, then click on the image.

3. Choose Image > Crop, then deselect (Ctrl-D/Cmd-D).

To quickly trim away excess transparent or color areas from around an image, use the Trim command.

To crop an image using the Trim command:

1. Choose Image > Trim.

2. Click a Based On option 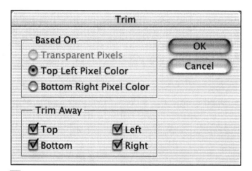:

Transparent Pixels trims away any extra transparency at the edges of the image, while preserving all image pixels.

Top Left Pixel Color removes any border areas that match the color of the upper-most-left pixel in the image.

Bottom Right Pixel Color removes any border areas that match the color of the lowermost-right pixel in the image.

3. Check which areas of the image you want the command to Trim Away: Top, Bottom, Left, or Right.

4. Click OK.

1 *The **Trim** command removes excess transparent areas or color areas, depending on which **Based On** option you click.*

1 *The original image*

Note: The Rotate Canvas > Flip Canvas Horizontal and Flip Canvas Vertical commands, discussed below, flip all the layers in an image. If you want to flip just one layer at a time, use Edit > Transform > Flip Horizontal or Flip Vertical instead.

To flip an image:

To flip the image left to right, choose Image > Rotate Canvas > Flip Canvas Horizontal **1**–**2**.

or

To flip the image upside-down to produce a mirror image, choose Image > Rotate Canvas > Flip Canvas Vertical **3**.

2 *The image **flipped horizontally***

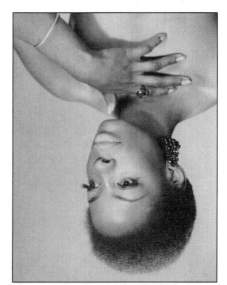

3 *The original image **flipped vertically***

Note: The Rotate Canvas commands, discussed below, rotate all the layers in an image. To rotate one layer at a time, use a rotate command from the Edit > Transform submenu instead.

To rotate an image by a preset amount:

Choose Image > Rotate Canvas > 180°, 90° CW (clockwise), or 90° CCW (counterclockwise).

To rotate an image by specifying a number:

1. Choose Image > Rotate Canvas > Arbitrary.

2. Enter an Angle between -359.99° and 359.99° **1**.

   TIP To straighten out a crooked scan, measure the angle using the Measure tool, then enter that angle.

3. Click °CW (clockwise) or °CCW (counterclockwise).

4. Click OK **2**–**3**.

1 *You can enter a custom Angle in the Rotate Canvas dialog box.*

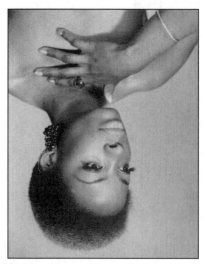

2 *The original image*

3 *The image rotated 180°. Compare with the flipped images on the previous page.*

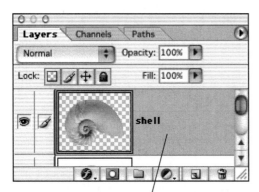

1 *Ctrl-click/Cmd-click a layer to **select** all the opaque pixels on that layer.*

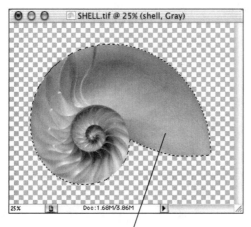

2 *Opaque pixels—**not** transparent areas—are selected on this layer.*

WHEN **A LAYER OR** part of a layer is selected, only that area is editable —the rest of the image is protected. A selection border has a "marching ants" marquee. This chapter covers the creation of selections using the Rectangular Marquee, Elliptical Marquee, Lasso, Polygonal Lasso, Magic Wand, and Magnetic Lasso tools, as well as the Color Range and Extract commands. You will also learn how to create selections of various shapes; how to select by color; how to deselect, reselect, invert, or delete a selection; how to move or hide a selection marquee; how to transform, add to, or subtract from a selection; and how to create a vignette.

Creating selections

A selection contains pixels from whichever layer is currently active. If the Move tool is used to move a selection on the Background of an image, the current Background color will be applied automatically to the exposed area. If a selection is moved on a layer using the Move tool, the exposed area will become transparent. (See Chapter 7, "Layers.")

TIP A selection can be converted into a path for precise reshaping, and then converted back into a selection (see pages 284 and 294). Quick Masks, which function like selections but can be painted on an image, are covered in Chapter 15.

To select an entire layer:

Choose a layer, then choose Select > All (Ctrl-A/Cmd-A). A marquee will surround the **entire** layer.
or
To select only **opaque pixels**—not any transparent areas—on a layer, Ctrl-click/Cmd-click the layer on the Layers palette **1**–**2**. Or right-click/Ctrl-click a layer thumbnail and choose Select Layer Transparency.

To create a rectangular or elliptical selection:

1. Choose a layer.

2. Choose the Rectangular Marquee  or Elliptical Marquee tool (M or Shift-M). Or to create the thinnest possible selection, choose the Single Row Marquee or Single Column Marquee tool.

3. *Optional:* To specify the exact dimensions of the selection, with the Rectangular or Elliptical Marquee tool highlighted, choose Fixed Size from the Style pop-up menu on the options bar , then enter Width and Height values. Remember though, you're counting pixels based on the file's resolution, not the monitor's resolution, so the same Fixed Size marquee will appear larger in a low-resolution file than in a high-resolution file.

   To specify the width-to-height ratio of the selection (3-to-1, for example), choose Constrained Aspect Ratio from the Style pop-up menu, then enter Width and Height values. Enter the same value in both fields to create a circle or a square.

4. *Optional:* To soften the edges of the selection before it's created, enter a Feather value above zero on the options bar 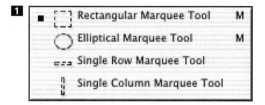. The Anti-aliased option can be checked on or off for the Elliptical Marquee tool.

5. If you specified Fixed Size values (or are using the Single Row or Single Column tool), click on the image. For any other Style, drag diagonally . A marquee will appear. To create a square or a circular selection for the Normal Style, start dragging, then finish the marquee with Shift held down.

   Hold down the spacebar to move the marquee while drawing it. To move the marquee after releasing the mouse, drag inside it.

TIP As you drag the mouse, the dimensions of the selection will be indicated in the W and H areas on the Info palette.

TIP To add to or subtract from a selection, see page 106.

see page 106.

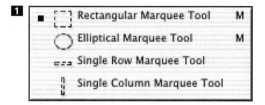

*Instead of drawing a marquee manually, you can choose **Fixed Size** from the **Style** pop-up menu, and then enter exact **Width** and **Height** dimensions.*

*Enter a **Feather** value to soften the edges of the selection.*

*Drag diagonally to create a **rectangular** selection...*

*...or an **elliptical** selection.*

Rectangular, Elliptical Marquee

Anti-aliasing

Check **Anti-aliased** on the options bar before using a selection tool to create a selection with a softened edge that steps gradually to transparency. Uncheck Anti-aliased to create a crisp, hard-edged selection.

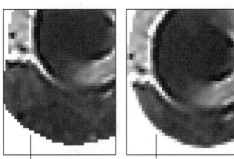

Aliased   *Anti-aliased*

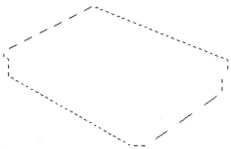

1 *A curved* ***Lasso*** *tool selection*

2 *A straight-edged* ***Polygon Lasso*** *tool selection*

Deleting Polygon Lasso corners

Press **Backspace/Delete** to erase the last-created corner. Hold down Backspace/Delete to erase multiple corners.

Note: Since it's difficult to precisely reselect an area (unless you save the selection in an alpha channel or as a path), try to refine your selection before you deselect it.

TIP If the shape you want to select isn't too complex, use the Pen or Freeform Pen tool to trace it (and then convert the path into a selection) instead of using the Lasso—you'll get a smoother selection. You can also convert a selection into a path for precise reshaping.

To create a freeform selection:

1. Choose a layer.

2. Choose the Lasso tool (L or Shift-L).

3. *Optional:* Enter a Feather value above zero on the Lasso tool options bar to soften the edges of the selection.

4. Drag around an area of the layer **1**. When you release the mouse, the open ends of the selection will join automatically.

TIP To feather a selection after it's created, use the Select > Feather command (Ctrl-Alt-D/Cmd-Option-D).

TIP To create a straight side using the Lasso tool, with the mouse button still down, press Alt/Option, and click to create corners. Drag, then release Alt/Option to resume drawing a freehand selection.

To create a polygonal selection:

1. Choose a layer.

2. Choose the Polygon Lasso tool (L or Shift-L).

3. To create straight sides, click to create points **2**. To join the open ends of the selection, click on the starting point (a small circle will appear next to the pointer). Or Ctrl-click/Cmd-click or double-click anywhere on the image to have the selection close automatically.

Alt-drag/Option-drag to create a curved segment as you draw a polygonal selection. Release Alt/Option to resume drawing straight sides.

Lasso; Polygon Lasso

If you click on a layer pixel with the Magic Wand tool, a selection will be created that includes adjacent pixels of a similar shade, color, or transparency level to the one you clicked on. You can then add similarly colored, nonadjacent pixels to the selection using the Similar command, or add non-similar colors by Shift-clicking.

To select by color (Magic Wand):

1. Choose a layer.

2. Choose the Magic Wand tool (W).

3. Check **Contiguous** on the Magic Wand tool options bar **1** to limit the selection to areas that are connected to the first pixel you click on, or uncheck this option to select noncontiguous areas.

4. On the Magic Wand options bar, check **Use All Layers** to sample from colors in all the currently displayed layers in order to create the selection. Only pixels on the current layer can be edited, but you can apply changes within the same selected area through successive layers.
or
Uncheck **Use All Layers** to sample colors only on the current layer.

Also, check **Anti-aliased**, if desired, for a smoother selection edge.

5. Click on a shade or color in the image window.

6. *Do any of these optional steps:*

To enlarge the selection based on the current Tolerance setting on the Magic Wand options bar, choose Select > **Grow** as many times as you like (use a low Tolerance). You can also access this command by right-clicking/Ctrl-clicking in the image window.

Magic Wand

1 *The **Magic Wand** tool options bar*

PHOTO: PAUL PETROFF

*A selection created using the **Magic Wand** with a **Tolerance** of 10*

*A selection created using the **Magic Wand** with a **Tolerance** of 40: At a higher Tolerance, more pixels are selected.*

To select additional, noncontiguous areas of similar color or shade based on the current Tolerance setting on the Magic Wand tool options bar, choose Select > **Similar**. You can also access this command by right-clicking/Ctrl-clicking in the image window.

To change the range of shades or colors within which the Magic Wand tool selects, enter a **Tolerance** value (0–255) on the Magic Wand tool options bar, then click on the image again. For example, at a Tolerance of 32, the Magic Wand will select within a range of 16 shades below and 16 shades above the shade it's clicked on. Enter 0 to select only one color or shade.

To gradually expand or narrow the range of shades or colors the Magic Wand tool selects, modify the Tolerance value between clicks. The higher the Tolerance, the broader the range of colors the wand selects.

TIP Choose Edit > Undo (Ctrl-Z/Cmd-Z) to deselect the last-created selection area.

TIP To quickly select all the opaque and partially opaque pixels on a layer (not the Background or any fully transparent areas), Ctrl-click/Cmd-click the layer.

TIP To add to or subtract from a selection, see page 106.

TIP To Expand or Contract a selection by a specified number of pixels, choose either command from the Select > Modify submenu.

TIP To remove a flat-color background from around a shape, first select the background of the image using the Magic Wand tool, then press Backspace/Delete.

Magic Wand

In creating the Magnetic Lasso tool (and the Extract command, discussed on page 108), Adobe has tried to make the difficult task of selecting irregular shapes and furry, fuzzy, or complex edges a little easier. Neither technique solves the problem completely, but they're useful tools nevertheless.

The Magnetic Lasso tool creates a free-form selection automatically as you move or drag the mouse. It snaps to the nearest distinct shade or color that defines the edge of a shape. *Note:* This tool utilizes a lot of processor time and RAM. If you move or drag the mouse quickly, the tool may not keep pace with you.

To select using the Magnetic Lasso tool:

1. Choose the Magnetic Lasso tool (L or Shift-L).

2. *Optional:* Change any of the tool's options bar settings. See "Magnetic Lasso tool options bar" on the next page.

3. Click to establish a fastening point. Move the mouse, with or without pressing the mouse button, along the edge of the shape that you want to select **1**. As you move or drag the mouse, the selection line will snap to the edge of the shape. The temporary points that appear will disappear when you close the selection.

4. If the selection line starts to follow adjacent shapes that you don't want to select, click on the edge of the shape that you do want to select to add a fastening point manually, then continue to move or drag to complete the selection.

5. To close the selection line: **2**

Double-click anywhere over the shape.
or
Click the starting point (a small circle will appear next to the Magnetic Lasso tool pointer).
or
Press Enter/Return.
or

Magnetic Lasso (side tab)

Make your life easier

To temporarily heighten the contrast in an image in order to enhance the Magnetic Lasso tool's effectiveness, choose **Brightness/Contrast** from the "Create new fill or adjustment layer" pop-up menu at the bottom of the Layers palette, move the Contrast slider to the right, then click OK. Delete this adjustment layer when you're done using the Magnetic Lasso.

1 *Move the mouse **slowly** around a shape.*

2 *After **closing** the selection*

Scrap it

Press **Esc** to cancel a partial selection line (then you can start again).

Press **Backspace/Delete** to erase the last-drawn fastening points in succession.

Ctrl-click/Cmd-click.
or
Alt-double-click/Option-double-click to close with a straight segment.

6. Choose a layer to be edited using the selection.

TIP Alt-click/Option-click to use the Polygon Lasso tool temporarily while the Magnetic Lasso tool is selected, or Alt-drag/Option-drag to use the Lasso tool.

🚩	▢▢◰▢	Feather: 0 px	☑ Anti-aliased	Width: 10 px	Edge Contrast: 10%	Frequency: 57	☑ Pen Press

1 *The **Magnetic Lasso** tool options bar*

2 *When **Other Cursors: Precise** is chosen in Edit (Photoshop, in OS X) > Preferences > **Display & Cursors**, the pointer will be a circle with a crosshair in the center, and its diameter will be the current Lasso Width. To use a temporary Precise pointer, press Caps Lock.*

Magnetic Lasso tool options bar **1**

The **Feather** amount is the softness of the edges of the selection.

The **Width** (1–40) is the size of the area in pixels under the pointer that the tool considers when it places a selection line **2**. Use a wide Width for a high-contrast image that has strong edges. Use a narrow Width for an image that has subtle contrast changes or small shapes that are close together; the selection will be more precise and the line won't flip-flop back and forth across the edge.

TIP To decrease the Width setting by one pixel as you create a selection, press "[". To increase it, press "]".

Edge Contrast (1–100) is the degree of contrast needed between shapes for an edge to be discerned. Use a low Edge Contrast for a low-contrast image.

TIP If you enter a low or high Width, do the same for the Edge Contrast.

Frequency (0–100) controls how often fastening points are placed as a selection is made. The lower the Frequency, the less frequently points are placed. Use a high Frequency to select an irregular contour.

Magnetic Lasso

Using the Color Range command, you can select areas based on colors in the image or based on a luminosity or hue range.

To select by color (Color Range):

1. Choose a layer. The Color Range command samples colors from all the currently visible layers, but only the current layer will be available for editing. You can limit the selection range by creating a selection first.

2. Choose Select > Color Range.

3. Choose from the Select pop-up menu. You can limit the selection to a preset color range (e.g., Reds, Yellows), to a luminosity range (Highlights, Midtones, or Shadows), or to Sampled Colors (shades or colors you'll click on with the Color Range eyedropper). The Out of Gamut option can only be used on an image that's in Lab Color or RGB Color mode. If you choose a preset color range, and the image contains only light saturations of that color, an alert box will warn you that the selection marquee will be present but invisible.

4. Choose a Selection Preview option for previewing selection areas on the image.

5. To preview the selection, click the Selection button; to redisplay the whole

image, click the Image button. Or hold down Ctrl/Cmd with either option chosen to toggle between the two. If the image extends beyond the edges of the image window, use the Image option; the entire image will be displayed in the preview box to facilitate sampling.

6. If you chose Sampled Colors in step 3, click or drag in the preview box or in the image window with the eyedropper cursor to sample colors in the image.

7. *Optional:* Move the Fuzziness slider to the right to expand the range of colors or shades selected, or move it to the left to narrow the range.

8. *Optional:* If you chose Sampled Colors for step 3, Shift-click in the image window or in the preview box to add more colors or shades to the selection; Alt-click/ Option-click to remove colors or shades from the selection. Or click the "+" or "-" eyedropper icon button in the Color Range dialog box, then click on the image or in the preview box without holding down Shift or Alt/Option.

9. Click OK.

*Choose a color or a luminosity range from the **Select** pop-up menu, or choose **Sampled Colors** to sample colors from the image using the Color Range eyedropper.*

*Move the **Fuzziness** slider to the left to reduce the range of selected colors, or to the right to expand the range of selected colors.*

*Choose a **Selection Preview** method for the image in the image window.*

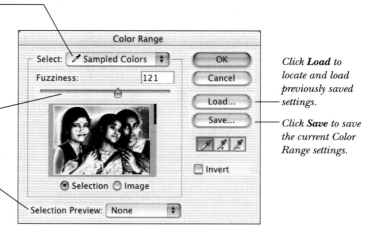

*Click **Load** to locate and load previously saved settings.*

*Click **Save** to save the current Color Range settings.*

1 *A frame selection created using the Rectangular Marquee tool*

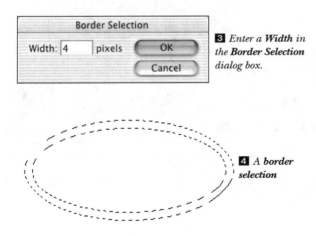

2 *Here's another option. The Marquee tool was used to select the center area, then Select > Inverse was used to reverse the selected and nonselected areas and cause the outer area to become selected. (We used the Levels command to screen back the selected area.)*

3 *Enter a Width in the Border Selection dialog box.*

4 *A border selection*

To create a frame selection:

1. Choose a layer.

2. Choose the Rectangular or Elliptical Marquee tool (M or Shift-M).

3. Drag to create a selection or choose Select > Select All (Ctrl-A/Cmd-A).

4. Alt-drag/Option-drag a smaller selection inside the first selection **1**. To subtract from a selection using another method, see page 106. See also **2**.

To select a narrow border around a selection:

1. Create a selection.

2. Choose Select > Modify > Border.

3. Enter the desired Width (1–200) of the border in pixels **3**. *7.0!*

4. Click OK. The new selection will evenly straddle the edge of the original selection **4**.

Frame Selection; Border Selection

Working with selections

To deselect a selection:

With any selection tool chosen, right-click/ Ctrl-click on the image and choose Deselect.
or
With any tool chosen, press Ctrl-D/Cmd-D (or if you want to be slow about it, choose Select > Deselect).
or
Click inside the selection with any selection tool .

Note: If you click *outside* the selection with the Magic Wand, Polygon Lasso, or Magnetic Lasso tool, you will create a new selection.

TIP It's difficult to reselect the same area twice, so deselect a selection only when you're sure you've finished using it. If you unintentionally deselect, choose Undo immediately. If you think you might want to reuse a selection, save it as a path or in an alpha channel.

To reselect the last selection:

With any selection tool chosen, right click/ Ctrl-click on the image and choose Reselect.
or
With any tool chosen, press Ctrl-Shift-D/ Cmd-Shift-D (or choose Select > Reselect).

TIP If you click a prior state on the History palette that involved a selection, the Reselect command will reselect the selection from that prior state.

If you delete a selection from a layer, the original selection area will become transparent . If you delete a selection from the Background, the selection area will fill with the current Background color 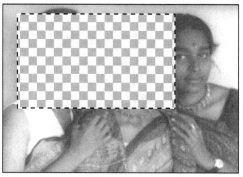.

To delete a selection:

Press Backspace/Delete.
or
Choose Edit > Clear.
or
Choose Edit > Cut (Ctrl-X/Cmd-X) to place the selection on the Clipboard.

PHOTO: PAUL PETROFF

1 *Click **inside** a selection to **deselect** it.*

2 *A selection deleted from a **layer***

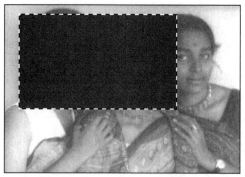

3 *A selection deleted from the **Background***

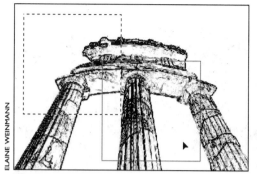

ELAINE WEINMANN

1 *Moving a marquee*

Follow these instructions to move only the selection marquee—**not** its contents.

To move a selection marquee:

1. *Optional:* To aid in positioning the marquee, choose View > Show > Grid or drag a guide or guides from the horizontal or vertical ruler. Also, turn on View > Snap To > Guides and/or View > Snap To > Grid.

2. Choose any selection tool.

3. Drag inside the selection **1**. Hold down Shift after you start dragging to constrain movement to a multiple of 45°.
or
Press any arrow key to move the marquee one pixel at a time.

TIP You can drag a selection marquee from one image window into another image window using a selection tool.

TIP If you drag a selection on a layer using the Move tool, the selection's pixel contents will be cut from that layer and the empty space will be replaced by layer transparency. If a selection is moved on the Background, on the other hand, the empty space will be filled with the current Background color.

Move Selection Marquee

To switch the selected and unselected areas:

With any selection tool chosen, right-click/
Ctrl-click and choose Select Inverse.

or

With any tool chosen, press Ctrl-Shift-I/
Cmd-Shift-I (or choose Select > Inverse)
1–**2**.

Choose the same command again (or use
the same shortcut) to switch back to the
original selection.

TIP It's easy to select a shape on a solid-color
background: Choose the Magic Wand
tool, enter 5 or less in the Tolerance
field on the Magic Wand options bar,
click the solid-color background to select
it entirely, then choose Select > Inverse.

Sometimes selection edges ("marching
ants") can be annoying or distracting. To
hide them temporarily, follow the instructions below. You can even hide selection
edges while some Image menu and Filter
menu dialog boxes are open.

To hide a selection marquee:

Choose View > Show > **Selection Edges** to
uncheck the command. The selection will
remain active.

To redisplay the selection marquee, choose
View > Show > Selection Edges (it should
have a checkmark).

The Ctrl-H/Cmd-H shortcut hides/shows
whichever options are currently available
on the Show submenu. The **Show Extras
Options** dialog box **3** (View > Show > Show
Extras Options) controls what options are
listed on the Show submenu.

TIP To verify that a selection is still active,
press on the Select menu. Most of the
commands will be available if a selection
is active.

1 *The original selection: The* **angels** *are selected.*

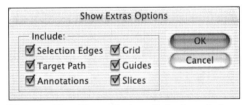

2 *After inverting the selection: Now the* **background**
is selected.

3 *In the* **Show Extras Options** *dialog box, check or
uncheck the onscreen features you want to show/hide
using the Ctrl-H/Cmd-H shortcut.*

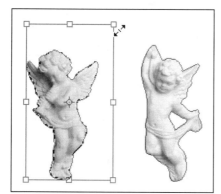

1 *Scaling a selection marquee*

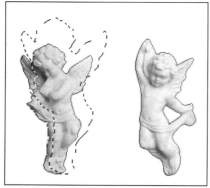

2 *The marquee is enlarged—not its contents.*

3 *You can use any of the Select > Modify submenu commands to modify an existing selection.*

Note: The Transform Selection command (discussed below) affects only the selection marquee—not its contents. To transform pixel contents, you can either use a command on the Edit > Transform submenu or you can transform selection contents using the bounding box (see page 138).

To transform a selection marquee:

1. With any selection tool chosen, right-click/Control-click on the image and choose Transform Selection from the context menu.
or
With any tool chosen, choose Select > Transform Selection.

2. Follow the instructions on pages 138–140 to flip, rotate, scale, etc. **1**–**2**.

To modify a selection marquee via a menu command:

Choose Select > Modify > Smooth (see page 132) **3** or choose Select > Modify > Expand or Contract, enter a value, then click OK.
or
Choose Select > Grow or Similar. These two commands use the current Magic Wand Tolerance setting (see page 97). You can repeat either command to further expand the selection.
or
Choose the Magic Wand tool, then right-click/Ctrl-click and choose Grow or Similar.

Transform, Modify Selection Marquee

To add to a selection:

Choose any selection tool other than the Magic Wand, click the "Add to selection" button on the options bar **1**, choose other options bar settings for the tool, if desired, then drag across the area to be added **2**–**3**. (To bypass the "Add to selection" button, position the cursor over the selection, then Shift-drag over the area to be added.)

or

Click the Magic Wand tool, click the "Add to selection" button on the options bar, then click outside the selection. (To bypass the "Add to selection" button, Shift-click outside the selection.)

TIP If the additional selection overlaps the original selection, it will become part of the new, larger selection. If the addition doesn't overlap the original selection, a second, separate selection will be created.

To subtract from a selection:

Choose any selection tool other than the Magic Wand, click the "Subtract from selection" button on the options bar **1**, choose other options bar settings, if desired, then drag around the area to be subtracted. (To bypass the "Subtract from selection" button, Alt-drag/Option-drag around the area to be subtracted.)

or

Click the Magic Wand tool, click the "Subtract from selection" button on the options bar, then click inside the selection. (To bypass the "Subtract from selection" button, Alt-click/Option-click inside the selection.)

To select the intersection of two selections:

1. With a selection present, choose a selection tool.

2. Click the Intersect with selection button on the options bar **1**, then create a new selection that overlaps the current selection **4**–**5**. (To bypass the button, Alt-Shift-drag/Option-Shift-drag.)

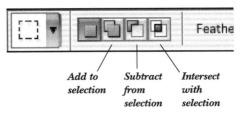

Add to   Subtract   Intersect
selection   from   with
        selection selection

1 *Use any of these buttons on the options bar to amend a selection.*

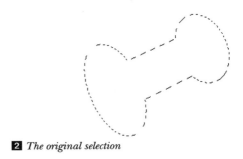

2 *The original selection*

3 *After **adding** an additional selection area*

4 *A circular selection is drawn over an existing selection with **Alt/Option** and **Shift** held down.*

5 *Only the **intersection** of the two selections remains selected.*

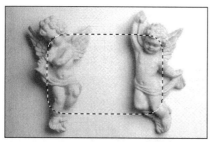

1 *First create a **feathered**-edge selection.*

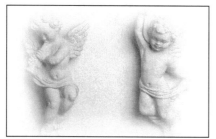

2 *The **vignette***

3 *The original image (Peter's relatives—no kidding)*

To vignette an image:

1. For a multi-layer image, choose a pixel layer, and unselect the Lock: transparent pixels button, if necessary. The vignette you create is going to appear to fade into the layer or layers below it.

For an image with a Background only, choose a Background color (see pages 179–182) for the area around the vignette.

2. Choose the Rectangular Marquee or Elliptical Marquee tool (M or Shift-M), or the Lasso tool (L or Shift-L).

3. Enter 15 or 20 px in the Feather field on the options bar. Alternatively, you can feather the selection after it's created (after step 4) using Select > Feather.

4. Create a selection **1**.

5. With the selection tool still chosen, right-click/Ctrl-click on the image and choose Select Inverse.

6. Press Backspace/Delete.

7. Right-click/Ctrl-click on the image and choose Deselect **2**–**5**.

4 *The **vignette***

5 *For this image, we applied the Glass filter after step 5.*

If you've ever torn your hair out trying to mask a shape with an irregular edge (a figure with curly hair or an animal in a landscape), you'll appreciate the Extract command. The nicest thing about this feature is that you'll create the mask on a full-size preview right in the dialog box **1**, so you can tweak it until you're certain you've got it just right. When you click OK, the masked area will be preserved, and the remaining areas will be erased to transparency.

To mask a shape using the Extract command:

1. *Note:* For safety's sake, work on a copy of the image—or at least on a duplicate layer. You could also make a snapshot of the original image.

Choose the layer from which you want to extract imagery.

2. Choose Filter > Extract (Ctrl-Alt-X/ Cmd-Option-X). A full-screen, resizable dialog box will open.

3. You'll use the Edge Highlighter to mask the object border first, and then click on the interior with the Fill tool to define the fill.

Choose the **Edge Highlighter** tool from the toolbox in the dialog box (B) **2**. *and*

In the Tool Options area **3**, enter or choose a Brush Size in pixels for the marker. The sharper the edge of the object you're going to extract, the smaller the brush you can use. Use a large brush if the shape has wide, choppy edges. *and*

Choose Red, Green, or Blue as the Highlight color for the mask. Or choose Other and choose a color from the Color Picker.

4. *Optional:* If you're going to trace a crisp-edged shape (e.g., a geometric shape), check Smart Highlighting. The highlight will be the minimum width necessary to cover the edge of the

1 *After outlining the chimp with the **Edge Highlighter** tool and filling the interior of the chimp with the **Fill** tool.*

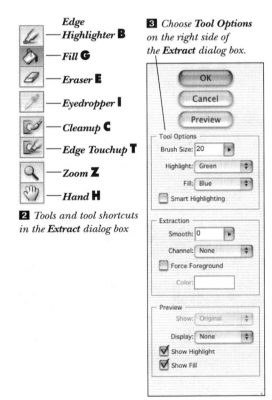

2 *Tools and tool shortcuts in the **Extract** dialog box*

3 *Choose **Tool Options** on the right side of the **Extract** dialog box.*

7.0!

Extract

Channel it

To make the marker highlight conform to the shape of a selection, create a selection, choose Select > Modify > **Border** (Width about 12 pixels), then click OK. **Inverse** the selection, and save the selection in an **alpha channel** (see page 276). Choose Filter > **Extract**, then choose that alpha channel from the Extraction: **Channel** pop-up menu. Finally, click with the **Fill** tool (G) inside the highlighted area.

shape, regardless of the current brush size.

5. Drag around the border of the area of the image you want to extract. Complete the loop to make a closed shape. Drag right along the object's border so as to catch any frizz or fringe. You don't need to drag along the edge of the canvas area if the imagery extends that far.

6. *Optional:* Raise the Extraction: Smooth value to eliminate extraneous pixels.

7. Choose the **Fill** (second) tool (G) from the toolbox in the dialog box.
and
Choose Red, Green, or Blue as the Fill color for the mask. Or choose Other and choose a color from the Color Picker.
and
Click on the area of the image that you want to extract. (Click again to un-fill.)

Note: To extract pixels of one color, instead of using the Fill tool, check Force Foreground, choose the Eyedropper tool in the dialog box (I), then click a color in the preview window. Or click the Color swatch and choose a color from the Color Picker.

8. Use the **Eraser** tool (E) from the dialog box if you need to unmask any masked areas. Choose a Brush Size for the Eraser in the Tool Options area of the dialog box.

TIP To zoom in on the preview, press Ctrl-+/Cmd-+. To zoom out, press Ctrl--/Cmd--. You could also use the Zoom tool in the dialog box (Alt-click/Option-click to reduce the view).

TIP If the preview is at greater than 100% view, you can use the Hand tool from the dialog box (H) to move it around in the preview window (press the spacebar to access the Hand tool temporarily).

(Continued on the following page)

Extract

9. Click Preview, then in the Preview area of the dialog box, do any of the following:

Check Show Highlight and/or Show Fill.

Choose Show: Extracted to toggle to the extracted image view; choose Original to toggle back to the original image.

Choose Display: None to display the background as transparent; choose Black Matte, Gray Matte, or White Matte to display the extracted shape on a background of black, gray, or white, respectively; choose Other to choose a custom color; or choose Mask to display the discarded area as black and the protected area as white.

10. To refine the mask further, do any of the following:

Use the Cleanup tool (C) to gradually subtract opacity. (Alt-drag/Option-drag to restore opacity.)

Use the Edge Touchup tool (T) to gradually sharpen edges.

Change the Smooth value.

11. Click OK. If you want to restore lost areas now, use the History Brush tool **1**–**2** (see pages 160–161). Or to erase further by hand, use the Background Eraser (see pages 228–229).

*The **Extract** command overdid it in these areas.*

1 *After extracting (chimp not in the mist)*

2 *This is after using the **History Brush** tool to restore areas of the chimp's face and arm. The Cleanup tool could have been used instead (see step 10).*

COMPOSITING 6

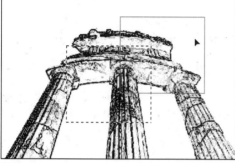

1 *If you move a selection on a **layer**...*

2 *...a **transparent** hole is left behind.*

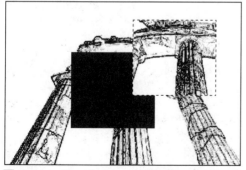

3 *If you move a selection on the **Background**, the exposed area fills with the current **Background color**.*

THIS **CHAPTER** covers methods for composing image elements: the Clipboard (Cut, Copy, Paste, and Paste Into), drag-and-drop, cloning, pattern stamping, and the new Healing Brush and Patch tools. Also covered are techniques for precisely positioning and aligning image elements and smoothing the seams between them.

Moving

In these instructions and in the "drag-copy" instructions on the next page, you'll be moving actual image pixels. (To move just a selection marquee without moving its contents, see page 103.)

To move a selection's contents:

1. *Optional:* To help you position the selection, choose View > Show > Grid (Ctrl-'/Cmd-') or drag a guide or guides from either ruler, and turn on View > Snap To > Guides and View > Snap To > Grid.

2. If the selection is on the Background, choose a Background color. The area exposed by the moved selection will fill with this color automatically. If the selection is on a layer, the exposed area will fill with transparency.

3. Choose the Move tool (V). (You can use Ctrl/Cmd to access the Move tool when most other tools are chosen.)

4. Position the pointer over the selection (the pointer will have a scissors icon), then drag. The selection marquee and its contents will move together **1**–**3**.

   Beware! When you deselect the selection, its pixel contents will drop back into its original layer, in its new location, regardless of which layer is currently active.

TIP Press an arrow key (Move tool chosen) to move a selection marquee in one-pixel increments.

To drag-copy a selection:

1. Choose the Move tool (V). ⊹ (You can use Ctrl/Cmd to access the Move tool when most other tools are chosen.)

2. Alt-drag/Option-drag the selection you want to copy. (Ctrl-Alt-drag/Cmd-Option-drag if you didn't choose the Move tool.) The copied pixels will remain selected **1**–**2**.

TIP Press Alt-arrow/Option-arrow with the Move tool chosen to offset a copy of a selection by one pixel from the original. Press Alt-Shift-arrow/Option-Shift-arrow to offset a copy by 10 pixels.

The Align to Selection commands align layer pixels to a currently active selection marquee. If you need to align objects from different layers, you can align each one individually to the same marquee, or you can link them first (see page 273) and then align them all at once.

To align a layer or layers to a selection marquee:

1. Create a selection.

2. Choose a layer or one layer in a set of linked layers.

3. Choose the Move tool (V), ⊹ then click an align button on the Move tool options bar **3**.
   or
   Choose Layer > Align To Selection > Top Edges, Vertical Centers, Bottom Edges, Left Edges, Horizontal Centers, or Right Edges.

   The layer pixels will align to the edges or center of the selection marquee, depending on which alignment option you chose.

1 *Alt-dragging/Option-dragging a selection*

PHOTO: ELAINE WEINMANN

2 *A copy of the selected pixels is moved.*

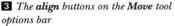

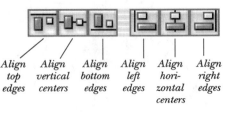

Align top edges *Align vertical centers* *Align bottom edges* *Align left edges* *Align horizontal centers* *Align right edges*

3 *The align buttons on the Move tool options bar*

Purge thy Clipboard

If the Clipboard imagery is large, the remaining available memory for other processing functions will be reduced. To empty the Clipboard and reclaim memory, choose Edit > **Purge** > **Clipboard**. This can't be undone.

Clipboard basics

You can use the Edit > **Cut** or **Copy** command to save a selection to a temporary storage area called the **Clipboard**, and then use Edit > **Paste** or **Paste Into** to paste the Clipboard pixels onto another layer in the same image or in another image. The Cut, Copy, and Paste Into commands are available only while a selection is active.

If you create a selection and choose Edit > **Cut**, the selection will be placed on the Clipboard. (The **Clear** command doesn't use the Clipboard.) If you Cut or Clear a selection from the Background, the exposed area will be filled with the current Background color. If you remove a selection from a layer, the area left behind will be transparent.

TIP For a soft transition between pasted imagery and a layer, check Anti-aliased on the options bar for your selection tool (if available) before you use it.

The Edit > **Paste** command pastes the Clipboard contents into a new layer, all the while preserving any pasted pixels that extend beyond the image window. You can move the entire layer to reveal the extended pixels. If you then save your document, the extended areas will save with it. If you subsequently crop the layer, however, click **Cropped Area: Hide** on the Crop options bar if you don't want the extended pixels to be discarded.

You can paste the same Clipboard contents an unlimited number of times. If **Export Clipboard** is checked in Edit (Photoshop, in OS X) > Preferences > General, the Clipboard contents will be stored in temporary system memory even if you exit/quit Photoshop. The Clipboard can contain only one selection at a time, however, and the Clipboard contents are replaced each time the Cut or Copy command is chosen.

TIP The dimensions in the New dialog box automatically match the dimensions of imagery currently on the Clipboard.

Clipboard Basics

Copying

Before using either the Clipboard commands or the drag-and-drop method to copy imagery, compare the **dimensions** of the source image with the dimensions of the destination image. If the imagery being copied is larger than the destination image, some of the copied pixels will extend beyond the image window when they're pasted or dropped, and they will be hidden from view. Move the layer using the Move tool if you want to bring the hidden pixels into view.

The size of a selection may also change when it's pasted or dropped for another reason: it's rendered in the **resolution** of the destination image. If the resolution of the destination image is higher than that of the source imagery, the copied image will appear smaller when it's pasted or dropped. Conversely, if the resolution of the destination image is lower than that of the source image, the source imagery will look larger when it's pasted or dropped.

TIP If you want the imagery to stay the same size, before copying it, standardize the resolution (and dimensions, if desired) of the source and destination images using Image > Image Size. To paste into a smaller image, see page 117.

To copy and paste a selection:

1. Select an area on a layer or on the Background. *Optional:* To feather the selection, right-click/Ctrl-click and choose Feather, enter a Feather Radius value, then click OK.

2. Choose Edit > Copy  (Ctrl-C/Cmd-C) (or choose Edit > Cut to cut the selection).

3. Choose a layer to paste onto.

4. Choose Edit > Paste (Ctrl-V/Cmd-V) 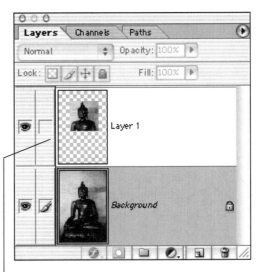. Restack the newly-created paste layer, move it using the Move tool, or defringe it (see page 132).

TIP To turn a selection into a new layer, right-click/Ctrl-click and choose Layer Via Copy or Layer Via Cut (see page 135).

1 *An area of the Background is placed on the* **Clipboard** *via Edit > Copy.*

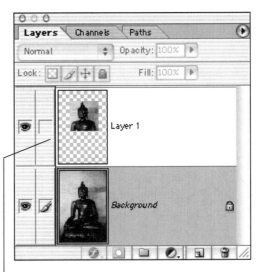

2 *The* **pasted** *imagery appears on a new layer.*

Copy/Paste a Selection

1 *A selection is dragged from the **Background**. The exposed area **temporarily** fills with the Background color.*

If you drag selected pixels from one image to another, presto, those selected pixels will be copied onto a new layer in the destination image. This drag-and-drop method bypasses the Clipboard, so it both saves memory and preserves the current contents of the Clipboard. If your monitor is too small to display two image windows simultaneously, use the copy-and-paste method instead (see the previous page).

To drag-and-drop a selection between images:

1. Open the source and destination images, and arrange them so their windows don't completely overlap.

2. In the source image, select an area on a layer or on the Background.

3. Choose the Move tool (V). (You can use Ctrl/Cmd to access the Move tool when most other tools are chosen.)

4. *Optional:* Check Show Bounding Box on the Move options bar to make the selection's bounding box visible.

5. Drag the selection into the destination image window, and release the mouse where you want the pixels to be dropped **1**–**3**. The copied imagery will automatically appear on a new layer. You can reposition the imagery using the Move tool.

TIP Shift-drag with the Move tool to drop the selection in the exact center of the destination image. You can release the mouse when the pointer is anywhere inside the destination image window.

TIP To drag-and-drop a whole layer to another image, see pages 149–150.

TIP Drag-and-drop is the only way to copy a shape layer from one document to another.

2 *A **dark border** appears in the destination image window.*

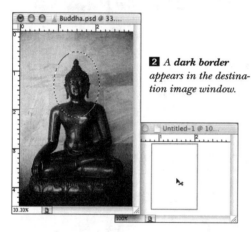

3 *The mouse is released, and the copied pixels appear in the **destination** image window. The source image is unchanged.*

If you use the Paste Into command to paste the Clipboard contents inside a selection, a new layer will be created automatically and the active marquee will become a layer mask. The pasted imagery can then be repositioned within the layer mask or the mask itself can be reshaped to reveal more or reveal less.

To paste into a selection:

1. Select an area of a layer. *Optional:* Right-click/Ctrl-click and choose Feather, enter a value, then click OK.

2. Choose Edit > Copy to copy pixels from the active layer only, or choose Edit > Copy Merged (Ctrl-Shift-C/Cmd-Shift-C) to copy pixels within the selection area from all the currently visible layers.

3. Leave the same layer active, or choose a different layer, or choose a layer in another image.

4. Select the area (or areas) that you want to paste the Clipboard contents into.

5. Choose Edit > Paste Into (Ctrl-Shift-V/ Cmd-Shift-V). A new layer and layer mask will be created **1**–**3**.

6. *More options:*

The entire Clipboard contents were pasted onto the layer, but the layer mask is probably hiding some of those pixels. To **move** the **layer mask** relative to the layer, choose the Move tool, click the layer mask thumbnail (the thumbnail on the right), then drag in the image window. To **move** the **layer contents**, click the layer thumbnail, then drag in the image window.

Click the layer mask thumbnail, then paint on the layer mask in the image window with white to **expose** more of the image or with black to **hide** more of the image.

To move the layer and layer mask in **unison**, click between the layer and layer mask thumbnails to link the two layer components together, choose the Move tool, then drag in the image window. Re-click the link icon to unlink.

1 *To create this effect in one image, a music layer was selected and copied. In another image, the type layer was Ctrl-clicked/Cmd-clicked, then Edit > **Paste Into** was chosen. A new layer resulted.*

2 *The layer contents can be repositioned within the layer mask because the two thumbnails aren't linked together. For this image, the music layer thumbnail was activated and then the layer contents were moved upward using the Move tool.*

Layer thumbnail   *Layer mask thumbnail*

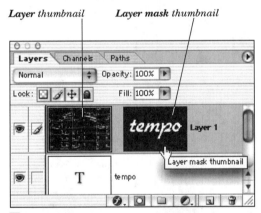

3 *When the **Paste Into** command is chosen, the pasted image appears on a new layer, and a layer mask is created automatically for it. The pasted image (the music) is visible only within the white areas in the layer mask (the letter shapes).*

Off the edge?

■ To **remove** pixels that extend beyond the edge of a layer, make sure the layer is active, choose Select > All, then choose Image > Crop. Trimming off the extra pixels will reduce the file's storage size.

■ If you apply an image-editing command, such as a filter, to a whole layer, any pixels beyond the edge of the layer will also be **modified**. (If you want to enlarge the canvas size to make all those pixels visible in the image window, use Image > Canvas Size).

■ To **select** pixels that extend beyond the edge of a layer, Ctrl-click/Cmd-click the layer name on the Layers palette. Don't use Select > All.

---

1 *Use the* **Image Size** *dialog box to change an image's* **resolution** *and/or* **dimensions**.

Normally, in Photoshop, if you move a large selection or layer, or paste a layer into another image, all the moved or pasted pixels on a layer are preserved, even if they extend beyond the visible edge of the layer. If you want the imagery to be trimmed as it's pasted, follow these instructions, but read "Copying" on page 114 first.

To paste into a smaller image:

1. Click in the destination image window, then Alt-press/Option-press and hold on the status bar at the bottom of the image window. Note (or jot down) the image's width, height, and resolution.

2. Click in the source image window, choose Image > Duplicate, then click OK.

3. With the duplicate image window active, choose Image > Image Size.

4. Check Resample Image, and change the resolution to the same value as that of the destination image **1**. In the Document Size: Width or Height field, enter a smaller number than the dimensions that you noted for step 1, then click OK.

5. Choose the layer you want to copy.

6. Choose Select > All (Ctrl-A/Cmd-A) to select the layer, choose Edit > Copy, click in the destination image, then choose Edit > Paste.
or
Shift-drag the source layer name into the destination image window.

7. Close the duplicate image. Save the original image, if desired.

TIP In lieu of steps 3 and 4 above, you can choose File > Automate > Fit Image and enter the desired pixel dimensions for the width or the height (from step 1). Fit Image won't change the image resolution. Instead, the copied or dragged layer will take on the resolution of the destination file.

Paste into a Smaller Image

Sharpening and blurring

The Blur tool decreases contrast between pixels, and is used to soften edges between shapes. The Sharpen tool increases contrast between pixels, and is used to delineate edges between shapes. Neither tool can be used on an image in Bitmap or Indexed Color mode.

To sharpen or blur edges:

1. Choose the Blur tool 🖋 or the Sharpen tool △ (R or Shift-R). Each tool keeps its own options bar settings.

2. On the Sharpen or Blur tool options bar **1**:

   Click the Brush picker arrowhead, then click a hard-edged or soft-edged **brush**. *and*

   Choose a blending **Mode**. Normal sharpens/blurs pixels of any shade or color. Darken sharpens/blurs only pixels that are darker than the Foreground color. Lighten sharpens/blurs only pixels that are lighter than the Foreground color. Hue or Color mode will cause a slight buildup of complementary colors. Saturation mode will cause a buildup of existing colors. Luminosity mode will intensify the existing luminosity. (The blending modes are described on pages 32–35.) You'll see a greater distinction between modes with the Sharpen tool than with the Blur tool.

   Choose a **Strength** percentage. Try a low setting at first (oh, say, around 30%).

3. *Optional:* Check Use All Layers on the options bar to pick up pixels from other visible layers under the pointer to place onto the active layer (see the sidebar).

4. Drag across an area in the image window to sharpen or blur pixels **2**–**3**. To intensify the effect, stroke again.

TIP To avoid creating an overly grainy texture, use the Sharpen tool with a medium Strength setting and stroke only once on a given area.

Use all you've got

With **Use All Layers** unchecked on the options bar for the Magic Wand, Smudge, Sharpen, Blur, or Clone Stamp tool, you will sharpen, blur, etc. using pixels from the currently chosen layer only. With Use All Layers checked, you will sharpen, blur, etc. using sampled data from all the currently visible layers under the pointer. With this option on, try applying pixels onto a new layer.

1 *The options bar for the **Blur** tool*

2 *The original image*

3 *After using the **Sharpen** tool on the strawberry in the center to bring it into sharper focus, and the **Blur** tool on the rest of the image to make it recede*

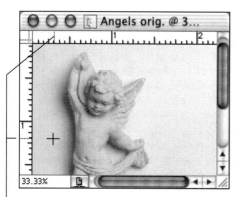

1 *The **location** of the **pointer** is indicated by a dotted marker on each ruler.*

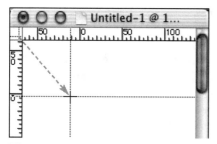

2 *Dragging the **ruler origin***

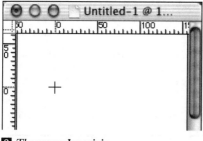

3 *The **new ruler origin***

Using rulers and guides

Grids, rulers, and guides can help you position objects more precisely than you can do "by eye."

To hide or show rulers:

Choose View > Rulers (Ctrl-R/Cmd-R) (when rulers are visible, the command has a check mark). Rulers will appear on the top and left sides of the image window, and the current position of the pointer will be indicated by a dotted marker on each ruler **1**. To hide the rulers, choose View > Rulers again.

TIP To change the ruler units quickly, right-click/Ctrl-click over either ruler and choose a unit from the context menu. Or to change units via the Units & Rulers Preferences dialog box, double-click either ruler.

The rulers' zero origin is the point from which an object's location is measured.

To change the rulers' zero origin:

1. *Optional:* To make the new ruler origin snap to a gridline, first display the grid by choosing View > Show > Grid (Ctrl-'/ Cmd-'). Then you can choose View > Snap To > Grid.

   To make the ruler origin snap to a guide, choose View > Snap To > Guides, then drag a guide into the image window, if you haven't already done so.

   See also "To use the Snap feature" on the following page.

2. Drag from the intersection of the rulers in the upper-left corner of the image window diagonally into the image **2**–**3**. Note where the zeros are now located on the rulers.

TIP To reset the ruler origin, double-click the square where the rulers intersect in the upper-left corner of the image window.

The Snap feature works like an electronic "tug." When View > Snap is on, as you move a selection border, slice, drawing tool pointer, path, or shape, that item will snap to the nearest guide, grid, slice, or document edge, depending on which of those options is chosen on the View > Snap To submenu.

To use the Snap feature:

1. Choose View > Snap To > Guides, Grid, Slices, Document Bounds, All [of the above], or None.

> *Note:* To turn on the Snap To > Grid function, the grid must be showing (View > Show > Grid).

2. Make sure View > Snap is on (has a checkmark) (New shortcut: Ctrl-Shift-;/ Cmd-Shift-;).

The grid is a non-printing framework that can be used to align image elements. Guides are individual guidelines that you drag into the image window yourself. With View > Snap To > Guides turned on, a selection or tool pointer will snap to a guide if it's moved within eight screen pixels of the guide. Ditto for View > Snap To > Grid.

To hide or show the grid:

Choose View > Show > Grid (Ctrl-'/Cmd-') **3**. To hide the grid, choose the command again. The grid can be turned on or off for individual files.

Show or snap it all

Show or hide Selection Edges, the Target Path, Grid, Guides, Slices, Annotations, or all of the above, via the View > **Show** submenu **1** (or via the View > Show > Show Extras Options dialog box). The **Extras** command (Ctrl-H/Cmd-H) shows/hides the items that are currently enabled on the Show submenu.

Turn on the snap feature for Guides, Grid, Slices, Documents Bounds, or all of the above, via the View > **Snap To** submenu **2**. The **Snap** command turns all of the current chosen Snap To options on and off.

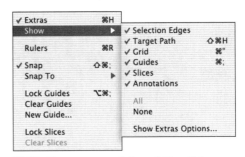

1 *The Extras command shows/hides all the currently enabled items on the Show submenu.*

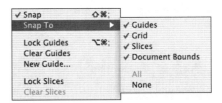

2 *The Snap command turns all the currently enabled commands on the Snap To submenu on or off.*

3 *Grid lines*

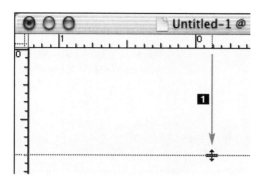

Use the **New Guide** dialog box to place a new guide at a specific location.

To create a guide:

Make sure the rulers are displayed, then drag from the horizontal or vertical ruler into the image window **1**.

If View > Snap is checked, you can Shift-drag to snap the guide to a ruler increment. If the grid is displayed and View > Snap To > Grid is on, the guide can be snapped to a grid line. A guide can also be snapped to a selection marquee.

TIP To **lock** all guides so they can't be moved using the Move tool, choose View > Lock Guides (Ctrl-Alt-;/Cmd-Option-;).

TIP Alt-drag/Option-drag as you create a guide to **switch** it from vertical to horizontal (or vice versa).

TIP To **move** an existing guide, drag it using the Move tool (make sure the guides aren't locked). Guides will keep their relative positions if you resize the image—provided they're not locked.

TIP You can choose a new guide **color** or **style** in Edit (Photoshop, in OS X) > Preferences > Guides, Grid & Slices. To quickly open that dialog box, double-click a guide with the Move tool (this works only if guides aren't locked).

To place a guide at a specified location:

1. Choose View > New Guide.

2. Click Orientation: Horizontal or Vertical **2**.

3. Enter a Position in any measurement unit.

4. Click OK.

To remove guides:

To remove one guide, choose the Move tool (V), then drag the guide out of the image window (this works only if guides aren't locked).

or

To remove all guides, choose View > Clear Guides.

Create, Place, Remove Guide

To use the Measure tool:

1. Choose the Measure tool (I or Shift-I). It's on the Eyedropper tool pop-out palette. And display the Info palette.

2. Drag in the image window **1**. The angle (A) and distance (D) of the measure line will be displayed on the Info palette **2**. Shift-drag to constrain the angle to a multiple of 45°.

3. *Optional:* After dragging with the Measure tool, Alt-drag/Option-drag from either end of the line to create a protractor **3**. The angle (A) formed by the two lines will display on the Info palette **4**. You can readjust the angle at any time by dragging either end of the line.

4. Choose another tool when you're finished using the Measure tool. If you choose it again, the measure line will redisplay.

To remove a measure line, drag it off the image using the Measure tool or click Clear on the Measure tool options bar.

TIP You can drag a measure line or protractor to another area of the image using the Measure tool. Drag any part of the line except an endpoint, unless you want to change its angle.

1 *If you drag in the image window using the **Measure** tool...*

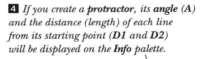

2 *...Angle (A) and **distance** (D) readouts will appear on the **Info** palette.*

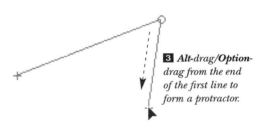

3 *Alt-drag/Option-drag from the end of the first line to form a protractor.*

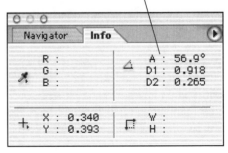

4 *If you create a **protractor**, its **angle** (A) and the distance (length) of each line from its starting point (**D1** and **D2**) will be displayed on the **Info** palette.*

Measure Tool

1 *The options bar for the **Clone Stamp** tool*

2 *Drag the mouse where you want the clone to appear. To produce this illustration, the **Aligned** option was turned **on** for the Clone Stamp tool.*

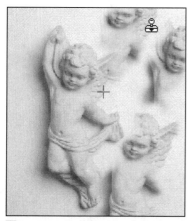

3 **Uncheck** *the **Aligned** option for the Clone Stamp tool to create multiple clones from the same source point.*

Cloning

The Clone Stamp tool is used to clone imagery from one layer to another within the same image, or to clone imagery from one image to another.

To clone areas in the same image:

1. Choose the Clone Stamp tool (S or Shift-S).

2. On the Clone Stamp tool options bar **1**:

Click the Brush picker arrowhead, then click a **brush** whose size is appropriate for the area you want to clone.
and
Choose a blending **Mode**.
and
Choose an **Opacity** percentage.
and
Set the **Flow** percentage to control the rate of application.
and
Check **Aligned** to create a single, uninterrupted clone from the same source point; you can release the mouse and drag in another area, or even switch modes or brushes between strokes **2**. Or uncheck Aligned to create repetitive clones from the same source point; in this case, the crosshair pointer will return to the same source point each time you release the mouse **3**.
and
Check **Use All Layers** to sample pixels from all currently visible layers that you Alt-click/Option-click over. Or uncheck Use All Layers to sample pixels from the current layer only.

3. *Optional:* To apply the cloning in an airbrush style, click the Airbrush icon.

(Continued on the following page)

4. On the Layers palette, choose the layer that you want to clone from.

5. In the image window, Alt-click/Option-click the area of the layer you want to clone from, to establish a source point. Don't click a transparent part of a layer —there will be nothing to clone.

6. On the same layer, drag the mouse back and forth where you want the clone to appear.
or
Choose or create another layer, then drag the mouse. Two pointers will appear on the screen: a crosshair pointer over the source point and a Clone Stamp pointer (or Brush Size pointer) where you drag the mouse. Imagery from the source point will appear where the mouse is dragged, and it will replace any underlying pixels.

Note: If the "Lock transparent pixels" button is selected on the Layers palette, the cloned imagery will replace only existing pixels.

7. *Optional:* To establish a new source point to clone from, Alt-click/Option-click a different area in the source image.

TIP You can change options bar settings for the Clone Stamp tool between strokes. To create a "double-exposure" effect, choose a low Opacity percentage so the underlying pixels will partially show through the cloned pixels **1**.

TIP To paint areas from earlier stages of the same editing session, use the History Brush tool.

1 *An **Opacity** of 50% was chosen for the **Clone Stamp** tool to create this double-exposure effect.*

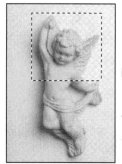

1 *Select an area of an image, then choose Edit > Define Pattern.*

To use the Pattern Stamp tool:

1. To create a custom pattern, choose the Rectangular Marquee tool, ⬚ select an area of an image for the tile **1**, choose Edit > Define Pattern, type a Name, click OK, then deselect (Ctrl-D/Cmd-D).

2. Choose the Pattern Stamp tool (S or Shift-S). 🖎

3. On the Pattern Stamp tool options bar, choose options as per steps 2–3 on page 123. Check Aligned to stamp pattern tiles in a perfect grid, regardless of how many separate strokes you use; or uncheck Aligned if you don't want the tiles to align.

Click the Pattern arrowhead or thumbnail, then click a pattern on the picker **3**. Your custom pattern from step 1 will be the last pattern on the picker.

4. *Optional:* Check Impressionist to apply a blurry, fragmented version of the pattern.

5. Drag on a layer in the same image or in another image to stamp the pattern **2**. No source point is required for this tool.

2 *The pattern is then applied in another image using various opacities for the **Pattern Stamp** tool.*

Pattern Stamp

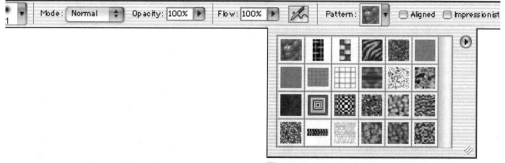

3 *You can choose a **preset** pattern from the **pattern picker** on the options bar.*

1 *The options bar for the Clone Stamp tool*

You can use the Clone Stamp tool to clone imagery from one image to another. Try using it to gather imagery from several open images into one final image. To create a brushstroke version of an image or images, clone to a new document that has a white or solid-colored background using a soft brush.

To clone from image to image:

1. Open two images, and position the two windows side-by-side.

2. If they're both color images, choose the same image mode for both. You can also clone between a color image and a grayscale image. *Note:* Choose the Don't Flatten option to preserve layers.

3. Choose the Clone Stamp tool (S or Shift S).

4. On the Clone Stamp tool options bar **1**:

Click the Brush picker arrowhead, then click a **brush**.
and
Choose a blending **Mode**.
and
Choose an **Opacity**.
and
7.0! Set the **Flow** percentage to control the rate of application.
and
Check **Aligned** to reproduce a continuous area from the source point, or uncheck Aligned to produce multiple clones from the source point.

5. *Optional:* To apply the cloning in an air-
7.0! brush style, click the Airbrush icon.

6. Click in the image window that you want to clone to, and choose a layer.

7. Alt-click/Option-click the area of the source (non-active) image that you want to clone from **2**.

8. Drag back and forth on the destination (active) image to make the clone appear **3**–**4**.

2 *Alt-click/Option-click on the non-active (source) image to establish a source point...*

3 *...then drag back and forth in short strokes on the active (destination) image to make the clone appear.*

4 *To create this effect, an image was cloned to a new document with a white background.*

⬦	Brush: ● 19 ▾	Mode: Normal ▾	Source: ◉ Sampled ○ Pattern: ▾	☐ Aligned

1 *The options bar for the **Healing Brush** tool*

The Healing Brush tool, and the related **7.0!**
Patch tool, offer touch-up precision that the
Clone Stamp and Pattern Stamp tools don't
offer. Whereas the Stamp tools copy the
source area's color to a target area, this new
pair of tools samples the source area's texture, applies that texture to the target area,
and finally matches it to the target area's surrounding color and brightness values. This
makes it much easier to fix, say, a facial
blemish in a photograph or a paper crinkle
in a vintage photo and blend it seamlessly
into the surrounding pixels. The Healing
brush usually is applied in a freehand man-
ner, whereas the Patch tool confines the
change to pre-selected areas.

To repair areas using the Healing Brush tool ("boo-boo brush"):

1. Choose the Healing Brush tool (J or Shift-J). ⬦

2. On the Healing Brush tool options bar **1**:

Click the Brush picker arrowhead, then
click a **brush** that's appropriate for the
area you want to sample. In general,
a small, hard tip will give you greater
control.
and
Choose **Replace** from the Mode pop-up
menu to have your brush stroke preserve
the grain, texture, and noise of the
area surrounding the target. Choose a
different mode if you don't care if those
attributes are preserved.
and
Click Sampled as the **Source**.
and
Check **Aligned** to create a single, uninterrupted sampling from the same
source point, or uncheck Aligned to
create repetitive samplings from the
same source point.

(Continued on the following page)

Healing Brush

3. Alt-click/Option-click the area to be used as the source sample **1**.

4. Drag across the area you want to repair **2**. When you release the mouse, the source texture will be applied to the target area and will be blended with its surrounding pixels. It will render in two stages, though: at first a full clone will appear, and then the source color will disappear, leaving just the source texture.

Shift-drag to constrain the stroke to the horizontal or vertical axis.

5. *Optional:* To establish a new source point for further repairs, Alt-click/Option-click a different area, then continue on your way.

TIP To confine the repair to a specific area, and avoid picking up colors from around that area, lasso the area you want to repair using the Healing Brush before clicking a source point.

TIP When using the Healing Brush tool, either work on a duplicate layer to preserve the original pixels, or make a snapshot of the file before using it so you'll be able use the History Brush tool to selectively restore the original pixels.

TIP The Healing Brush tool works like the Clone Stamp tool if it's used in Replace mode with a hard-edged brush.

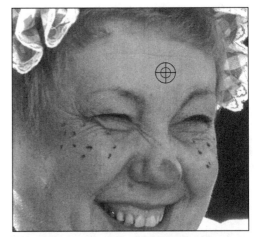

1 *With the **Healing Brush** tool, **Alt-click/Option-click** the area you want to use as **replacement** pixels...*

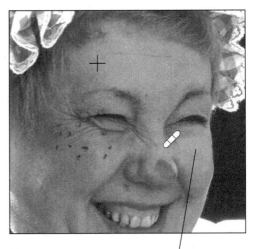

2 *...then drag across the area you want to **repair**.*

1 *Click **Source** on the **Patch** tool options bar.*

2 *Using the **Patch** tool, select the area you want to repair.*

3 *Drag from the selected area to the area that you want to **sample** pixels from...*

4 *...and the patch will be applied to the original **selected area**.*

You can use the Patch tool to quickly repair tears, stains, and dust marks. Use this tool instead of the Healing Brush if you want to avoid sampling a particular color. This tool also lets you fine-tune and modify a selection (e.g., feather the edges) before the repair is applied to it.

To use the Patch tool: 7.0!

1. Choose the Patch tool (J or Shift-J).

2. Click Patch: Source on the Patch tool options bar **1**.

3. Drag around the area you want to repair (this is called the Destination) **2**. Alt-click/Option-click if you want to create a straight-edged selection.

4. Add to (Shift-drag) or subtract from (Alt-drag/Option-drag) the selection as needed, or use any Select menu commands to feather or otherwise modify the selection.

5. Drag from inside the selection to the area you want to sample **3**, then release the mouse **4**. The patch will bounce back, and the sampled pixels will be applied automatically to the area you originally selected (see also **1**–**2** on the following page).

TIP You could also click Destination instead of Source for step 2, above, select the area you want to sample from, and then for step 5, drag to the area you want to repair (the Destination). However, you'll have more control over which area is repaired if you do it in the reverse order, as in our instructions above.

TIP To patch (fill) the selection with a pattern, choose a pattern from the picker on the options bar, then click Use Pattern.

Patch Tool

1 *The original image*

2 *After using the **Patch** tool to remove the damaged area on the left side*

To produce this image, entitled **Physique Medley**, David Humphrey composited scans of embroidery and his own charcoal drawings and photographs, among other things. He then adjusted the luminosity levels of the various components on individual layers using blending modes (Darken, Multiply) and the Eraser and Burn tools.

1 The original image, with a **feathered** selection

2 After inversing the selection and pressing Delete

Apply the Feather command to fade the edge of a selection by a specified number of pixels inward and outward from the marquee. A feather radius of 5, for example, would create a feather area 10 pixels wide.

Note: The feather won't be visible until the selection is modified with a painting tool, copied/pasted, moved, or filled, or a filter or Image menu command is applied to it.

To feather an existing selection:

1. With a selection active, right-click/ Ctrl-click and choose Feather, or choose Select > Feather, or press Ctrl-Alt-D/ Cmd-Option-D.

2. Enter a Feather Radius value (.2–250 pixels). The feather width is affected by the image resolution. The higher the image resolution, the wider you need to make the feather Radius.

3. Click OK **1**–**2**. *Note:* If the feather radius is too wide for the selection area, the message "No pixels are more than 50% selected…" will appear.

TIP To specify a feather radius before creating the selection, choose a Marquee or Lasso tool, then enter a Feather value on the options bar.

Feather

To eliminate a noticeable seam after pasting or moving layer pixels, use the Defringe command. It recolors pixels on the edge of the selection with pixel colors from just inside the edge, within a specified radius.

Note: If the imagery you moved or pasted was originally on a black background, and was anti-aliased, you can try using the Layer > Matting > Remove Black Matte command to remove unwanted remnants from the black background. Choose Layer > Matting > Remove White Matte command if the imagery was originally on a white background. Feathered selections will be more noticeably affected by the Matting commands.

To defringe a layer:

1. With the paste layer chosen, choose Layer > Matting > Defringe.

2. Enter a Width for the Defringe area (1–200) pixels **1**. Try a low number first (1, 2, or 3 pixels) so your edges won't lose definition. Some non-edge areas may also be affected.

3. Click OK.

The Smooth command adds unselected pixels to, or removes unselected pixels from, a selection from within a specified radius. It's a good way to eliminate extraneous selection areas, particularly after using the Magic Wand tool.

To smooth a selection:

1. Choose Select > Modify > Smooth.

2. Enter a Sample Radius value (1–100 pixels) **2**. If most pixels within the specified radius are selected, any unselected pixels in that radius will be added to the selection; if most pixels are unselected within the specified radius, any selected pixels will be removed from the selection.

3. Click OK **3**–**4**.

1 *Use the **Defringe** command to make montaged imagery look more seamless.*

2 *Use the **Smooth Selection** command to clean up selections.*

3 *The original Magic Wand tool selection*

4 *After applying the **Smooth** command*

Defringe; Smooth

LAYERS 7

For additional layer topics, see Chapter 14

*The currently **active** layer (note the brush icon)*

Add layer style *Create new set* *Create new layer* *Delete layer*

Add layer/ vector mask *Create new fill or adjustment layer*

Show/hide layer

LAYERS ARE LIKE clear acetate sheets: opaque where there is imagery and transparent where there is no imagery. To each layer, you can assign a different opacity and mode to control how that layer blends with the layers below it. You can change the stacking order of layers, and you can also assign a layer mask to any layer. Only one layer can be edited at a time, which means you can easily modify one part of an image without disturbing the other layers.

Layers basics

If you choose Contents: White or Background Color for a new image (File > New), the bottommost area of the image will be the Background, which is not a layer. If you choose Contents: Transparent, the bottommost component of the image will be a layer. Layers can be added to an image at any time.

Layers are listed on the Layers palette from topmost to bottommost, with the Background, of course, at the bottom of the list. The layer that is currently highlighted (active) on the palette is the only layer that can be edited. Click a layer name to activate that layer. The name of the currently active layer (or the Background) is listed on the title bar of the image window.

Layers Palette

If you've already learned how to paste a selection or create type, you know that both operations create a new layer automatically. And in Chapter 9, you'll learn about a special variety of layers called adjustment layers, which are used to preview color adjustments on underlying layers. In this chapter, you'll learn the layer basics.

Beware! If you save your image in any file format except Photoshop (.psd) or advanced TIFF (.tif), all layers will be flattened and any transparency in the bottommost layer will become opaque white. Also, if you change image modes (e.g., from RGB to CMYK), remember to click Don't Flatten or Don't Merge if you want to preserve layers.

Note: An image can contain as many layers as available memory and storage allow. However, because the pixel areas on a layer occupy storage space, when you finish a large image, you can merge or flatten its layers together to reduce its storage size **1**.

To create a new layer:

1. To create a layer with 100% opacity and Normal mode, click the "Create new layer" button 🔲 at the bottom of the Layers palette and skip the remaining steps.

or

To choose options for the new layer as it's created, choose New Layer from the Layers palette menu or Alt-click/Option-click the "Create new layer" button at the bottom of the palette, then follow the remaining steps.

2. *Do any of the following optional steps:*

Change the layer Name **2**.

Click Group With Previous Layer to make the new layer a part of a clipping group (see page 271).

Choose a color for the area on the Layers palette behind the layer's eye and brush/link icons (see the sidebar).

Choose a different blending Mode or Opacity (both can be changed later).

Dress it up

To help you identify layers quickly (and to make your Layers palette look "purty"), right-click/Ctrl-click in the eye column and choose a **color**.

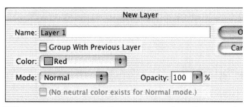

1 *Before adding a new layer to your image, choose* **Document Sizes** *from the Status bar drop-down menu, and note the current image size.*

The second figure is the amount of **RAM** *the layered, unflattened file is using. Note how much the file's storage size increases when you add a new layer. The image in this illustration contains two layers.*

2 *Enter a name and choose options for a layer in the* **New Layer** *dialog box.*

3 *Click a different* **Thumbnail Size** *or turn off thumbnail display altogether (None) in the* **Layers Palette Options** *dialog box.*

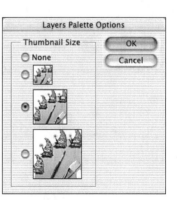

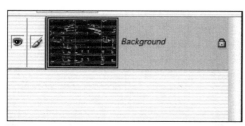

1 *A detail of the Layers palette, showing the original* **Background**

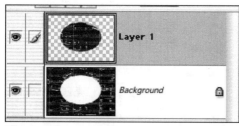

2 *After choosing the* **Layer Via Cut**, *a selection is cut from the Background and placed on its own layer.*

3 *Right-click/Ctrl-click a layer name, then choose* **Duplicate Layer** *from the context menu.*

4 *The* **duplicate** *layer appears on the palette.*

3. Click OK. The new layer will appear directly above the previously active layer.

TIP To improve Photoshop's performance, especially if you're working on a large file, choose Palette Options from the Layers palette menu, then click the smallest thumbnail size (**3**, previous page).

To turn a selection into a layer:

1. Create a selection.

2. To place a **copy** of the selected pixels on a new layer and leave the original layer untouched, right-click/Ctrl-click and choose Layer Via Copy (Ctrl-J/Cmd-J).
or
To place the selected pixels on a new layer and **remove** them from the original layer, right-click/Ctrl-click and choose Layer Via Cut (Ctrl-Shift-J/Cmd-Shift-J) **1**–**2**.

3. *Optional:* Click the eye icon for the original layer to temporarily hide it from view.

To duplicate a layer in the same image:

To create a new layer with a generic name, drag the name of the layer you want to duplicate over the "Create new layer" button **□** at the bottom of the Layers palette. The duplicate layer will appear above the original layer, and it will be the active layer.
or
To name the duplicate as you create it, right-click/Ctrl-click the name of the layer you want to duplicate and choose Duplicate Layer, or Alt-drag/Option-drag the layer over the "Create new layer" button. Type a name for the duplicate layer in the "As" field, then click OK **3**–**4**.

Selection into a Layer; Duplicate Layer

We can think of at least two reasons to hide the layers you're not currently working on: one, to remove them as a visual distraction and two, to improve Photoshop's performance.

Note: If you're going to be printing your image, remember that only visible layers will print. Ditto for merging layers: Only visible layers can be merged (you'll learn about merging and flattening at the end of this chapter). Be especially careful when using the Flatten Image command—it discards hidden layers!

To hide or show layers:

Click the eye icon on the Layers palette for any individual layer you want to hide ■–■. Click in the eye column again to redisplay the layer.

or

Drag upward or downward in the eye column to hide or show multiple layers.

or

Alt-click/Option-click an eye icon to hide all other layers except the one you click on (including the Background). Alt-click/Option-click the remaining eye icon again to redisplay all layers.

or

Right-click/Ctrl-click in the eye column and choose "Show/Hide all other layers" from the context menu ■.

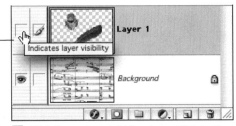

1 *Click the eye icon to hide a layer. Click in the eye column again to redisplay it.*

2 *Layer 1 hidden*

3 *Layer 1 redisplayed*

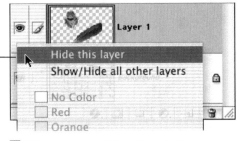
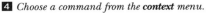

4 *Choose a command from the context menu.*

1 *The original image*

2 *Layer 1 flipped horizontally*

3 *Deleting Layer 1 via the context menu*

4 *After deleting Layer 1*

To flip a layer:

1. On the Layers palette, choose the layer that you want to flip. Any layers that are linked to the active layer will also flip.

2. Choose Edit > Transform > Flip Horizontal **1**–**2** or Flip Vertical.

To delete a layer:

On the Layers palette, click the layer you want to delete. Then click the "Delete layer" (trash) button and click Yes, or Alt-click/ Option-click the "Delete layer" button to bypass the prompt.

or

Right-click/Ctrl-click the layer you want to delete, choose Delete Layer from the context menu, then click Yes **3**–**4**.

TIP Change your mind? No problem. Choose Edit > Undo or click a prior state on the History palette.

To rename a layer: *7.0!*

1. Double-click a layer name on the Layers palette.

2. Type in a new name.

3. Press Enter/Return.

TIP You can rename a layer set using the same method.

Flip Layer; Delete Layer; Rename Layer

Transform layers

To transform (scale, rotate, skew, distort, or apply perspective to) a layer by dragging:

1. On the Layers palette, activate the layer you want to transform. Any layers that are linked to the active layer will also transform. You can't transform a 16 bits/channel image.

Optional: Create a selection to limit the transformation to those pixels.

2. Choose Edit > Transform > Scale, Rotate, Skew, Distort, or Perspective. A solid bounding box will appear around the opaque part of the layer or the selection.

3. *Optional:* To transform the layer or selection from a location other than its center, move the reference point . You can move it outside the bounding box.

4. *Note:* If you're going to perform multiple transformations, to save time and preserve image quality, after performing this step for the first command, choose and then perform additional transform commands, and then accept them all at once (step 5).

To **Scale** the layer horizontally and vertically, drag a corner handle ▪. To scale only the horizontal or vertical dimension, drag a side handle. Shift-drag to scale proportionately. Alt-drag/Option-drag to scale from the reference point.

For **Rotate**, position the pointer near a bounding box handle, either inside or outside the box (the pointer will become a double-headed arrow), then drag in a circular direction ▪. Shift-drag to constrain the rotation to a multiple of 15°.

For **Skew**, drag a corner handle to reposition just that handle or drag a side handle to skew along the current horizontal or vertical axis. Alt-drag/Option-drag to skew symmetrically from the center of the layer.

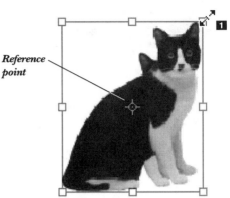

Reference point

Scale

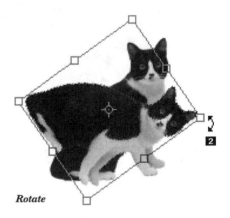

Rotate

Distort

Transform Commands

General information

Choose an **interpolation** method for the transform commands in Edit (Photoshop, in OS X) > Preferences > General (Ctrl-K/Cmd-K). Bicubic (Better)—the slowest method—causes the least degradation to the image.

To **repeat** the last transformation, choose Edit > Transform > Again (Ctrl-Shift-T/Cmd-Shift-T).

To transform a **duplicate** of a selection, hold down Alt/Option as you choose the command or press Ctrl-Alt-T/Cmd-Option-T.

In addition to transforming a layer, you can also transform an **alpha channel**, a **selection border** (see page 105), a **path** (see page 289), or an unlinked, active **layer mask**.

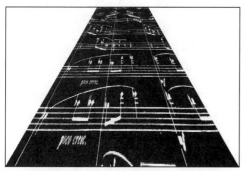

1 *The original image*

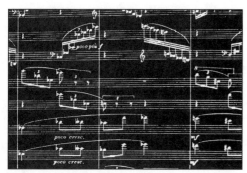

2 *A **perspective** transformation*

For **Distort** (**3**, previous page), drag a corner handle to freely reposition just that handle or drag a side handle to distort the side of the bounding box along the horizontal and/or vertical axis. Alt-drag/Option-drag to distort symmetrically from the center of the layer. Distort can be more drastic than Skew.

For **Perspective**, drag a corner handle along the horizontal or vertical axis to create one-point perspective along that axis **1**–**2**. The adjacent corner will move in unison. Or drag a side handle to skew along the current horizontal or vertical axis.

5. To accept the transformation, double-click inside the bounding box or click the ✔ on the options bar (Enter/Return). To cancel the transformation, click the ⊘ (Esc).

TIP To undo the last handle modification, choose Edit > Undo.

TIP To move the entire layer (or selection), drag inside the transform bounding box.

TIP Choose the Measure tool (I or Shift-I), drag in the image window to define an angle, then with the Measure tool still selected, choose Edit > Transform > Rotate. The layer will rotate automatically along the angle you defined.

Transform Commands

Once you're acquainted with the individual Transform commands, you'll probably want to start using the Free Transform command, especially if you want to perform a series of transformations. With Free Transform, the various commands are accessed using keyboard shortcuts—you don't have to choose each command individually from a menu. And best of all, image data is resampled only once: when you accept the changes.

To free transform a layer:

1. On the Layers palette, activate the layer you want to transform. Any layers that are linked to the active layer will also transform. You can't transform a 16-bits/channel image.

Optional: Create a selection to limit the transformation to those pixels.

2. Choose Edit > Free Transform (Ctrl-T/ Cmd-T).
or
Choose the Move tool (V) and check Show Bounding Box on the options bar. *Note:* This option can interfere with the Auto Select Layer option (see page 144).

3. Follow step 4 on the previous page, with these exceptions:

To **Skew**, Ctrl-Shift-drag/Cmd-Shift-drag.

To **Distort**, Ctrl-drag/Cmd-drag.

To apply **Perspective**, Ctrl-Alt-Shift-drag/ Cmd-Option-Shift-drag a corner handle.

The transformation will automatically occur from the current reference point, which is chosen on the options bar (see step 3 on the next page).

4. To accept the transformation, double-click inside the bounding box or click the ✔ on the options bar (Enter/Return). To cancel the transformation, click the ⊘ (Esc). You must accept or cancel to return to normal editing.

TIP As you transform a layer or a selection, note the width (W), height (H), rotation angle (A), and horizontal skew (H) or vertical skew (V) readout(s) on the options bar or the Info palette.

What's left?

If you transform a **layer** (or a selection on a layer), any empty space remaining after the transformation will become **transparent**.

If you transform a selection on the **Background**, any remaining empty space will be filled with the current **Background color**.

1 *Sections of the options bar with the **Free Transform** command chosen:*

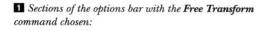

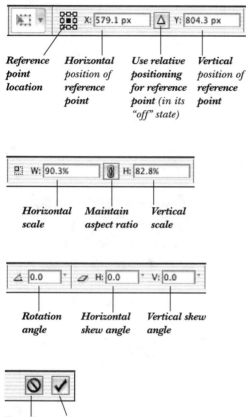

Reference point location *Horizontal position of reference point* *Use relative positioning for reference point (in its "off" state)* *Vertical position of reference point*

Horizontal scale *Maintain aspect ratio* *Vertical scale*

Rotation angle *Horizontal skew angle* *Vertical skew angle*

Cancel transform *Commit transform*

Follow these instructions if you'd rather transform a layer by entering exact numeric values than by dragging the mouse. The controls for numeric transforms display on the options bar whenever a transform function is chosen.

To transform a layer by entering numeric values:

1. On the Layers palette, activate the layer that you want to transform. Any layers that are linked to it will also transform.

2. Choose Edit > Free Transform (Ctrl-T/ Cmd-T).

3. On the options bar, choose the reference point location for the move, rotate, and flip transformations by clicking one of the nine little reference point squares **1**.
or
In the document window, drag the reference point to the desired location.
or
Click the "Use relative positioning for reference point" button △ to set the X and Y fields to 0; otherwise those values will reflect the absolute position of the reference point as measured from the upper-left corner of the layer. (Click the icon again to turn off the option. To change the units, right-click/Ctrl-click either value.)

4. Do any of the following:
To **move** the layer, enter new X and Y Position values.

To **scale** the layer, enter W (width) and/or H (height) values. (Right-click/ Ctrl-click either value to choose different units from the pop-up menu.) Click the Maintain Aspect Ratio button to preserve the current width-to-height ratio.

To **rotate** the layer, enter a rotation angle.

To **skew** the layer, enter a Horizontal and/or Vertical Skew angle (the amount of slant).

(Continued on the following page)

5. To accept the transformation, double-click inside the bounding box or click the ✓ on the options bar (Enter/Return). To cancel the transformation, click the Ⓢ (Esc).

Managing layers

To restack a layer:

1. On the Layers palette, click the name of the layer you want to restack.

2. Drag the layer name upward or downward on the palette, and release the mouse when a dark horizontal line appears in the desired location **1**–**4**.

TIP You can also restack an active layer by choosing Layer > Arrange > Bring to Front, Bring Forward, Send Backward, or Send to Back, or by using any of the shortcuts listed in the sidebar below. A layer can't be stacked below the Background.

TIP To move the Background upward on the list, it must first be converted into a layer (see the following page).

1 *The original image*

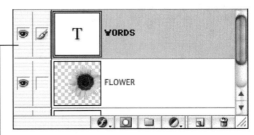

2 *Dragging the WORDS layer **upward***

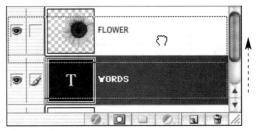

3 *Now the WORDS layer is above the FLOWER layer.*

Restack an active layer

Windows		Macintosh	
Bring Forward	Ctrl-]	Bring Forward	Cmd-]
Bring to Front	Ctrl-Shift-]	Bring to Front	Cmd-Shift-]
Send Backward	Ctrl-[	Send Backward	Cmd-[
Send to Back	Ctrl-Shift-[	Send to Back	Cmd-Shift-[

4 *Here's how it looks.*

Restack a Layer

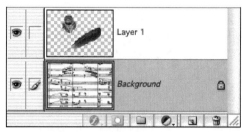

1 *Double-click the **Background**.*

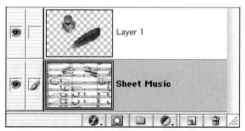

2 *Name the layer.*

3 *The former Background is now a **layer**.*

The standard things you can do to a layer (e.g., move it upward or downward in the layer stack, choose a blending mode or opacity for it, or create a layer mask for it) can't be done to the Background—unless it's first converted into a layer.

To convert the Background into a layer:

Double-click the Background on the Layers palette **1**, type a new Name **2**, choose a Mode and Opacity for the layer, then click OK **3**.

or

Alt-double-click/Option-double-click the Background on the Layers palette to bypass the dialog box.

If you need to create a Background for a file that doesn't have one, you can convert an existing layer into the Background.

To convert a layer into the Background:

1. Choose a layer.

2. Choose Layer > New > Background From Layer (at the top of the Layer menu). The new Background will be placed at the bottom of the stack on the Layers palette.

To move multiple layers in unison, see page 273.

To move a layer:

1. On the Layers palette, choose the layer you want to move.

2. Choose the Move tool (V) ⊹ or hold down Ctrl/Cmd if any other tool is chosen.

3. Drag in the image window. The entire layer will move **2**–**3**.

TIP Press an arrow key with the Move tool chosen to move an active layer one pixel at a time. Press Shift-arrow to move a layer 10 screen pixels at a time. (Don't use Alt/Option arrow—that shortcut duplicates the layer.)

TIP If pixels are moved beyond the existing edge of the image, don't worry—they'll be saved with the image, and you can always move them back into view.

TIP If Auto Select Layer is checked (options bar), you can quickly select a layer by clicking any visible pixels in that layer with the Move tool. However, if this option is on, you may not be able to select a layer if you click pixels on that layer that have an opacity below 50%.

TIP For faster previewing of high-resolution images when using the Move tool, choose Edit (Photoshop, in OS X) > Preferences > Display & Cursors, then check Use Pixel Doubling. Pixels will temporarily double in size while you drag (they'll be half their normal resolution).

Quick layer select

■ With the Move tool chosen, right-click/Ctrl-click in the image window and choose a layer from the context menu **1**. (Ctrl-right-click/Cmd-Ctrl-click with any other tool selected.) Only layers containing non-transparent pixels under the pointer will appear on the menu.

■ With the Move tool chosen, Ctrl-click/Cmd-click an object in the image window to quickly activate that object's layer. (*Mac OS:* Cmd-Option-Ctrl-click if any other tool is chosen.)

1 *Choosing a layer from a context menu*

2 *The original image*

3 *After **moving** the type layer with the **Move** tool*

Out, set, out!

To move a layer out of its set, drag the layer name over the current set name, or over another set name, or above or below a layer name outside the set.

1 *Click the triangle to expand or contract the layer set list.*

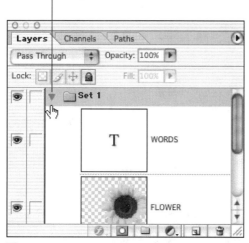

2 *The WORDS and FLOWER layers were dragged into the Set 1 folder.*

3 *Lock position   Lock all*

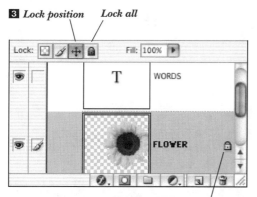

*The **lock icon** appears next to the layer **name.***

Layer sets are a very useful organizational tool. Once layers are organized into a set, you can display just the name of the set on the Layers palette, or you can click the arrow to reveal all the layer names within the set **1**. Sets make the Layers palette easier to work with, especially for images that contain many layers.

A second reason for using sets is to limit the effect of blending modes and adjustment layers. When a layer set's blending mode is other than the default Pass Through mode, adjustment layers and blending modes applied to layers within the set affect only layers within that set, as if all the layers in the set were merged into one. Keep in mind also that when a layer mask or vector mask is applied to a set, it affects the whole set.

To create a layer set:

1. Click the "Create new set" button ⬜ at the bottom of the Layers palette.
   or
   Choose Layer > New > Layer Set, change the Name, Color, blending Mode, or Opacity setting for the new set, if desired, then click OK.

2. On the Layers palette, drag each layer you want to include in the set onto the set's folder icon **2**.

The Lock feature helps to prevent inadvertent edits.

To lock a layer:

1. On the Layers palette, choose the layer you want to lock.

2. Click the "Lock position" button **3** (formerly a checkbox) to lock only the layer's location. Now the layer can't be moved, but its pixels can still be edited.
   or
   Click the "Lock all" button to protect the layer from any and all edits.

TIP To learn about the "Lock transparent pixels" and "Lock image pixels" buttons (the first two buttons) on the Layers palette, see page 147.

A fill layer works like an adjustment layer, except in this case it contains a solid color, gradient, or pattern. Like an adjustment layer, a fill layer can be edited or removed without affecting any other layers. (Read about adjustment layers on pages 166–169.)

To create a Fill layer:

1. On the Layers palette, activate the layer that you want the fill layer to appear above (you can restack it later).

2. Choose Solid Color, Gradient, or Pattern from the "Create new fill or adjustment layer" pop-up menu at the bottom of the Layers palette **1**.
or
To choose options for the Layer as you create it, choose Layer > New Fill Layer > Solid Color, Gradient, or Pattern, then do any of the following: change the layer Name; choose a Color for the area on the Layers palette behind the layer's eye and brush/link icons; choose a different Opacity or Mode; or check Group With Previous Layer to make the new layer a part of a clipping group (see page 271). Click OK. All of these options can be changed later.

3. For a **Solid Color** layer, choose a color from the Color Picker, then click OK.

For a **Gradient** layer, choose from the gradient picker and set its Style, Angle, and Scale. (For the Reverse, Dither, or Align with layer options, see page 234).

For a **Pattern** layer, choose from the pattern picker and choose a Scale percentage (1–1000) **2**. *All optional:* Uncheck Link with Layer to keep the pattern stationary if the layer is moved; click Snap to Origin to make the pattern snap to the current ruler origin (the location where the zeros on the horizontal and vertical rulers meet; click the "Create new preset" button to create a preset.

4. Click OK.

TIP Adjust the mode or opacity of the fill layer by using the Layers palette.

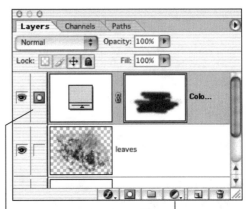

—*The adjustment layer for a **Solid Color** fill (with a modified layer mask)*

1 *Choose **Solid Color, Gradient,** or **Pattern** from the **Create new fill or adjustment layer** pop-up menu.*

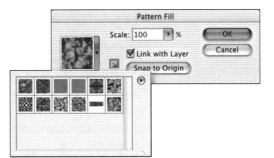

2 *Choose options for a pattern fill layer in the **Pattern Fill** dialog box.*

Fill Layer

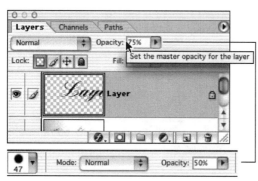

1 *This **layer's** opacity is 75% (Layers palette) and the Paintbrush **tool** opacity is 50% (options bar); the opacity of the resulting stroke will be 37%.*

2 *A rasterized type layer is recolored with **Lock transparent pixels** turned **on**.*

3 *Only the **type** is recolored—not the transparent pixels.*

Tools and layers

You can use any painting or editing tool to edit pixels on the currently active layer, but keep in mind that in addition to the blending Mode, Opacity, and Fill settings chosen for each **tool** from the options bar, the blending Mode, Opacity, and Fill of the currently active **layer** also contribute to a tool's effect **1**. (Learn more about the Opacity and Fill commands on page 243.)

For example, if a layer has a 60% opacity, a painting or editing tool with an opacity of 100% will work at a maximum opacity of 60% on that layer; at an even lower opacity if the tool opacity is below 100%.

Lock transparent pixels

With the **Lock transparent pixels** button selected on the Layers palette, only **non-transparent** pixels on a layer can be edited or recolored **2**–**3**; blank areas will remain transparent. Turn this option off if you want to **create visible pixels**. It can be turned on or off for individual layers.

Note: "Lock transparent pixels" is in a fixed "on" position for an editable type layer. It can be turned on or off for a rasterized type layer.

If you use the Eraser tool with "Lock transparent pixels" on, you will recolor visible pixels with the current background color rather than remove them.

TIP Press / to toggle the "Lock transparent pixels" option on and off.

You can change the size or color of the checkerboard pattern that is used to indicate transparent areas on a layer or turn off the checkerboard pattern altogether in Edit (Photoshop, in OS X) > Preferences > Transparency & Gamut (Ctrl-K/Cmd-K, then Ctrl-4/Cmd-4).

Tools and Layers; Lock Transparent Pixels

Use all layers

With **Use All Layers** checked on the options bar for the Blur, Sharpen, Smudge, Paint Bucket, Magic Eraser, Magic Wand, or Clone Stamp tool, the tool will sample pixels from all the currently visible layers. Regardless of whether Use All Layers is on or off, pixels can be modified only on the currently active layer.

Copy layers

Let's say you're about to perform an operation that requires or causes your file to become flattened, such as converting it to Indexed Color mode (which does not support multiple layers), or saving it to a format other than Photoshop. If you want to preserve a copy of a few individual layers from the file before it's flattened, the following instructions will come in handy. You can save individual layers to a new document or to an existing, open document.

To save a copy of a layer in a new file:

1. On the Layers palette, choose the layer that you want to save a copy of.

2. Right-click/Ctrl-click that layer, and choose Duplicate Layer from the context menu.

3. Choose Destination Document: New 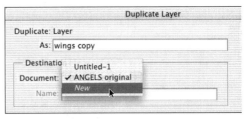.

4. In the As field, enter a name for the layer to appear in the new file.

5. In the Destination: Name field, enter a name for the new file.

6. Click OK, and save the new document.

1 *Choose a **Destination Document** in the **Duplicate Layer** dialog box.*

Save Layer in Separate File

1 *Choose a layer in a **source** image, then **drag** the layer name into the **destination** image window.*

There are two methods for drag-copying layers between images. Choose your method based on how much of each layer you need to copy (area-wise) and whether you want to copy linked layers. If you drag a layer name from the Layers palette to the destination image window, any areas that extend beyond the edge of the image boundary will be copied along with it. This method is described in the instructions below. To copy linked layers, follow the instructions on the next page. To trim any overhanging areas as you copy a layer, follow the instructions on page 151.

To drag-and-drop a layer to another image (Layers palette):

1. Open both the image that contains the layer you want to copy and the image the layer will be copied to (the "destination image"), and make sure the two windows don't completely overlap.

2. Click in the source image window.

3. On the Layers palette, click the layer you want to copy **1**. Any tool can be chosen.

4. Drag the layer from the Layers palette into the destination image window, and release the mouse when the darkened border is in the desired spot. The added layer will be stacked above the previously active layer in the destination image **2**.

TIP Shift-drag to place the layer in the center of the destination image.

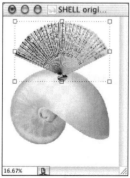

2 *This is the destination image after the SHELL layer was **added**.*

Use this method to copy individual layers or a series of linked layers from one file to another.

To drag-and-drop a layer to another image (Move tool):

1. Open the image that contains the layer that you want to copy (the "source" image) and the image to which the layer is to be copied (the "destination" image).

2. On the Layers palette, click the layer that you want to copy.
   or
   To move multiple layers, make sure they're linked (see page 273).

3. *Optional:* Click in the destination image window, then click the name of the layer on the Layers palette above which you want the added layer to appear.

4. Choose the Move tool (V).

5. Click in the source image window. Drag the active layer(s) from the source image window into the destination image window **1**. The new layer(s) will be positioned where you release the mouse, above the currently active layer in that file **2**.

6. *Optional:* Use the Move tool to reposition the layer in the destination image window.

7. *Optional:* Restack the new layer or layers (drag them upward or downward on the Layers palette).

TIP To copy a layer into the center of another image, start dragging the layer, hold down Shift, then continue to drag.

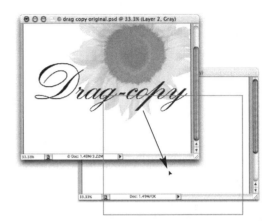

1 *The flower layer is dragged from the* **source image window** *into the* **destination image window**.

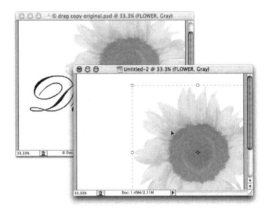

2 *The new layer appears in the* **destination** *image.*

Honey, I shrunk the layer

When you copy-and-paste or drag-and-drop imagery between files, it is rendered in the resolution of the destination image. If the resolution of the destination file is **higher** than that of the source file, the layer will look **smaller** when it's pasted or dropped.

Conversely, if the resolution of the destination file is **lower** than that of source file, the layer will look **larger** when it's pasted or dropped. If the pasted or dropped imagery extends beyond the edge of the live canvas area in the destination file, you can use the Move tool to move the hidden parts into view. The hidden pixels will save with the image.

Use the Clipboard (Copy and Paste commands) if you want to copy only the visible portion of a layer (when displayed at 100% view) and you don't want to copy any pixels that may extend beyond the layer's edge.

To copy and paste only the visible part of a layer to another image:

1. On the Layers palette, activate the layer you want to copy.

2. Choose Select > All (Ctrl-A/Cmd-A). The selection will not include any areas that extend beyond the edge of the canvas area.

3. Choose Edit > Copy (Ctrl-C/Cmd-C).

4. Click in the destination image window.

5. Choose Edit > Paste (Ctrl-V/Cmd-V). The pasted pixels will appear on a new layer. The layer can be restacked using the Layers palette.

6. Click back in the original image window, then right-click/Ctrl-click and choose Deselect (Ctrl-D/Cmd-D) to deactivate the selection.

Merge or flatten layers

The sad truth is, most file formats other than Photoshop (.psd), Photoshop PDF (.pdf) and advanced TIFF (.tif) don't support multiple layers. In order to export your file to another application, it's going to have to get flattened. We think the best way to do this is to save a flattened copy of it using File > **Save as** with **As a Copy** checked (the layered version will remain open). This way, the layered version will be preserved so you can overwork it to death at some later date.

If you're the cocky sort and you're positive your image is totally and completely done, *finis,* you can flatten it yourself down into the Background using the **Flatten Image** command (see page 154). Actually, because flattened files are smaller than layered files, flattening the stuff you're done with is a good way to free up storage space—if you happen to need storage space. (My, how times have changed. We had to save our first book, QuarkXPress layout, illustrations, and all, onto 12 floppy disks!)

Whereas the Flatten Image command is used when a file is complete, the two merge commands, **Merge Down** and **Merge Visible**, are normally used as an image is being edited. Using either of these commands, you can merge two or more layers together on a case-by-case basis, while leaving the remaining layers intact.

To merge two layers together:

1. Click the top layer of the two layers you want to merge **1**. Either layer can have a layer mask or be an adjustment layer. The topmost layer can be a shape layer; the bottom layer cannot. If you choose a layer set, all the layers in the set will be merged into one layer.

2. Choose Merge Down (Ctrl-E/Cmd-E) from the Layers palette menu. The active layer will merge into the layer directly below it **2**. For a layer set, choose Merge Layer Set. If the underlying layer contains a mask, an alert dialog box will appear **3**; click Apply or Preserve.

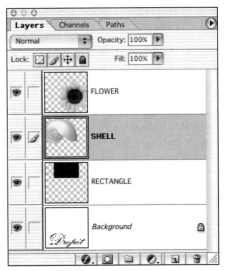

1 *The SHELL layer is chosen.*

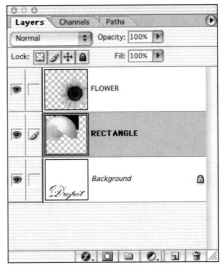

2 *After choosing the **Merge Down** command*

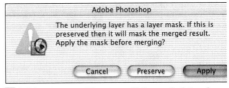

3 *This prompt will appear if the underlying layer being merged contains a **layer mask**.*

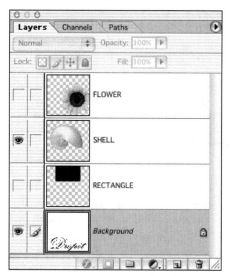

1 *The SHELL layer and background are visible and the Background is chosen; the FLOWER and RECTANGLE layers are hidden.*

The Merge Visible command merges all the currently visible layers into the active layer and **preserves** hidden layers.

To merge multiple layers:

1. Make sure only the layers you want to merge are visible (all should have eye icons on the Layers palette) and **hide** any layers you **don't** want to merge. They don't have to be consecutive. Hide the Background if you don't want to merge layers into it.

2. Activate any one of the layers to be merged. *Beware!* If you merge an editable type layer or an adjustment layer, it will no longer be editable.

3. Choose Merge Visible (Ctrl-Shift-E/ Cmd-Shift-E) from the Layers palette menu **1**–**2**.

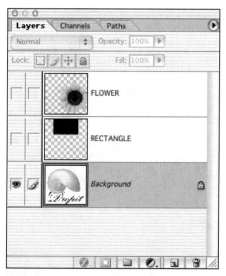

2 *After choosing the **Merge Visible** command, the SHELL layer merges into the Background. The FLOWER and RECTANGLE layers stay as they are.*

Merge Multiple Layers

Beware! The Flatten Image command merges currently displayed layers into the bottommost visible layer and **discards hidden layers**.

To flatten layers:

1. Make sure all the layers you want to flatten are visible (have eye icons) **1**. It doesn't matter which layer is currently active.

2. Choose Flatten Image from the Layers palette menu. If the file contains any hidden layers, you'll get a warning prompt; click OK **2**. If there were any transparent areas in the bottommost layer, they will become white.

Other merge commands

To merge a **copy** of the pixels on currently visible (or linked) layers or layer sets into the active layer (it can be a new layer that you create just for this purpose), hold down **Alt/Option** and choose **Merge Visible** (or **Merge Linked**) from the Layer menu or Layers palette menu. **Alt/Option + Merge Down** also leaves existing layers intact, but copies pixels to the layer below the current layer.

To merge linked layers, choose **Merge Linked** from the Layers palette menu or the Layer menu. The Merge Linked command **discards** hidden, linked layers and ignores non-linked layers. You have to link layers in a set (not the set itself) to use this command.

To merge layers in a clipping group, activate the underlined layer name, then choose **Merge Group** from the Layers palette menu or the Layer menu. The Merge Group command **discards** hidden layers or hidden layers within a group.

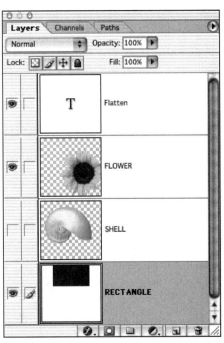

1 *Before choosing the Flatten Image command, make sure all the layers you want to merge are visible!*

2 *After choosing the **Flatten Image** command, all the **visible** layers are flattened into the bottommost visible layer. Photoshop **discarded** the SHELL layer, because it was **hidden**.*

HISTORY 8

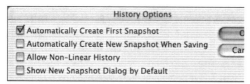

1 *Allow Non-Linear History and other options are turned on or off in the History Options dialog box.*

— Source for the **History Brush**   A history **state**

— *History state slider and current state*   *Create new document from current state*   *Create new snapshot*   *Delete current state*

2 *This is the History palette in linear mode. Note that some steps are grayed out. Figure* **2** *on page 157 shows the palette in non-linear mode.*

IN THIS CHAPTER you'll learn how to use the History palette to selectively undo up to 1,000 previous stages (called "states") of a work session. You'll also learn how to restore selective areas to a prior state using the History Brush or Art History Brush tool, by filling a selection with a history state, and by erasing to a history state.

The History palette displays a list of the most recent states (edits) that were made to an image, with the bottommost state being the most recent. Clicking on a prior state restores the image to that stage of the editing process. What happens to the image when you do this depends on whether the palette is in linear or non-linear mode, so the first step is to learn the difference between these two modes.

Using the History palette

Linear and non-linear

There are two ways in which the History palette can be used: linear mode or non-linear mode. This option is turned on/off via the **Allow Non-Linear History** box in the History Options dialog box **1**, which opens if you choose History Options from the palette menu. You can switch between these two modes at any time during an editing session.

In **linear** mode, if you click back on an earlier state and resume image-editing from that state or delete it, all subsequent (dimmed) states will be deleted **2**.

In the History palette's **non-linear** mode, if you click back on or delete an earlier state, subsequent states won't be deleted (or dimmed). If you then resume image-editing while that earlier state is selected, the new edits will show up as the latest states on the palette and earlier states will be preserved.

(Continued on the following page)

If you delete an earlier state and then click on the latest state, the deleted edits will still appear in the actual image. Non-linear is the more flexible of the two modes.

When would you want to work in non-linear mode? When you need flexibility. Let's say you apply paint strokes to a layer, try out different blending modes for that layer, and then settle on a mode that you like. If you want to reduce the number of states on the palette, you can then delete any of the other blending mode states, whether they're before or after the one you've settled on. You can pick and choose.

When would you want to work in linear mode? If you find non-linear mode confusing or disorienting, or if you want the option to revert back to an earlier state with a nice, clean break.

As long as Automatically Create First Snapshot is checked in the History Options dialog box, the History palette will automatically make a snapshot of the original state of the image when it was opened (see page 158). This is a good option to use in case you edit and save the document and then want to restore the original file.

Clearing the palette

To deliberately clear the History palette for all currently open images in order to free up memory, choose Edit > Purge > Histories, then click OK. To clear the History palette for just the current document, choose Clear History from the History palette menu. The Purge command can't be undone, the Clear History command can.

What's the max? 7.0!

To specify the number of states that can be listed on the palette for an editing session, enter a number in the **History States** field in Edit (Photoshop, in OS X) > Preferences > General. The maximum number was beefed up from 100 in Photoshop 6 to **1000** in Photoshop 7. If the maximum is exceeded during an editing session, earlier steps will automatically be **removed** to make room for the new ones. *Note:* The maximum number of states may be limited by various factors, including the image size, the kind of edits that are made to the image, and currently available memory. Each open image keeps its own list of states.

Clear the History Palette

History shortcuts

Step Forward one state   Ctrl-Shift-Z/Cmd-Shift-Z

Step Backward one state Ctrl-Alt-Z/Cmd-Option-Z

1 *After clicking a prior state with the **History** palette in **linear** mode*

2 *After clicking a prior state with the **History** palette in **non-linear** mode*

Note: If the palette is in linear mode (Allow Non-Linear History is off), the states below the one you click on will become dimmed. If you delete the state you click on or edit the image at that state, all the dimmed states will be **deleted**. If you change your mind, choose Undo immediately to restore them. If the palette is in non-linear mode, you can restore the document to the latest stage of editing by clicking the bottommost state.

To revert to a prior history state:

Click a prior state on the History palette **1**–**2**.
or
Choose Step Forward or Step Backward from the palette menu (see the shortcuts at left).
or
Drag the slider on the left side of the palette upward or downward to the desired state.

To duplicate a state:

1. Turn on Allow Non-Linear History.

2. Alt-click/Option-click a state. The duplicate will be listed as the latest (bottommost) state.

Note: If Allow Non-Linear History is checked and you delete a state, **only** that state will be deleted. If Allow Non-Linear History is unchecked and you delete a state, **all** subsequent states will be deleted along with it (you can choose Edit > Undo to restore them).

To delete a state:

Drag the name of the state that you want to delete over the "Delete current state" (trash) button on the History palette.

TIP Keep Alt-clicking/Option-clicking the trash button to delete a series of consecutive states from the current state backward.

TIP When File > Revert is chosen, like other commands, it becomes a state on the History palette, and all the states preceding it are retained. So you can restore an image to a state before the Revert command (or restore a state selectively using the History Brush).

Revert to Prior State; Duplicate, Delete State

Using snapshots

A snapshot is like a copy of a history state, with one major difference: unlike a state, a snapshot will stay on the palette even if the state from which it was created is deleted due to the maximum number of history states being reached or the palette being cleared or purged. It's a good idea to create a snapshot before performing a long series of editing steps or running an action on an image. *Beware!* All snapshots are deleted when an image is closed.

To have a snapshot be created automatically each time a document is opened, check **Automatically Create First Snapshot** in History Options. To have a snapshot be created each time a file is saved, check **Automatically Create New Snapshot When Saving**.

To create a snapshot of a history state:

1. Click the state that you want to create a snapshot of **1**.

2. Click the "Create new snapshot" button **2**. If Show New Snapshot Dialog by Default is checked in History Options, the New Snapshot dialog box will open; follow the remaining steps.

or

To choose options for the snapshot as you create it, choose New Snapshot from the palette menu; or Alt-click/Option-click the "Create new snapshot" button; or right-click/Control-click the state and choose New Snapshot from the context menu.

3. Type a Name for the snapshot **3**.

4. Choose From: Full Document to make a snapshot of all the layers in the image at that state; or choose Merged Layers to create a snapshot that merges all layers in the image at that state; or choose Current Layer to make a snapshot of only the currently active layer at that state.

5. Click OK. A new snapshot thumbnail will appear near the top of the palette **4**.

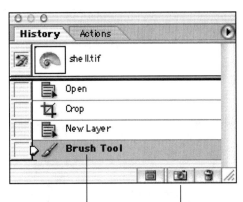

1 *First click a state on the History palette.*   **2** *Then click or Alt-click/ Option-click the **Create new snapshot** button.*

3 *In the **New Snapshot** dialog box, enter a **Name** and choose which part of the image you want the snapshot to be created **From**.*

4 *A **thumbnail** for the new snapshot appears on the History palette.*

Create Snapshot

To replace the contents of one image with a history state from another image, drag the state from the source document's history palette into the destination image window.

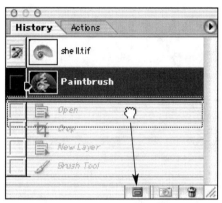

1 *Drag a snapshot or state over the* **Create new document from current state** *button.*

2 *A* **duplicate** *of the snapshot appears in a new document.*

To make a snapshot become the latest state:

Click a snapshot thumbnail. If the Allow Non-Linear History option is turned off and edits were made to the image since that snapshot was taken, the document will revert to the snapshot stage of editing and all the states will be dimmed. If you then resume editing, all dimmed states will be deleted. If Allow Non-Linear History was on, subsequent states will remain on the palette.
or
With either History option chosen, Alt-click/Option-click a snapshot thumbnail. The other states will remain available and that snapshot will become the latest state.

To delete a snapshot:

Click the snapshot thumbnail, choose Delete from the palette menu or click the "Delete current state" (trash) button, then click Yes.
or
Drag the snapshot to the "Delete current state" (trash) button.

If you turn a history snapshot or state into a new document, you'll have a sort of freeze insurance—something to fall back on in the event of a system or power failure. *Note:* Only one history state can be copied at a time.

To create a new document from a history state or snapshot:

Drag a snapshot or a state over the "Create new document from current state" button **1**.
or
Click a snapshot or a state, then click the "Create new document from current state" button.
or
Right-click/Control-click a snapshot or a state, then choose New Document from the context menu.

A new image window will appear, bearing the title of the state from which it was created, and "Duplicate State" will be the name of the starting state for the new image **2**. Save this new image!

Restoring and erasing

You can select any snapshot or state on the History palette to use as a source of earlier pixel data for the History Brush tool. Dragging with the brush restores pixels from that prior state of editing.

Note: The History Brush tool can't be used on an image if you've changed its pixel count since it was opened (e.g., by resampling or cropping, or by changing its image mode or canvas size).

To use the History Brush tool:

1. Choose the History Brush tool (Y or Shift-Y).

2. From the History Brush tool options bar :

   7.0! Choose a blending Mode, Opacity percentage, and Flow percentage. Click the Airbrush button, too, if desired.
   and
   Click the Brush picker arrowhead, then click a brush on the picker.

3. On the History palette, click the blank box at the left side of the palette for the state or snapshot that you want to use as a source for the History Brush tool (the History Brush icon will appear where you click).

4. Choose the layer that you want to restore pixels on.

5. Draw strokes on the image. Pixel data from the prior state of that layer will replace the current pixel data where you draw strokes –.

TIP Here's an example of how the History Brush tool could be used to restore an earlier stage of an image. You add brushstrokes to a layer and then decide several editing steps later that you want

Snapshot as History Brush source

Modify a layer (e.g., apply an Adjust command, a filter, or paint strokes), take a snapshot of the current state, and then delete that state or choose Undo. Set the **History Source** icon to the **snapshot**, then stroke with the History Brush tool on the part of the layer that you modified to selectively restore it.

2 *The original image*

3 *After applying the Graphic Pen filter, positioning the **History Source** icon at a prior state, and then painting on parts of the image using the **History Brush** tool at 95% opacity*

1 *Choose settings from the **History Brush** tool options bar.*

1 *The original image*

2 *Choose **Use: History** in the **Fill** dialog box.*

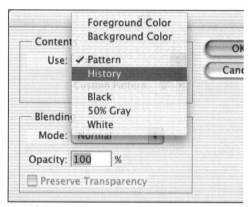

3 *We applied the Glass filter to a layer, selected the area around the tree, and then filled the selection with an earlier history state (**Use: History**). Try doing the same thing using the Distort > Wave or Ripple filter or an Artistic or Sketch filter.*

to remove them. Clicking on the state prior to brushstrokes state could cause other edits to be deleted. Instead, click in the box next to any state prior to the state in which the strokes were added to set the source for the History Brush tool, click the layer on the Layers palette to which the brush strokes were added, choose the History Brush tool (Y), then paint out the added strokes.

TIP When restoring from a snapshot, you can choose a layer if the snapshot you're using as a source was created with the Full Document or Merged Layers option on. If the Current Layer option was chosen, you will paint on the layer that was preserved in the snapshot.

Note: The Fill > Use: History command can't be used on an image if you've changed its pixel count since it was opened (e.g., by resampling or cropping or by changing its image mode or canvas size). Furthermore, you can't restore vector data layers (type or shapes) using the History Brush tool, or restore a vector mask on an image layer that has been modified.

To fill a selection or a layer with a history state:

1. Choose a layer that contains pixels **1**.

2. *Optional:* Create a selection.

3. On the History palette, click in the left-most column for the state you want to use as a fill (a History Brush icon will appear where you click).

4. Choose Edit > Fill (Shift-Backspace/Shift-Delete).

5. Choose Use: History **2**.

6. Choose a Blending Mode and an Opacity percentage.

7. *Optional:* Check Preserve Transparency to replace only existing pixels.

8. Click OK **3**.

Using the Art History Brush tool, you can paint a designated history state or snapshot back onto an image in an assortment of different-shaped brushstrokes (actually, in our humble opinion, all the different brush choices—Tight Long, Loose Curl, etc.—look like worms). Adjacent colors are blended to produce a painterly effect, and those colors will vary depending on the current Tolerance setting for the Art History Brush tool. By all means use a stylus if you have one.

To use the Art History Brush tool:

1. Perform some edits on a layer, if you haven't already done so, to create states on the History palette 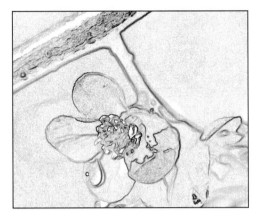 .

> **TIP** If you're working on the Background, before using the Art History Brush tool, fill the layer with white or a solid color to create a clean background to apply the Art History strokes to.

2. On the History palette, click in the leftmost column at the state or snapshot that you want the brushstrokes to take their pixel data from. The source icon for the Art History Brush tool will appear there.

3. Choose the Art History Brush tool (Y or Shift-Y).

4. From the Art History Brush tool options bar **2**:

Click the Brush picker arrowhead, then click a **brush** on the picker.
and
Choose a blending **Mode** and an **Opacity** percentage.
and
Choose a painting **Style** from the pop-up menu.
and

1 *A continuous-tone image, after applying Photoshop's* **Find Edges** *filter*

	Brush: 21	Mode: Normal	Opacity: 100%	Style: Tight Short	Area: 100 px	Tolerance: 0%

2 *The* **Art History Brush** *tool options bar*

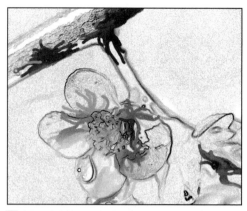

1 *After clicking in the leftmost column on the History palette at a prior state (the original photo), and then adding brushstrokes here and there using the **Art History Brush** tool (Darken mode, Loose Long, Tolerance 0%)*

Choose an **Area** (0–500 pixels) for the size of the overall area the strokes can cover. The wider the area, the greater the number of strokes will be applied.
and

Choose a **Tolerance** value (0–100%) to control, based on color, where strokes can be applied. Choose a low Tolerance to have strokes appear anywhere in the image; choose a high Tolerance to allow strokes to appear only over pixels that differ markedly from the source color. To be honest, in our testing, the Tolerance setting didn't seem to make much of a difference.

5. Choose a layer, and then draw strokes in the image window **1**. The longer you keep the mouse button down in the same spot, the more colors will blend in that area.

Feel free to switch stroke shapes or adjust other parameters on the Art History Brush tool options bar between strokes, or choose different source states on the History palette. You'll achieve a less machine-made look by doing so, in fact. Another way to achieve a more personalized look with this tool is by using custom brush shapes (see pages 222 and 223).

TIP For the brush preset you've chosen to use with the Art History Brush tool, you can create your own variations using the Shape Dynamics, Scattering, Texture, Color Dynamics, or Other Dynamics pane(s) on the Brushes palette.

Art History Brush

You can use the Eraser tool with its Erase to History option to restore pixels from the currently active state on the History palette. An advantage of using the Eraser is that in addition to choosing a mode, opacity, and flow percentage for the tool, you can also choose a tool type (Brush, Pencil, or Block).

Note: The Erase to History feature can't be used on an image if you've changed its pixel count since it was opened (e.g., by resampling or cropping, or by changing its image mode or canvas size).

To erase to history:

1. Choose the Eraser tool (E or Shift-E). 

2. Select an image layer—not a shape layer **1**.

3. On the Eraser tool options bar:

Click the brush picker arrowhead, then click a brush on the picker (or from the Brushes palette).
and
Choose a Mode (Brush, Pencil, or Block).
and
Choose an Opacity percentage.
and
Choose a Flow percentage. **7.0!**
and
Check Erase to History.

7.0! **4.** *Optional:* Click the Airbrush button.

5. Establish the History source by clicking the box next to a state or a snapshot at the far left side of the History palette.

6. Choose a layer on the Layers palette.

7. Draw erasure strokes in the image window **2**.

1 *A **snapshot** is made of the original image, and then the Rough Pastels filter is applied.*

2 *Next, the **Eraser** tool is used with its **Erase to History** option to restore the angel's face, belly, and toes from the snapshot.*

ADJUSTMENTS 9

1 *The Image > Adjustments submenu*

THIS CHAPTER covers many methods for adjusting an image's light and dark values. Using commands on the Image > Adjustments submenu **1**, you can make simple adjustments, like Invert a layer to make it look like a film negative, or Posterize it to restrict its luminosity levels to a specified number. Or you can make more precise lightness or contrast adjustments to a layer's highlights, midtones, or shadows using such features as Levels or Curves. You can also darken smaller areas by hand using the Burn tool, or lighten areas using the Dodge tool.

Adjustment basics

Here are a few pointers for applying the adjustment commands:

- For flexibility in editing, use **adjustment layers** (instructions begin on the following page).

- To apply any adjustment command to a selected area of a layer rather than to an entire layer, create a **selection** before you choose the command.

- To **reset** the settings in a dialog box, hold down Alt/Option and click Reset.

- Check **Preview** in an adjustment dialog box to see how the adjustment will affect the image. CMYK color displays more acccurately with Preview on.

- To progressively reduce an adjustment command's effect in increments, use Edit > **Fade** (Ctrl-Shift-F/Cmd-Shift-F).

- To reopen a dialog box with its **last-used** settings rather than the default settings, hold down Alt/Option while choosing the command, or include Alt/Option if you use a shortcut to invoke the command.

Adjustments Basics

(sidebar tab)

165

Adjustment layers

There are two ways to apply adjustment commands: They can be applied directly to the current layer (or to a selection on the current layer), or they can be applied via an adjustment layer. We prefer the latter method because it offers the most flexibility.

Unlike a normal layer, an adjustment layer affects all the visible layers below it—not just the current layer. But the beauty of an adjustment layer is that it doesn't actually change pixels until it's merged with the layer below it (Ctrl-E/Cmd-E), so you can use it to try out various effects. We think of adjustment layers as a handy way to preview color and tonal adjustments.

On this page and the following three pages we explain how to create and use adjustment layers. If you prefer, you can skip ahead and read about the individual adjustment commands first (starting on page 170), and then return to these pages.

To create an adjustment layer:

1. Choose the layer above which you want the adjustment layer to appear.

2. Choose an adjustment command from the "Create new fill or adjustment layer" pop-up menu ◷. at the bottom of the Layers palette **1–2**.
or
Choose a command from the Layer > New Adjustment Layer submenu, then click OK.

3. Make the desired adjustments, then click OK.

To modify an adjustment layer:

1. On the Layers palette, double-click the adjustment layer thumbnail (the thumbnail on the left).
or
The slow way: Click the adjustment layer name, then choose Layer > Layer Content Options.

2. Make the desired changes in the adjustment dialog box, then click OK.

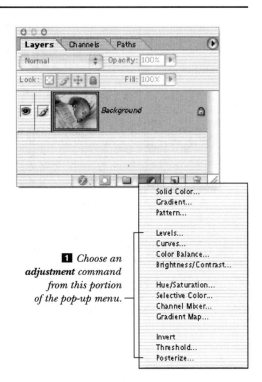

1 *Choose an* ***adjustment*** *command from this portion of the pop-up menu.*

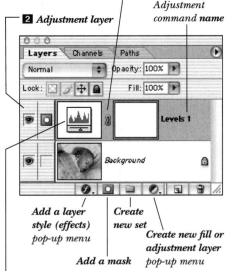

Link layer mask to layer button

2 *Adjustment layer*

Adjustment command ***name***

Add a layer style (effects) pop-up menu

Create new set

Add a mask

Create new fill or adjustment layer pop-up menu

The top part of the ***adjustment command*** ***thumbnail*** *is the icon for that command (each command has a different symbol). The slider signifies that the adjustment command is editable or changeable.*

File to file

To copy an adjustment layer from one image to another, **drag-and-drop** it from the source image's Layers palette into the destination image window.

1 *Choose **Blending Options** for an adjustment layer in the **Layer Style** dialog box.*

You can control how an adjustment layer blends with underlying layers. This is accomplished via the Layer Style dialog box.

To choose blending options for an adjustment layer (or any layer):

1. On the Layers palette, double-click the blank area to the right of an adjustment layer (or ordinary layer) name.

2. Make sure Blending Options is chosen on the left side of the Layer Style dialog box.

3. Change the **General Blending: Blend Mode** and/or **Opacity** settings **1**.

4. Change any of these **Advanced Blending** options:

Uncheck any **Channels** you want to exclude from blending with the underlying layer. To set the blend range for each channel one at a time, choose a channel from the Blend If pop-up menu; or to work on all the channels simultaneously, leave Gray as the choice on that pop-up menu. The current image mode (e.g., RGB Color, CMYK Color) determines which Channels are available.

Move the leftmost Blend If: **This Layer** slider to the right to remove shadow areas from the active layer. Move the rightmost This Layer slider to the left to remove highlights from the active layer.

Move the leftmost **Underlying Layer** slider to the right to restore shadow areas from the layer directly below the active layer. Move the rightmost Underlying Layer slider to the left to restore highlights from the layer directly below the active layer.

(To read about Knockout and the two "Blend..." checkboxes, see pages 260–264.)

5. Click OK.

Blending Options for Adjustment Layer

You can keep an adjustment layer right where it is, but change the adjustment command that it contains (e.g., Levels, Curves, Brightness/Contrast).

To choose a different command for an existing adjustment layer:

1. Choose an adjustment layer on the Layers palette.

2. Choose the command you want to switch to from the Layer > Change Layer Content submenu.

3. Make the desired adjustments, then click OK.

TIP To discard an adjustment layer, drag it to the "Delete layer" (trash) button.

When you merge down an adjustment layer, the adjustments become permanent for the image layer below it, so be certain you want the effect to become permanent before you perform another operation. If you change your mind, choose Edit > Undo or click the prior state on the History palette.

To merge an adjustment layer:

1. Choose the adjustment layer you want to merge downward **1**.

2. Choose Merge Down from the Layers palette menu (Ctrl-E/Cmd-E) **2**.

Note: An adjustment layer can't be merged with another adjustment layer; because they don't contain pixels, there's nothing to merge. You can, however, merge multiple adjustment layers into an image layer (or layers) by using either the Merge Visible or the Flatten Image command (see pages 152–154).

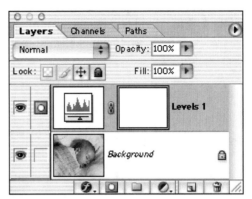

1 *An **adjustment layer** is chosen.*

2 *After applying the **Merge Down** command, the Levels values from the adjustment layer are permanently applied to the layer below it (in this case, the Background).*

Change Layer Content; Merge Adjustment Layer

1 *Choose a **blending mode** for an adjustment layer.*

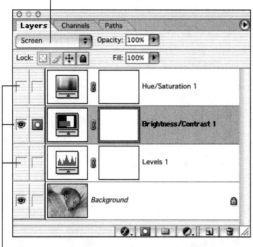

2 *Show/hide adjustment layers to compare their effects.*

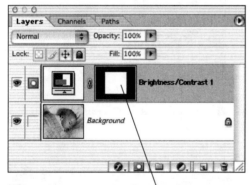

3 *A **rectangular selection** was created before the adjustment layer command was chosen.*

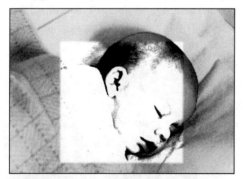

4 *The **Brightness/Contrast** adjustment affected only the **rectangular selection** area.*

Ways to use adjustment layers

Change an adjustment layer's **blending mode** via the pop-up menu on the Layers palette to produce a variety of visual effects in relationship to its underlying layers **1**. For example, try Overlay mode to heighten contrast, Multiply mode to darken the image, or Screen mode to lighten the image. You can stack several adjustment layers, then hide, or lower the opacity of, each layer to see how the underlying image is altered **2**.

To **compare** different settings for the same adjustment command, create multiples of the same adjustment layer (e.g., Levels), hide all the adjustment layers, and then show/hide them one at a time. You can also restack adjustment layers among themselves or place them at different locations within the overall layer stack.

To **prevent** an underlying layer from being affected by an adjustment layer, restack it so it's above the adjustment layer.

To limit the area an adjustment layer affects, create a **selection** before you create it. The selection area is shown in white on the layer mask thumbnail **3**–**4**.

You can also **paint** or **fill** with black on the adjustment layer to remove the adjustment effect or white to reveal the adjustment effect. The strokes will display on the layer mask thumbnail. To read more about adjustment layer masks, see page 177.

Normally, an adjustment layer will affect all the currently visible layers below it, but you can use a **clipping group** to limit an adjustment layer's effect to only the layer or layers it's grouped with (see page 271). If you choose a command from the Layer > New Adjustment Layer submenu, you'll have the option to check Group With Previous Layer in the New Layer dialog box.

Using Adjustment Layers

Adjustment commands

Next we'll show you how to use the individual commands on the Image > Adjustments submenu. They can be applied to a layer directly or via an adjustment layer. Try applying the adjustment commands to a grayscale image first to learn how they work, then use them on color images.

We'll begin with the simple, one-step Auto Contrast command, which turns the almost-lightest pixels in an image white and the almost-darkest pixels black, and then redistributes the gray levels in-between.

To adjust an image using Auto Contrast:

Choose Image > Adjustments > Auto Contrast (Ctrl-Alt-Shift-L/Cmd-Option-Shift-L) **1**–**2**.

TIP To learn about the Auto Color Correction options, see page 203.

The Equalize command redistributes the active layer's brightness values. It may improve an image that lacks contrast or is too dark. But then again, it may not!

To equalize a layer:

Choose Image > Adjustments > Equalize.
or
To limit the adjustment to an area of a layer, select that area, choose Image > Adjustments > Equalize, then click "Equalize selected area only." Or to equalize the entire layer based on the values within the selected area, click "Equalize entire image based on selected area." **3**–**5**

1 *The original image*

2 *After applying **Auto Contrast***

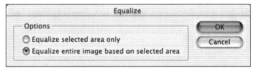
3 *You can **Equalize** a selected area or the entire layer.*

4 *The original image*

5 *After applying the **Equalize** command*

PHOTO: PAUL PETROFF

PHOTO: NADINE MARKOVA

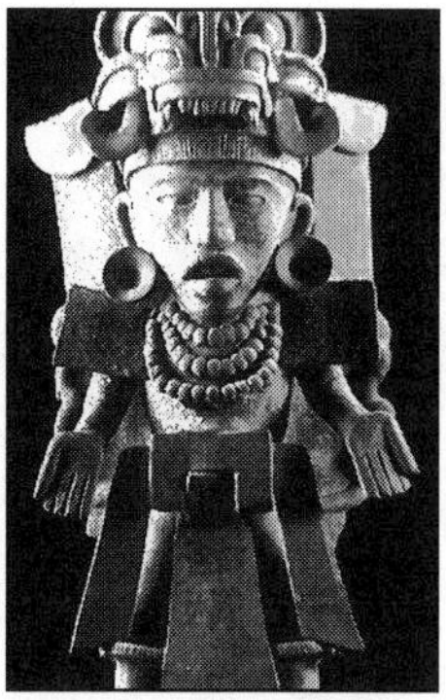

1 *The original image*

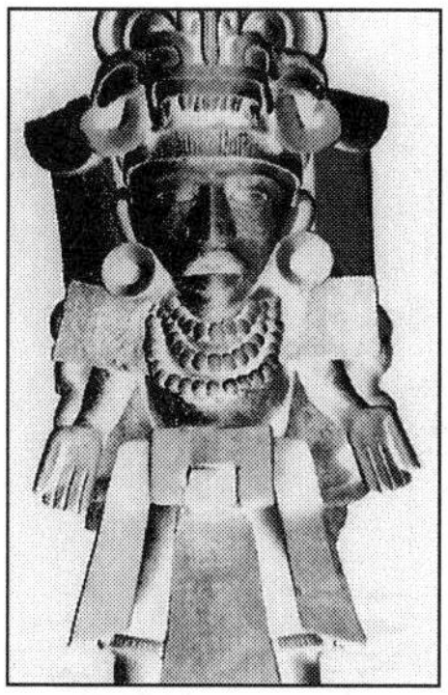

2 *The image **inverted***

PHOTO: PAUL PETROFF

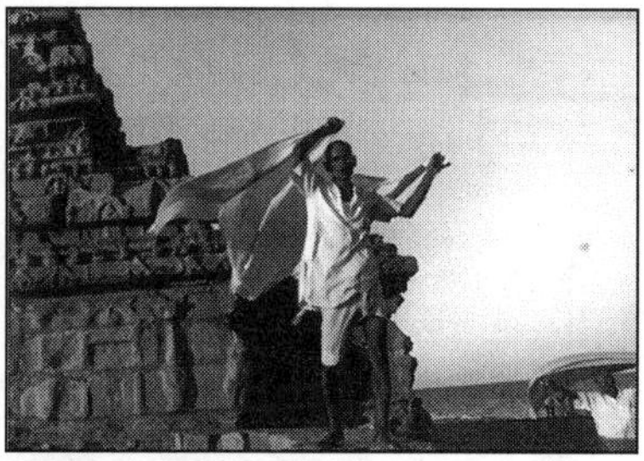

3 *The original image*

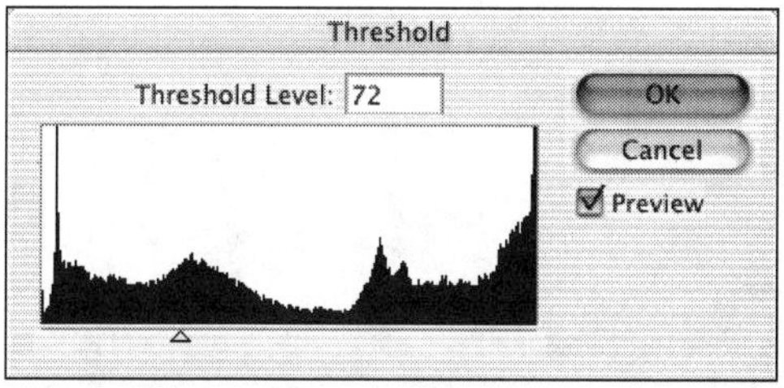

4 *Move the **Threshold** slider to control the cutoff point for black/white values.*

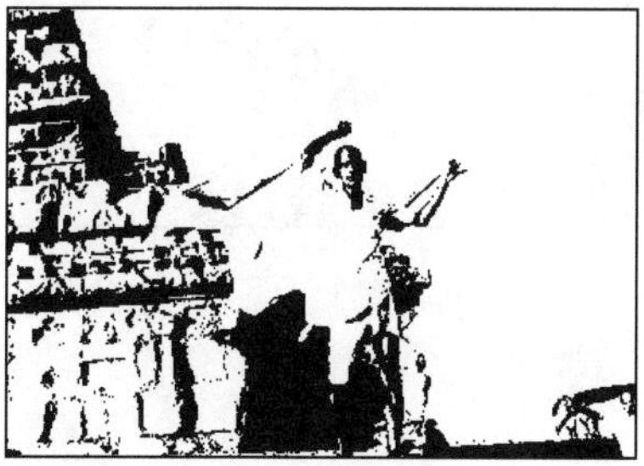

5 *After applying the **Threshold** command*

Choose the Invert command to make a layer or the Background look like a film negative. Each pixel is replaced with its opposite brightness and/or color value. You can also use this command to make a negative look like a positive, though this may not be the most exacting way to do it, at least from a photographer's point of view.

To invert lights and darks:

Choose a layer, then choose Image > Adjustments > Invert (Ctrl-I/Cmd-I) **1**–**2**. You can use the same shortcut again to undo the Invert command.

or

To use an adjustment layer to invert the layers below it, choose Invert from the "Create new fill or adjustment layer" pop-up menu at the bottom of the Layers palette.

The Threshold dialog box makes the current layer or the Background high-contrast by converting color or gray pixels into pure black and white pixels.

To make a layer high contrast:

1. Choose a layer or the Background **3**, then choose Image > Adjustments > Threshold.

   or

   To use an adjustment layer, choose Threshold from the "Create new fill or adjustment layer" pop-up menu at the bottom of the Layers palette.

2. Move the slider to the right to increase the number of black pixels **4**.

   or

   Move the slider to the left to increase the number of white pixels.

   or

   Enter a value (1–255) in the Threshold Level field. Pixels lighter than the value you enter will become white, pixels darker than the value you enter will become black.

3. Click OK **5**.

Use the Posterize command to reduce the number of color or value levels in the current layer or the Background to a specified number. We love the arty effects that this simple command can produce.

To posterize:

1. Choose a layer 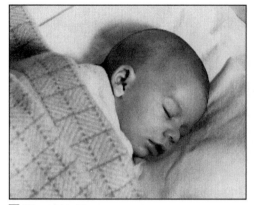, then choose Image > Adjustments > Posterize.

or

To use an adjustment layer, choose Posterize from the "Create new fill or adjustment layer" pop-up menu 🖌, at the bottom of the Layers palette.

2. Make sure Preview is checked, then enter the desired number of Levels (2–255) **2**. To make the image look like a poster or silkscreen, try a Levels value between 4 and 8.

3. Click OK **3**.

TIP If the number of shades in an image is reduced using the Posterize command (or any other tonal adjustments are made, for that matter), without using an adjustment layer, and then the image is saved and closed, the original shade information will be permanently lost.

TIP Create a gradient using two or more colors, then create a Posterize adjustment layer above the gradient layer—the gradient will have obvious color bands.

1 *The original image*

2 *Enter the desired number of color or value* **Levels** *in the* **Posterize** *dialog box.*

3 *Posterized*

1 *The original image*

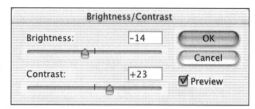

2 *Move the **Brightness** and/or **Contrast** sliders in the **Brightness/Contrast** dialog box.*

3 *The **Brightness** slider moved to the right*

4 *The **Brightness** and **contrast** adjusted*

The Brightness/Contrast command, discussed below, is easy to use, but is also limited in scope. If you want to adjust the shadows, midtones, and highlights in an image separately and with more precision, use the Levels dialog box, which is discussed on the following page.

To adjust brightness and contrast (Brightness/Contrast):

1. Choose a layer **1**, then choose Image > Adjustments > Brightness/Contrast.
or
To use an adjustment layer, choose Brightness/Contrast from the "Create new fill or adjustment layer" pop-up menu **◑.** at the bottom of the Layers palette.

2. To lighten the layer, move the brightness slider to the right **2**.
or
To darken the layer, move the Brightness slider to the left.
or
Enter a Brightness value (−100 to 100).

3. To intensify the contrast, move the Contrast slider to the right.
or
To lessen the contrast, move the Contrast slider to the left.
or
Enter a Contrast value (−100 to 100).

4. Click OK **3**–**4**.

Use the Levels dialog box to make fine adjustments to a layer's highlights, midtones, or shadows. We use this dialog box, day in and day out, for most of our adjustments.

To adjust brightness and contrast using Levels:

1. Choose a layer **1**, then choose Image > Adjustments > Levels (Ctrl-L/Cmd-L).
or
To use an adjustment layer, choose Levels from the "Create new fill or adjustment layer" pop-up menu ⚫, at the bottom of the Layers palette.

2. Do any of the following **2**:

To brighten the highlights and intensify the contrast, move the **Input highlights** slider to the left. The midtones (middle) slider will move along with it. Readjust the midtones slider, if necessary.

To darken the shadows, move the **Input shadows** slider to the right. The midtones slider will move along with it. Readjust the midtones slider, if necessary.

To adjust the midtones independently, move the **Input midtones** slider.

To decrease contrast and lighten the image, move the **Output shadows** slider to the right.

To decrease contrast and darken the image, move the **Output highlights** slider to the left.

Note: You can enter values in the Input Levels or Output Levels fields instead of moving the sliders. To save the current settings, click Save. Use Load to reapply the saved settings to other images.

3. Click OK **2**–**4**.

TIP To adjust levels automatically, choose Image > Adjustments > **Auto Levels** (Ctrl-Shift-L/Cmd-Shift-L) or click Auto in the Levels dialog box. For the Auto Color Correction options, see page 203.

TIP To intensify contrast in the image, move the Input shadows and highlights sliders closer together.

1 *The original image*

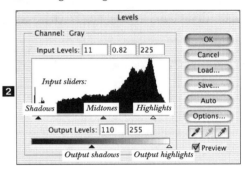

3 *After* **Levels** *adjustments*

PHOTO: PAUL PETROFF

4 *To produce this image, an area of the image was* **selected** *before the Levels adjustment layer was made.*

1 *The original image*

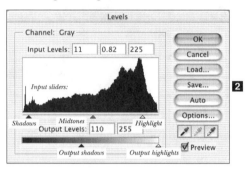

2

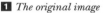

3 *The music layer screened back*

4 *The Output slider positions reversed*

This is just another way to use the Levels command.

To screen back a layer:

1. Choose a layer or the Background **1**, then choose Image > Adjustments > Levels (Ctrl-L/Cmd-L).
or
To use an adjustment layer, choose Levels from the "Create new fill or adjustment layer" pop-up menu ![icon] at the bottom of the Layers palette.

2. To reduce contrast, move the Input highlights slider slightly to the left **2**.
and
Move the Output shadows slider to the right.

3. To lighten the midtones, move the Input midtones slider to the left.

4. Click OK **3**, **5**–**6**.

TIP To make a layer look like a film negative, reverse the position of the two Output sliders **4**. The farther apart you move the sliders, the more brightness and contrast attributes will be reversed. Or try the Invert command for a similar effect.

PHOTO: PAUL PETROFF

5 *The original image*

6 *The screened-back version*

Screen Back a Layer

To lighten pixels by hand in small areas, use the Dodge tool; to darken pixels, use the Burn tool. You can choose separate brushes and options bar settings for each tool.

1 *Choose settings for the **Dodge** or **Burn** tool from the options bar.*

To lighten using the Dodge tool or darken using the Burn tool:

1. Choose a layer. *Note:* The Dodge and Burn tools can't be used on a image in Bitmap or Indexed Color mode.

2. Choose the Dodge 🔍 or Burn 🖐 tool (O or Shift-O).

3. On the tool's options bar **1**:

   7.0! Click the brush picker arrowhead, then click a hard-edged or soft-edged **brush**. A large, soft brush will produce the smoothest result. You can also choose a brush from the Brushes palette.
   and
   Choose Shadows, Midtones, or Highlights from the **Range** pop-up menu to Dodge or Burn only pixels in that value range.
   and
   Choose an **Exposure** setting between 1% (low intensity) and 100% (high intensity). Try a low exposure first (20%–30%) so the tool won't bleach or darken areas too quickly.
   and
   7.0! Click the **Airbrush** button, 🖌 if desired.

4. Stroke on any area of the layer. Pause between strokes, if necessary, to allow the screen to redraw **2**–**3**. To dodge or burn in a straight line, click on the image, move the pointer, then Shift-click on the image again.

TIP If you Dodge or Burn an area too much, choose Edit > Undo or use the History palette to remove those states. Don't use the opposite tool to fix it—it will end up looking blotchy.

TIP To create a smooth, even highlight or shadow line, dodge or burn a path using the Stroke Path command with the Dodge or Burn tool chosen (see page 295).

2 *The **Dodge** tool with **Shadows** chosen from the options bar was used to eliminate dark spots in the background of this image.*

3 *After **dodging***

Layer mask shortcuts

View the mask in image window	Alt-click/Option-click adjustment layer mask thumbnail
View the mask in a **rubylith** color (red)	Alt-Shift-click/Option-Shift-click adjustment layer mask thumbnail
Temporarily turn **off** the mask for an adjustment layer	Shift-click adjustment layer mask thumbnail
Convert non-masked area into a **selection**	Ctrl-click/Cmd-click adjustment layer mask thumbnail

1 *We painted with black on the left side of the* **Threshold** *adjustment layer. The Threshold effect is visible only in the areas we didn't paint on.*

2 *In this image, the adjustment layer's* **opacity** *was lowered to 60%, which causes the Threshold effect to blend with the overall underlying image.*

There are two ways to restrict an adjustment layer effect to a portion of an image. One way is to create a selection before you create the adjustment layer. Another way is to create a selection or paint with black on the adjustment layer after it's created, which we discuss below. More about layer masks on pages 266–270.

To restrict an adjustment layer's effect using a mask:

1. Choose an adjustment layer, and choose black as the Foreground color. The Color palette will reset automatically to the Grayscale model.

2. To mask the adjustment layer effect:

Create a selection using any selection tool (e.g., Rectangular Marquee, Lasso, or Magic Wand), choose Edit > Fill (Shift-Backspace/Shift-Delete), choose Use: Foreground Color, then click OK. *or*
Choose the Brush tool (B), choose Mode: Normal and Opacity 100% from the options bar, then paint on the image **1**. Or to partially mask the adjustment layer effect, choose a lower Opacity for the Brush tool.

3. *More options:*

To restore the adjustment layer effect, paint or fill with white.

To reveal just a small area of the adjustment effect, fill the entire layer with black and then paint with white over specific areas.

To make the adjustment effect visible on the entire image, fill the whole adjustment layer with white.

TIP To diminish the adjustment layer's effect over the entire layer by a percentage, lower the opacity of the adjustment layer via the Opacity slider on the Layers palette **2**.

TIP By default, an adjustment layer contains a pixel-based layer mask. To create a vector mask for an adjustment layer, see page 298.

To make a layer grayscale using the Channel Mixer:

1. Choose a layer or the Background, then choose Image > Adjustments > Channel Mixer.

or

To use an adjustment layer, choose Channel Mixer from the "Create new fill or adjustment layer" pop-up menu ⬤, at the bottom of the Layers palette.

2. Check Monochrome **1**. The layer or image will become grayscale and Gray will be the only choice on the Output Channel pop-up menu.

3. Move any Source Channels slider to modify how much that color channel is used as a source for the luminosity levels in the grayscale image. Drag a slider to the left to decrease the amount of that color in the output channel, or to the right to increase the amount of that color.

4. Move the Constant slider to the left to add black or to the right to add white.

5. Click OK. Despite the layer's appearance, the image is still in its original color mode. If you like, you can now convert it to Grayscale mode.

TIP If you applied the Channel Mixer to a layer, you can choose a different layer opacity or blending mode for the layer.

TIP To add a color tint to a layer, check Monochrome in the Channel Mixer dialog box, then uncheck it to restore the color Output Channels. Choose an Output Channel and move the Source Channel sliders to produce a different color tint. Repeat for any other Output Channel(s).

Try one of theirs

To use a **preset Channel Mixer** effect (e.g., RGB Rotate Channels or CMYK Swap Cyan & Magenta), first make sure the Channel Mixer Presets folder has been copied from the Goodies folder on the Adobe Photoshop 7 CD-ROM into the Adobe Photoshop 7 > Presets folder.

To load an effect, click Load in the Channel Mixer dialog box, open the Presets > Channel Mixer Presets folder inside the application folder, open any one of the four folders there, then double-click a mixer. In Windows, the abbreviated names represent Channel Swap, Grayscale, Special Effects, and YCC Color.

1 *Check* **Monochrome** *in the* **Channel Mixer** *dialog box to make the layer grayscale.*

CHOOSE COLORS 10

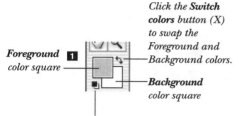

*Click the **Switch colors** button (X) to swap the Foreground and Background colors.*

Foreground 1
color square

Background
color square

*Click the **Default colors** button (D) to make the Foreground color **black** and the Background color **white**.*

The currently active square has a double frame. This is the **Foreground** *color square.*

2 **Background**
color square

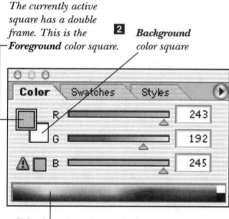

Color bar

N THIS CHAPTER, you will learn how to choose colors. In the next chapter, you will learn how to apply colors using various painting and editing tools, as well as some commands.

Foreground and Background colors

When you use a painting tool, create type, or use the Stroke command, the current **Foreground** color is applied.

When you use the Eraser tool, increase an image's canvas size, or move a selection on the Background using the Move tool, the hole that's left behind is automatically filled with the current **Background** color. The Gradient tool can produce blends using the Foreground and/or Background colors.

The Foreground and Background colors are displayed in the Foreground and Background color squares on the Toolbox 1 and on the Color palette 2. (When written with an uppercase "F" or "B," these terms refer to those colors, not the foreground or background areas of a picture.)

The many ways to choose a Foreground or Background color are described on the following pages. In brief, you can:

- Enter values in fields or click the large color square in the **Color Picker**.
- Choose a premixed color from a matching system using the **Custom Colors** dialog box.
- Enter values in fields or move sliders on the **Color** palette.
- Click a swatch on the **Swatches** palette.
- Pluck a color from an image using the **Eyedropper** tool.

To choose a color using the Color Picker:

1. Click the Foreground or Background color square on the Toolbox.
or
Click the Foreground or Background color square on the Color palette, if it's already active (has a double frame).
or
Double-click the Foreground or Background color square on the Color palette, if it's not active.

Note: If the color square you click on is a Custom color, the Custom Colors dialog box will open. Click Picker to open the Color Picker dialog box.

2. *Optional:* In the Photoshop Color Picker, check Only Web Colors to make only Web-safe colors available.

3. Click a color on the vertical color slider to choose a hue **1**, then click a variation of that hue in the large square **2**.
or
To choose a specific process color for print output, enter percentages from a matching guide in the C, M, Y, and K fields.
or
For on-screen output, enter a value (0–255) for the R, G, and B components. When all these components are set to 0, black is produced; when all three are set to 255, white is produced. You can also enter numbers in the HSB or Lab fields.

4. Click OK.

TIP To make the Photoshop Color Picker available, choose Edit (Photoshop, in OS X) > Preferences > General (Ctrl-K/Cmd-K), then choose Color Picker: Adobe. You can choose the Windows/Apple color picker from the same pop-up menu. Only one color picker is accessible at a time.

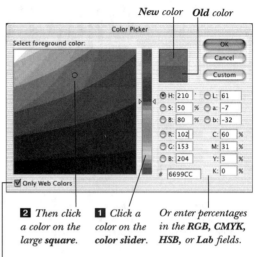

New color   Old color

2 *Then click a color on the large* **square**.   **1** *Click a color on the* **color slider**.   *Or enter percentages in the* **RGB**, **CMYK**, **HSB**, *or* **Lab** *fields.*

Check **Only Web Colors** *in the* **Color Picker** *to make only Web-safe colors available.*

An **exclamation point** in the Color Picker or on the Color palette indicates there is no ink combination for the color you chose—meaning it's outside the **printable gamut**. If you're planning to print your image, choose an in-gamut color or click the exclamation point to have Photoshop substitute the closest printable color (shown in the swatch next to or below the exclamation point). If you convert your image to CMYK Color mode, the entire image will be brought into printable gamut. The out-of-gamut range is defined by the CMYK output profile currently chosen in Edit (Photoshop, in OS X) > Color Settings.

A **cube** in the Color Picker indicates that the chosen color isn't **Web-safe**. Click the swatch under the cube to have Photoshop choose the closest Web-safe color to yours.

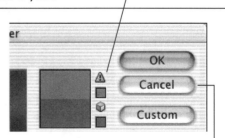

Click **Custom** *to choose a predefined color.*

Color Picker

Color separate from elsewhere

To color separate a Photoshop image that contains spot color channels using QuarkXPress, InDesign 1.x, Illustrator, or FreeHand, first convert the file to CMYK Color mode and save it in the Photoshop DCS 2.0 format (see page 423).

1 *Choose a matching system from the* **Book** *pop-up menu, then type a* **number***.*

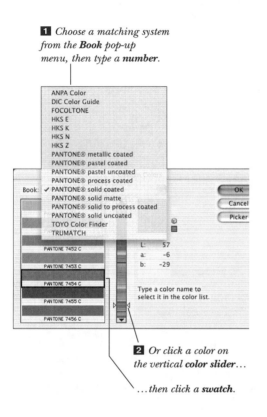

2 *Or click a color on the vertical* **color slider** *…*

…then click a **swatch***.*

Normally, Photoshop separates all colors in an image into the four process colors, regardless of whether they are process or spot colors. In order to separate a spot color to a separate plate from Photoshop, you must create a spot color channel for it (see page 207).

Note: Don't rely on your monitor to represent matching system colors accurately—you must choose them from a printed PANTONE, TRUMATCH, TOYO, DIC, FOCOLTONE, or ANPA Color swatch book. But before you do so, find out which brand of ink your printer is planning to use.

For online output, you can choose Hexadecimal colors (HKS E, HKS K, HKS N, or HKS Z).

To choose a custom color:

1. Click the Foreground or Background color square on the Toolbox.
or
Click the Foreground or Background color square on the Color palette, if it's already active.
or
Double-click the Foreground or Background color square on the Color palette, if it's not active.

Note: If the color square you click on isn't a Custom color, the Color Picker dialog box will open. Click Custom to open the Custom Colors dialog box.

2. Choose a matching guide system from the Book pop-up menu **1**. You'll notice some new PANTONE choices.

3. Type a number—that swatch will become selected.
or
Click a color on the vertical color slider, then click a swatch on the left side of the dialog box **2**.

4. *Optional:* Click Picker to return to the Color Picker.

5. Click OK.

TIP To load a matching system palette onto the Swatches palette, see page 184.

Custom Colors

To choose a color using the Color palette:

1. Click the Foreground or Background color square, if it isn't already active **1**.

2. Choose a color model for the sliders from the Color palette menu **2**.

3. Move any of the sliders **3**.
or
Click or drag on the color bar.
or
Enter values in the fields.

TIP In the RGB model, white (the presence of all colors) is produced when all the sliders are in their rightmost positions, black (the absence of all colors) is produced when all the sliders are in their leftmost positions, and gray is produced when all the sliders are vertically aligned in any other position.

TIP Right-click/Control-click the color bar to choose a different spectrum style for the color bar from a context menu.

Color palette tips

■ Alt-click/Option-click the color bar to choose a color for the **non-selected** color square.

■ Colors inside the slider bars will update as you drag a slider. To turn this feature off, uncheck **Dynamic Color Sliders** in Edit (Photoshop, in OS X) > Preferences > General.

1 *Click the **Foreground** or **Background** color square. The currently active square has a white border.*

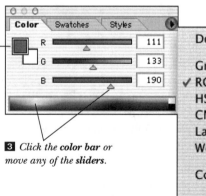

3 *Click the **color bar** or move any of the **sliders**.*

*Choose **Make Ramp Web Safe** to make the color bar contain only Web-safe colors. Choose this option again to restore the normal color spectrum.*

Dock to Palette Well
Grayscale Slider
✓ RGB Sliders
HSB Sliders
CMYK Sliders
Lab Sliders
Web Color Sliders
Copy Color as HTML
RGB Spectrum
✓ CMYK Spectrum
Grayscale Ramp
Current Colors
Make Ramp Web Safe

2 *Choose a **model** for the sliders. Choose **Web Color Sliders** to have the RGB sliders mix only Web-safe colors.*

*Choose **Copy Color as HTML** to copy the currently selected color on the palette as HTML code to the Clipboard. Paste the code into an HTML editor.*

*Choose a **spectrum** or **ramp** for the color bar.*

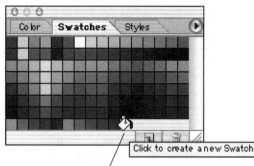

1 *Click in the* **white** *(blank) area below the swatches to* **add** *a color to the palette.*

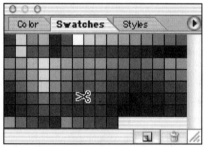

2 *Alt-click/Option-click a swatch to* **delete** *it.*

Swatches palette

You may want to detach the Swatches palette from the Color palette group for these instructions.

To choose a color from the Swatches palette:

To choose a color for the currently active color square, click a color swatch.

or

To choose a color for the square that isn't currently active, Ctrl-click/Cmd-click a color swatch. **7.0!**

TIP To display a different set of swatches on the palette, see the following page. To restore the default Swatches palette, choose Reset Swatches from the Swatches palette menu, then click OK.

To add a color to the Swatches palette:

1. Mix a color using the Color palette.

2. Click the Swatches tab to display the Swatches palette, if it isn't on its own.

3. Position the cursor in the blank area below the swatches on the palette, and click (paint bucket pointer) **1**.
   or
   Right-click/Ctrl-click a swatch and choose New Swatch.

4. Enter a Name, then click OK. The new color will appear where you clicked.

To rename a swatch:

Double-click an existing swatch, type a name, then click OK. To see the swatch name, display the palette in Small List mode or use tool tips.

To delete a color from the Swatches palette:

Alt-click/Option-click the swatch to be deleted (scissors cursor) **2**. This can't be undone. **7.0!**

Note: If you edit the Swatches palette, exit/ quit Photoshop, and then re-launch, your edited palette will reopen.

Choose, Add, Rename, Delete Swatches

To save an edited swatches library:

1. Choose Save Swatches from the Swatches palette menu.

2. Enter a Name for the edited library **1**.

3. Choose a location in which to save the library, then click Save (see the sidebar).

You can load any of the 24 preset color swatch libraries that are supplied with Photoshop, or any preset palette that you've created, onto the Swatches palette. You can either replace the existing preset library with the new one or append the additional library to the existing one.

To replace or append a swatches library:

1. Choose a library name from the bottom of the palette menu. You'll notice some new library names on the list.

2. Click Append to add the new library swatches to the current palette.
or
Click OK to replace the current palette with the new library swatches.

TIP To enlarge the palette to display the loaded swatches, drag the palette resize box or click the palette zoom box.

Follow the instructions below to open any swatches library that isn't in the default location (see the sidebar).

To load a swatches library:

1. Choose Load Swatches from the Swatches palette menu.

2. Locate and highlight the swatches library you want to open.

3. Click Load. The loaded swatches will appear below the existing swatches on the Swatches palette.

Finding the defaults

■ In Windows, the swatches libraries are stored in Program Files > Adobe > Photoshop 7.0 > Presets > Color Swatches.

■ In the Mac OS, the swatches libraries are stored in Applications > Adobe Photoshop 7 > Presets > Color Swatches, or in the Adobe Photoshop Only folder in the Color Swatches folder.

■ To restore the default palette, choose **Reset Swatches** from the Swatches palette menu.

1 *Enter a **Name** and open the **Color Swatches** folder.*

1 *Sampling a color from an image using the **Eyedropper** tool*

Sample Size : • Point Sample / 3 by 3 Average / 5 by 5 Average

2 *Choose a **Sample Size** for the **Eyedropper** tool from the options bar.*

To choose a color from an image using the Eyedropper:

1. On the Color palette, click the Foreground or Background color square if it's *not* already active.

2. Choose the Eyedropper tool (I or Shift-I).

3. Click on a color in any open image window **1**.
  or
  Move the tool over the image with the mouse button up to preview various colors (watch the color square change on the Toolbox or the Color palette, or note the color percentages on the Info palette), then click when the pointer is over the desired color.

TIP To change the area within which the Eyedropper tool samples, choose Point Sample (the exact pixel that's clicked on), or 3 by 3 or 5 by 5 Average (an average within a 3-by-3-pixel or 5-by-5-pixel square) from the Eyedropper options bar **2**. If you right-click/Control-click on the image with the Eyedropper, you can choose any of those settings from a context menu. (For the Copy Color as HTML option, see the next page.)

TIP Alt-click/Option-click or drag in the image window with the Eyedropper tool to choose a Background color when the Foreground color square is active, or to choose a Foreground color when the Background color square is active.

Eyedropper

Colors can be copied as hexadecimal values from a file in Photoshop or ImageReady and then pasted into an HTML file. There are two methods for doing this.

To copy a color as a hexadecimal value:

Method 1

1. Choose the Eyedropper tool (I or Shift-I).

2. In Photoshop: Right-click/Ctrl-click a color in the image window, then choose Copy Color as HTML.
or
In ImageReady: Click the color that you want to copy in the image window (it will become the Foreground color). Then with the Eyedropper tool still over the image, right-click/Control-click and choose Copy Foreground Color as HTML.

The selected color will be copied to the Clipboard as a hexadecimal value.

3. To paste the color into an HTML file, display the HTML file in your HTML-editing application, then choose Edit > Paste. You can insert the code for any HTML element that allows a color property.

Method 2

1. Choose a Foreground color via the Color palette, Color Picker, or Swatches palette.

2. In Photoshop or ImageReady: Choose Copy Color As HTML from the Color palette menu.
or
In ImageReady: Choose Edit > Copy Foreground Color as HTML.

The Foreground color will be copied to the Clipboard as a hexadecimal value.

3. To paste the color into an HTML file, open the destination application, display the HTML file, then choose Edit > Paste.

RECOLOR 11

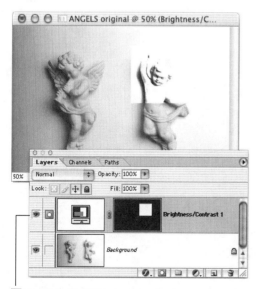

1 *Your changes will preview in the image window or a selection when* **Preview** *is checked.*

2 *For more flexibility, try out adjustments via an* **adjustment layer**.

IN THIS CHAPTER, you will learn to fill a selection with color, a pattern, or imagery; apply a stroke to a selection or a layer; adjust a color image using the Hue/Saturation, Color Balance, Variations, Curves, and Levels commands; use the Color Sampler tool to get multiple color readouts; change colors using the Replace Color command; strip color from a layer; saturate or desaturate colors using the Sponge tool; use a neutral color layer to heighten color; tint a grayscale image; and create and print spot color channels.

Note: Make sure your monitor is calibrated before performing color adjustments! See pages 38–41.

Adjustment basics

Every Image > Adjustments submenu dialog box has a **Preview** box. Changes preview in the image or selection when Preview is checked **1**.

TIP While a dialog box is open, you can Ctrl-Spacebar-click/Cmd-Spacebar-click to **zoom in**; or hold down Spacebar, then Alt-click/Option-click to **zoom out**; or press Spacebar to **move** the image around in the image window.

In addition to the standard method for applying Adjustments submenu commands, many of those commands can also be applied via an **adjustment layer 2**. Unlike the standard method, which affects only the currently active layer, the adjustment layer affects all the currently visible layers below it. The adjustment layer, however, doesn't actually change pixels until it's merged with the layer below it. Adjustment layers are used in this chapter, but to learn how to create and use them, follow the instructions

(Continued on the following page)

Adjustment Basics

on pages 166–169. Similarly, you can use a **fill layer** to apply a solid color, gradient, or pattern (see page 146).

You can use the **Save** command in the Levels, Curves, Replace Color, Selective Color, Hue/Saturation, Channel Mixer, or Variations dialog box to save color adjustment settings. You can then apply them to another layer or to another image via the **Load** button in the same dialog box. And for even more efficiency, any Adjustments submenu command can be recorded and applied via an **action**.

Some of the Adjustments submenu commands, such as Variations, Color Balance, and Brightness/Contrast, produce broad, overall changes. Other commands, such as Levels, Curves, Hue/Saturation, Replace Color, Selective Color, and Channel Mixer, offer more control, but are a little trickier to use. Which command you decide to use will depend on the kind of imagery you're working with and whether it will be color separated or output online. For example, a color cast (e.g., too much blue or too much magenta) will be most noticeable in flesh tones, so this kind of imagery would require careful color adjustment.

TIP To restore the original settings to any Adjustments submenu dialog box while it's still open, Alt-click/Option-click Reset.

Fill shortcuts

Windows

Fill with Foreground color, 100% opacity	Alt-Backspace
Fill with Background color, 100% opacity	Ctrl-Backspace
Fill visible pixels (not transparent areas) with the Foreground color	Alt-Shift-Backspace
Fill visible pixels (not transparent areas) with the Background color	Ctrl-Shift-Backspace

Mac OS

Fill with Foreground color, 100% opacity	Option-Delete
Fill with Background color, 100% opacity	Cmd-Delete
Fill visible pixels (not transparent areas) with the Foreground color	Option-Shift-Delete
Fill visible pixels (not transparent areas) with the Background color	Cmd-Shift-Delete

1 *Select an area to use as a **tile** for a pattern.*

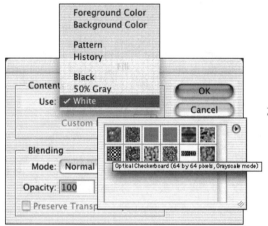

2 *Choose options in the **Fill** dialog box.*

To fill a selection or a layer with a color, a pattern, or imagery:

1. To fill with a flat Foreground or Background **color**, choose that color from the Color or Swatches palette.
or
To fill with **history**, click in the box next to a state on the History palette to establish a source for the History Brush.
or
To tile an area using a **pattern** preset, you don't need to do anything. Or if you'd like to create a custom pattern now, select an area on a layer in any open image using the Rectangular Marquee tool (no feathering) **1**, choose Edit > Define Pattern, enter a Name, then Deselect (Ctrl-D/Cmd-D).

2. Choose a layer. To fill only non-transparent areas on the layer, click the "Lock Transparent pixels" button on the Layers palette (the button will darken); or to fill the entire layer, turn that option off.

To restrict the fill area, create a **selection** using any selection method (no feathering).

3. Choose Edit > Fill (Shift-Backspace/ Shift-Delete).

4. From the **Use** pop-up menu, choose what you want to fill the selection or layer with: **2**

Foreground Color, Background Color, Black, 50% Gray, or White.

Pattern; click the Custom Pattern picker arrowhead, then choose a pattern from the picker.

History to fill the selection or layer with imagery from the active layer at the state that you chose as a source.

5. Choose a blending Mode and an Opacity percentage.

6. *Optional:* If you forgot to click the "Lock transparent pixels" button on the

(Continued on the following page)

Layers palette, you can check Preserve Transparency here instead.

7. Click OK –.

TIP If you dislike the new fill color, choose Edit > Undo now so it won't blend with your next color or mode choice.

TIP To fill a layer using a layer effect, double-click next to the layer name, then, in Layer Style, click Color Overlay, Gradient Overlay, or Pattern Overlay. The gradient picker is accessible in the Gradient Overlay pane, the pattern picker in the Pattern Overlay pane. Adjust the settings, then click OK. You can apply one, two, or all three of the Overlay effects to the same layer (see pages 254–255).

It's a pattern

Using the **presets** feature in Photoshop 7, it's easy to save patterns for future use. To learn more about presets, see pages 404–406. Nevertheless, for safe-keeping, you should hold onto any files that contain imagery you've used as the source for a pattern tile in case the presets are accidentally deleted.

You're not limited to the Fill command to apply patterns. You can also apply a pattern using the **Pattern Stamp** tool (see page 125) or the **Paint Bucket** tool.

1 *The tile used as a* **fill pattern** *in another image*

2 *To produce this image, the pattern layer was duplicated, the opacity of the duplicate was lowered to 43%, its blending mode was changed to Multiply, and the duplicate layer was offset from the original.*

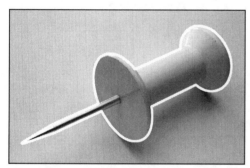

1 *Choose options in the **Stroke** dialog box.*

*A white **stroke** was applied to the pushpin.*

To apply a stroke to a selection or a layer:

1. *Optional:* If you'd rather choose a stroke color using the Color palette or Swatches palette than with the Color Picker, do so now. If you want to use the Color Picker, you can access it when you get to the Stroke dialog box (step 5).

2. Choose a layer. If you don't want the stroke to extend into transparent areas on the layer, click the "Lock transparent pixels" button ▣ on the Layers palette; and for step 6, below, don't click the Location: Outside option.

Optional: Select an area on the layer.

3. Choose Edit > Stroke.

4. Enter a Width (1–250 pixels) **1**.

5. If you didn't choose a stroke color for step 1, click the Color swatch, then choose a color from the Color Picker.

6. Click Location: Inside, Center, or Outside for the position of the stroke on the edge of the selection or layer imagery.

7. Choose a blending Mode and an Opacity.

8. Click OK **2**.

TIP To apply a stroke as a layer effect, double-click a layer name, check Stroke in the Layer Style dialog box, adjust the settings, then click OK. The Stroke style ignores the Lock transparent pixels setting.

TIP To stroke a path, see page 295.

Stroke

Hue/Saturation

To adjust a color image using Hue/Saturation:

1. Choose a layer. *Optional:* Select an area of the layer to recolor only that area.

2. Choose Image > Adjustments > Hue/Saturation (Ctrl-U/Cmd-U).
or
Create an adjustment layer by choosing Hue/Saturation from the "Create new fill or adjustment layer" pop-up menu ◑ at the bottom of the Layers palette.

3. From the Edit pop-up menu, choose Master to adjust all the image colors at once or choose a preset range to adjust only colors within that range **1**.

4. Make sure Preview is checked.

5. Do any of the following:
Move the **Hue** slider **2** to the left or the right to shift colors to another part of the color bar.

Move the **Saturation** slider to the left to decrease saturation or to the right to increase saturation.

To lighten the image or layer, move the **Lightness** slider to the right. To darken the image or layer, move it to the left.

TIP To add Color Sampler points while the Hue/Saturation dialog box is open, choose Edit: Master, then Shift-click on the image (see pages 194–195).

6. When a color range is chosen from the Edit pop-up menu (step 3), the adjustment slider and color selection droppers become available **3**. You can use the adjustment slider to narrow or widen the range of colors that the Hue, Saturation, and Lightness sliders will affect. By default, the slider covers 90° of the color bar, the areas to the left and right of the vertical bars (the fall-off) each occupy 30°, and the center area between the vertical bars (the color range) occupies 30°.

Do any of the following to the adjustment slider:

Drag the center area to move the whole slider, as is, to a new spot on the color

Colorize a color or grayscale image

Check **Colorize** in the Hue/Saturation dialog box to tint the current layer. Move the Hue slider to apply a different tint; move the Saturation slider to reduce/increase tint color intensity; move the Lightness slider to lighten or darken the tint (and the image or layer). The Edit pop-up menu defaults to Master when the Colorize option is on. To tint a grayscale image using this method, convert it to RGB Color or CMYK Color mode first. To produce a duotone, see page 426.

1 *From the **Edit** pop-up menu, choose **Master** or choose a preset **color** range...*

2 *...then move the **Hue, Saturation,** or **Lightness** sliders.*

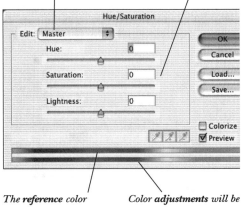

*The **reference** color bar won't change.*

*Color **adjustments** will be displayed in this color bar.*

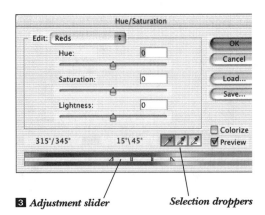

3 *Adjustment slider*

Selection droppers

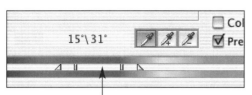

1 *The adjustment slider is moved into a different range.*

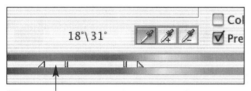

2 *The vertical white bar is moved inward to **narrow** the **color range** (the center area).*

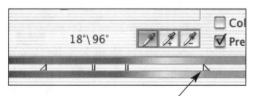

3 *The outer area (the fall-off) is moved outward to **widen** the **color range** (the center area). The fall-off is unchanged.*

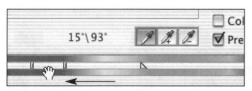

4 *The triangle is moved outward to **widen** the **fall-off**. The color range is unchanged.*

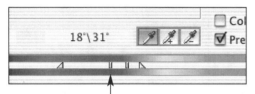

5 ***Ctrl-drag/Cmd-drag** to change where colors display on the color bars.*

bar and shift it into a different color range **1**. The Edit pop-up menu will update to reflect your new color range choice.

Drag either or both of the vertical white bars on the slider to narrow or expand the range. Narrowing the range increases the fall-off area, and vice versa **2**.

Drag either or both of the areas outside the vertical bars to widen or narrow that range without altering the fall-off area **3**.

Drag the outer triangles on the slider to change how much of the current range falls off into adjacent colors **4**. Drag outward to increase the fall-off or inward to decrease it. *Note:* A very short fall-off may produce dithering in the image.

Ctrl-drag/Cmd-drag either color bar to adjust where colors are visible on the bar **5**. Colors wrap from one edge to the other. This won't affect the actual image.

If you alter the slider for any of the six preset color ranges, then that current color adjustment will become the new listing on the Edit pop-up menu. If, for example, you move the preset Reds range slider so it enters the Yellows range, then the menu will list Yellows and Yellows 2, and will no longer list Reds, since the Yellows range now includes Reds.

Click a color in the image window—related colors will be adjusted. Or use the Add to Sample eyedropper 🖊 or Subtract from Sample 🖊 eyedropper to add to or subtract from any current color range by clicking on the image.

TIP Hold down Shift with the first dropper chosen to make it function temporarily like an Add to Sample eyedropper; or hold down Alt/Option to make it function temporarily like a Subtract from Sample dropper.

7. Click OK.

TIP To restore the original dialog box settings, Alt-click/Option-click Reset.

Hue/Saturation

Instead of using the Eyedropper tool to get a color readout from one spot, you can use the Color Sampler tool to place up to four color readout markers, called color samplers, on an image. As you perform color and shade adjustments, before and after color breakdown readouts will display on the Info palette. You can also add color samplers while a color adjustment dialog box is open (Shift-click on the image). Color samplers save with the file in which they're created.

To place color samplers on an image:

1. Choose the Color Sampler tool (I or Shift-I).

2. Click up to four locations on the image to position color samplers .

Note: If you choose a tool other than the Color Sampler, Eyedropper, or a painting or editing tool, the samplers will disappear from view. To redisplay them, choose one of the above-mentioned tools or open a dialog box from the Adjustments submenu. To deliberately hide them, choose Color Samplers from the Info palette menu to uncheck that command.

TIP You can also add samplers by Alt-Shift/ Option-Shift-clicking with the Eyedropper tool.

TIP Color samplers gather data from the topmost visible layer that contains pixels in the spot where the sampler is located. If you hide a layer from which a sampler is reading, the sampler will then read from the next layer down that contains visible pixels in that spot. The Info palette will update if you hide a layer from which it was reading sampler data.

TIP The samplers are located on the canvas. They won't move if a layer is flipped, but they *will* move if the whole canvas is rotated.

1 *Click on an image with the **Color Sampler** tool to create up to four sampler locations.*

Color Samplers

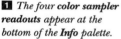

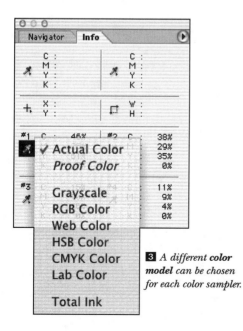

1 *The four color sampler readouts appear at the bottom of the Info palette.* **Before adjustment** **After adjustment**

2 *Choose a Sample Size from the Color Sampler tool options bar.*

3 *A different color model can be chosen for each color sampler.*

To move a color sampler:
Choose the Color Sampler tool (I or Shift-I), then drag a color sampler.
or
Choose the Eyedropper tool (I or Shift-I), then Ctrl-drag/Cmd-drag a color sampler.

Using the Info palette with the Color Sampler tool
The Info palette displays before-adjustment (and after-adjustment) color breakdowns of the pixel or pixel area under each color sampler **1**. The size of the sample area depends on which **Sample Size** setting is chosen on the Color Sampler options bar **2**. Choose Point Sample to sample only the pixel under the pointer; choose 3 by 3 Average or 5 by 5 Average to sample an average color from a 3- or 5-pixel-square area. If you change the Sample Size for the Color Sampler tool, that setting will also change for the Eyedropper, and vice versa.

To choose a **color model** (Grayscale, RGB Color, etc.) for a section of the Info palette, click the tiny arrowhead next to a dropper icon on the palette, then choose from the pop-up menu **3**. Actual Color is the image's current color mode; Proof Color is the current color profile mode chosen in View > Proof Setup; and Total Ink is the total percentage of CMYK under the pointer based on the current settings in CMYK Setup. The model you choose for the Info palette doesn't have to match the current image mode. You can also choose a color model in the Info Options dialog box (choose Palette Options from the Info palette menu).

To remove a color sampler:
Choose the Color Sampler tool, 🖋 then Alt-click/Option-click a sampler (the pointer will become a scissors icon) or drag the sampler out of the image window. That sampler's readout area will be removed from the Info palette, and the remaining samplers will be renumbered automatically.
or
Choose the Eyedropper tool, 🖋 then Alt-Shift-click/Option-Shift-click a sampler.

Color Samplers

Use the Replace Color command to change colors in an image without having to first select them.

To replace colors:

1. *Optional:* For an RGB image, choose View > Proof Setup > Working CMYK to see a soft proof of the actual image and modifications to it in CMYK color. (The Sample swatch in the Replace Color dialog box will continue to display in RGB.) You can choose this command even while the dialog box is open.

2. Choose a layer.

3. *Optional:* Create a selection to restrict color replacement to that area.

4. Choose Image > Adjustments > Replace Color.

5. Click the color you want to replace either in the preview window in the Replace Color dialog box or in the image window **1**.

> **TIP** Initially, the preview window will be solid black. Click the Selection button to preview the selection in the preview window, or click the Image button to display the entire image *(Mac OS:* press Control to toggle between the two display modes). If your image extends beyond the edges of your monitor, click Image so you'll be able to sample from the entire image preview with the eyedropper.

6. *Optional:*
Move the Fuzziness slider to the right to add related colors to the selection.
or
Shift-click in the preview window or image window to add other color areas to the selection. Or choose the 🖋 eyedropper and click without holding down Shift.
or
With the first eyedropper chosen, Alt-click/Option-click in the preview window or image window to subtract color areas from the selection.
or

1 *The **white** areas in the preview window are the areas that will be modified.*

1 *The original image*

2 *After a **Lightness** adjustment to the background*

Choose the ✐ eyedropper, then click without holding down Shift.

7. Move the Hue, Saturation, or Lightness sliders to change the selected colors (only the Lightness slider will be available for a Grayscale image). The Sample swatch will change as you move the sliders.

The Transform sliders will stay in their current positions even if you click on a different area of the image.

8. Click OK **1**–**2**.

TIP The Sample swatch color from the Replace Color dialog box will also display in the currently active square on the Color palette, and the Color palette sliders will reflect its individual components. If the gamut alarm displays, it means you have produced a non-printable color using the Transform sliders. Note also that the Transform sliders won't change the amount of Black (K) in a color for an image in CMYK Color mode. That component is set by Photoshop's Black Generation function.

TIP To restore the original dialog box settings, hold down Alt/Option, then click Reset.

Use the Desaturate command to strip color from a layer (convert it to grayscale) without having to change the color mode for the whole image.

To convert a layer or the Background to grayscale:

1. Choose a layer or the Background.

2. Choose Image > Adjustments > Desaturate (Ctrl-Shift-U/Cmd-Shift-U).

Use the Color Balance dialog box to apply or correct a warm or cool cast in a layer's highlights, midtones, or shadows. Color adjustments will be easier to see in an image that has a wide tonal range.

To colorize or color correct using Color Balance:

1. Make sure the composite color image is displayed (Ctrl-~/Cmd-~) (all the channels on the Channels palette should have eye icons, including the topmost one). To colorize a Grayscale image, first convert it to a color image mode.

2. Choose a layer.

3. Choose Image > Adjustments > Color Balance (Ctrl-B/Cmd-B).
or
Create an adjustment layer by choosing Color Balance from the "Create new fill or adjustment layer" pop-up menu ⬤. at the bottom of the Layers palette.

4. At the bottom of the dialog box, click the tonal range you want to adjust: Shadows, Midtones, or Highlights **1**.

5. *Optional:* Check Preserve Luminosity to preserve brightness values.

6. Move a slider toward any color you want to add more of. Cool and warm colors are paired opposite each other. Pause to preview.

> **TIP** Move sliders toward related colors to make an image warmer or cooler. For example, move sliders toward Cyan and Blue to produce a cool cast.

7. *Optional:* Repeat the previous step with any other Tone Balance button selected.

8. Click OK.

Hand tinting

To tint small areas manually, use the **Brush** tool with the **Airbrush** button 🖌 pressed on the options bar, and a low Opacity. *7.0!*

1 *First click* ***Tone Balance: Shadows, Midtones,*** *or* ***Highlights,*** *then move any of the sliders.*

*Click the **Original** thumbnail to restore the unmodified layer.*

1 *First click **Shadows, Midtones, Highlights,** or **Saturation.***

*The **Current Pick** thumbnail represents the modified layer.*

2 *Second, move the **Fine/Coarse** slider to control the degree of adjustment.*

3 *Click any **More**... thumbnail to add more of that color to the layer. Click the diagonally opposite thumbnail to undo the modification.*

4 *Click **Lighter** or **Darker** to modify the luminosity without modifying the hue.*

Thumbnail previews in the Variations dialog box represent how an image would look with various color adjustments. The Variations command can't be used on an Indexed Color image. *Note:* To make more precise adjustments and preview the changes in the image window, use the Color Balance or Levels dialog box instead.

To adjust color using thumbnail Variations:

1. Choose a layer.

2. Choose Image > Adjustments > Variations.

3. Click Shadows, Midtones, or Highlights at the top right of the dialog box to modify only those areas **1**.
or
Click Saturation to adjust only saturation.

4. Position the Fine/Coarse slider to the right of center to make major adjustments or to the left of center to make minor adjustments **2**. Each notch to the right doubles the adjustment per click; each notch to the left halves the adjustment per click.

5. Click any "More..." thumbnail to add more of that color to the layer **3**. To lessen the amount of a color, click its diagonally opposite color. As you do this, compare the Current Pick thumbnail, which represents the modified layer, with the Original thumbnail. Click the Original thumbnail to undo all the Variations adjustment(s).

6. *Optional:* Click Lighter or Darker to change the luminosity without changing the hue **4**.

7. *Optional:* If you chose to adjust Shadows, Highlights, or Saturation, and Show Clipping is checked, areas that will be converted to black or white will have neon highlights in the dialog box.

8. *Optional:* Repeat steps 3–6 with a different tonal range chosen.

9. Click OK.

Variations

Use the Sponge tool to make color areas on the current layer more or less saturated. (The Sponge tool is also discussed on page 431, where it's used to bring colors into the printable gamut.) This tool can't be used on a Bitmap or Indexed Color image.

1 *The Sponge tool options bar*

To saturate or desaturate colors using the Sponge tool:

1. Double-click the Sponge tool (O or Shift-O). ◉ It's on the pop-out menu with the Dodge and Burn tools.

2. On the Sponge tool options bar **1**:

Click the Brush picker arrowhead, then click a brush. A soft brush will produce the smoothest result. You can also choose a brush from the Brushes palette.
and
Choose Mode: Desaturate or Saturate.
and
Choose a Flow percentage between 1% (low intensity) and 100% (high intensity). Try a lowish Flow percentage first (20%–30%) so the tool won't saturate or desaturate areas too quickly. (Flow was called "Pressure" in Photoshop 6.)

> **TIP** Press a single number on the keyboard to get a Flow percentage of 10 times that number (e.g., press "4" to get 40 percent). Press two numbers to enter an exact percentage.

3. Choose a layer.

4. Stroke on any area of the layer **2**. Pause to allow the screen to redraw, if necessary. Stroke again to intensify the effect.

> **TIP** If you Saturate or Desaturate an area too much, choose Edit > Undo or click an earlier state or snapshot on the History palette. Don't try to use the tool with its opposite setting to fix it—the results will be uneven.

> **TIP** You can also adjust saturation in an image using the Image > Adjustments > Hue/Saturation or Replace Color command.

2 *Using the Sponge tool to desaturate colors in an image*

7.0!

7.0!

```
                    New Layer
Name: neutral color layer                        OK
      ☐ Group With Previous Layer               Canc
Color: ☐None              ↕
■ Mode: Color Dodge  ↕    Opacity: 100 ▸ %
      ☑ Fill with Color-Dodge-neutral color (black)
```

2 *The original image*

3 *After painting on the Color Dodge mode layer, choosing Color Burn as the layer mode, and painting medium gray strokes on the Color Burn mode layer*

4 *The original image*

5 *After choosing Overlay mode, checking the "Fill with…" option for the neutral layer, and applying Dodge and Burn strokes to the neutral layer to heighten the highlights and shadows*

In this exercise, you'll be painting shades of gray on a special neutral black or white layer in Color Dodge or Color Burn mode in order to heighten or lessen color in the underlying layer. You're welcome to try out other layer modes.

To heighten color or silhouette color areas on black:

1. Convert the image to RGB image mode, and activate the layer that you want to affect.

2. Alt-click/Option-click the "Create new layer" button ▣ on the Layers palette.

3. Type a name for the layer.

4. Choose a Mode. We chose Color Dodge mode for our illustration **■**, but you can choose any mode other than Normal, Dissolve, Hue, Saturation, Color, or Luminosity.

5. Check "Fill with [mode name]-neutral color [color name]," then click OK. Our layer was filled with black.

6. Choose the Brush tool (B or Shift-B), ✐ and choose a brush from the brush picker or Brushes palette.

7. Choose Grayscale Slider from the Color palette menu.

8. Paint with a 60–88 percent gray. You'll actually be changing the neutral black on the layer. Areas you stroke over will become much lighter.

   If you're displeased with the results, paint over areas or fill the entire layer again with black to remove all the changes, and start over. Repainting or refilling with black will remove any existing editing effects, while preserving pixels in the underlying layers.

9. To heighten the color effect, you can choose another mode from the Layers palette. We chose Color Burn mode. Your image strokes will be silhouetted against black **2**–**5**.

   Or to restore more of the original color, paint with a medium gray.

Levels and Curves

If you use the Levels or Curves command to make color or tonal adjustments, you should adjust the overall tone of the image first (the composite channel), and then adjust individual color channels, if necessary (a bit more cyan, a bit less magenta, etc.).

To adjust individual color channels using Levels:

1. Display the Info palette.

2. Choose Image > Adjustments > Levels (Ctrl-L/Cmd-L).
or
Create an adjustment layer by choosing Levels from the "Create new fill or adjustment layer" pop-up menu ⬤. at the bottom of the Layers palette.

3. Check Preview.

4. If there's an obvious predominance of one color in the image (e.g., too much red or green), choose that channel from the Channel pop-up menu **1**.

Follow any of these steps for a CMYK Color image (the sliders will have the **opposite** effect in an RGB image!):

To increase the amount of that particular color, move the black or gray Input Levels slider to the right. The black triangle affects the shadows in the image, the gray triangle affects the midtones.
or
To decrease the amount of that color, move the gray or white Input Levels slider to the left. The white slider affects the highlights.
or
To tint the image with the chosen channel color, move the white Output Levels slider to the left. To lessen the chosen channel color, move the black Output Levels slider to the right. The Output sliders are particularly effective for adjusting skin tones in a photograph.

Repeat these steps for any other channels that need adjusting, bearing in mind that one channel adjustment may affect another.

1 *Choose an individual* **channel**, *if desired.*

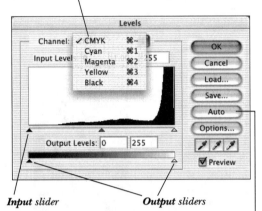

Input slider   *Output sliders*

Click **Auto** *to have Photoshop set the high-light and shadow values in an image and redistribute the midrange color values. Individual channel curves will be altered.*

Levels

The auto color correction algorithms

■ **Enhance Monochromatic Contrast** maintains the color relationships between channels because the black and white input sliders move inward by the same amounts on all individual channels. Moving the sliders inward lightens the highlights and darkens the shadows. (The Auto Contrast command uses this option.)

■ **Enhance Per Channel Contrast** moves the input sliders inward by different amounts for each individual channel. The correction produces more noticeable image contrast. Because each channel is adjusted differently, color casts (color changes) may result in the image. (The Auto Levels command uses this option.)

■ **Find Dark & Light Colors** finds the average darkest and lightest pixels in the image. Those darkest and lightest pixel values are used to position the black and white input sliders in each channel and increase image contrast. (The Auto Color command uses this option.)

Note: The Auto Color Correction options can also be accessed in the Image > Adjustments > Curves dialog box. Option changes will readjust an individual channel's curve chart.

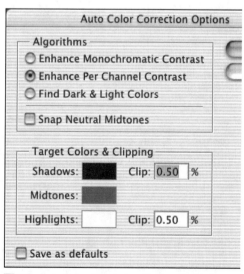

1 *The Auto Color Correction Options dialog box*

5. Click OK.

TIP Alt-click/Option-click Reset to restore the original dialog box settings.

TIP Shift-click the image to place Color Sampler points while the Levels dialog box is open.

The Auto Color Correction Options command can be used to automatically adjust the color, tonal range and contrast in an image and set target values for shadows, midtones, and highlights. We recommend using these auto correction options as a starting point for correcting an image.

To apply auto color correction options:

1. With a pixel (non-vector) layer chosen, choose Image > Adjustments > Levels.

2. Click the Options button. Move the Auto Color Correction Options dialog box so you'll be able to see the Levels histogram readjust as options are chosen.

3. Click an algorithm option to adjust color and tonal range (see the sidebar) **■**.

4. Check Snap Neutral Midtones to automatically locate average colors that are very close to the neutral value in the image, then adjust each channel's midpoint value to make those colors actually become neutral.

5. *Optional:* To alter the target value assigned to the shadow, midtone, and highlight areas of the image, click the respective swatch. In the Color Picker, drag the small circle up or down in the large square. Move the Color Picker so you'll be able to see how the histogram (when the composite RGB or CMYK channel is displayed) shifts left or right, remapping image pixels to the current color choice. Click OK when done.

6. Click OK twice.

TIP To view a channel's adjustments, set the channel pop-up menu to an individual channel before clicking Options in step 2, above.

Using the Curves command, you can correct a picture's highlights, quarter tones, midtones, three-quarter tones, or shadows separately. You can even use multiple adjustment layers to do this. Use one adjustment layer for the composite channel first and then use another one for each individual channel to fine-tune the color. And you can experiment with the layer opacity or use a layer mask to remove or lessen the effect in specific areas.

To adjust color or values using the Curves command:

1. *Optional:* To adjust a combination of two or more channels at the same time, Shift-click those channel names on the Channels palette now. *Note:* You can't do this for a Curves adjustment layer!

2. Choose Image menu > Adjustments > Curves (Ctrl-M/Cmd-M).
or
Create an adjustment layer by choosing Curves from the "Create new fill or adjustment layer" pop-up menu ⬤. at the bottom of the Layers palette.

3. Move the pointer over the grid. The default Input and Output readouts in the lower-left corner of the dialog box are either the brightness values for RGB Color mode or the percentage values for CMYK Color mode. Click the gradient bar below the grid to switch between those two readouts.

4. *Optional:* Choose a Channel to adjust it separately. If you chose more than one channel in step 1, you can select that combo now (e.g., "RB" for the red and blue channels).

5. If the gradient on the gradient bar is white on the left side (for CMYK mode), drag the part of the curve you want to adjust upward to darken or downward to lighten **1**. (Click the double arrow in the middle of the gradient bar to reverse the curve.) Reverse this instruction for RGB mode.
and/or

Changing channels

If you adjust an individual color channel, keep in mind that **color opposites** (cyan and red, magenta and green, yellow and blue) work in tandem. Lowering cyan, for example, adds more red; lowering red adds more cyan. In fact, you'll probably need to adjust more than one channel to remove an undesirable color cast. If you overzealously adjust only one channel, you'll throw off the color balance of the whole image.

Highlights

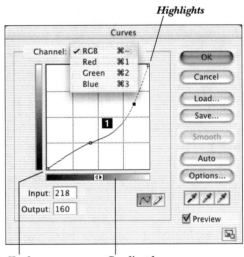

Shadows   *Gradient bar*

Curves

1 *The original image*

2 *After a **Curves** adjustment*

For more precise adjustments, click on the curve to create additional points (up to 14), then drag the segment between any pair of points to make subtle adjustments. (To remove a point, click on it and press Backspace/Delete; or Ctrl-click/Cmd-click on it.)
and/or
Move the extreme end of the curve to reduce absolute black to below 100%, or absolute white to above 0%.

Note: Once you've added a point, you can then enter numbers in the Input and/or Output fields for that point.

6. Click OK **1**–**2**.

TIP The Curves pencil tool tends to produce a bumpy curve, resulting in sharp color transition jumps.

TIP For an image in RGB Color mode, click on the image to see that pixel's placement on the curve. Ctrl-click/Cmd-click on the image to place that point on the curve. For a CMYK Color image, you can click an individual C, M, Y, or K channel to show that pixel's value, but not on the composite CMYK channel.

TIP Alt-click/Option-click the grid in the Curves dialog box to toggle between a 4 by 4 and 10 by 10 grid spacing.

TIP Shift-click on the image to place Color Sampler points while the Curves dialog box is open.

TIP Click the Auto button to have Photoshop set the highlight and shadow values in the image and redistribute the midrange color values. Individual channel curves will be altered.

TIP Click the button on the lower right of the Curves dialog box to expand the dialog box, in case you need to adjust your curve more precisely. Click the button again to restore the dialog box to its original size.

7.0!

Curves

Convert to Grayscale, then Restore Color

To convert a color layer to grayscale and selectively restore its color:

1. Choose a layer in a color image. Layers below this layer will be affected by the adjustment layer you're about to create.

2. Create an adjustment layer by choosing Hue/Saturation from the "Create new fill or adjustment layer" pop-up menu at the bottom of the Layers palette.

3. Move the Saturation slider all the way to the left (to –100) **1**.

4. Click OK.

5. Set the Foreground color to black.

6. With the adjustment layer chosen, paint across the image where you want to restore the original colors from the underlying layers **2**. Paint with white to restore grayscale areas.

   You can also restack a layer above the adjustment layer to fully restore that layer's color.

TIP Choose any of the following mode and opacity combinations for the adjustment layer:

   Dissolve with a 40%–50% Opacity to restore color with a chalky texture.

   Multiply with a 100% Opacity to restore subtle color in the darker areas of the image.

   Color Dodge to lighten and intensify color or Color Burn to darken and intensify color.

TIP To limit the adjustment layer effect to just the layer directly below it, Alt-click/Option-click the line between them on the Layers palette. This creates a clipping group.

Hide behind a mask

Duplicate a color layer, choose Image > Adjustments > **Desaturate** (Ctrl-Shift-U/Cmd-Shift-U), choose Layer > Add Layer Mask > **Hide All** to create a layer mask for that layer, and then paint with white to reveal parts of the grayscale layer above the color layer. You can gradually reshape the mask this way, alternately painting with black to add to the mask or white to remove parts of the mask.

1 *In the **Hue/Saturation** dialog box, move the **Saturation** slider all the way to the left to remove color from the layer.*

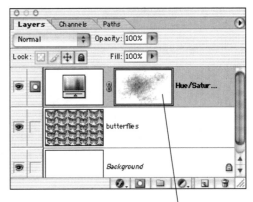

2 *Brushstrokes are applied to an **adjustment layer**.*

Copy to a spot color channel

■ To copy an image shape to a spot color channel, first make a selection on a layer. Then, with the selection active, create a new spot color channel. Or choose an existing spot color channel and fill the selection with black.

■ To copy an image's light and dark values to a spot color channel, first create a selection and copy it to the Clipboard. Then create or choose a spot color channel, and paste onto that channel.

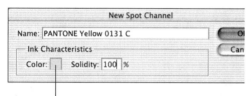

1 *Click the* **Color** *swatch in the* **New Spot Channel** *dialog box.*

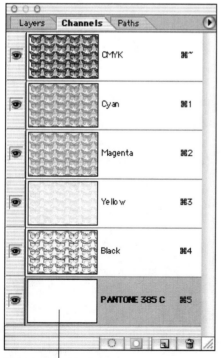

2 *The new spot channel*

Spot color channels

A spot color can be placed in its own separate channel. Then when the image is color separated, this spot color channel will appear on its own plate.

To create a spot color channel:

1. Display the Channels palette, and drag it away from the Layers palette so you can see both palettes at once.

2. Choose New Spot Channel from the Channels palette menu.

3. Click the Color swatch, **1** and if necessary, click Custom to open the Custom Colors dialog box.

4. Choose a Pantone or other spot color matching system name from the Book pop-up menu, choose a color, then click OK.

5. *Optional:* To change the way color in the spot channel displays on screen, enter a new Ink Characteristics: Solidity percentage. At 100%, it will display as a solid color; at a lower percentage, it will appear more transparent (as a preview for, say, a spot color varnish).

6. Click OK. The name of the color you chose will be listed next to the spot channel name on the Channels palette **2**. Any stroke that is applied or image element that is created while the spot color channel is active will appear in that color (see the following page).

TIP To change the spot color in a channel, double-click the channel name, then follow steps 3–6, above. The channel will automatically be renamed for the new color, and all the pixels on the channel will display in that new color.

To paint on a spot color channel:

1. Create a spot color channel (instructions on the previous page).

2. Double-click the spot color channel name, enter 100 as the Solidity value, then click OK.

3. Choose the Brush tool. (The Color palette will display in grayscale mode while the spot color channel is active.) Choose black as the Foreground color.

4. On the Brush tool options bar, choose Normal as the painting Mode and choose an Opacity percentage to establish the tint percentage for the spot color ink on the spot color plate.

5. Make sure the spot color channel is still active, then paint on the image.

Spot color channel basics

When the **eye** icon is present for both the spot color channel and the topmost (composite) channel on the Channels palette, the spot channel is displayed along with the other image layers. To display the spot channel by itself, hide the composite channel by clicking its eye icon.

If you want to know the **opacity** of a spot color area, choose the spot color channel, choose Actual Color mode for the readout on the Info palette, move the pointer over the image, and then note the K (grayscale percentage) on the Info palette.

When a spot color channel is active, the thumbnail for the most recently active **layer** will have a black border and edits will affect only the spot channel. If you click the topmost (composite) channel on the Channels palette, edits will now affect the most recently active layer, not the spot channel.

To add **type** to a spot color channel, see page 335.

If a color image with a spot color channel (or an image in Duotone mode), is converted to Multichannel mode, any spot colors in the image (or duotone) will be placed in separate spot channel(s). Preexisting

Lighten/darken spot channel tint

Click the spot channel on the Channels palette, then choose Image > Adjustments > **Levels**. To darken the tint, move the black Input slider to the right; to lighten the tint, move the black Output slider to the right. Position the pointer over the image so you can get an opacity readout on the Info palette (choose Actual Color mode for the readout). Readjust either slider, if desired.

spot channels, if any, will remain after the conversion. To **tint** an entire image with a spot color, convert the image to Duotone mode and specify the desired spot color as the monotone color (see page 427).

To **export** a file that contains spot channels, save it in the DCS 2.0 format (make sure Spot Colors is checked in the options pane). Each spot channel will be preserved as a separate file, along with the composite DCS file. Also, let Photoshop assign the spot channel name for you. Then other applications will recognize it as a spot color. The Photoshop PDF format also supports spot colors.

Printing spot color channels

Spot channel colors **overprint** all other image colors. The stacking order of spot color channels on the Channels palette controls the order in which spot colors overprint each other. To prevent a spot color from overprinting, you must manually knock out (delete) any areas from other channels that fall beneath the spot color shapes (read more about this in the Photoshop documentation). Talk with your print shop, though, to see if this step is necessary.

Choosing **Merge Spot Channel** (Channels palette menu) merges the spot color into the existing color channels and flattens all layers, so you can then print a composite (single-page) proof on a color printer. If you don't merge spot channels, they will print as separate pages. Merging a spot color channel into the other color channels changes the actual spot color, because CMYK inks can't exactly replicate spot color inks. When a spot color channel is merged into other color channels, its Solidity value determines the tint percentage of merged spot color. The lower the Solidity, the more transparent the newly merged color will be. All image layers are flattened when spot channels are merged.

TIP Use the Solidity option in the Spot Channel Options dialog box to produce

(Continued on the following page)

an on-screen simulation of the ink opacity for the spot plate. For an opaque ink, such as a metallic ink, use 100% Solidity. For a transparent, clear varnish, use 0% Solidity.

To convert an alpha channel into a spot color channel:

1. Double-click an alpha channel on the Channels palette.

2. Choose Color Indicates: Spot Color **1**.

3. Click the Color swatch, click Custom, if necessary, to open the Custom Colors dialog box, choose a spot color, then click OK.

4. Click OK. Former non-white (black or gray) areas on the channel will now display in the chosen spot color.

TIP To reverse the spot color and white areas, deselect any selections, choose the channel, then choose Image > Adjustments > Invert (Ctrl-I/Cmd-I).

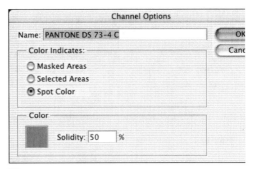

1 *Choose Color Indicates:* **Spot Color** *in the* **Channel Options** *dialog box.*

PAINT 12

Brush Tool

Tool shortcuts

Cycle through the blending Modes on the options bar	Shift + or Shift -
Decrease/increase a brush's Master Diameter	"[" or "]"
Change Opacity level* (Shift-press a number to change the Flow level)	0 through 9 on the keypad (e.g., 2 = 20%) or quickly type a percentage (e.g. "38")

*If the Airbrush option is on, Shift-press a number to change the Opacity level.

IN THIS CHAPTER, you will learn how to use Photoshop's Brush, Paint Bucket, Eraser, Background Eraser, Magic Eraser, Smudge, and Gradient tools to embellish or edit a scanned image, or paint a picture from scratch. You will also learn how to use the Brushes palette to save and load brush libraries and create custom brush presets for the painting tools.

Brush tool

First, just to get started, let's get acquainted with the Brush tool. In these instructions, you will choose an existing brush preset (brush tip) for the Brush tool, and then choose various options bar settings to customize how the tool applies pigment. In the next section, starting on page 213, you will learn how to customize a brush preset using a wide assortment of options on the Brushes palette.

Brush preset picker arrowhead

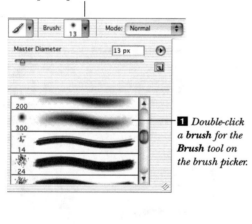

1 *Double-click a brush for the Brush tool on the brush picker.*

To use the Brush tool:

1. Choose a layer. Create a selection on the layer if you want to restrict the brush-strokes to that area.
2. Click the Brush tool (B), formerly called the Paintbrush tool. **7.0!**
3. Choose a Foreground color (see pages 179–182).
4. On the options bar:

   Click the Brush preset picker arrowhead, then double-click a brush **1**. The picker will close automatically.
   and
   Choose a blending Mode (see "Blending modes" on pages 32–36).
   and
   Choose an Opacity percentage **2**. At 100%, the stroke will completely cover underlying pixels.
   and

2 *Choose an **Opacity** percentage.*

(Continued on the following page)

Choose a Flow percentage to control how quickly and smoothly the paint is applied.

5. *Optional:* Turn on the Airbrush option  to have the brush continue to dispense paint for as long as you hold down the mouse button, simulating traditional airbrushing **1**–**2**.

6. Drag across any area of the picture. If you press and hold on a spot when the Airbrush option is on, the paintdrop will gradually widen (up to the brush's maximum diameter), and become more dense and opaque.

Note: Click the "Lock transparent pixels" button 🔲 on the Layers palette to have the brush recolor only non-transparent areas, not any fully transparent areas.

Each brush preset has its own Master Diameter setting, but you can temporarily change the diameter of any brush preset.

To temporarily change the diameter of a brush preset:

1. Choose any tool that uses a brush (e.g., the Brush, Pencil, Dodge, Burn, or Eraser tool).

2. Right-click/Ctrl-click in the image window, move the Master Diameter slider **3**, then press Enter/Return.

This setting will remain in effect until you choose a different preset. If you choose a different preset, and then click back on the previous preset, the original Master Diameter will be restored.

TIP To draw a straight stroke, click once to begin the stroke, then Shift-click or Shift-drag in a different location to complete the stroke.

TIP Alt-click/Option-click in any open image to sample a color while a painting tool is chosen (this is a temporary Eyedropper).

Hey, where'd the Airbrush tool go?

The **Airbrush** function can be turned on or off for the Brush tool via a button on the options bar.  This option is also available for the Clone Stamp, Pattern Stamp, History Brush, Eraser, Dodge, Burn, and Sponge tools.

1 *A **Brush** stroke created with the **Airbrush** option **off***

*A brush stroke created with the **Airbrush** option **on***

2 *A brush stroke created with the **Airbrush** option **on***

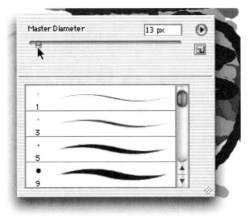

3 *You can change the **Master Diameter** on the fly using the **context menu**.*

Master Diameter

Dock it

Once the Brushes palette is displayed, if your monitor is wide enough to display the palette well at the right side of the options bar, drag the Brushes palette tab there or choose **Dock to Palette Well** from the Brushes palette menu. Thereafter, to display the palette, just click its tab. To access the palette menu when the palette is docked, click its tab, then click the arrowhead on the tab.

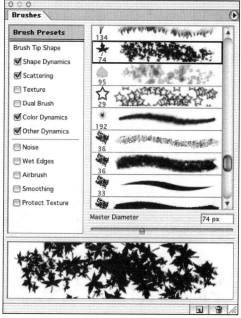

1 *The* **Brushes** *palette*

Brushes palette 7.0!

The new Brushes palette offers a myriad of options for customizing brush tips for the Brush, Pencil, History Brush, Art History Brush, Clone Stamp, Pattern Stamp, Eraser, Background Eraser, Blur, Sharpen, Smudge, Dodge, Burn, and Sponge tools. The options are organized into categories, such as Shape Dynamics, Scattering, Texture, and Color Dynamics. You can also use the Brushes palette to choose options for a stylus or for an airbrush input device.

The first step is to get acquainted with the palette. This is "Brushes Palette 101."

To use the Brushes palette:

1. Choose any of the tools that are listed above in the introductory paragraph.

2. To display the Brushes palette **1**:
   Choose Window > Brushes.
   or
   Click the Brushes palette button 📷 toward the middle of the options bar.

3. If you don't see a list of categories on the left side of the palette, choose Expanded View from the palette menu. If the palette is just a bar, double-click the bar.

4. Check the box for any of the first six categories to activate the features for that category. If a category is dimmed, it means it's not available for that tool. The categories are discussed in depth in the next set of instructions.

5. To display the pane for a category, click the category name. The options listed below the horizontal line are individual features; there is no pane for them.

6. To choose a different display option for the palette, click Brush Presets at the top of the palette, click the arrowhead in the circle on the right side of the palette, then choose Text Only, Small Thumbnail, Large Thumbnail, Small List, Large List, or Stroke Thumbnail from the menu. The Small options compact the list; the Large options allow you to see the brush shapes more clearly.

7.0!

Given the enormous range of options on the Brushes palette, your choices are endless. For example, you can make subtle adjustments to a hard-edged brush or create a simulation of a natural-media bristle brush. Start by editing the preset brushes that are supplied with Photoshop. Later, you'll learn how to save your customized presets as well as create brand new brushes.

Steps 2 through 9 in the following instructions are optional; just pick and choose which options you want to experiment with. And remember, though we talk here about applying "pigment," the brushes are used with many other tools besides the Brush.

Note: A brush's settings remain in effect until they're changed.

To edit a brush preset:

1. Click **Brush Presets** **1** in the upper-left corner of the Brushes palette, then click a preset. Use the scroll arrows to scroll down the list, if necessary

2. To change any of the basic shape or size settings for the brush, click **Brush Tip Shape** at the top of the list **2**, then watch the brush preview at the bottom of the palette as you make any of these changes:

For the brush size, enter a Diameter value (1–2500 pixels) or move the slider. If the brush was originally created from a selection, you can check Use Sample Size to make the brush the same size as the original selection (see "To Create a Brush from an image" on page 223.)

Enter a new Angle or drag the arrowhead around the circle to alter the brush slant.

Enter a new Roundness value (0–100%) or drag one of the two tiny dark circles inward to make the brush tip more elliptical, less round **3**.

Change the Hardness value (0–100%) to feather or sharpen the edge of a round tip **4**.

To control the distance between brush tips within the stroke, check Spacing, then enter or choose a value (1–1000%) **5**.

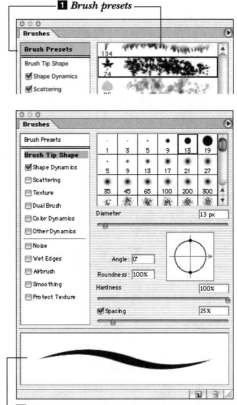

1 *Brush presets*

2 *You can watch the brush **preview** at the bottom of the Brushes palette as you change the settings.*

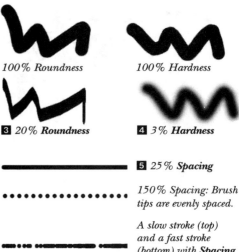

100% Roundness

100% Hardness

3 *20% **Roundness***

4 *3% **Hardness***

5 *25% **Spacing***

150% Spacing: Brush tips are evenly spaced.

*A slow stroke (top) and a fast stroke (bottom) with **Spacing** unchecked: Brush tips are unevenly spaced.*

Edit Brush Preset

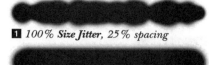

1 *100% Size Jitter, 25% spacing*

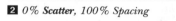

0% Size Jitter

2 *0% Scatter, 100% Spacing*

*500% Scatter, **Both Axes** option **checked***

*500% Scatter, **Both Axes** option **unchecked***

3 *0% Count Jitter, 100% Spacing*

*100% **Count Jitter**: The Count varies randomly from 1% to 100% of the Count value.*

4 *Painting with a **texture** brush with **Pen Pressure** chosen as the Opacity Jitter Control (see the following page).*

3. To control how much variety there can be in the brush tip shape, click **Shape Dynamics** (click the words—the box will become checked automatically), then do any of the following:

Change the Size Jitter **1**, Angle Jitter, and Roundness Jitter values to establish variation parameters for those attributes. ("Jitter" means the amount of random variation that is allowed for that option.)

From the Control pop-up menus, choose what mouse or stylus feature that attribute looks to for the variation (see page 218).

Change the Minimum Diameter value for the brush size variations.

Change the Minimum Roundness value.

4. To control the placement of pigment in the stroke, click **Scattering**, then do any of the following:

Change the Scatter value **2** to control how far pigment can veer off the path drawn by the mouse. The lower the Scatter value, the more solid the stroke.

Check Both Axes to allow pigment to be scattered both along and perpendicular to the path. Uncheck Both Axes to have strokes be scattered perpendicular to, but not along, the path. Choose a Control option, if desired.

Change the Count value to control the stroke's overall density (the amount of pigment).

Change the Count Jitter **3** value to control how much the Count (density) can vary.

5. To use the texture from a pattern in a brush stroke, click **Texture 4**, then do any of the following:

Click the preset arrowhead, then choose a texture from the pattern picker.

Check Invert to swap the light and dark areas in the pattern.

Change the texture's Scale (1–1000%).

(Continued on the following page)

Edit Brush Preset

Check Texture Each Tip to allow the Depth (covered next) to vary within each stroke. Uncheck this option to have the Depth value remain constant.

Choose a blending Mode to control how the texture mixes with the brush stroke.

Choose a Depth value 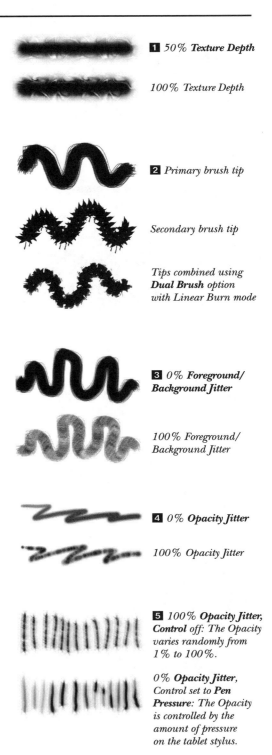 to control how deeply paint sinks into the texture. At a high Depth value, paint will be applied only to the high points in the texture, and the texture will appear more prominent. Choose a Minimum Depth to keep a texture from appearing too flat. Some brushes reveal texture more than others.

Choose a Depth Jitter value to control how much the Depth can vary. Choose an option from the Control pop-up menu to specify if and how the brush stroke can fade (see page 218).

6. *Optional:* As an added bonus to make the brush preset more interesting, add another preset to it. Click **Dual Brush** ❷, click a preset, then choose Diameter, Spacing, Scatter, and Count values.

7. To control how much the color can vary as you use the brush, click **Color Dynamics**, then do any of the following:

Enter a Foreground/Background Jitter value ❸ for the amount of variation between the Foreground and Background colors. Choose an option from the Control pop-up menu to specify if and how colors can fade.

Enter Hue Jitter, Saturation Jitter, and Brightness Jitter values to establish variation parameters for those attributes.

Enter a Purity value to control how much of the Foreground color can appear in the stroke. The lower the Purity, the grayer the stroke.

8. To control how the overall stroke opacity can vary as you paint, click **Other Dynamics**, then do any of the following:

Change the Opacity Jitter ❹–❺ for the amount the opacity can vary. Choose a Control option to control fading.

❶ *50% **Texture Depth***

100% Texture Depth

❷ *Primary brush tip*

Secondary brush tip

*Tips combined using **Dual Brush** option with Linear Burn mode*

❸ *0% **Foreground/ Background Jitter***

100% Foreground/ Background Jitter

❹ *0% **Opacity Jitter***

100% Opacity Jitter

❺ *100% **Opacity Jitter**, **Control** off: The Opacity varies randomly from 1% to 100%.*

*0% **Opacity Jitter**, Control set to **Pen Pressure**: The Opacity is controlled by the amount of pressure on the tablet stylus.*

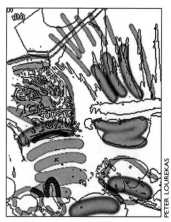

1 *Strokes created with the Brush tool with* **Wet Edges** *checked*

2 *More* **Wet Edges**

Change the Flow Jitter to control how smoothly the pigment is applied. A high Flow Jitter makes for a blotchy stroke; but that may be what you're aiming for. Choose a Control option.

9. And last but not least (you're almost done!), check any or all of these options:

Noise to add random grain to brush strokes to make them look rougher.

Wet Edges to simulate the buildup of pigment at the edges of the strokes, as in traditional watercolors **1**–**4**.

Airbrush to allow a stroke to build up for as long as the mouse button is held down in the same spot. You can also press the ⟨button⟩ button on the options bar.

Smoothing **5**–**6** to convert straight segments into smooth curves.

To apply the same texture pattern and scale to other brushes that currently use a texture option, or to which you add a texture option, check **Protect Texture**. This method will create a uniform surface texture for the entire canvas.

TIP To copy the currently chosen texture and texture settings to the non-painting tools that have a Texture option, choose Copy Texture to Other Tools from the Brushes palette menu.

3 *Wet Edges* **unchecked**

4 *Wet Edges* **checked**

5 *Smoothing* **is off**: *Straight segments and corners are visible in this rapidly-drawn stroke.*

6 *Smoothing* **is on**: *This stroke was drawn as quickly as the one above, but it's smooth and has no corners.*

Edit Brush Preset

7.0! If you want to make your brush strokes look more painterly, or to take advantage of the capabilities of a pressure-sensitive tablet, you can specify how gradually you want some or all of a brush preset's attributes to vary (e.g., its opacity, size, texture).

Some of the variation options work only with certain kinds of graphics tablets. For example, some tablet models may not sense the tilt of the stylus (Pen Tilt) or support airbrush devices. The Fade, Initial Direction, and Direction options, on the other hand, work with a mouse or with any other input device.

To choose variation options:

1. Display the Brushes palette.

2. Click any of these categories:

Shape Dynamics to choose variation controls for Size Jitter, Angle Jitter, or Roundness Jitter.

Scattering to choose variation controls for Scatter or Count Jitter.

Texture to choose variation controls for Depth Jitter.

Color Dynamics to choose variation controls for Foreground/Background Jitter.

Other Dynamics to choose variation controls for Opacity Jitter and Flow Jitter.

3. For any option that offers variation controls, choose one of these options from the Control pop-up menu (not all of these options will be available for every attribute) 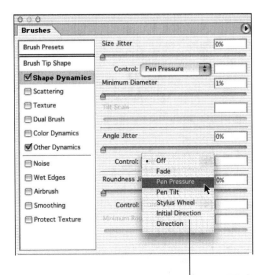:

Off prevents fading.

Fade decreases the attribute over the length of the stroke, using the number of steps you specify.

Pen Pressure varies the attribute based on how hard you press with a stylus on a pressure-sensitive tablet.

Pen Tilt lets you control how a brush attribute varies by changing the angle at which you hold a stylus.

1 *Choose a method from the **Control** pop-up menu below any brush option.*

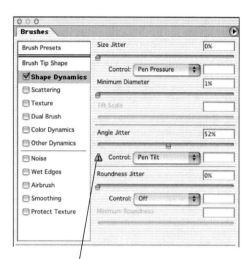

1 *If you choose a Control pop-up menu option that isn't supported by any of the graphics tablet devices that you have connected, this **warning icon** will appear. If you think an option should work, double-check that the tablet device is on the tablet and that its driver software is set up correctly.*

Airbrush Wheel lets you control the brush option using the wheel found on an airbrush input device (this is available for some pressure-sensitive tablets).

Initial Direction sets the angle of an option based on the direction in which you first drag the brush.

Direction sets the angle of an option based on the direction the mouse is dragged; the Direction changes as you drag.

TIP If you have a pressure-sensitive graphics tablet, keep an eye out for any Jitter or Scatter attribute you find in the Brushes palette **1**. To have an attribute vary randomly as you paint with a stylus or other tablet device, choose an option from the Control pop-up menu below any Jitter or Scatter attribute. For example, to allow the stylus to control opacity, choose an option from the Control pop-up menu below Opacity Jitter in the Other Dynamics pane.

Variation Options

7.0! Choosing Clear Brush Controls from the Brushes palette menu resets all the brush options to their defaults so you can start over. However, any custom settings that you chose for any presets will be wiped out if you choose this command (or if the current brush library is replaced). Follow these instructions if you want to preserve your customized brushes in a library for future use. Custom brushes that are saved and loaded as a library display as presets on the Brush Preset pane of the Brushes palette. These custom brushes can also be selected and modified at any time, and can be used with any tool.

Note: On page 222, you will learn how to save custom brushes as presets for specific tools (for example, a custom brush, including a Foreground color, for the Brush tool). Instead of saving brushes in a brush library, you will save them in a tool preset library.

To save brush presets in a new library:

1. Make sure Brush Presets is chosen at the top of the Brushes palette, then choose Save Brushes from the palette menu.

2. Enter a Name for the set. Keep the default extension for the brush library (.abr).

3. Choose a location in which to save the set, then click Save (Enter/Return). If you want the new brush library to display at the bottom of the Brushes palette menu, store the library in Adobe Photoshop 7 > Presets > Brushes > Adobe Photoshop Only, then relaunch Photoshop.

Save Brush Presets

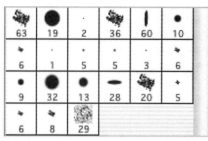

1 *Dry Media Brushes*

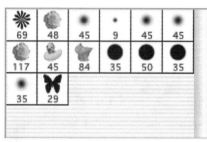

2 *Special Effect Brushes*

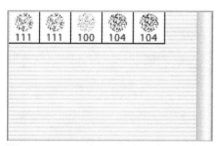

3 *Thick Heavy Brushes*

4 *Wet Media Brushes*

Eleven brush libraries are supplied with Photoshop, in addition to the default brushes. Brushes that were also included in previous versions of Photoshop include Assorted Brushes, Calligraphic Brushes, Drop Shadow Brushes, Faux Finish Brushes, Natural Brushes, Natural Brushes 2, and Square Brushes. The Dry Media, Special Effect Brushes, Thick Heavy Brushes, and Wet Media Brushes are new **1**–**4**. **7.0!**

To load a brush library:

1. Click Brush Presets at the top of the Brushes palette, click the arrowhead in the circle on the right side of the Brushes palette, then choose a brush library name from the lower portion of the menu.

2. Click Append to add the additional brushes to the current picker.
or
Click OK to replace the current brushes on the picker with those in the library.

TIP To append all brushes within a library to the current preset list, choose Load Brushes from the picker menu, locate the library you want to load, then click Load. Use this method to locate and open any brush library that isn't in the default location (either the Adobe Photoshop 7 > Presets > Brushes folder or the Adobe Photoshop Only folder inside the Brushes folder).

The brushes that were on the brush preset picker when you last exit/quit Photoshop will still be there next time you launch Photoshop. Follow these instructions if you want to restore the default set.

To restore the default brushes:

Choose Reset Brushes from the brush preset picker menu or the Brushes palette menu, then click OK.

Load Brush Library; Reset Brushes

7.0! **Customizing brushes**

By turning a brush into a tool preset, you'll preserve it for future use, and you will also be able to access it quickly. The presets you save for a particular brush are listed on the Tool preset picker on the far left side of the options bar when that brush is chosen. To create a variation on an existing brush, make your change, and then save the alteration with an appropriate name as a new tool preset. No brush variation is too minor to be saved this way. Even a color can be saved with a preset.

To make a brush into a tool preset:

1. Create a custom brush.

2. On the options bar, click the Tool Preset picker thumbnail or arrowhead **1**.
or
Display the Tool Presets palette **2**.

3. Check Current Tool Only to have only brush tool presets display. (If unchecked, presets for all tools will display.)

4. Click the "Create new tool preset" button, enter a brush name **3**, check Include Color to have the current Foreground color save with the preset, then click OK. The new tool preset will display on the Tool preset picker and palette (not on the Brushes picker or palette).

7.0! Tool presets can also be saved in a library.

To save the tool presets to a library:

1. From the Tool preset picker menu or the Tool Preset palette menu, choose Save Tool Presets.

2. Enter a name, choose a location for the library, then click OK. If you want the tool preset library to display at the bottom of the preset picker menu or palette menu when you relaunch Photoshop, save the preset file in the Adobe Photoshop 7 > Presets > Tools folder.

TIP Use Load Tool Presets to load in a tool preset library to the palette or picker.

Preview it

To preview a selected brush tool preset, look at the stroke **preview** at the bottom of the Brushes palette.

1 *Click the thumbnail or arrowhead to open the* **Tool Preset** *picker.*

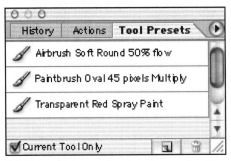

2 *The* **Tool Presets** *palette has the same function as the Tool Preset picker.*

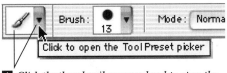

3 *Check* **Include Color** *in the* **New Tool Preset** *dialog box to save the preset with the current Foreground color.*

Create, Save Tool Preset

Walter Robertson

Wendy Grossman

Wendy Grossman

Wendy Grossman

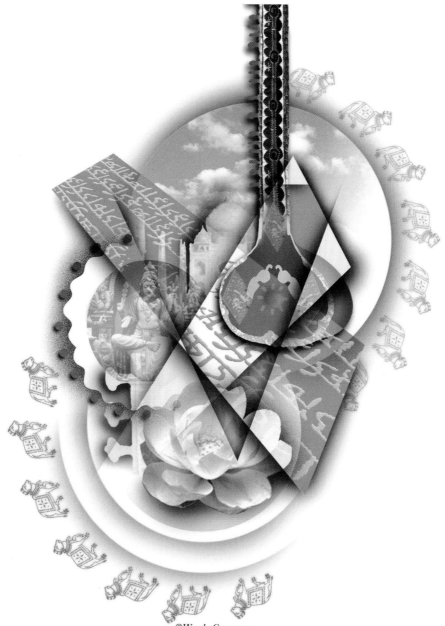

Naomi Shea

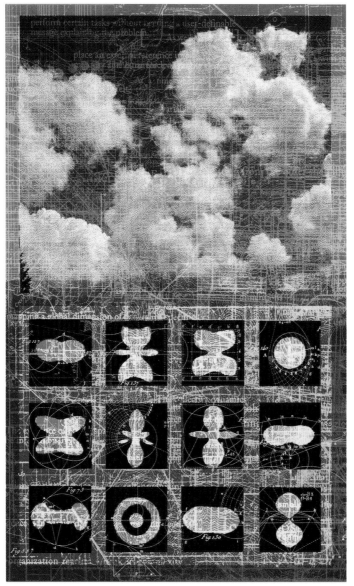

Jeff Brice

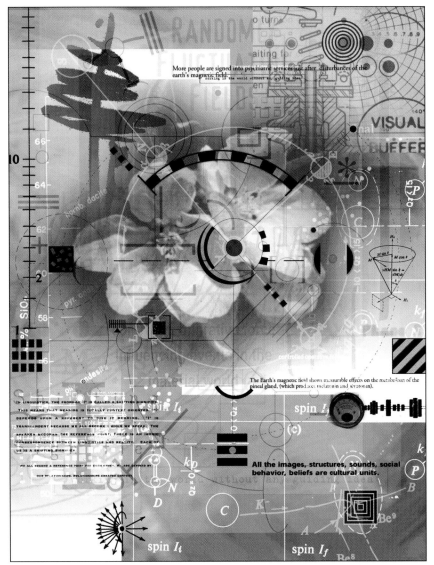

Jeff Brice

Suling Wang

Alicia Buelow

Alicia Buelow

Stephanie Dalton Cowan

Foot leads eye, eye instructs foot, alternatingly.
Walking takes on the movement of soul
because, as the great philosopher Plotinus said,
the soul's motion is not direct

©Stephanie Dalton Cowan

William Cook, a sailor in the US Navy, lies buried at the foot of Monkey Mountain in Vietnam. But he wasn't killed fighting the Viet Cong. He died in 1845, aboard the USS Constitution, during a good-will tour around the world. When the ship put into Da Nang Harbor for food and water, Cook was taken ashore, buried, and all but forgotten – until this year, when a group of Massachusetts veterans set out to find the grave of the first US serviceman buried on Vietnamese soil.

The search for
Seaman
Cook
By Peter Kneisel

1 *The commands for managing brushes that appear on the **preset picker menu**...*

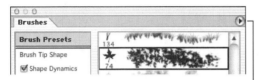

2 *...are also found on the **Brushes palette** menu.*

3 *Select an area of an **image**.*

Brush Name

Name: Zigzagger

4 *Type a **Name** for the new brush.*

5 *A **custom brush** used with the Brush tool at various opacities (Wet Edges checked)*

There are two ways to create a new brush. One way is to use the New Brush command. Or for an entirely different approach, you can use the Define Brush command to create a brush from imagery in an existing file.

If you modify an existing preset, you are actually modifying an unsaved copy of the preset—not the original brush that's in the current library. If you like a brush, you should make a new brush from it and save it to a library so you can use it again.

To create a new brush based on an existing brush:

1. Click the Brush preset picker arrowhead on the options bar, then choose New Brush from the Brush picker menu **1**.
   or
   Choose New Brush from the Brushes palette menu **2**.
   or
   Right-click/Control-click a brush on the Brushes palette, then choose New Brush from the context menu.

2. Type a name for the new brush, then click OK.

3. To customize the brush, follow the steps starting on page 214. The new brush will appear after the last brush on the brush preset picker and on the Brushes palette. To save it to a library, see page 220.

To create a brush from an image:

1. Choose the Rectangular Marquee tool (M or Shift-M).

2. Marquee an area of a picture (maximum 1,000 by 1,000 pixels). Try using a distinct shape on a white background **3**.

3. Choose Edit > Define Brush.

4. Enter a Name for the new brush **4**, then click OK.

5. Deselect the selection (Ctrl-D/Cmd-D), then choose the Brush tool. The new brush will appear after the last brush on the picker **5**. Adjust any of the settings for the brush by using Brushes palette.

Create New Brush

Deleting a brush has no effect on any existing strokes that have been created. (This is the opposite of what could potentially happen if you delete a brush in Adobe Illustrator).

To delete a brush:

On the brush picker, click the brush you want to delete, choose Delete Brush from the picker menu, then click OK.

or

On the Brushes palette, click the brush you want to delete, choose Delete Brush from the palette menu, then click OK.

or

On the Brushes palette or brush preset picker, right-click/Control-click the brush you want to delete, choose Delete Brush from the context menu, then click OK.

TIP To bypass the prompt, Alt-click/Option-click the brush you want to delete. You can't undo this.

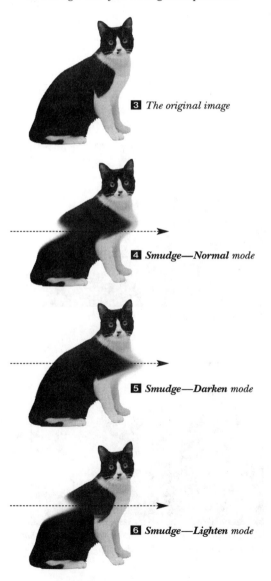

1 *The left side of the* ***Smudge*** *tool options bar*

2 *The right side of the* ***Smudge*** *tool options bar*

3 *The original image*

4 *Smudge—Normal mode*

5 *Smudge—Darken mode*

6 *Smudge—Lighten mode*

Other painting tools

In this section, you'll learn how to use the Smudge, Paint Bucket, Eraser, Background Eraser, and Magic Eraser tools, and the Auto Erase function of the Pencil tool.

To smudge colors:

1. Choose a layer. *Note:* The Smudge tool can't be used on an image in Bitmap or Indexed Color mode.

2. Choose the Smudge tool (R or Shift-R).

3. On the Smudge tool options bar **1**–**2**:

Click the Brush preset picker arrowhead, then click a **brush**; or click a brush on the Brushes palette.
and
Choose a blending **Mode** (see pages 32–36). Try Normal to smudge all shades or colors, Darken to push dark colors into lighter colors, or Lighten to push light colors into darker colors.
and
Move the **Strength** slider below 100%.

4. Check **Use All Layers** on the options bar to start the smudge with colors from all the currently visible layers in the image (uncheck Finger Painting if you use this option). Or uncheck Use All Layers to smudge only with colors from the active layer. In either case, of course, pixels will be smudged only on the currently active layer.

5. To start the smudge with the Foreground color, check **Finger Painting** on the options bar. Uncheck Finger Painting to have the smudge start with the color under the pointer where the stroke begins. The higher the Strength percentage, the more the Foreground color will be applied.

> **TIP** Hold down Alt/Option to toggle the Finger Painting option on/off.

6. Drag across an area of the image **3**–**6**. Pause, if necessary, to allow the screen to redraw.

Smudge Colors

The Paint Bucket tool replaces pixels with the Foreground color or a pattern, and fills areas of a similar shade or color within a specified Tolerance range. You can use the Paint Bucket without creating a selection.

To fill an area using the Paint Bucket:

1. Choose a layer. If you don't want to fill transparent areas on the layer, click the "Lock transparent pixels" button. *Note:* The Paint Bucket tool won't work on an image in Bitmap color mode.

2. Choose the Paint Bucket tool (G or Shift-G). It's on the Gradient tool pop-out menu.

3. On the Paint Bucket options bar –:

Choose Fill: **Foreground** to fill with a solid color. Or choose **Pattern**, then click a pattern on the pattern picker. *and*
Choose a blending **Mode** (press Shift + or Shift - to cycle through the modes). Try Multiply, Soft Light, or Color Burn. *and*
Choose an **Opacity** percentage. *and*
Enter a **Tolerance** value (0–255). The higher the Tolerance, the wider the range of colors the Paint Bucket can fill. Try a low number first. *and*
Check **Anti-aliased** to smooth the edges of the fill area. *and*
Check **Contiguous** to permit only areas that are contiguous to the one you click on to be filled, or uncheck this option to allow non-contiguous areas to be filled. *and*
Check **All Layers** to have the Paint Bucket fill areas on the active layer based on colors the tool detects on all the currently visible layers, instead of just the colors it detects on the current layer.

4. Choose a Foreground color.

5. Click on the image **3**–**4**. As you click, keep an eye on the little black spill in the tool pointer.

Defining a pattern

To apply a pattern using a custom pattern, create a rectangular selection, choose Edit > **Define Pattern**, enter a name, click OK, then deselect. The custom pattern will be the last pattern swatch in the picker.

1 *The left side of the **Paint Bucket** tool options bar*

2 *The right side of the **Paint Bucket** tool options bar*

PHOTO: PAUL PETROFF

3 *The original image*

4 *After clicking with the **Paint Bucket** tool, pixels that fall within the specified Tolerance range are recolored.*

Paint Bucket

1 *The left side of the **Eraser** tool options bar*

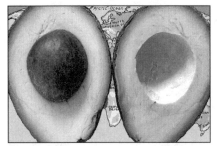

2 *The original image*

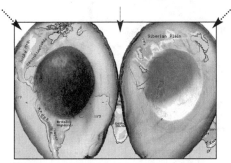

3 *After **erasing** part of the avocados layer to reveal the map underneath it (Airbrush option on, 55% opacity), and erasing part of the map layer to white (Brush option, 100% opacity)*

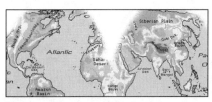

4 *A detail of the **partially erased** map layer*

To erase part of a layer:

1. Choose a layer **2**. If you use the Eraser tool on a layer when the "Lock transparent pixels" button is on or use it on the Background of an image, the erased area will be replaced with the current Background color. If the "Lock transparent pixels" button is off for the layer, the erased area will be replaced with transparency.

2. Choose the Eraser tool (E or Shift-E).

3. On the Eraser tool options bar **1**:

Click the Brush preset picker arrowhead, then click a brush in the picker, or choose a brush from the Brushes palette. *7.0!*
and
Choose Mode: Brush, Pencil, or Block (square eraser)
and
Choose an Opacity percentage.
and
If you chose the Brush mode, you can choose a Flow percentage. The lower *7.0!* the Flow percentage, the rougher the erasure stroke. *7.0!*

4. Click the Airbrush button on or off.

5. If you're going to erase the Background of the image or if "Lock transparent pixels" is on, choose a Background color.

6. Click on or drag across the layer **3**–**4**.

TIP To restore areas on the current layer from a history state, move the History source icon to the desired state on the History palette, then use the Eraser tool with Erase to History checked on the options bar (or Alt-drag/Option-drag to turn on Erase to History temporarily). The Erase to History option won't be available if you added a new layer or changed the number of pixels in (resampled) the file after using the eraser.

Eraser Tool

1 *The **Background Eraser** tool options bar*

The Background Eraser tool erases to transparency or the current Background color by dragging. This tool's strength is that you can control several criteria, such as whether the tool erases contiguous or non-contiguous pixels. By choosing your brush carefully, you can control how large the erasure will be and how soft the edges of the erased area will be.

To use the Background Eraser tool:

1. Choose the Background Eraser tool (it has a scissors icon) (E or Shift-E).

2. To control where the erasure occurs, from the **Limits** pop-up menu on the options bar, choose **1**:

Discontiguous to erase all pixels within the current Tolerance range, whether or not they are next to one another. If you choose this option, also choose Once from the Sampling pop-up menu (see step 5).
or
Contiguous to erase only adjacent pixels within the current Tolerance range that match the first pixel that you click on.
or
Find Edges to erase contiguous pixels, but preserve object edges (high-contrast borders) **2**.

3. Click the Brush tip thumbnail on the options bar to open the pop-up palette, then modify the tip size and/or shape.

4. Choose a **Tolerance** percentage. The higher the Tolerance value, the wider the range of colors similar to the first color clicked on will be erased.

5. From the **Sampling** pop-up menu on the options bar, choose:

Continuous to erase to transparency all the pixels you drag across within the current Tolerance range.

2 *With **Find Edges** chosen from the **Limits** pop-up menu on the **Background Eraser** tool options bar, the tool successfully erased the background area on this image.*

1 *The original image*

Find Edges, Once,
Tolerance 18,
Brush size 45

Contiguous, Once,
Tolerance 40,
Brush size 65

2 *After using the*
Background Eraser *tool with*
various options bar settings

Contiguous, Once,
Tolerance 18,
Brush size 45

Once to erase to transparency only the pixels that closely match the first pixel you drag across. To erase only one color, choose Once and make the Tolerance 1%.

Background Swatch to erase only pixels that match the current Background color. Choose a Background color now. Use a low Tolerance with this option.

6. *Optional:* To protect a particular color from erasure, check Protect Foreground Color and make sure Once is chosen from the Sampling pop-up menu. Make the Foreground color square active on the Color palette, hold down Alt/Option, and then in the image window, click to sample the color that you want to protect. This can be anywhere on the image —background, foreground, whatever.

7. If you're using a pressure-sensitive tablet, you can set the brush size and tolerance to respond to pen pressure. Click the Brush tip thumbnail, then set these options using the pop-up palette.

8. Choose the layer from which you want to erase pixels.

9. Drag across the area of the image that you want to erase **1**–**2**. The active part of the tool is the crosshair.

If you're unhappy with the results, undo or click on an earlier history state, change any of the parameters described in steps 2–5 starting on the previous page, then try again. To widen or narrow the range of colors that the tool erases, change the Tolerance value on the Background Eraser tool options bar.

Background Eraser

7.0!

1 *The **Magic Eraser** tool options bar*

The Magic Eraser tool erases by clicking with the mouse—not by dragging. It erases pixels that are similar in color to the pixel you click on, within a defined Tolerance range. It works like the Paint Bucket tool, except it removes, rather than adds, pixels from a layer. Used with an Opacity setting below 100%, the Magic Eraser tool can be used to make target areas of a layer partially transparent.

To use the Magic Eraser tool:

1. Choose the Magic Eraser tool (E or Shift-E).

2. On the Magic Eraser tool options bar **1**:

Enter a **Tolerance** value. The higher the Tolerance, the wider the range of colors that will be erased. Enter a low Tolerance if you want to erase only colors that are very similar to the color you click on. Enter "0" to erase one color.
and
Check **Anti-aliased** to slightly soften the edges of the erased area.
and
Check **Contiguous** to erase only pixels that are next to one another, or uncheck this option to erase similarly colored pixels throughout the layer **2**–**3** (and **1**, next page).
and
Check **Use All Layers** to have the Magic Eraser tool erase areas on the active layer based on colors the tool detects on all the currently visible layers. With this option unchecked, the tool will detect only the colors on the currently active layer. In either case, only pixels on the currently active layer will be erased.
and
Choose an **Opacity** percentage. Enter 100% to erase to transparency or a lower opacity to erase partially.

2 *The original image*

3 *After clicking on the rightmost leaf, with the **Contiguous** option turned off on the **Magic Eraser** tool options bar*

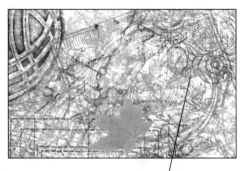

1 *After clicking with the **Magic Eraser** tool on the rightmost leaf in the original image, with the **Contiguous** option turned **on**: The three dark leaves disappear.*

2 *Using the **Pencil** tool with **Auto Erase** checked on the options bar*

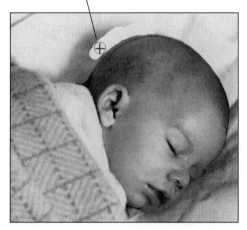

3. Choose the layer from which you want to erase pixels.

4. In the image window, carefully position the tool's crosshair on the area that you want to erase, then click.

If the erasure is too large or too small, undo, change the Tolerance value on the Magic Eraser tool options bar, then try clicking again on the image.

The auto eraser (the Pencil tool with the Auto Erase option, actually) applies the Background color if you start dragging the mouse with the pointer over a Foreground color pixel. The tool paints the Foreground color if you begin dragging with the pointer over any other color.

To auto erase:

1. Choose a Foreground color and a Background color. You can use the Eyedropper tool to sample a color from the image.

2. Choose a layer.

3. Choose the Pencil tool (B or Shift-B).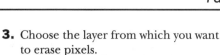

4. Check Auto Erase on the Pencil tool options bar.

5. Draw strokes on the image **2**. Start dragging with the pointer over a Foreground color pixel (if any) to apply the Background color. Start dragging with the pointer over a non-Foreground color pixel to apply the Foreground color.

TIP To make the color under the pointer into the Foreground color when using the Auto Erase function of the Pencil tool, Alt-click/Option-click the color, then drag.

In these "added bonus" instructions, you'll learn a nice technique for applying tints to a grayscale image. By drawing colored strokes on a separate layer, you'll have the flexibility to change the blending mode or opacity for your painting tool or for the color layer, or erase or dodge here or there—all without changing the underlying grayscale image at all.

To apply tints to a grayscale image:

1. Open a Grayscale mode image and convert it to RGB Color mode (Image > Mode > RGB Color).

2. Alt-click/Option-click the "Create new layer" button at the bottom of the Layers palette to add a new layer above the grayscale imagery, choose Mode: Color or Overlay for the new layer, then click OK.

3. Choose the Brush tool (B or Shift-B).

4. Choose a Foreground color.

5. From the Brush tool options bar:

Choose a brush from the brush picker (or from the Brushes palette).
and
Choose an Opacity percentage below 100%. Choose a low opacity for a subtle tint. You can change opacities between strokes. You can also lower the opacity of the whole layer via the Layers palette.
and

7.0! Choose a Flow percentage.
and

Turn on the Airbrush option for a
7.0! simulation of traditional airbrushing.

6. Paint strokes on the new layer ▪.

7. *Optional:* Use the Eraser tool to remove areas of unwanted color, then repaint, if desired. Or use the Dodge tool at a low Exposure percentage to gently lighten the tints.

8. *Optional:* Try a different blending mode for the color layer. Try Multiply, Soft Light, Color Burn, or Color. You can also use the Channel Mixer to apply colors.

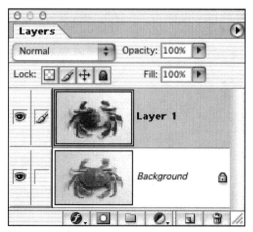

1 *The **color tints** are on Layer 1. The original Background image still looks like it's grayscale (even though the image is now in RGB Color mode).*

GRADIENTS 13

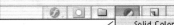

1 *Choose* **Gradient** *from the "Create new fill or adjustment layer" pop-up menu at the bottom of the Layers palette.*

2 *Click the gradient arrowhead, then choose from the* **gradient** *picker.*

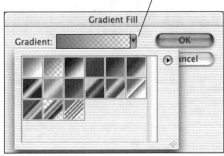

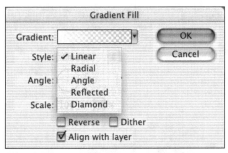

3 *Choose gradient* **Style**, **Angle**, *and* **Scale** *percentages in the* **Gradient Fill** *dialog box.*

4 *The five basic gradient* **Styles**

Linear *gradient*

Radial *gradient*

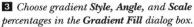

Reflected *gradient*

Angular *gradient*

Diamond *gradient*

A **GRADIENT IS A GRADUAL** blend between two or more colors, and there are two ways to apply one. One way is to use the **Gradient tool** to apply a gradient directly to a content layer. This tool is a good choice if you want to custom fit a gradient by hand in a particular area. You could also use the tool to fill a layer mask in a fill or adjustment layer with a gradient to create a gradual masking effect.

A second option is to use a **gradient fill layer**. A gradient applied using this feature appears in its own layer, with a layer mask that can be used to mask gradient layer pixels. This type of gradient is easier to edit.

To apply a gradient as a fill layer:

1. Choose a layer. The Gradient tool can't be used on an image in Bitmap or Indexed Color mode.

2. *Optional:* Select an area of a layer to limit the gradient fill to that area (see also the sidebar on the next page). Otherwise, the gradient will fill the entire layer.

3. Choose Gradient from the "Create new fill or adjustment layer" pop-up menu  at the bottom of the Layers palette, **1**.

4. Click the gradient arrowhead at the top of the dialog box, choose a preset gradient from the picker, then click back in the dialog box **2**.

5. Choose a gradient **Style**: Linear, Radial, Angular, Reflected, or Diamond **3**–**4**. *and*

(Continued on the following page)

Gradient Fill Layer

Choose an **Angle** by moving the dial or by entering a value.

and

Use the **Scale** slider to scale the gradient relative to the layer. The higher the scale value, the more gradual the transition between gradient colors.

6. *Optional:* Drag in the image window to reposition the gradient in the image. Cool!

7. Do any of the following:

Check/uncheck **Reverse** to reverse the order of colors in the gradient.

Check **Dither** to minimize banding (stripes) in the gradient.

Check **Align with layer** to have the length of the gradient fill be calculated based on visible pixels on the layer or a selection on the layer. Or uncheck this option to have the gradient stretch across the whole layer, whether or not the layer contains transparent pixels or a selection is present.

8. Click OK.

9. *Optional:* Use the Layers palette to change the gradient fill layer's opacity or blending mode. You can get some beautiful effects this way. If the layer imagery has transparent edges, double-clicking a layer opens the Layer Style dialog box, which you can use to apply an effect to the layer.

Note: To adjust any of the gradient settings, double-click the gradient fill layer thumbnail—the Gradient Fill dialog box reopens. This is what we meant before when we said this method offers the most flexibility.

TIP To hide a gradient fill layer, click the eye icon for the layer. To delete a gradient fill layer, drag it over the "Delete layer" (trash) button.

Mask a gradient fill

If you create a selection before creating a gradient fill layer, the gradient will be limited to the selection area. The former selection will be displayed as a white area within the gradient fill layer mask **1**–**2**.

To limit a gradient fill any time after a fill layer is created, click the layer mask thumbnail and paint on the layer mask.

Gradient fill thumbnail 　　**1** *A **mask** on the **gradient fill** layer limits the fill effect.*

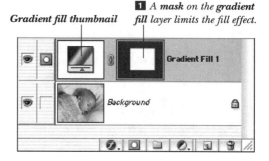

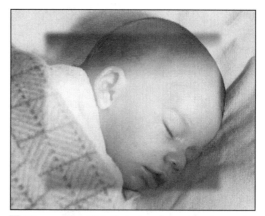

2 *The **gradient fill** is limited to the rectangular **mask**. We chose **Hard Light** blending mode for the gradient layer.*

Gradient Fill Layer

1 *The left side of the **Gradient** tool options bar*

2 *The right side of the **Gradient** tool options bar*

3 *This is after dragging the Gradient tool from the middle to the right. This is a **Linear** gradient.*

4 *This is after dragging the Gradient tool a **short** distance in the middle using the same colors. The transitions are more abrupt.*

5 *The **gradient tool** was used in different directions to fill a rasterized type layer (with the **Lock transparent pixels** button clicked).*

Use the Gradient tool if you want to apply a gradient by dragging. Each time you drag with this tool, an additional gradient is applied. Any additional gradient that you create at less than 100% opacity will only partially cover over the existing one(s). Unlike a gradient fill layer, once this type of gradient is applied, it can't be edited easily.

To apply a gradient using the Gradient tool:

1. Choose a layer or create a new layer.

2. *Optional:* Select an area of a layer. Otherwise, the gradient will fill the entire layer.

3. Choose the Gradient tool (it shares a pop-out menu with the Paint Bucket tool) (G or Shift-G).

4. On the Gradient tool options bar **1**–**2**:

Click the gradient picker arrowhead, then click a gradient preset.
and
Click a gradient style button: Linear, Radial, Angular, Reflected, or Diamond.
and
Choose a blending Mode.
and
Choose an Opacity.

5. *Do any of these optional steps:*

Check Reverse to reverse the order of colors in the gradient.

Check Dither to minimize banding (stripes) in the gradient.

Check Transparency to enable any transparency that was edited into the gradient (see page 239).

6. For a linear gradient, drag from one side or corner of the image (or selection) to the other. For any other gradient style, drag from a center point outward. Shift-drag to constrain the gradient to a multiple of 45°. To delete a Gradient tool fill, remove its state from the History palette.

Drag a long distance to produce a subtle transition area or drag a short distance to produce an abrupt transition **3**–**5**. This works like the Scale slider in the Gradient Fill dialog box.

Gradient Tool

When you revise or delete a preset swatch, the actual gradient in the current gradient library isn't affected; you'll automatically be working on or deleting a copy of the preset.

To create or edit a gradient preset:

1. *Optional:* Open the Swatches palette if you're going to use it to choose colors for the gradient, and move it to the corner of your screen. Weirdly enough, you won't be able to move it around once the Gradient Editor is open.

2. Choose the Gradient tool (G or Shift-G), then click the Gradient sample **1** on the options bar to open the Gradient Editor.
or
Double-click an existing Gradient Fill layer thumbnail on the Layers palette, then click the gradient sample at the top of the Gradient Fill dialog box.

3. In the Gradient Editor, click the Presets swatch you want to create a variation of.

4. To choose a starting color, click the starting (left) color stop under the gradient bar **2**.

5. Click a color on the Swatches palette that you so conveniently stuck in a corner, or on the spectrum bar at the bottom of the Color palette, or in any open image window.
or
To create a gradient that will use the current Foreground or Background color, choose Foreground or Background from the Color pop-up menu at the bottom of the dialog box.
or
Click the Color swatch at the bottom of the Gradient Editor, choose a color from the Color Picker, then click OK.

6. Click the ending (right) color stop under the gradient bar to set the ending color, then repeat the previous step.

7. *Do any of these optional steps:*
To **add** an intermediate color to the gradient, click below the gradient bar to produce a new stop, then choose a

1 *Click the gradient **sample** to open the Gradient Editor.*

2 *Starting color stop*

Starting opacity stop
Intermediate opacity stop   Ending opacity stop

Color swatch   Midpoint diamond   Intermediate color

Ending color stop

Create or Edit a Gradient Preset

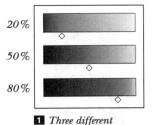

20%

50%

80%

1 *Three different* **Location** *settings*

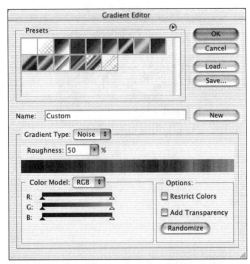

2 *Here's another option. From the* **Gradient Type** *pop-up, choose* **Noise** *to create a gradient composed of randomly chosen colors within the color range and* **Roughness** *you specify. The lower the* **Roughness**, *the smoother the color transitions. Choose a* **Color Model** *for the sliders, then move the sliders to define the color range.*

color for the new stop, as per step 5 on the previous page.

Move any color stop by dragging it or by changing its **Location** value.

To control the **abruptness** of a color transition, drag a midpoint diamond. The diamond marks the point where the two colors it's between are evenly blended (50% of each color). Clicking the diamond, then changing its Location percentage does the same thing **1**. 0% is for the far left, 100% is for the far right.

To **remove** a color, drag its stop downward off the bar.

Use Ctrl-Z/Cmd-Z to undo the previous operation.

8. Enter a name in the Name field, then click New. (Any time you edit a gradient, the Name changes to "Custom" automatically to ensure that you'll be working on a copy of the gradient—not the original.)

9. Click OK. The new gradient preset is now available for use on the gradient picker.

To save the presets currently on the gradient picker to a file for future use, see the instructions on the following page!

TIP To rename a gradient swatch, double-click it in the Gradient Editor, change the Name, then click OK.

TIP To delete a preset, Alt-click/Option-click on it in the Gradient Editor.

Create or Edit a Gradient Preset

To save the current gradients to a file:

1. To open the Gradient Editor, choose the Gradient tool, then click the Gradient sample on the options bar. Or double-click an existing Gradient Fill layer thumbnail on the Layers palette, then click the gradient sample at the top of the Gradient Fill dialog box.

2. Click Save, enter a name (keep the .grd extension), leave the default location as is (in Windows: Program Files > Adobe > Photoshop 7.0 > Presets > Gradients; in the Mac OS: Applications > Adobe Photoshop 7 > Presets > Gradients), then click Save. All the gradients currently displayed in the Presets panel will be saved to that separate file, and that file name will appear on the gradient picker menu after you relaunch Photoshop. (Read about the Preset Manager on pages 404–406.)

3. Click OK.

To use alternate gradient libraries:

1. Open the Gradient Editor (see step 1 in the previous set of instructions).
   or
   Click the gradient arrowhead to open the gradient picker.

2. Click the arrowhead in the circle at the top of the palette, then choose a gradient library from the bottom of the picker menu **1**. Custom libraries saved as per the previous set of instructions on this page will appear on this menu below the Adobe Photoshop default libraries.

3. Click Append to add the selected library to the bottom of the current presets.
   or
   Click OK to replace the current presets with the gradient library you've chosen.

Wendy Grossman combined Photoshop gradients and Illustrator patterns to produce this **Guitar with Wine** *image.*

1 *Choose an alternate* **gradient library** *from the bottom of the pop-up menu in the* **Gradient Editor**.

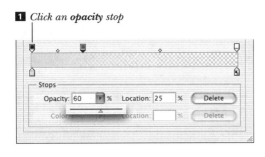

1 *Click an opacity stop*

2 *Two gradients, on separate layers, were applied to this image. The middle of the gradients fade to a 20% opacity to allow the balloons on an underlying layer to peek through.*

To restore the default gradients:

Click the arrowhead in the circle in the Gradient Editor or on the gradient picker, choose Reset Gradients, then click OK. Any newly created or newly modified presets will be removed!

To change the opacity of gradient colors:

1. Open the Gradient Editor, then click the gradient swatch you want to edit.

2. Click an opacity stop, located above the gradient bar **1**.

3. Choose an Opacity percentage (you can enter a percentage or use the slider). Look at the gradient bar to see a preview of the transparency effect.

4. *Do any of the following optional steps:*

To add other opacity level stops, click just above the gradient bar, then choose an opacity percentage for each one.

To delete a stop, drag it upward off the bar.

To move a stop, drag it or change its Location percentage.

To adjust the location of the opacity midpoint, drag one of the diamonds above the transparency bar or click a diamond, then change the Location percentage.

5. Enter a Name, then click New.

6. Click OK **2**. The exercise on the following page uses semi-transparent gradients on different layers.

To create a multicolor wash:

1. Choose a layer.

2. *Optional:* Select an area of a layer.

3. Choose Gradient from the "Create new fill or adjustment layer" pop-up menu ⬤, at the bottom of the Layers palette.

4. In the Gradient Fill dialog box, click the gradient sample to open the Gradient Editor.

5. In the Gradient Editor, either choose an existing gradient preset that finishes with transparency or create a new gradient that fades to (finishes with) transparency, then click OK.

6. Choose a Style, Angle, and Scale for the gradient fill layer, then click OK.

7. Create another gradient fill layer, then repeat steps 4 and 5. Try out different Style, Angle, and Scale settings, or drag the gradient in the image window **1**–**2**.

8. *Optional:* Using the Layers palette, change the opacity or blending mode for, or restack, the gradient fill layers.

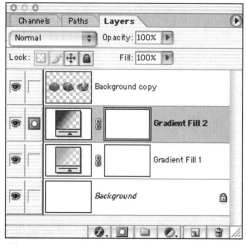

1 *You can create a painterly effect by placing translucent gradient washes on separate **layers**.*

2 *A diamond gradient and a linear gradient*

Multicolor Wash

240

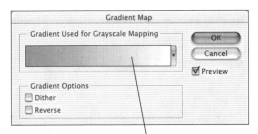

1 *Click the gradient* **thumbnail** *in the* **Gradient Map** *dialog box.*

The Gradient Map command applies (maps) a gradient based on luminosity levels (lights and darks) in the layer below it. This command can be used to colorize a grayscale image or re-render a color image in new tonalities, and the result can be anything from subtle to Day-Glo. If you apply the Gradient Map via an adjustment layer, it will be fully reeditable.

The starting (left) color of the selected gradient is applied to the shadow areas of the layer. The ending (right) color of the gradient is applied to the highlight areas of the layer. Any color stops that are added to the gradient are applied to the midtone areas of the layer. The number of color transitions in the resulting layer will be based on the number of color stops in the selected gradient.

To apply a gradient map to a layer:

1. Choose a layer.

2. Choose Gradient Map from the "Create new fill or adjustment layer" pop-up menu ⊘, at the bottom of the Layers palette.

You can also apply the gradient map directly to a layer by choosing Image > Adjustments > Gradient Map, but we prefer the adjustment layer approach because it offers more flexibility. A gradient map that is applied directly to an image layer can't be reedited or removed.

3. Click the Gradient arrowhead to open the gradient picker, then click a preset gradient.

4. Click the gradient thumbnail **1** to open the Gradient Editor.

5. *Do any of the following optional steps:*

Change the starting and/or ending stop **colors**.

Add more color stops to the middle of the gradient ramp to add color to the midtone areas of the image. For example, if your gradient contains four

(Continued on the following page)

color stops, the layer will contain four major color transition areas.

Move any of the color stops to change the distribution of colors within the layer's tonal range

6. Click OK.

7. *Optional:* Check Dither to have random noise be added to color transitions in the layer to help prevent color banding.

8. *Optional:* Check Reverse to reverse the direction of the gradient colors. This will reverse the color distribution in the layer.

9. Click OK **1**–**3**.

To reedit a gradient map at any time, double-click the gradient map layer thumbnail on the Layers palette.

TIP To heighten the contrast in the colors produced from a gradient map adjustment layer, create an adjustment layer > Posterize command using four, five, or six levels, then restack the posterize layer between the image layer and the gradient map layer.

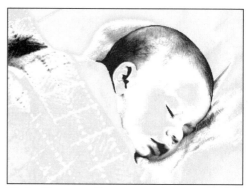

1 *Gradient map* effect

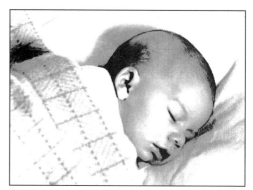

2 *Gradient map* effect

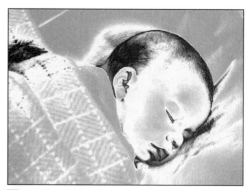

3 *Gradient map* effect

Gradient Map

N THIS CHAPTER, you will learn about Photoshop's intermediate and advanced layers features. Be sure to read Chapter 7, Layers first, though, to learn about basic layer operations. (Adjustment layers are discussed on pages 166–169.)

Layer opacity

To change a layer's opacity or fill: 7.0!

Choose an Opacity or Fill percentage from the Layers palette **1**. The lower the Opacity or Fill, the more pixels from the layer below will show through the active layer **2**–**3**. You can't change the Opacity or Fill of the Background.

or

Choose a tool other than a painting tool, then press 1 on the keyboard to change the opacity of an active layer to 10%, 2 to change the Opacity to 20%, and so on. Or type both digits quickly (e.g., 15, for 15%). *Mac OS:* Hold down Shift using the above method to change the Fill of the active layer.

Note: The Fill percentage changes the opacity of user-created pixels or shapes, but not the opacity of layer effects.

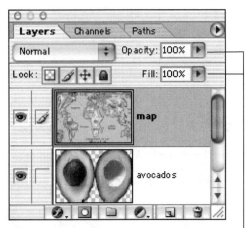

1 *Each layer can have a different* **Opacity** *and/or* **Fill** *percentage.*

Layer Opacity

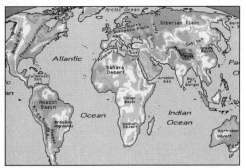

2 *The map layer, 100% Opacity, on top of the avocados layer*

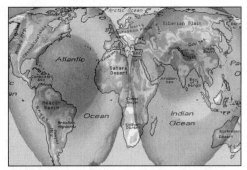

3 *The map layer opacity reduced to 50%*

Layer effects

Applying layer effects

The special effects that can be applied to a layer are as follows **1**: Drop Shadow, Inner Shadow, Outer Glow, Inner Glow, Bevel and Emboss, Satin, Color Overlay, Gradient Overlay, Pattern Overlay, and Stroke. A layer effect (or effects) can be applied to any layer, even an editable type layer, and it can be turned on or off at any time. Layer effects automatically affect all the visible pixels on a layer, and will update if pixels are added, modified, or deleted from the layer.

TIP Don't confuse styles with effects. A style is simply a combination of one or more layer effects.

Effects are applied and edited from one central, chock-full dialog box—the **Layer Style** dialog box **2**—and they are displayed on the Layers palette as indented (nested) layers below the name of the layer to which they're applied. Effects are attached to, and move with, the main layer that they're applied to. Layer effects can't be applied to the Background of an image.

Before we get into specific effects, here are some general pointers:

■ To **apply** an effect to a layer, double-click the layer (or for an image layer—not a type layer—you can double-click the thumbnail). In the Layer Style dialog

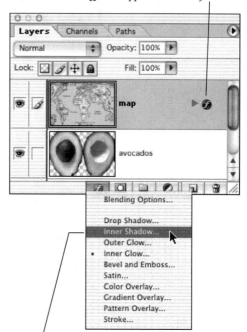

*The "f" icon indicates that a **layer effect** is applied to that layer.*

1 *Choose an effect name from the **Add layer style** pop-up menu. A bullet next to an effect signifies that that effect is currently applied to the active layer. The same effects can also be chosen from the* **Layer > Layer Style** *submenu.*

2 *The **Layer Style** dialog box is used to choose settings for layer effects.*

Copying effects from layer to layer

Click the layer that contains the effect or effects you want to copy, right-click/Ctrl-click and choose **Copy Layer Style**, choose another layer, then right-click/Ctrl-click and choose **Paste Layer Style**.

or

Expand the effects list for a layer, then **drag** an individual **effect name** over another layer name or over another layer's Effects bar.

or

To copy multiple effects from one layer to another, expand the effects list for a layer, then **drag** the **Effects bar** over another layer or another layer's Effects bar. In this case, the duplicated effect(s) will replace any existing effects on the destination layer.

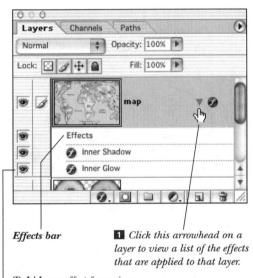

Effects bar

1 *Click this arrowhead on a layer to view a list of the effects that are applied to that layer.*

To hide an effect from view temporarily, click the eye icon.

box, click an effect name (don't just click the check box!), and choose settings for the effect. More than one effect can be applied to the same layer. Check **Preview** to preview the effect in the image window. You can also apply an effect by choosing a layer, and then choosing an effect from the **Add layer style** pop-up menu at the bottom of the Layers palette.

■ On the Layers palette, any layer to which a layer effect is currently applied will have an 🅕 icon. Click the arrowhead next to the 🅕 to view a list of the effects that are applied to that layer **1**. Each effect has its own hide/show (eye) icon.

■ To **edit** an existing layer effect (or add another one), double-click the 🅕; or double-click the effect name nested under the layer name; or choose an effect from the 🅕 (Add layer style) pop-up menu at the bottom of the Layers palette.

■ To **hide** a layer effect, expand the effects list for the layer in question, then click the eye icon for the effect you want to hide. (Click again in the same spot to redisplay the effect.)

To temporarily **hide all** effects from all layers and speed performance, choose Layer > Layer Style > Hide All Effects. Choose Show All Effects to redisplay them.

TIP If you recheck an effect that was turned off or deleted, the last-used options for that effect will redisplay.

TIP Alt/Option-click Reset to restore the Layer Style dialog box to the settings it had when it was opened.

To remove an individual layer effect:

Double-click a layer or an individual effect name on the Layers palette, then uncheck the box next to the effect name.

or

Drag an individual effect name over the Delete Layer (trash) button at the bottom of the Layers palette.

Remove Layer Effect

To apply the Drop Shadow or Inner Shadow effect:

1. Double-click a layer.

2. Click Drop Shadow or Inner Shadow.

3. Change any of the following settings: **1**

Choose a **Blend Mode** from the pop-up menu.

To choose a different **shadow color**, click the color swatch, choose a color from the Color Picker (the new color will preview immediately), then click OK.

Choose an **Opacity** percentage for the transparency of the shadow.

Choose an **Angle** for the angle of the shadow relative to the original layer shapes. Check Use Global Light to use the angle that was entered in the Layer > Layer Style > Global Light dialog box. Uncheck this option if you want to use a unique angle setting for this particular effect. *Note:* If you readjust the Angle for an individual effect while Use Global Angle is checked, all effects that utilize the Global Angle option will also be modified. This option makes the lighting in multiple layer effects look more uniform.

Choose a **Distance** for the distance (in pixels) of the drop shadow from the original layer shapes, or for the width of an inner shadow **2**–**3**. We usually like to increase the Distance a bit.

TIP You can drag the actual shadow in the image window while the dialog box is open, but this will also move all effects that use the Global Light option.

Choose a **Spread** (mask enlargement width, before blurring) for the shadow. For Inner Shadow, choose a **Choke** (mask reduction) value for the shadow.

Choose a **Size** for the shadow.

In the Quality section, click the arrowhead, then choose a preset **Contour** from the Contour picker for the edge

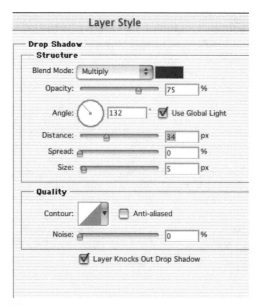

1 *Choose settings in the **Drop Shadow** or **Inner Shadow** pane of the **Layer Style** dialog box.*

2 *Drop Shadow*

3 *Inner Shadow (with a drop shadow, too)*

1 *The original layer with a **Drop Shadow***

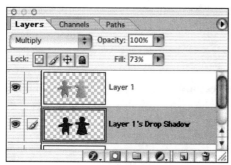

2 *Choosing the new **Drop Shadow** layer*

3 *Distorting the Drop Shadow*

4 *The final image*

profile of the shadow (see also page 252). The profiles can change the shadow dramatically.

Check **Anti-aliased** to soften the jagged edges between the shadow and other parts of the image.

Set the **Noise** level to adjust the amount of speckling in the shadow.

Check **Layer Knocks Out Drop Shadow** to prevent the shadow from showing through any layer pixels that have a low fill opacity.

4. Click OK.

To transform a Drop Shadow effect:

1. Apply the Drop Shadow effect (instructions on the previous page) **1**, and keep the layer selected.

2. Choose Layer > Layer Style > Create Layer to transfer the shadow effect to its own layer.

3. Click the new shadow layer **2**.

4. Choose Edit > Transform > Distort, drag the handles of the bounding box to achieve the desired shape, then press Enter/Return **3**–**4**.

5. *Optional:* Change the luminosity of the shadow via an adjustment layer, or choose a different blending mode or opacity for the shadow layer. Click the "Lock transparent pixels" button ▦ on the Layers palette to limit any painting or fill changes to just the shadow shape.

TIP Link the shadow layer and its original object layer to move them in unison.

Transform Drop Shadow

Note: To use a type mask selection for these steps, save the active selection to a channel first, and then load the channel as a selection. You can save any active selection as a channel for later use.

To create a drop shadow without using an effect:

1. Create a selection to become the shadow shape. To select a silhouetted object, Ctrl-click/Cmd-click the object's layer.

2. Choose Select > Feather (Ctrl-Alt-D/ Cmd-Option-D), enter a Feather Radius above zero, then click OK.

3. Choose Select > Transform Selection or right-click/Ctrl-click and choose Transform Selection from the context menu, transform and/or move the selection marquee, then press Enter/Return.

4. Click the "Create new layer button" 🖿 at the bottom of the Layers palette, then restack the new layer directly below the layer that contains the silhouetted object.

5. Choose Edit > Fill; choose Fill: Black, Mode: Normal or Multiply, and Opacity: 75%; click OK; then deselect (Ctrl-D/ Cmd-D).

6. Choose the Move tool (V), then move the shadow layer to the desired position. You can also change its blending mode or opacity.

To apply an Outer or Inner Glow effect:

1. Display the Swatches palette.

2. Double-click a layer.

3. Click Outer Glow or Inner Glow.

4. Choose **Structure** settings **1**:

   Choose a **Blend Mode** (see "Blending modes" on pages 32–36).

   Choose an **Opacity** for the transparency level of the glow.

   Set the **Noise** level for the amount of speckling in the glow.

   To change the glow **color**, click the color square in the Structure area, choose a

1 *Choose Structure, Elements, and Quality settings for an* **Inner Glow** *effect in the* **Layer Style** *dialog box.*

1 *Inner Glow (Center) (with a Drop Shadow, too)*

2 *Outer Glow*

color from the Color Picker (or while the Picker is open, from the Swatches palette). Choose a color that contrasts with the background color. It might be hard to see a light Outer Glow color against a light background color. The new color will preview on the image. Click OK.

or

To create a glow with a **gradient**, click the arrowhead to choose a gradient from the Gradient picker; or click the gradient thumbnail to edit one of the presets or create a new gradient (see page 236–237).

5. Choose **Elements** settings:

Choose Softer or Precise from the **Technique** pop-up menu to control how closely the mask follows the contours of areas that contain pixels.

For an Inner Glow, click **Center** to create a glow that spreads outward from the center of the layer pixels **1**. (Suggestion: Try this on type.) Click **Edge** to create a glow that spreads inward from the inside edges of the layer pixels.

For Outer Glow, set the **Spread** to define the width of the glow (a mask, actually) before it starts to blur **2**.

For Inner Glow, adjust the **Choke** to define the width of the glow before it starts to blur.

Choose a **Size** for the glow.

6. Choose **Quality** settings:

Click the arrowhead to choose a preset **Contour** from the Contour picker for the edge profile of the glow (see page 252).

Set the **Range** to control the placement of the contour along the width of the glow.

If the glow contains a gradient, set the **Jitter** to randomize the distribution of colors in the gradient.

7. Click OK.

TIP To apply a layer effect to type, make the type large, and don't track it tightly.

Outer or Inner Glow

The Bevel and Emboss command creates an illusion of depth by adding a highlight and a shadow to layer shapes.

To apply the Bevel or Emboss effect:

1. Display the Swatches palette.

2. Double-click a layer on the Layers palette. It can be a type layer.

3. Click Bevel and Emboss.

4. Choose **Structure** settings **1**:

Choose a **Style**: Outer Bevel **2**, Inner Bevel **3**, Emboss, Pillow Emboss (**1**–**2** next page), or Stroke Emboss.

From the **Technique** pop-up menu, choose Smooth, Chisel Hard, or Chisel Soft.

Choose a **Depth** for the amount the highlight and shadow are offset from the layer shapes.

Click the **Up** or **Down** button to switch the highlight and shadow positions.

Choose a **Size** for the bevel or emboss effect.

Raise the **Soften** value to soften the shadows and highlights along the edge.

5. Choose **Shading** settings:

Choose an **Angle** and an **Altitude** to change the location of the the light source. These settings will in turn affect the highlight and shadow. Check Use Global Light to use the current Angle and Altitude settings from the Layer > Layer Style > Global Light dialog box. Or uncheck this option to use a unique setting for this particular style. *Beware!* If you readjust an individual style's Angle or Altitude while Use Global Light is checked, all other styles that utilize the Global Light option will update, too.

Click the **Gloss Contour** arrowhead, then choose from the Contour picker (see page 252).

Choose a **Highlight Mode** and **Opacity** and a **Shadow Mode** and **Opacity** for

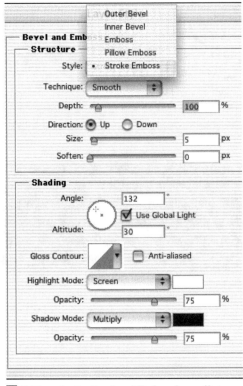

1 *Settings for the **Bevel and Emboss** layer effect*

2 *Outer Bevel*

3 *Inner Bevel (with a Drop Shadow, too)*

Bevel and Emboss

1 *Emboss*

2 *Pillow Emboss*

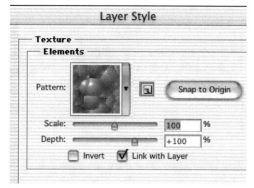

3 *The* **Texture** *options for the* **Bevel and Emboss** *layer effect*

4 *Adobe's Tie Dye* **texture** *used with the* **Bevel and Emboss** *layer effect (Style: Emboss)*

image highlight and shadow areas (see "Blending modes" on pages 32–36).

To change the highlight or shadow **color**, click either color swatch, then choose a color from the Color Picker (or, while the Picker is open, you can also choose from the Swatches palette). The color will preview on the image. Click OK.

6. To add a **Contour** to the edges of the bevel or emboss, click Contour at the left side of the dialog box, under Bevel and Emboss. Click the Contour arrowhead, then click a preset contour in the picker (see page 252). This can dramatically change the appearance of the effect.

Set the **Range** to determine the placement of the contour along the width of the glow. The Range option has no effect on the Emboss effect.

Check **Anti-aliased** to soften the hard edges between adjoining areas.

7. To add a texture to a bevel or emboss, click **Texture** at the left side of the dialog box, click the Texture arrowhead, choose a pattern from the picker, then do any of the following **3**–**4**:

Adjust the **Scale** of the pattern.

Change the **Depth** to adjust the contrast of shadows and highlights in the pattern.

Check **Invert** to flip the shadows and highlights. This has the same effect as changing the Depth percentage from negative to positive, or vice versa.

Check **Link with Layer** to ensure that the texture and the layer move in unison.

Drag in the image window to reposition the texture within the effect. Click **Snap to Origin** to realign the pattern to the upper-left corner of the image.

If you've loaded in a custom pattern, click the "Create new preset" button to add it to the presets.

8. Click OK.

For all the layer effects except the Overlay effects and the Stroke effect, you can choose an edge style, called a contour. The contours control such elements as the fade on a drop shadow or a highlight on a bevel. Follow these steps if you want to modify the contour for an effect.

To change the profile of a contour:

1. Double-click a layer or an effect name to open the Layer Style dialog box. For the Bevel and Emboss effect only, also click Contour at the left side of the dialog box.

2. Click the Contour thumbnail (not the arrowhead).

3. *Optional:* In the Contour Editor, choose a preset contour from the Preset pop-up menu to use as a starting point **2**.

4. Click on the graph to add points. Drag points to adjust the graph. To delete a point, drag it off the graph. The name "Custom" will automatically appear on the Preset pop-up menu.

   Check Corner to convert the currently selected point into a corner point.

5. To save the custom graph as a preset contour, click New, enter a name, then click OK. The custom contour will be listed on the Contour picker.

6. To save the custom graph as a file for reuse, click Save, enter a file name, then click Save again. Click Load to retrieve it.

7. Click OK to close the Contour Editor.

TIP To delete a contour, open the Contour picker, Alt-click/Option-click the contour you want to delete, then close the picker. *Note:* The contour will be deleted only from the current picker—not from the actual preset library.

TIP To restore the default contour library, open the Contour picker, choose Reset Contours from the Contour picker menu, then click OK. To open a different library, choose a library name from the bottom of the Contour picker menu (click Append, or click OK to replace).

Pick from the picker

The profile thumbnails in the **Contour** picker illustrate different edge styles **1**. The gray areas in the profile represent opaque pixels; the white areas represent transparency. To close the picker, click the Contour arrowhead or click somewhere outside the picker in the Layer Style dialog box.

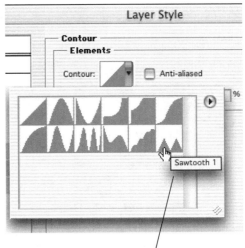

1 *You can use tool tips to learn the **names** of the various contours in the **Contour** picker.*

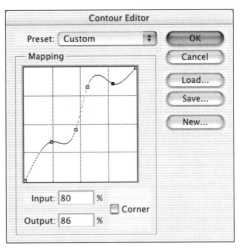

2 *Customize a contour using the **Contour Editor**.*

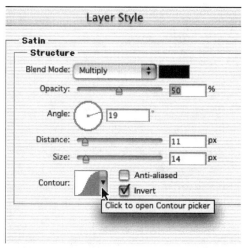

1 *Options for the **Satin** layer effect*

2 *The **Satin** layer effect applied to editable type*

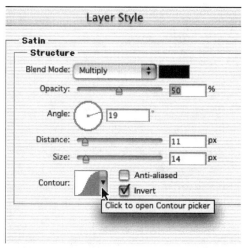

3 *The **Satin** layer effect (**Invert** unchecked)*

To apply the Satin effect :

1. Double-click a layer on the Layers palette.

2. Click Satin.

3. Do any of the following **1**:

Change the Blend Mode (see "Blending Modes" on pages 32–36).

To change the overlay color, click the color swatch, then choose a color from the color picker.

Adjust the Opacity of the effect.

Change the Angle of the effect. This angle is independent of the Global Light settings.

Set the Distance and the Size of the effect. You can also drag in the image window to adjust the distance.

Click the Contour arrowhead, then choose from the Contour picker for the edge profile of the effect.

Check Anti-aliased to soften the hard boundary between the effect and the underlying shape.

Check Invert to swap the shadows and highlights.

4. Click OK **2**–**3**.

Satin

To apply the Color Overlay effect :

1. Double-click a layer on the Layers palette.

2. Click Color Overlay.

3. Do any of the following **1**:

Choose a Blend Mode.

Click the color swatch, then choose a different color for the overlay.

Adjust the Opacity of the overlay.

4. Click OK.

To apply the Gradient Overlay effect:

1. Double-click the layer on the Layers palette.

2. Click Gradient Overlay.

3. Do any of the following **2**:

Choose a **Blend Mode**.

Adjust the **Opacity** of the overlay.

Click the **Gradient** arrowhead, then choose a preset gradient from the Gradient picker.

Check **Reverse** to change the direction of the gradient.

Choose a **Style** (Linear, Radial, Angle, Reflected, or Diamond).

Check **Align with Layer** to align the gradient with the shapes in the layer.

Set the **Angle** of the gradient.

Choose a **Scale** percentage for the placement of the midpoint of the gradient.

You can also drag in the image window to reposition the gradient.

4. Click OK **3**. Read more about gradients on page 233.

Layer Style

Color Overlay

Color

Blend Mode: Normal

Opacity: 50 %

1 *Options for the Color Overlay layer effect*

Layer Style

Gradient Overlay

Gradient

Blend Mode: Normal

Opacity: 100 %

Gradient: ☑ Reverse

Style: Reflected ☑ Align with Layer

Angle: 90 °

Scale: 100 %

2 *Options for the Gradient Overlay layer effect*

3 *Gradient Overlay (Style: Reflected, Reversed)*

1 *Options for the **Pattern Overlay** layer effect*

2 *The **Pattern Overlay** effect applied to a shape layer object*

To apply the Pattern Overlay effect:

1. Double-click a layer on the Layers palette.

2. Click Pattern Overlay.

3. Do any of the following **1**:

Choose a Blend Mode.

Adjust the Opacity of the overlay.

Click the Pattern arrowhead, then choose a preset pattern from the picker.

Click Snap to Origin to align the pattern with the upper-left corner of the image. You can also drag in the image window to reposition the pattern.

Choose a Scale percentage for the pattern.

Check Link with Layer to link the pattern to the layer.

If you have loaded in a custom pattern, click the "Create new preset" button 🖫 to add it to the presets.

4. Click OK **2**.

To apply a Stroke effect:

1. Double-click a layer on the Layers palette.

2. Click Stroke.

3. Do any of the following **1**:

Choose a Size (width) for the stroke.

From the Position pop-up menu, choose whether you want the stroke to be Outside, Inside, or Centered on the edges of shapes in the layer.

Choose a Blend Mode.

Choose an Opacity percentage.

Choose a Fill Type (Color, Gradient, or Pattern), and specify its details using the controls that become available. See Color Overlay and Gradient Overlay information on page 254, or Pattern Overlay information on page 255.

4. Click OK **2**.

1 *Options for the **Stroke** layer effect*

2 *The **Stroke** effect applied to a shape layer object*

Stroke

*Right-click/Ctrl-click a layer's **effects icon** and choose an effects command.*

Other effects commands

The effects commands that are discussed in this section can be accessed either by right-clicking/Ctrl-clicking an existing effects icon 🗌 for a layer on the Layers palette or via Layer > Layer Style.

Copy Layer Style copies all effects from a selected layer so they can be pasted into another layer.

Paste Layer Style pastes effects onto the current layer in the same document or in a different document; **Paste Layer Style to Linked** [layers] pastes effects onto any layers that are linked to the currently selected layer. In either case, the pasted effects will override any existing effects.

Clear Layer Style eliminates all styles from the selected layer. It also restores the Blending Options to their default settings.

Global Light establishes a common Angle and Altitude for all current and future effects for which the Use Global Light option is on. And conversely, if you change the Angle or Altitude of any individual layer effect when Use Global Light is on, all the other effects that have a Global Light option will update, as will the Angle and Altitude in the Global Light dialog box. Using a Global Light helps to unify lighting across multiple effects.

If more than one effect has been applied to a layer and you choose **Create Layers,** each effect will be placed on its own layer. The image won't look substantially different after this command is chosen, but the effects will no longer be editable via the Layer Style dialog box, and they will no longer be associated with the layer that they were originally applied to. You may get a warning that effects may not completely carry over to the layers. You don't have much choice, though, if you want to proceed.

(Continued on the following page)

After applying the Create Layers command, any layer effect that is inside a shape (an inner glow, or a highlight or a shadow for a bevel or an inner emboss) will be placed on a new, separate layer, but it will be joined with the original shape layer in a clipping group, with the original layer being the base layer of the group. Any effect that is outside a shape (a drop shadow, an outer glow, or a shadow for a bevel or an outer emboss) will be converted into separate layers below the original shape layer.

Use Create Layer(s) before exporting a layered file to a multimedia program, such as Adobe After Effects 4.x or Adobe LiveMotion 1.0. The Create Layer(s) command can't be applied to the Background of an image.

After Effects 5.x can import a layered Photoshop file. In After Effects, choose Composition from the Import As pop-up menu in the Import File dialog box. Not all layer effects can be imported to AfterEffects, but most can.

LiveMotion 2.x can import Photoshop layer effects correctly as effects, without the need for creating separate layers. Place a layered file, then choose Object > Convert Into > Objects, Group of Objects, Sequence, or Sequence with Background.

Hide All Effects temporarily hides layer effects for all the layers in the document. To redisplay them, choose Layer > Layer Style > Show All Effects.

Scale Effects opens a dialog box that allows you to increase or decrease the size of all the current effects on the selected layer. Only parameters defined in pixels (not those defined by a percentage) are affected.

Save it!

Layer effects can be saved as a style on the **Styles** palette in ImageReady or Photoshop. See pages 497–498 to learn how to save effects as a style, and how to apply a style to a layer.

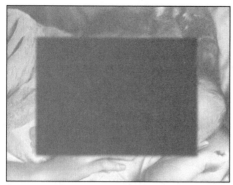

1 *The original image*

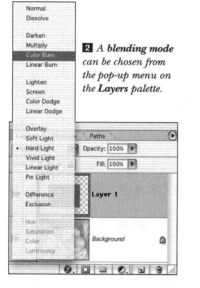

2 *A blending mode can be chosen from the pop-up menu on the **Layers** palette.*

Blending layers

The layer blending modes

The layer blending mode you choose for a layer affects how that layer's pixels blend with pixels in the layer directly below it. Some modes produce subtle effects (e.g., Soft Light), whereas others produce dramatic color shifts (e.g., Difference). Normal is the default mode. The blending modes are discussed in detail on pages 32–36.

There are four ways to choose a blending mode for a layer:

■ From the mode pop-up menu in the top-left corner of the Layers palette **2**.

■ By pressing Shift + or Shift -. This shortcut cycles through the modes for the currently active layer (don't have a painting tool selected when you do this).

■ By double-clicking the layer, then choosing a Blend Mode in the Layer Style dialog box.

TIP You can choose Behind mode for the Brush, Paint Bucket, Pencil, History Brush, Clone Stamp, Pattern Stamp, or Gradient tool from the options bar, but not for a layer. In Behind mode, it will appear as if you're painting on the back of the current layer.

For the Paint Bucket tool, or for any shape tool with the "Fill pixels" button ⬚ clicked on the options bar, you can choose Clear mode. This mode works like an eraser.

Note: To access Behind and Clear modes, make sure neither the "Lock image pixels" button ⟋ nor the "Lock transparent pixels" button ⬚ are selected on the Layers palette.

3 *After choosing **Color Burn** mode for the top layer*

Using the Blend If sliders in the Blending Options section of the Layer Style dialog box, you can control which pixels in the current layer will remain visible and which pixels from the underlying layer will show through the upper layer.

To fine-tune the blending between two layers:

1. Double-click a layer name on the Layers palette, then click Blending Options at the top left side of the dialog box.
or
Click a layer, then choose Blending Options from the Layers palette menu.

2. *Optional:* In the General Blending section, modify the current layer's Blend Mode or Opacity .

3. Check Preview.

4. In the Advanced Blending section, do any of the following:

To control the opacity of user-created layer pixels without affecting pixels in any layer effects, adjust the **Fill Opacity**.

Uncheck any **Channels** you want to prevent from blending with the underlying layer.

5. The first two check box options control how single layers or layers in a clipping group blend with underlying layers (more about clipping groups on pages 271–272).

Let's say you double-clicked a base layer in a clipping group that has a blending mode other than Normal. With **Blend Clipped Layers as Group** checked (the default setting), the blending mode applied to the base layer of the clipping group will control how all the layers of the group as a whole blend with any underlying layers in the image **2**.

With Blend Clipped Layers as Group unchecked, individual layers in a clipping group will blend with layers below the clipping group using each layer's own current blending mode—not the blending mode of the base layer **3** (and **1**, next page).

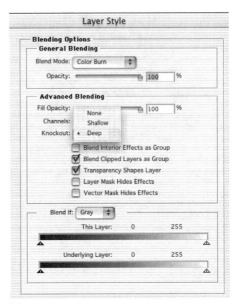

1 *The **Blending Options** settings in the **Layer Style** dialog box*

2 *Blend Clipped Layers as Group checked: The bottom layer of the clipping group (dune) controls the blending. (See **1**, next page.)*

3 *Blend Clipped Layers as Group unchecked: Here the layer blending mode of the clipping group layer ("Pattern") isn't controlled by the blending mode of the base layer of the clipping group.*

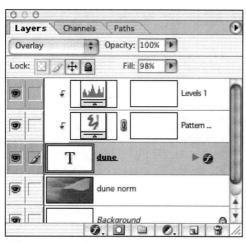

1 *The **clipping group** used for the previous two figures (not the next two)*

2 *Blend Interior Effect as Group unchecked: Linear Dodge was chosen as the blending mode for the Inner Glow effect, and Difference was chosen as the blending mode for the Gradient Overlay effect. Both of these layer effects are more visible than the layer's blending mode (Difference).*

3 *Blend Interior Effect as Group checked: The Inner Glow and Gradient Overlay effects have the same blending modes as in the previous figure, but those modes are less obvious because the layer's blending mode (Difference) now controls the overall blending with underlying layers.*

If **Blend Interior Effect as Group** is unchecked (the default setting) for a layer that has a blending mode other than Normal, the layer's interior effects (e.g., Inner Glow, Satin, Color Overlay, Pattern Overlay, or Gradient Overlay) will be used to blend the layer with underlying layers, and the layer's overall blending mode will be less evident.

With Blend Interior Effect as Group checked, the layer's interior effects will blend first with the layer's own blending mode, then the whole blended collection of the layer will blend with underlying layers, thus diminishing the visual impact of the interior effects **2**–**3**.

6. Check any of these options, if desired:

Transparency Shapes Layer (checked by default) to prevent effects from displaying over transparent areas of the layer. Uncheck this option to permit effects to cover the whole layer, including any transparent areas.

Layer Mask Hides Effects to hide portions of layer effects that fall outside the layer mask shape.

Vector Mask Hides Effects to hide portions of layer effects that fall outside the vector mask shape.

7. To set the blend range for each channel one at a time, choose a channel from the **Blend If** pop-up menu; to work on all the channels simultaneously, leave Gray as the choice on this pop-up menu. The current image mode (e.g., RGB or CMYK) determines which channels are available.

Move the leftmost Blend If: This Layer slider to the right to remove shadow areas from the active layer.

Move the rightmost This Layer slider to the left to remove highlights from the active layer.

(Continued on the following page)

Blending Options

Move the leftmost Underlying Layer slider to the right to restore shadow areas from the layer directly below the active layer.

Move the rightmost Underlying Layer slider to the left to restore highlights from the layer directly below the active layer.

8. Click OK **1**–**2**.

TIP To adjust the midtones independently for either slider, Alt-drag/Option-drag the slider (it will divide in two).

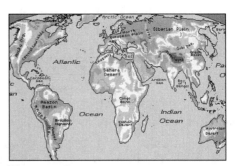

1 *The map layer is above an avocados layer.*

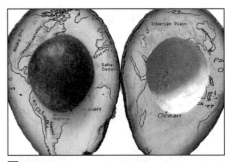

2 *The same image after dividing and moving the white* ***This Layer*** *slider and the black* ***Underlying*** *slider in the* ***Layer Style*** *dialog box*

Knockout tips

- If the **layer set** that the knockout layer is a part of has a blending mode other than Pass Through, then the knockout will stop at the layer directly below the layer set, whether Shallow or Deep is chosen. The blending mode chosen for other layer sets has no effect on how a knockout layer and its layer set behave.

- If the knockout layer is in a **clipping group**, then Shallow would stop at the layer directly below the clipping group. Deep would knock out through to the Background if Blend Clipping Layers as Group (under Blending Options–Advanced Blending) is unchecked for the base (underlined) layer of the clipping group.

- If the image contains **no** clipping groups or layer sets, then Shallow or Deep will knock out to the **Background**.

You can control how many layers down a chosen layer will knock out (cut away) underlying pixels: Either all the way to the Background or just down to a default stopping point among the layers below it.

To choose a knockout option for a layer:

1. On the Layers palette, arrange layers into the desired stacking order, or put layers into a layer set.

2. Double-click a layer, then click Blending Options at the left side of the dialog box.

3. Make sure Preview is checked.

4. In the Advanced Blending area, choose from the Knockout pop-up menu (**1**, next page):

   None for no knockout.

   Shallow to knock out down to the default stopping point for a layer. The default stopping point will either be the layer directly below the layer set that the knockout layer is a part of, or if Blend Clipped Layers as Group is checked, the bottommost layer in a clipping group.
   or
   Deep to knock out all the way down to the Background.

5. Choose a blending mode other than Normal in the Blending Options area of the Layer Style dialog box.

6. Click OK.

Knockout Options

1 *In this example, the **sand** layer is part of a layer **set**. Therefore, **Shallow** knocks out to the layer below the set, whereas **Deep** knocks out all the way to the Background.*

None

Shallow

Deep

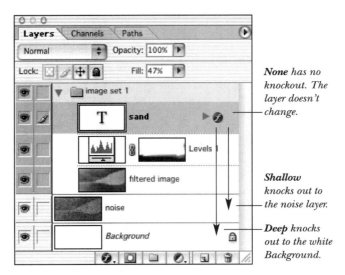

None has no knockout. The layer doesn't change.

Shallow knocks out to the noise layer.

Deep knocks out to the white Background.

1 *The original image*

2 *After applying the **Mezzotint** filter to the **duplicate** layer, then lowering the **opacity** of the duplicate layer*

3 *Blended layers, with the **Grain** filter applied*

In these instructions, a filter is applied to a duplicate layer and then the original and duplicate layers are blended using Layers palette opacity and mode controls. Use this technique to soften the effect of an image-editing command, such as a filter, or to experiment with various blending modes or adjustment commands. You can also use a layer mask to limit the area of an effect. If you don't like the results, you can just delete the duplicate layer and start over.

To blend a modified layer with the original layer:

1. Choose a layer **1**.

2. Right-click/Ctrl-click and choose Duplicate Layer from the context menu (or choose Duplicate Layer from the Layers palette menu), then click OK.

3. Modify the duplicate layer (e.g., apply a filter or other image-editing command).

4. On the Layers palette, adjust the Opacity to achieve the desired degree of transparency between the original layer and the modified, duplicate layer **2** and/or choose a different blending mode.

5. *Optional:* Create a layer mask to partially hide pixels on the duplicate layer. You could also add a gradient to the layer mask to gradually fade the blend effect.

TIP To create a beautiful textural effect, duplicate a layer in a color image (not a solid white layer), click the new layer, and choose Image > Adjustments > Desaturate (Ctrl-Shift-U/Cmd-Shift-U) to make it grayscale. Next, apply the Artistic > Film Grain, Noise > Add Noise, or Texture > Grain filter **3**. And finally, lower the opacity of, and try out different blending modes for, the new layer via the Layers palette.

TIP You could also click different channels in the Layer Style dialog box to control which channels in the duplicate layer blend with the underlying layer.

Blend Modified Layer

Layer masks

A layer mask is an eight-bit grayscale channel that has white or black as its background color. By default, white areas on a layer mask permit pixels to be seen, black areas hide pixels, and gray areas partially mask pixels. You can use a mask to temporarily hide pixels on a layer so you can view the rest of the composite picture without them. Later, you can modify the mask, apply the mask effect to make it permanent, or discard the mask altogether.

An advantage of using a layer mask is that you can access it from both the Layers and Channels palettes. You'll see a thumbnail for the layer mask on the Layers palette and on the Channels palette when a layer that contains a mask is highlighted. Unlike an alpha channel selection, however, which can be loaded onto any layer, a layer mask can only be turned on or off for the layer or clipping group (group of layers) with which it's associated.

To create a layer mask:

1. Choose the layer you want to add a mask to **1**.

2. *Optional:* Create a selection if you want to create a mask in that shape.

3. To create a white mask in which all the layer pixels are visible, choose Layer > Add Layer Mask > Reveal All or click the "Add a mask" button  on the Layers palette **2**–**3**.
   or
   To create a black mask in which all the layer pixels are hidden, choose Layer > Add Layer Mask > Hide All or Alt-click/ Option-click the Add a mask button on the Layers palette.
   or
   To reveal only layer pixels within an active selection, choose Layer > Add Layer Mask > Reveal Selection or click the "Add a mask" button at the bottom of the Layers palette.
   or

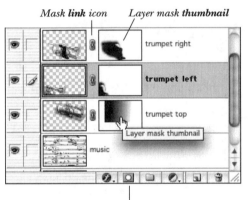

1 *The trumpets **without layer masks***

Mask **link** icon   Layer mask **thumbnail**

2 *Add a mask button*

*The Layers palette, showing the three trumpet layers, each with its own **layer mask***

3 *The trumpets **with layer masks:** The topmost trumpet fades out due to a gradient in its layer mask, and portions of the middle and bottom trumpets are hidden via a black-and-white layer mask.*

Other tools for modifying a mask

Try using the Eraser, Burn, Dodge, Sponge, Sharpen, Blur, Smudge, Paint Bucket, or Gradient tool. If you want to use any of the shape tools, you must first display the mask by itself (see step 3, at right).

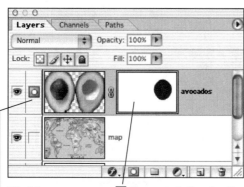

Mask icon   **1** *Layer mask thumbnail*

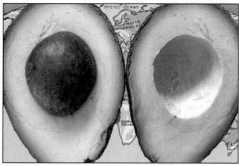

2 *The original image*

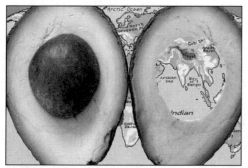

3 *The center of the avocado on the right is blocked by a layer mask.*

To hide layer pixels within the selection, choose Layer > Add Layer Mask > Hide Selection or Alt-click/Option-click the "Add a mask" button at the bottom of the Layers palette.

To reshape a layer mask:

1. Choose the Brush tool (B or Shift-B).

2. On the options bar, choose 100% Opacity (or a lower Opacity to partially hide layer pixels), choose Mode: Normal, and click a brush on the Brush picker.

3. To reshape the layer mask while viewing the layer pixels, click the layer mask thumbnail (not the layer name) on the Layers palette **1**. The thumbnail will have a dark border and a mask icon will appear for that layer.
   or
   To display the mask by itself in the image window, Alt-click/Option-click the layer mask thumbnail. (Alt-click/Option-click the layer mask thumbnail to redisplay the mask on the image.)
   or
   Alt-Shift-click/Option-Shift-click the layer mask thumbnail to display the mask as an overlay on the image. (Alt-Shift-click/Option-Shift-click the thumbnail again to restore the normal display.)

4. Paint on the picture with black as the Foreground color to enlarge the mask and hide pixels on the layer.
   and/or
   Paint with white as the Foreground color to reduce the mask and restore pixels on the layer.
   and/or
   Paint with gray as the Foreground color to partially hide pixels on the layer.

5. When you're finished modifying the layer mask, click the layer thumbnail **2**–**3**.

TIP To invert the effect of a layer mask, click the layer mask thumbnail, then choose Image > Adjustments > Invert (Ctrl-I/Cmd-I). Hidden areas will be revealed, and formerly visible areas will be hidden.

Reshape Layer Mask

By default, a layer and its layer mask move in unison. Follow these steps if you want to move layer pixels or a layer mask independently of one another.

To move layer pixels or a layer mask indpendently:

1. On the Layers palette, click the link icon 🔗 between the layer thumbnail and the layer mask thumbnail **1**. The link icon will disappear.

2. Click the layer thumbnail or the layer mask thumbnail.

3. Choose the Move tool (V). 🖐⊕

4. Drag the layer in the image window.

5. Click again between the layer and layer mask thumbnails to re-link them.

To duplicate a layer mask:

1. Choose the layer you want the duplicate mask to appear on.

2. From another layer, drag the thumbnail of the layer mask you want to duplicate over the "Add layer mask" button ▣ at the bottom of the palette.
   or
   To have the hidden and revealed areas be switched in the duplicate, Alt-drag/Option-drag the thumbnail of the layer mask you want to duplicate over the "Add layer mask" button.

On the previous page, we showed you how to display the mask overlay with the image (Alt-Shift-click/Option-Shift-click the layer mask thumbnail). If you like, you can change the color of the overlay to make it contrast more effectively with colors in the image, and also change its opacity.

To choose layer mask display options:

1. Double-click a layer mask thumbnail.

2. Click the Color square, then choose a different Overlay color.
   and/or
   Change the Opacity percentage **2**.

3. Click OK.

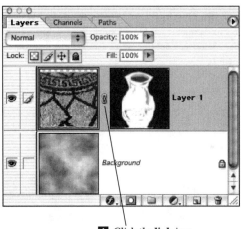

1 *Click the* **link** *icon*

2 *You can change the* **Overlay** *color and/or* **Opacity** *for a* **layer mask**.

Move Mask; Duplicate Mask; Mask Display

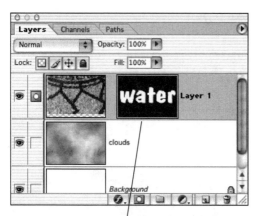

1 *This is the **layer mask thumbnail.** Layer 1 pixels are revealed through the **white** areas in the layer mask.*

2 *In this image, the water layer is visible only through the letter shapes of the **layer mask.***

To fill type with imagery using a layer mask:

1. Activate a layer that contains non-transparent pixels (not the Background).

2. Choose the Horizontal Type Mask tool (T or Shift-T).

3. Choose a font and other type specifications, then click on the image. The image will temporarily display in Quick Mask mode. (If Color Indicates: Masked Areas is chosen in the Quick Mask options dialog box, then the mask will cover the whole image; if Selected Areas is chosen, then the mask will cover only the letters you type.)

Type the letters you want to appear. When you're ready to turn the type into a selection, click the ✔ on the options bar, or click Enter (on the keypad), or choose any other tool.

4. Reposition the type selection using the Rectangular Marquee tool. (Don't use the Move tool to move the selection—that would remove image pixels from the selection on the current layer.)

5. Choose Layer > Add Layer Mask > Reveal Selection to reveal layer pixels within the selection.
or
Choose Layer > Add Layer Mask > Hide Selection to hide layer pixels within the selection.

The type will now display as white or black pixels in the layer mask thumbnail **1**–**2**.

TIP To reposition the type area within the layer mask, first unlink the layer mask from the layer (click the link icon to make the icon disappear), use the Move tool (V) to drag within the layer mask in the image window, then relink the mask to the layer.

TIP To fill type with imagery using a vector mask (instead of a layer mask), see pages 302–303.

Fill Type with Imagery

To temporarily deactivate a layer mask:

Shift-click the layer mask thumbnail on the Layers palette (this won't select the layer mask thumbnail). A red "X" will appear over the thumbnail and the entire layer will be visible **1**. (Shift-click the layer mask thumbnail again to remove the "X" and restore the mask effect.)

Layer masks take up storage space, so you should discard any that you no longer need.

To apply or discard the effects of a layer mask:

1. On the Layers palette, click the thumbnail of the layer mask you want to apply or discard **2**.

2. Click the Delete Layer (trash) button. To make the mask effect permanent, click Apply **3**, or to remove the mask without applying its effect, click Discard.
or
Right-click/Ctrl-click and choose Discard Layer Mask or Apply Layer Mask.

Clip it

Image layer pixels can also be masked using a **vector mask** that you create using the Pen tool or a shape tool (see page 298).

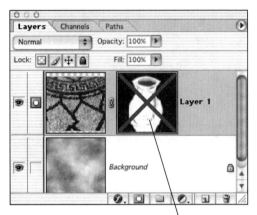

1 *Shift-click the layer mask thumbnail.*

2 *Click the layer mask thumbnail.*

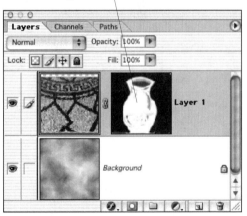

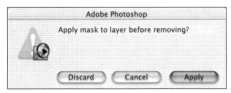

3 *Click **Apply** to make the mask effect permanent.*

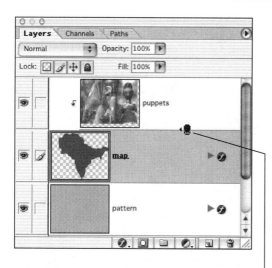

1 *Alt-click/Option-click between two layers to join them together as a **clipping group**. A dotted line will appear, and the **base** layer will be underlined.*

2 *The map of India is **clipping** (limiting) the view of the puppets.*

Clipping groups

The bottommost layer of a clipping group of layers (the base layer) clips (limits) the display of pixels, and (by default) controls the mode and opacity of the layers above it. Only pixels within the group of layers that overlap pixels on the base layer are visible. You can achieve very artful effects using this feature. Try it on various kinds of imagery.

To create a clipping group of layers:

1. Click a layer name in a multi-layer image.

2. Alt-click/Option-click the line between that layer name and the name just above it (the pointer will be two overlapping circles) **1**–**2**. *Note:* The layers to be joined in a clipping group must be listed **consecutively** on the palette. A clipping group can be formed using layers within a layer set; but not with layers from both inside and outside a set.

3. *Optional:* Repeat the previous step to add more layers to the clipping group.

The base layer name will be underlined, and the thumbnails for the other layers in the group will be indented above it.

TIP To create a clipping group from linked layers, choose Layer > Group Linked (Ctrl-G/Cmd-G).

TIP To fill type with imagery using a clipping group, see page 331.

TIP To learn how clipping group layers blend with underlying layers, see pages 260–261.

Clipping Group

When you remove (ungroup) a layer from a clipping group, any grouped layers above the ungrouped one will also ungroup.

To remove a layer from a clipping group:

Alt-click/Option-click the line below the layer that you want to remove **1**. The layer will no longer be indented.

or

Click the name of the layer you want to remove, then choose Layer > Ungroup (Ctrl-Shift-G/Cmd-Shift-G).

To ungroup an entire clipping group:

1. Click the base layer in the group.

2. Choose Layer > Ungroup (Ctrl-Shift-G/Cmd-Shift-G) **2**.

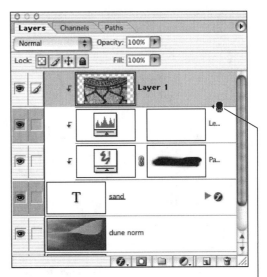

1 *Alt-click/Option-click below a layer to be removed from a clipping group.*

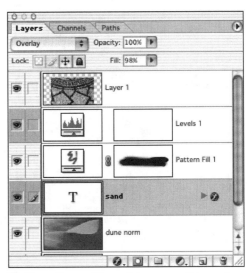

2 *Choose Layer > **Ungroup** to remove all layers from a clipping group.*

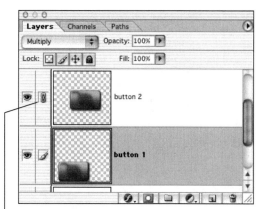

1 *Click to display the **link** icon in the second column on the Layers palette for any layers you want to link to the active layer. In this illustration, the "button 1" and "button 2" layers are linked.*

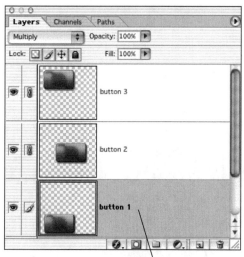

2 *Choose a **linked** layer.*

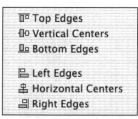

3 *Choose one of these options from the Layer > **Align Linked** or **Distribute Linked** submenu...*

Linking layers

Linking is used to secure the position of multiple layers in relationship to one another. Once layers are linked together, they can be moved as a unit in the image window or drag-copied to another image, and they can be distributed or aligned.

Note: You can transform linked layers. In fact, you'll minimize image distortion due to resampling by transforming multiple layers all at once instead of one by one.

To link layers (and move them as a unit):

1. On the Layers palette, click one of the layers that you want to link.

2. Click in the second column for any other layer you want to link to the layer you chose in the previous step. The layers you link don't have be consecutive. The link icon will appear next to any non-active, linked layers **1**.

3. *Optional:* Choose the Move tool (V), then drag the linked layers in the image window.

TIP To unlink a layer, click the link icon.

The Align Layers command is used to align the pixel edges of linked layers.

To align two or more linked layers:

1. Choose a layer that one or more other layers are linked to **2**. The layer you choose will be the reference position that the other linked layers will align to.

2. Choose Layer > Align Linked > Top Edges, Vertical Centers, Bottom Edges, Left Edges, Horizontal Centers, or Right Edges **3** (and **1**–**2**, next page).
   or
   Choose the Move tool (V), then click an alignment button on the options bar **4**.

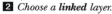

4 *...or click an **alignment** button on the **options** bar.*

To align the pixel edge of a layer with a selection:

1. Create a selection.

2. Choose a layer to align with the selection.

3. Choose an align command from the Layer > Align To Selection submenu.
or
Choose the Move tool (V), ⊹ then click an alignment button on the options bar.

TIP Any layers linked to the chosen layer will also be aligned.

You can distribute the pixel areas in linked layers using the Distribute Linked command.

To distribute three or more linked layers:

1. Choose a layer to which two or more other layers are linked (not the Background).

2. Choose Layer > Distribute Linked > Top Edges, Vertical Centers, Bottom Edges, Left Edges, Horizontal Centers, or Right Edges.
or
Choose the Move tool (V), ⊹ then click a distribute button on the options bar **1**.

The layers will be distributed evenly between the two layers that are furthest apart **2**–**4**.

TIP If you don't like the results and you want to apply a different align or distribute command, undo the last command before applying a new one.

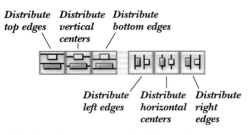

Distribute *Distribute* *Distribute*
top edges *vertical* *bottom edges*
centers

Distribute *Distribute* *Distribute*
left edges *horizontal* *right*
centers *edges*

1 *Distribute* buttons on the *Move* tool options bar.

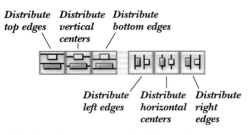

2 *The original image*

3 *The layers* **aligned**: *Bottom*

4 *The layers* **distributed**: *Horizontal Center*

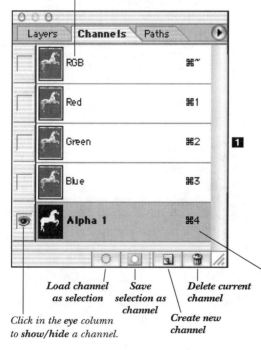

The active (selected) area is clear, the
Quick Mask *is semi-transparent.*

The **composite color channel**

THIS CHAPTER COVERS two special methods for saving and reshaping a selection: alpha channels and Quick Mask mode.

If you save a selection to a specially created grayscale channel, called an **alpha channel**, you can load the selection onto the image at any time. A selection that has an irregular shape that would be difficult to reselect would be a logical candidate for this operation. A file can contain up to 24 channels, though from a practical standpoint, because each channel increases a picture's storage size (depending on the size of the selection area), you should be judicious about adding alpha channels. Alpha channels are accessed via the Channels palette **1**, and are saved or loaded onto an image via Select menu commands or the Channels palette. (To create a vector mask instead of an alpha channel to conserve file storage space, see page 298.)

Using Photoshop's **Quick Mask** mode, the selected or unselected areas of an image can be covered with a semi-transparent colored mask, which can then be reshaped using any editing or painting tool. Masked areas are protected from editing. Unlike an alpha channel, a Quick Mask cannot be saved, but when you return to Standard (non-Quick Mask) mode, the mask will turn into a selection, which can be saved.

Note: If you're unfamiliar with Photoshop's basic selection tools, read Chapter 5 before reading this chapter.

Layer masks are covered in Chapter 14.

1

Load channel as selection   **Save selection as channel**   **Delete current channel**

Click in the **eye** *column to* **show/hide** *a channel.*

Create new channel

Only the currently highlighted channel or channels can be edited. A non-color channel is called an **alpha channel**.

Alpha channels

A selection that's saved in an alpha channel can be loaded onto any image whenever it's needed.

Note: To convert an alpha channel into a spot color channel, see page 210.

To save a selection to a channel using the current options settings:

1. Create a selection **1**.

2. Click the "Save selection as channel" (second) button ◻ at the bottom of the Channels palette **2**.

To save a selection to a channel and choose options:

1. Create a selection **1**. It can be a type mask selection. *Optional:* Also choose a layer if you want to create a layer mask for it.

2. Choose Select > Save Selection.
or
Right-click/Ctrl-click and choose Save Selection from the context menu.

3. Leave the Document setting as the current file, or choose **Document: New** to save the selection to an alpha channel in a new, separate document **3**.

4. *Optional:* Choose **Channel:** "[   ] **Mask**" to turn the selection into a layer mask for the current layer. Layer pixels will be visible only where the selection was.

5. Type a **Name** for the selection.

6. *Optional:* Choose an **Operation** option to combine the current selection with an existing alpha channel that you choose from the Channel pop-up menu. (The Operation options are illustrated on page 278.)

Note: You can save an alpha channel with an image in the BMP, Photoshop, TIFF, Photoshop PDF, PICT, or Pixar format. To save a copy of a file without alpha channels, uncheck Alpha Channels in the Save As dialog box, if it's available.

7. Click OK. The selection will remain active.

1 *Select an area on a layer.*

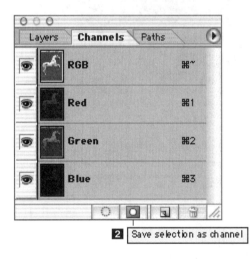

2 Save selection as channel

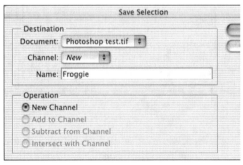

3 *In the **Save Selection** dialog box, choose **Document** and **Channel** options and give the channel a **Name**.*

Load channel to another image

Make sure the source and destination images have the same dimensions and resolution, activate the destination image, then follow steps 2–6 at below right, choosing the source document in the **Load Selection** dialog box. To load a layer mask selection, activate that layer first in the source image.

Just the pixels, please

To select only **non-transparent** pixels on an active layer, choose Channel: [ ] Transparency in the Load Selection dialog box. Or Ctrl-click/Cmd-click the layer thumbnail on the Layers palette.

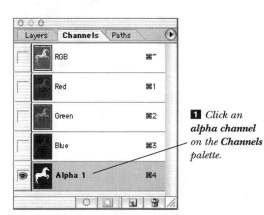

1 *Click an alpha channel on the Channels palette.*

2 *An alpha channel displayed in the image window: The selected area is white, the protected area is black.*

An alpha channel can be displayed without loading it onto the image as a selection.

To display a channel selection:

1. Click an alpha channel name on the Channels palette **1**. The selected area will be white, the protected area black **2**.

2. To restore the normal image display, click the top (composite) channel name on the palette (Ctrl-~/Cmd-~).

TIP If the selection has a Feather radius above zero, the feather area will be gray, and will only be partially affected by editing.

TIP Reshape the mask with any painting tool using black, gray, or white "paint."

To load a channel selection onto an image using the current options:

On the Channels palette, Ctrl-click/Cmd-click the name of the alpha channel that you want to load.

To load a channel selection onto an image and choose options:

1. If the composite image isn't displayed, click the top channel name on the Channels palette. You can combine the channel selection with an existing selection in the image (see the next page).

2. Choose Select > Load Selection.
or
If you didn't create a selection, you can right-click/Ctrl-click in the image window and choose Load Selection from the context menu.

3. Choose the alpha channel name from the Channel pop-up menu **3**.

4. To combine the channel with an existing selection in the image, click an Operation option (see the next page).

5. *Optional:* Check Invert to switch the selected and unselected areas in the loaded selection.

6. Click OK.

3 *Choose an alpha channel from the Channel pop-up menu.*

Save Selection Operations

When saving a selection, you can choose from these Operation options in the **Save Selection** dialog box:

New Channel *saves the current selection in a new channel.*

Shortcut: *Click the "Save selection as channel" button on the Channels palette.*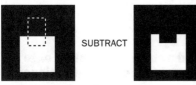

Channel and selection to be saved *Resulting channel*

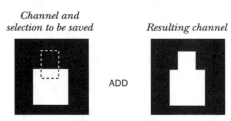

ADD

Add to Channel *adds the new selection to the channel.*

Channel and selection to be saved *Resulting channel*

SUBTRACT

Subtract from Channel *removes white or gray areas that overlap the new selection.*

INTERSECT

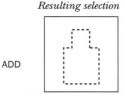

Intersect with Channel *preserves only white or gray areas that overlap the new selection.*

Load Selection Operations

If a channel is loaded while an area of a layer is selected, you can choose from these Operation options in the **Load Selection** dialog box:

New Selection: *the channel becomes the current selection.*

Shortcut: *Ctrl-click/Cmd-click the channel name or drag the channel name over the "Load channel as selection" button.*

Selection and channel to be loaded *Resulting selection*

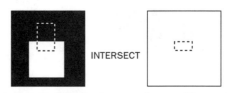

ADD

Add to Selection *adds the channel selection to the current selection.*

Shortcut: *Ctrl-Shift-click/Cmd-Shift-click the channel name.*

Selection and channel to be loaded *Resulting selection*

SUBTRACT

Subtract from Selection *removes areas of the current selection that overlap the channel selection.*

Shortcut: *Ctrl-Alt-click/Cmd-Option-click the channel name.*

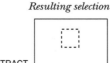 

INTERSECT

Intersect with Selection *preserves only areas of the current selection that overlap the channel selection.*

Shortcut: *Ctrl-Alt-Shift-click/Cmd-Option-Shift-click the channel name.*

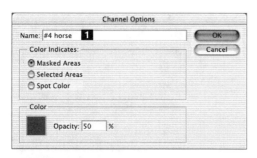

To choose channel options:

1. Double-click next to a channel name on the Channels palette.
or
Click next to a channel name, then choose Channel Options from the palette menu.

2. Type a new name in the Name field ■.
and/or
Normally, the selected areas of an alpha channel are white and the protected areas are black or colored. To reverse these colors without changing which area is actually selected, click Color Indicates: Selected Areas **2**–**3**.

3. Click OK.

TIP You can also change a channel name by double-clicking the existing name on the palette.

TIP To change the size of the channel thumbnails, choose Palette Options from the Channels palette menu, then click a different thumbnail size.

2 *The horse is the selected area.*

3 *The horse is still the selected area, but it is now* **black** *instead of white.*

To delete a channel:

Drag the channel over the "Delete current channel" (trash) button on the Channels palette.
or
Click the channel you want to delete, click the "Delete current channel" button at the bottom of the palette **4**, then click Yes. Or Alt-click/Option-click the "Delete current channel" button to bypass the prompt.
or
Right-click/Ctrl-click the Channel name, then choose Delete Channel from the context menu.

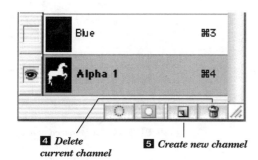

4 *Delete current channel*

5 *Create new channel*

To duplicate a channel:

Drag the name of the channel you want to duplicate over the "Create new channel" button or into another image window **5**.
or
Right-click/Ctrl-click the Channel name, choose Duplicate Channel from the context menu, change the name, if desired, then click OK **6**.

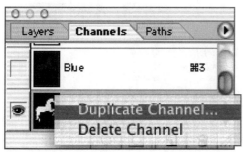

6 *Choose* **Duplicate Channel** *from the context menu.*

You can superimpose an alpha channel selection as a colored mask over an image, and then reshape the mask.

To reshape an alpha channel mask:

1. Make sure there is no selection on the image.

2. Click an alpha channel on the Channels palette. An eye icon will appear next to it **1**.

3. Click in the left column at the top of the palette. An eye icon will appear. The alpha channel should still be the only highlighted channel **2**.

4. Choose the Pencil 🖉 or Brush tool 🖌 (B or Shift-B).

5. On the options bar:

    Click the Brush preset picker arrowhead, then click a brush on the picker.
    and
    Choose Mode: Normal.
    and
    Choose 100% Opacity to create a full mask or a lower opacity to create a partial mask.

6. To enlarge the masked (protected) area, stroke on the cutout with black as the Foreground color **3**. You can click the "Switch colors" button 🔄 on the Toolbox (X) to swap the Foreground and Background colors **4**.

    To enlarge the unmasked area, stroke on the mask with white as the Foreground color **5**.

7. To hide the mask, click the alpha channel's eye icon or choose a layer on the Layers palette.

1 *Click an **alpha channel** on the **Channels** palette.*

2 *Click in the **left** column at the top of the palette. Make sure the alpha channel stays highlighted.*

3 *Enlarge the **masked** area by stroking on the cutout with **black** as the Foreground color.*

5 *Enlarge the **unmasked** area by stroking on the mask with **white** as the Foreground color.*

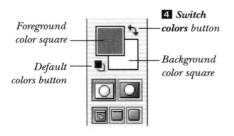

Foreground color square

Default colors button

4 *Switch colors* button

Background color square

1 *Select an area on a layer.*

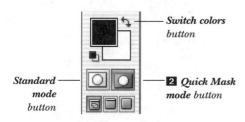

Switch colors button

Standard mode button

2 *Quick Mask mode button*

3 *The unselected area is covered with a mask.*

Quick Masks

If you choose Quick Mask mode when an area of a layer is selected, a semi-transparent tinted mask will cover the unselected areas, and the selected areas will be revealed in a cutout. You'll still be able to see the image under the mask. The cutout (mask) can be reshaped using the Pencil, Airbrush, or Brush tool.

Note: You can't save a Quick Mask to a channel (Select > Save Selection) while your image is in Quick Mask mode, but you can use Save Selection once you restore the standard screen display mode.

To reshape a selection using Quick Mask mode:

1. Select an area of a layer **1**.

2. Click the "Quick Mask mode" button on the Toolbox (Q) **2**. A mask will cover the unselected part of the picture **3**. (If it doesn't, double-click the "Quick Mask mode" button, click Color Indicates: Masked Areas, then click OK.)

3. Choose the Pencil 🖉 or Brush 🖌 tool. To use airbrush behavior, click the Airbrush button on the options bar. 🖌

4. On the options bar:

Click the Brush preset picker arrowhead, then click a brush on the picker.
and
Choose Mode: Normal.
and
Move the Opacity and Flow sliders to 100%.

5. Stroke on the cutout with **black** as the Foreground color to enlarge the **masked** (protected) area.
or
Stroke on the mask with **white** as the Foreground color to enlarge the **unmasked** area. You can click the "Switch colors" button on the Toolbox 🔁 (X) to swap the Foreground/Background colors.
or
Stroke with gray or a brush with an opacity below 100% (options bar) to create

(Continued on the following page)

Quick Mask

a partial mask. When you edit the layer, that area will be partially affected by modifications.

6. "Quick Mask" will be listed on the Channels palette and on the image window title bar while the image is in that mode. Click the "Standard mode" button on the Toolbox (Q) when you're ready to turn off Quick Mask mode 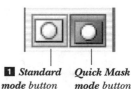. The non-masked areas will turn into a selection.

7. Modify the layer. Only the unmasked (selected) area will be affected.

In these instructions, you'll create a mask without first creating a selection.

To create a Quick Mask without using a selection:

1. Choose the Pencil or Brush tool, and choose options for the tool as per step 4 on the previous page.

2. Double-click the "Quick Mask mode" button on the Toolbox.

3. Click Selected Areas, then click OK.

4. Stroke with black on the layer 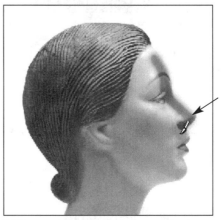. The selected areas (not the protected areas) will be covered with a mask; you'll be creating what will become the selection. Press Q to return to standard mode.

The Quick Mask options affect only how a Quick Mask looks on screen—not how it functions.

To choose Quick Mask options:

1. Double-click "Quick Mask" on the Channels palette.
   or
   Double-click the "Quick Mask mode" button on the Toolbox.

2. Do any of the following:

   Choose whether Color Indicates: Masked Areas or Selected Areas.

   Click the Color swatch, then choose a new Quick Mask color.

   Change the Opacity of the mask color.

3. Click OK.

Quick switch

To switch the mask color between the **selected** and **masked** areas without opening the Quick Mask Options dialog box, **Alt-click/Option-click** the "Quick Mask mode" button on the Toolbox.

---

1 *Standard mode* button **Quick Mask mode** button

2 *Painting a mask on an image in **Quick Mask** mode*

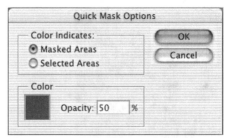

3 *In the **Quick Mask Options** dialog box, choose whether Color Indicates: **Masked Areas** or **Selected Areas**; click the **Color** swatch to choose a different mask color.*

PATHS/SHAPES 16

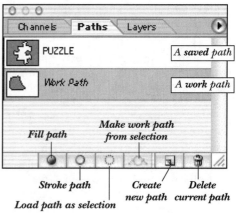

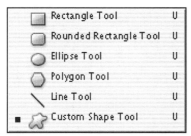

1 *The **pen** tools and path **reshaping** tools*

2 *The **shape** tools*

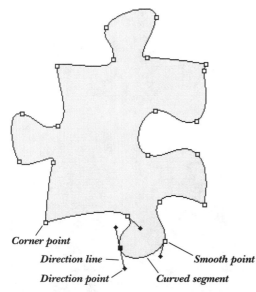

Corner point

Direction line

Direction point

Smooth point

Curved segment

3 *This is a **path**. To reshape a path or shape, you can drag, add, or delete an **anchor point** or move a **segment**. A curved line segment can also be reshaped by adjusting its **direction lines**.*

PHOTOSHOP'S pen tools **1** and shape tools **2** create precise vector shapes, called **paths**, that consist of anchor points connected by curved or straight line segments **3**. Before drawing a path, you'll decide whether you want to click the first button on the options bar ☐ for your pen tool to create a **shape layer** or click the second button ▨ to create a **work path**. Both kinds of paths can be reshaped and filled.

Paths created by the Pen tool and Freeform Pen tool are displayed, activated, deactivated, restacked, saved, and deleted using the Paths palette **4**.

Shapes automatically show up as layers on the Layers palette, along with a vector mask that controls which part of the layer will be visible and which areas will be hidden.

Vector masks (formerly called clipping paths) work like layer masks, but with an added bonus: They have sharp, precise path edges, and take up far less storage space than channels. The contour of the vector mask is defined using a clipping path (a pen path or shape). A vector mask can be used on any fill, type, or image layer.

7.0!

Paths and Shapes

4 *The **Paths** palette*

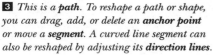

PUZZLE	A *saved* path
Work Path	A *work* path

Fill path

Make work path from selection

Stroke path

Create new path

Delete current path

Load path as selection

Creating paths

Before delving into the Pen tools, we'll show you how to create a path using a selection as a starting point. Once a selection has been converted into a path, you can precisely reshape it and then use it either as a standard path or as a vector mask. You can also convert it back into a selection, if need be.

To convert a selection into a path:

Method 1

1. Select an area of an image . *Note:* When the selection is converted into a path, any feathering on the selection will be removed.

2. Alt-click/Option-click the "Make work path from selection" button at the bottom of the Paths palette 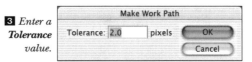.
or
Choose Make Work Path from the Paths palette menu.

3. Enter a Tolerance value (0.5–10) **3**. At a low Tolerance value, many anchor points will be created and the path will conform precisely to the selection marquee, but a low Tolerance could cause a printing error. At a high Tolerance value, fewer anchor points will be created and the path will be smoother, but it will conform less precisely to the selection. Try 4 or 5.

4. Click OK **4**–**5**. The new work path name will appear on the Paths palette. Don't leave it as a work path, though! Save the path by double-clicking the path name, entering a name, then clicking OK.

Method 2

To convert a selection into a path using the current Make Work Path Tolerance setting, click the "Make work path from selection" button ✎ at the bottom of the Paths palette. Now to save the path, double-click the path name, enter a name, then click OK.

TIP You can export a Photoshop path to Illustrator, where it can also be used as a path. You can also silhouette part of an image using a clipping path in the EPS format, then place it in an illustration or page layout program.

1 *The original selection*

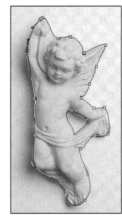

2 *Click the Make work path from selection button on the Paths palette.*

3 *Enter a Tolerance value.*

4 *The selection converted into a path: Tolerance 2*

5 *The selection converted into a path: Tolerance 6*

Selection into Path

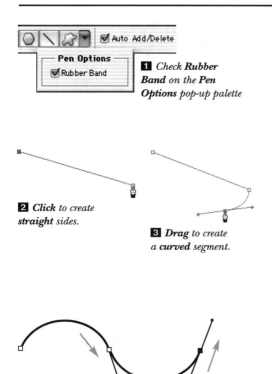

1 *Check Rubber Band on the Pen Options pop-up palette*

2 *Click to create straight sides.*

3 *Drag to create a curved segment.*

4 *Drag in the direction you want the curve to follow. Place anchor points at the **ends** of a curve, not at the height of a curve. The fewer the anchor points, the more graceful the curves.*

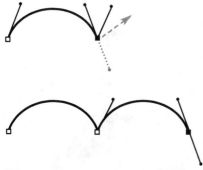

5 *To draw **non-continuous** curves, Alt-drag/Option-drag from the last anchor point in the direction you want the next curve to follow. Both direction lines will be on the same side of the curve segment.*

To draw a path using the Pen tool:

1. Choose the Pen tool (P or Shift-P).

2. Deselect all paths on the Paths palette.

3. On the options bar:

Click the Paths button.

and

To preview the line segments as you draw them, click the Geometry options arrowhead on the right side of the shape tools area, then check Rubber Band **1**.

4. Click in the image window, move the mouse, then click again to create a straight segment (Shift-click to draw the line at a multiple of 45°) **2**.

or

Drag to create a curved segment. Direction lines will appear **3**–**4**.

or

To create a non-continuous curve, starting from on top of the last anchor point, Alt-drag/Option-drag in the direction you want the next curve to follow, release Alt/Option and the mouse, then drag in the direction of the new curve **5**.

TIP As you draw, press Esc once to erase the last created anchor point, or twice to delete the entire path.

5. Repeat the previous step as many times as necessary to complete the shape.

6. To end the path but leave it open, Ctrl-click/Cmd-click outside the path or click any tool.

or

To close the path, click the starting point (a small circle appears in the pointer).

7. To save the new work path, double-click the path name on the Paths palette, enter a name, then click OK. Deselect the path or the path name if you don't want the next path you draw to share that name. To reshape the path, see page 292.

TIP Click the name of a saved path before using the Pen to add the new path to the existing name. Or to start off with a saved path (instead of a work path), click the "Create new path" button on the Paths palette, then draw the new path.

Pen Tool

Like the Magnetic Lasso tool, when the Freeform Pen tool is used with its Magnetic option on, it creates a path automatically as you move or drag along areas of high contrast. The path snaps to the nearest distinct shade or color edge that defines a shape.

To draw a magnetic Freeform Pen path:

1. Hide any layers you don't want to trace.

2. Choose the Freeform Pen tool (P or Shift P). 🖋

3. Deselect all paths on the Paths palette.

4. On the Freeform Pen tool options bar, click the Paths button 🔲 and check Magnetic. To choose Magnetic options, see the following page.

5. Click to begin the path, then slowly move the mouse—with or without pressing the mouse button—along the edge of the shape that you want the path to describe **1**. As you move or drag, the path will snap to the edge of the shape. If you move or drag the mouse quickly, the tool might not keep pace with you.

6. If the path snaps to any neighboring shapes that you *don't* want to select, click on the edge of the shape that you *do* want to select to manually create an anchor point, and then continue to move or drag to finish the path.

7. To **close** the path **2**:

Double-click anywhere over the shape to close with magnetic segments or Alt-double-click/Option-double-click to close with a straight segment.
or
Click the starting point (a small circle appears next to the tool pointer).
or
Ctrl-click/Cmd-click anywhere over the shape.

To end the path but leave it **open**, press Enter/Return. You can then reposition the Pen tool and click to start another path for the same Work Path.

TIP Press Esc to cancel a partial path.

Drawing straight lines

To draw straight segments with a temporary Pen tool while the Freeform Pen is chosen, **Alt-click/Option-click**, and continue clicking. Release Alt/Option to go back to the Freeform Pen.

1 *Click to start the path, then move the mouse around the object you want to select.*

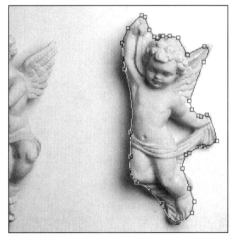

2 *The completed* **Magnetic Pen** *path*

Magnetic Path

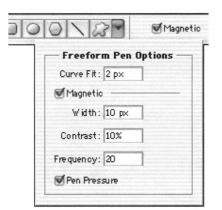

1 *When **Magnetic** is checked on the options bar for the **Freeform Pen** tool, you can then choose settings from the **Freeform Pen Options** palette.*

The Freeform Pen Options pop-up palette

Click the arrowhead in the shape tools area to open the Freeform Pen Options palette **1** (the tool tip says "Geometry options").

Curve Fit (0.5–10 pixels) controls how closely your Freeform Pen path will match the movement of your mouse. The higher the Curve Fit, the fewer the points, and thus the smoother the shape.

With Magnetic checked, the following options can be set:

The **Width** (1–40) is the width in pixels under the pointer that the tool considers when placing points. Use a wide Width for a high-contrast image that has clear delineations between shapes. For more exact line placement in a low-contrast image that contains subtle gradations or closely-spaced shapes, use a narrow Width.

TIP To have the Magnetic Freeform Pen pointer display as a circle in the current Width, click Other Cursors: Precise in File > Preferences > Display & Cursors. Or press Caps Lock to turn this option on temporarily.

TIP To decrease the Width incrementally while creating a path, press [. To increase the Width, press].

Contrast (0–100) is the degree of contrast needed between shapes for the tool to discern an edge. At a low Edge Contrast setting, even edges between low-contrast areas will be discerned.

Frequency (5–40) controls how quickly fastening points are placed as you draw a path. The lower the Frequency, the more frequently fastening points will be placed and the more anchor points will be created.

Check **Pen Pressure** if you have a stylus tablet and want to control the pen width using pen pressure. As you apply more pressure, the width decreases.

Freeform Pen Options

The Freeform Pen tool creates a path by dragging. Anchor points will appear automatically when you release the mouse.

To draw a path using the Freeform Pen:

1. Choose the Freeform Pen tool (P or Shift-P). 🖋 Deselect all paths on the Paths palette.

2. On the Freeform Pen tool options bar, click the Paths button 🔲 and uncheck Magnetic.

3. Draw a path in a freehand style.

   TIP To draw straight segments, Alt-click/ Option-click. To resume freehand drawing, release Alt/Option when the mouse button is down.)

4. To **close** the path:

   Drag back over the starting point **1**–**2**. A small circle will display next to the Freeform Pen tool pointer.
   or
   Hold down Ctrl/Cmd and release the mouse to close the path with a final straight segment.

   To end the path but leave it open, just release the mouse.

Working with paths

In this section, you will learn how to move, add to, transform, copy, display/hide, select, reshape, delete, and deselect a path; convert a path into a selection; apply a stroke or fill to a path; and finally, export a path to a drawing application.

To move a path:

1. On the Paths palette, click a path name.

2. Choose the Path Selection tool (A or Shift-A). ▶ **7.0!**

3. Click the path in the image window to select it, then drag the path **3**.

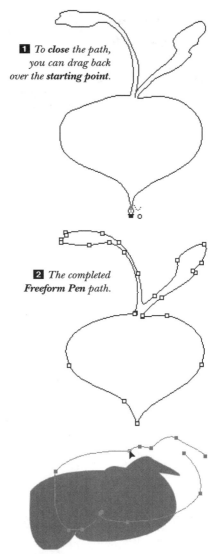

1 To **close** the path, you can drag back over the **starting point**.

2 The completed **Freeform Pen** path.

3 A path is **moved** using the **Path Selection** tool.

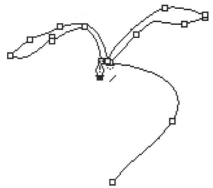

1 *To add to a path, drag from an endpoint using the Pen or Freeform Pen tool.*

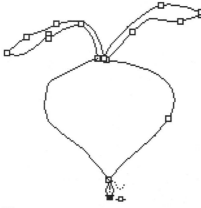

2 *Completing the addition*

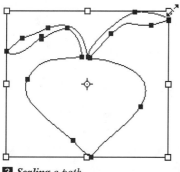

3 *Scaling a path*

To add to an existing, open path:

1. Choose the Freeform Pen tool, 🖋 or Pen tool 🖋 (P or Shift-P).

2. On the Paths palette, click the name of a work path or a saved open path.

3. Drag from either endpoint of the path **1**–**2**. To end the path, follow step 4 in the first set of instructions on the previous page.

To transform an entire path:

1. Choose the Path Selection tool (A or Shift-A). ▶

2. Activate the path name on the Paths palette, then click inside the path in the image window.

3. Choose Edit > Transform Path > Scale, Rotate, Skew, Distort, or Perspective; or right-click/Ctrl-click and choose Free Transform Path (Ctrl-T/Cmd-T).
   or
   Check Show Bounding Box on the options bar, then use the bounding box handles to transform a path as you would the handles on the Free Transform box.

4. Follow the instructions on pages 138–142 to perform the transformation.

TIP To repeat the transformation, choose Edit > Transform Path > Again (Ctrl-Shift-T/Cmd-Shift-T).

To transform points on a path:

1. Choose the Direct Selection tool (A), ▶ then select one or more individual points on a path (marquee or Shift-click multiple points).

2. Choose Edit > Transform Points > Scale, Rotate, or Skew (the Distort and Perspective commands won't be available); or right-click/Ctrl-click and choose Free Transform Points (Ctrl-T/Cmd-T).

3. Follow the instructions on pages 138–142 to perform the transformation **3**.

To copy a path in the same image:

To make the copy a separate path name, on the Paths palette, Alt-drag/Option-drag the path name over the "Create new path" button 🔳 at the bottom of the palette, enter a Name **1**, then click OK. (To copy the path without naming it, drag the path name without holding down Alt/Option.)
or
Choose the Path Selection tool, **↖** then Alt-drag/Option-drag the path in the image window. The two paths will share the same path name.

To drag-and-drop a path to another image:

1. Open the source and destination images, and click in the source image window.

2. Drag the path name from the Paths palette into the destination image window.
or
Choose the Path Selection tool (A), **↖** click the path in the image window, then drag it into the destination image window.
or
Click the path name on the Paths palette, choose Edit > Copy (Ctrl-C/Cmd-C), click in the destination image window, then choose Edit > Paste (Ctrl-V/Cmd-V).

Note: You can also copy and paste a vector mask that you've created for an image layer or shape layer.

A new path that's created with the Pen tool will be labeled "Work Path" automatically, and it will save with the file. The next path you create, however, will replace the existing one. Follow these instructions to save a path so it won't be deleted by a new path. Once a path is saved, it's resaved automatically each time it's modified.

To save a work path:

Double-click the path name, enter a Name **2**, then click OK.

Quick-save a work path

Drag the path name over the "Create new path" button 🔳 at the bottom of the Paths palette. Photoshop will assign a default name to it. To rename it at any time, double-click the path name, then type a new name.

1 *Type a Name in the* **Save Path** *dialog box.*

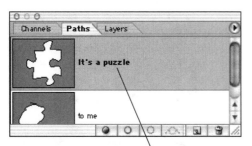

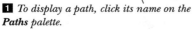

1 *To display a path, click its name on the* **Paths** *palette.*

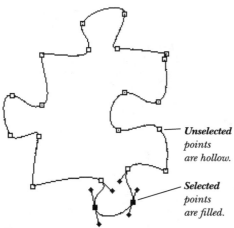

Unselected points are hollow.

Selected points are filled.

2 *Click with the* **Direct Selection** *tool to select* **individual** *points on a path.*

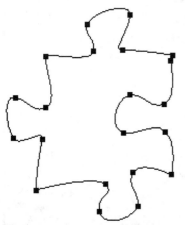

3 *Click with the* **Path Selection** *tool to select* **all** *the points on a path.*

To display a path:

Click the path name or thumbnail on the Paths palette **1**.

TIP To change the size of or turn off palette thumbnails, choose Palette Options from the Paths palette menu, then click a Thumbnail Size.

To hide a path:

Shift-click the path name on the Paths palette.
or
Click below the path names on the Paths palette.

To select anchor points on a path:

Method 1

1. Click a path name on the Paths palette.

2. Choose the Path Selection tool (A or Shift-A).

3. Click the path in the image window or draw a marquee around it. All the anchor points on the path will be selected.

Method 2

1. Click a path name on the Paths palette.

2. Choose the Direct Selection tool (A or Shift-A).

3. Click the path or subpath, then click on an anchor point **2**. Shift-click to select additional anchor points.
or
To select all the anchor points on the path, Alt-click/Option-click the path or subpath or draw a marquee around it **3**. An entire path can be moved when all its points are selected.

TIP To change the stacking position of a path, drag the path name up or down on the Paths palette. The "Work Path" will always remain on the bottom.

TIP Hold down Ctrl/Cmd to use the Direct Selection tool while any Pen tool is chosen.

Display/Hide Path; Select Anchor Points

291

To reshape a path, you can move, add, or delete an anchor point, or move a segment. To modify the shape of a curved line segment, move a direction line toward or away from its anchor point, or rotate it around its anchor point.

To reshape a path:

1. On the Paths palette, click the name of the path you want to reshape.

2. Choose the Direct Selection tool (A or Shift-A). To access the Direct Selection tool when another pen tool is chosen, press Ctrl/Cmd.

3. Click the path in the image window.

4. Do any of the following:

Drag an anchor **point** or a **segment** 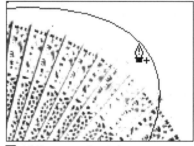. To select a segment, drag a marquee that includes both of the segment's endpoints. Shift-drag to marquee additional segments (or subpaths).

Drag or **rotate** a **direction line** 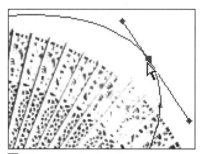. If you move a direction line on a smooth point, the two segments that are connected to that point will also move. If you move a direction line on a corner point, on the other hand, only one curve segment will move.

To **add** an anchor **point**, choose the Add Anchor Point tool, then click on a line segment (the pointer will be a pen icon with a plus sign when it's over a segment) 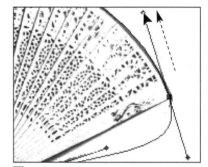–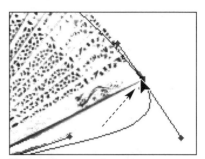.

TIP If Auto Add/Delete is checked on the options bar, the Pen tool will turn into the Add Anchor Point tool when it's over a segment, or into the Delete Anchor Point tool when it's over a point. To turn this function off temporarily, hold down Shift.

1 *Dragging an anchor point*

2 *Pulling a direction line*

3 *Adding an anchor point*

4 *The new anchor point*

Reshape Path

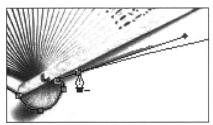

1 *Deleting an anchor point*

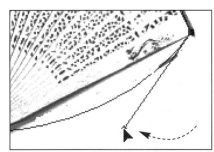

2 *Converting a direction line*

3 *To delete a path,* ***right-click/Control-click*** *the path name, then choose* ***Delete Path*** *from the context menu.*

To **delete** an anchor **point**, choose the Delete Anchor Point tool, then click on the anchor point (the pointer will be a pen icon with a minus sign when it's over a point) **1**.

To **convert** a **smooth point** into a **corner point**, choose the Convert Point tool (or hold down Ctrl-Alt/Cmd-Option if the Direct Selection tool is chosen or Alt/Option if a Pen tool is chosen), then click the anchor point (deselect the Convert Point tool by choosing another tool). To **convert** a **corner point** into a **smooth point**, choose the Convert Point tool, then drag away from the anchor point.

Use the Convert Point tool to rotate one direction line independently of the other direction line in the pair **2**. Once the Convert Point tool has been used on part of a direction line, you can use either the Convert Point tool or the Direct Selection tool to move its partner.

5. Click outside the path to deselect it.

Note: If the path you want to delete is a "Work Path," simply drawing a new work path with the Pen tool will cause the original "Work Path" to be replaced.

To delete a path:

1. On the Paths palette, activate the path you want to delete.

2. Right-click/Control-click the path name, then choose Delete Path from the context menu **3**.
or
Alt-click/Option-click the Delete Path (trash) button on the Paths palette.
or
Click the Delete Path (trash) button, then click Yes.
or
Drag the path name over the Delete Path (trash) button.

Is that enough options for ya?

Delete Path

To deselect a path:

1. Choose the Direct Selection tool ![tool] or the Path Selection tool ![tool] (A or Shift-A).

2. Click outside the path in the image window. The path will still be visible in the image window, but its anchor points and direction lines will be hidden.

To convert a path into a selection:

1. *Optional:* Create a selection if you want to add, delete, or intersect the new path selection with it.

2. Ctrl-click/Cmd-click the name of the path you want to convert into a selection.
or
On the Paths palette, activate the name of the path you want to convert into a selection, then click the "Load path as a selection" button ![button] **1** at the bottom of the palette. The last used Make Selection settings will apply.

To choose options as you load the path as a selection, right-click/Control-click the path name and choose Make Selection from the context menu **2**. You can apply a Feather Radius to the selection (enter a low number to soften the edge slightly) or add, subtract, or intersect the path with an existing selection on the image by clicking an Operation option. Operation shortcuts are listed in the sidebar on this page. Click OK. *Note:* If you check Anti-aliased, make the Feather Radius 0.

3. On the Layers palette, choose the layer you created the selection for.

2 *Choose options for a selection in the* **Make Selection** *dialog box.*

Path-into-selection shortcuts

WINDOWS

Make path current selection	Ctrl-click path name
Add path to current selection	Ctrl-Shift-click path name
Subtract path from current selection	Ctrl-Alt-click path name
Intersect path with current selection	Ctrl-Alt-Shift-click path name

MACINTOSH

Make path current selection	Cmd-click path name
Add path to current selection	Cmd-Shift-click path name
Subtract path from current selection	Cmd-Option-click path name
Intersect path with current selection	Cmd-Option-Shift-path name

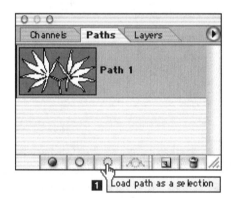

1 Load path as a selection

Make Selection

Rendering

Feather Radius: 10 pixels

☐ Anti-aliased

OK

Cancel

Operation

○ New Selection

○ Add to Selection

◉ Subtract from Selection

○ Intersect with Selection

1 *This is the original image. (The path is shown in the thumbnail in figure* **1** *on the previous page.)*

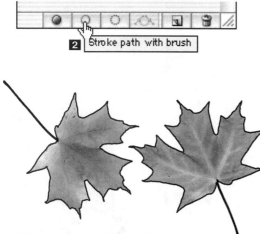

2 Stroke path with brush

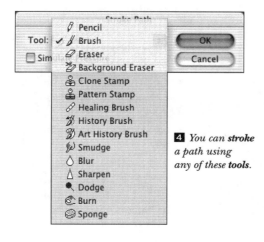

3 *A* **Pencil** *tool* **Stroke** *is applied to the* **path***.*

Tool:	✓		Pencil
		✓	Brush
☐ Sim			Eraser

Stroke Path

- ✎ Pencil
- ✓ 🖌 Brush
- ✐ Eraser
- ✐ Background Eraser
- 🖌 Clone Stamp
- 🖌 Pattern Stamp
- ✐ Healing Brush
- ✐ History Brush
- ✐ Art History Brush
- 🖐 Smudge
- ○ Blur
- △ Sharpen
- ✦ Dodge
- ✋ Burn
- 🧽 Sponge

OK
Cancel

4 *You can* **stroke** *a path using any of these* **tools***.*

When you apply color to (stroke) the edge of a path, the current tool and its current options bar attributes (e.g., Opacity and Mode) are used as the attributes for the stroke.

To stroke a path:
Method 1

1. On the Paths palette, click a closed or open path **1**.

2. Using the Layers palette, click the layer on which you want the stroke pixels to appear (not a shape layer).

3. From the Toolbox, choose one of the tools shown on the pop-up menu in figure **4** to be used to produce the stroke.

4. On the options bar:

Choose a Mode.

and

Choose an Opacity (or Pressure, Exposure, or Flow, depending on which tool you chose).

and

Click the Brush picker arrowhead, then click a brush on the picker. The stroke thickness will be the same as the diameter of the brush tip.

5. Choose a Foreground color.

6. Click the "Stroke path with brush" (second) button at the bottom of the Paths palette **2**–**3**.

Method 2

1. If you don't need to change the options bar settings for the tool used to produce the stroke, you can choose the tool directly from the dialog box. Alt-click/ Option-click the "Stroke path with brush" (second) button at the bottom of the Paths palette.

2. Choose a tool **4**.

3. *Optional:* Check Simulate Pressure to have the stroke thin out at the ends, if the path is open, or somewhere in the middle, if the path is closed.

4. Click OK.

7.0!

Stroke Path

Use the Fill Path command to fill a path with a color, a pattern, or imagery.

To fill a path:

1. On the Paths palette, activate an open or closed path.

2. On the Layers palette, choose the layer you want the fill pixels to appear on. Don't choose a shape layer!

3. To fill with a solid color other than white or black, choose a Foreground color.
or
To fill with imagery from a history state, move the History Brush icon to the state you want to use for the fill.

(To fill with a pattern, you'll choose an existing preset in step 5.)

4. Right-click/Ctrl-click and choose Fill Path from the context menu.
or
Alt-click/Option-click the "Fill path with foreground color" (first) button at the bottom of the Paths palette **1**.

5. Choose from the Contents: Use pop-up menu **2**. For a pattern, choose a pattern from the Custom Pattern picker.
and
Choose a Mode. Choose Clear mode if you want to fill the path on a layer with transparency.
and
Enter an Opacity percentage.

6. *Optional:* If a layer (not the Background) is active, check Preserve Transparency to recolor only existing, visible pixels on that layer, not any transparent areas.

7. *Optional:* Choose Rendering options (feathering and anti-aliasing).

8. Click OK **3**–**4**.

TIP To fill a path using the default dialog box settings, click the path name, then click the "Fill path with foreground color" button ● at the bottom of the Paths palette.

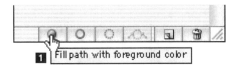

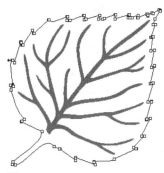

3 *The original path*

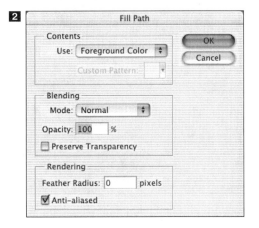

4 *The path **filled** with a **pattern**, 50% opacity*

1 *Windows: Choose a path from the **Paths** drop-down menu.*

2 *Mac OS: Choose a path from the **Write** pop-up menu.*

You can create a path in Photoshop, export it to Adobe Illustrator or Macromedia FreeHand, and then use it as an editable path in that program. What's more, you can then place the same path back into Photoshop (see page 70).

Note: You could also use the Path Selection tool to copy and paste or drag-and-drop an active path to another application (or to another open Photoshop image).

To export a path to Illustrator or FreeHand:

1. Create and save a path. You can also use a shape layer's vector mask (see the next page). *Note:* To make a vector mask available on the Write pop-up menu, choose that layer before performing the next step.

2. Choose File > Export > Paths to Illustrator.

3. *Optional:* Change the name in the File Name (Win)/Name (Mac OS) field.

4. From the Paths (Win)**1**/Write (Mac)**2** pop-up menu:

Choose an individual path name.
or
Choose All Paths to export all the paths in the image as one file. Document crop marks will be included in the export file.
or
Choose Document Bounds to export crop marks only for the current file.

5. Choose a location in which to save the path file.

6. Click Save. The path can be opened as an Adobe Illustrator document.

TIP To ensure that the path fits when you reimport it into Photoshop, don't alter its crop marks in Illustrator.

TIP You may have to choose Outline view in Illustrator to see the exported path, because it won't have a stroke.

Export Path to Illustrator or FreeHand

Vector masks

7.0! A vector mask (formerly called a layer clipping path) works like a layer mask, except in this case a vector path shape is used to delineate the visible and masked areas in the current layer. The path used for the mask can be created using the Pen tool, Freeform Pen tool, or a shape tool, or from a selection that is converted to a path. The vector mask produces a clean, sharp-edged shape that hides pixels on a layer. You can modify the path shape or discard the mask at any time.

A vector mask displays as a gray thumbnail on the Layers palette, and also on the Paths palette when the layer that contains the mask is selected. Like a layer mask, a vector mask is associated with only one layer.

To create a vector mask:

Method 1

1. On the Layers palette, choose the layer you want to add a vector mask to ■.

2. To create a white mask in which all the layer pixels are visible, choose Layer > Add Vector Mask > Reveal All or Ctrl-click/Cmd-click the "Add vector mask" button ◙ on the Layers palette.
or
To create a gray mask in which all the layer pixels are hidden, choose Layer > Add Vector Mask > Hide All or Ctrl-Alt-click/Cmd-Option-click the "Add vector mask" button ◙ on the Layers palette.

3. Choose the Pen, Freeform Pen, or any shape tool and create a clipping path in the desired shape ■–■.

Method 2

1. On the Layers palette, choose the layer you want to add a vector mask to.

2. To reveal only layer pixels within a selected, existing path, select a path on the Paths palette, then choose Layer > Add Vector Mask > Current Path.

■ *A layer with strokes that will be clipped*

■ *A vector mask is added,* **Hide All,** *and then the Pen tool is used to shape the path.*

■ *The effect of the* **vector mask** *on the layer imagery*

EPS clipping paths—a new way

If you save a file containing a vector mask as a Photoshop EPS for import into another program (e.g., InDesign or QuarkXPress), the masking effect of the vector mask will be preserved in the other program. This method has an advantage over the clipping path option on the Paths palette because you're working directly with the image layer and will see how the image will be clipped before it's exported. Just be sure **Include Vector Data** stays checked in the EPS Options dialog box.

Note: To import a Photoshop file that contains a vector mask into Illustrator 10, Place (Link option unchecked) or Open the file in Illustrator 10 and choose to convert layers to objects.

Add to shape area — Subtract from shape area — Intersect shape areas — Exclude overlapping shape areas

1 The **Pathfinder** buttons on the options bar

2 Using the Pen tool and the **Add to shape area** button, a second vector mask is added to a layer that already contains a vector mask.

The pathfinder operation buttons are used to create add-ons to, or cutouts from, an existing path, or to create a separate path.

To combine paths:

1. Click a layer that contains a vector mask. The vector mask thumbnail is now selected.

2. Choose a pen or shape tool.

3. On the options bar, click one of the four pathfinder buttons **1**.

4. Draw another path in the image window **2**–**3**.

If you reshape a vector mask, the masking effect in the image will change accordingly.

To reshape a vector mask:

1. Choose the Direct Selection tool (A or Shift-A).

2. Click the vector mask in the image window to select it.
or
Click the layer that has a vector mask. The vector mask thumbnail should be selected and the vector mask should now be visible in the image window.

3. Click the edge of the vector mask to reveal and select its anchor points.

4. Follow the steps on pages 291–293 to reshape the path.

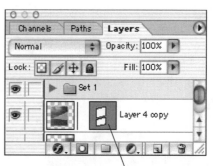

3 Now **two** vector mask shapes are displayed in the vector mask thumbnail.

Combine Paths; Reshape Vector Mask

A vector mask can be moved independently of its layer pixels at any time. It stays on its designated layer.

To reposition a vector mask:

1. Choose the Path Selection tool (A or Shift-A).

2. On the Layers palette, click the layer that contains the vector mask.

3. Drag the vector mask to a new location in the image window. A different area of layer pixels will now be visible within the confines of the path **1**.

To duplicate a vector mask:

1. Choose the layer you want the duplicate to appear on.

2. From another layer, drag the vector mask thumbnail you want to duplicate over the "Add vector mask" button ◻ **2**–**3**. The duplicate vector mask will appear on the active layer.

To deactivate a vector mask:

Shift-click the vector mask thumbnail on the Layers palette. A red "X" will appear over the thumbnail, and the entire layer will now be visible **4** (the vector mask thumbnail won't become selected).

(Shift-click the vector mask thumbnail again to remove the "X" and restore the clipping effect.)

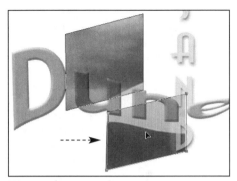

1 *The vector mask is **moved**, and now a different area of layer pixels is visible inside it.*

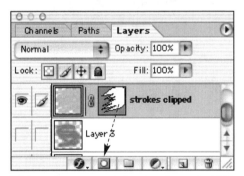

2 *Drag the vector mask thumbnail over the **Add vector mask** button.*

3 *A **copy** of the vector mask appears on the active layer (in this case, Layer 3).*

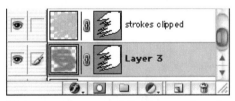

4 *The vector mask is **deactivated.***

Reposition, Duplicate, Deactivate Vector Mask

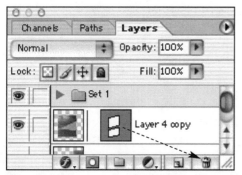

2 *Subtract from shape area* button

3 *The hidden and visible areas are* **reversed***.*

4 *Drag the* **vector mask thumbnail** *over the* **Delete Layer** *button.*

To reverse the visible and hidden areas in a vector mask:

1. Choose the Path Selection tool (A or Shift-A).

2. On the Layers palette, click the layer that contains a vector mask. The vector mask will be highlighted in the image window.

3. Click the vector mask in the image window. Now the anchor points and segments will become selected **1**.

4. Click the "Subtract from shape area" (second) button on the options bar **2**–**3**, or press "-" (minus or hyphen key).

To switch the revealed and hidden areas again, click the first button (Add to shape area) on the options bar, or press "+".

You can delete any vector masks that you no longer need, though you won't recoup any file storage space by doing so.

To discard a vector mask:

1. On the Layers palette, click the thumbnail for the vector mask that you want to remove.

2. Click the Delete Layer (trash) button, then click OK.
or
Drag the vector mask thumbnail over the Delete Layer button **4**.
or
Choose Layer > Delete Vector Mask, then click OK.

Reverse, Discard Vector Mask

Should you decide that you want a hard-edged mask to define an image layer, you can convert a layer mask into a vector mask.

To convert a layer mask into a vector mask:

1. Ctrl-click/Cmd-click a layer mask thumbnail on the Layers palette.

2. On the Paths palette, click the "Make work path from selection" button. Leave the path selected.

3. Choose Layer > Add Vector Mask > Current Path **1**.

4. *Optional:* To remove the layer mask, drag the layer mask thumbnail (first thumbnail) to the Delete Layer button on the Layers palette, then click Discard, or choose Layer > Remove Layer Mask > Discard. The vector mask will remain.

To create an adjustment layer that uses a vector mask:

1. Create a new shape layer (see page 304).

2. Choose a command from Layer > Change Layer Content submenu.

3. Make the desired adjustments in the dialog box, then click OK.

You can fill type shapes with imagery using a vector mask, and we offer two methods for doing this.

To create a vector mask from type:
Method 1

1. Create a type layer (**1**, next page).

2. With the type layer active, choose Layer > Type > Convert to Shape (**2**, next page).

3. From the Paths (yes Paths) palette menu, choose Save Path, change the path name, if desired, then click OK.

4. Leave path selected in the image window. On the Layers palette, choose the image layer you want the new vector mask to appear on (not a layer that already has a vector mask).

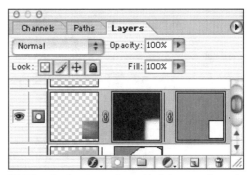

1 *The* **selection** *from a* **layer mask** *becomes the path for a* **vector mask***. The layer shown here now has two mask thumbnails.*

Layer Mask or Type into Vector Mask

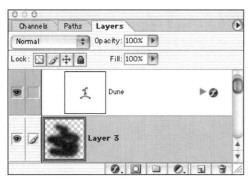

1 *Choose a type layer.*

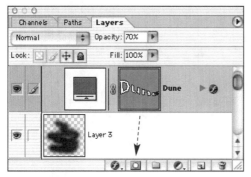

2 *Convert the type layer into a shape layer, then drag the vector mask thumbnail over the Add vector mask button.*

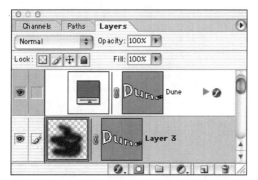

3 *The vector mask thumbnail is copied to the selected layer (Layer 3, in our example). (Any layer effects on the original layer can also be copied by dragging them over the selected layer.)*

5. Choose Layer > Add Vector Mask > Current Path.

6. Delete or hide the type shape layer.

Method 2

1. Create a type layer, and keep it active **1**.

2. Choose Layer > Type > Convert to Shape **2**.

3. Choose the layer you want the new vector mask to appear on (the layer shouldn't already contain a vector mask).

4. Drag the vector mask thumbnail that was created in step 2 over the "Add vector mask" button [icon] on the Layers palette. A new vector mask will be created for the active layer **3**.

5. Delete or hide the type shape layer.

TIP For both Method 1 and Method 2, you can do any of the following:

Duplicate the original type layer before converting it so you'll have it available for future type edits, and thus future vector masks. Hide the duplicate type layer.

Use the Path Selection tool to reposition the vector masks within the layer.

To reverse what is revealed and what is hidden on the layer, choose the Path Selection tool, Shift-click the character shapes in the image, then click the "Subtract from shape area" button [icon] on the options bar or press the hyphen ("-") key.

Type into Vector Mask

Shapes

A shape is a precise geometric or custom-shaped clipping path that reveals a solid color, gradient, or pattern fill within its contour and occupies its own layer 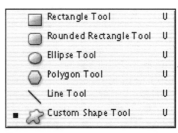. A shape can be repositioned, transformed, or reshaped at any time; its fill content can be modified or changed to a different type at any time; and the usual layer styles, effects, blending modes, opacity settings, and fill settings can be applied to it.

Unlike the main Photoshop image, which is a bitmap, shape layers are composed of vector data (think Adobe Illustrator or Macromedia Freehand). This means that shapes always look sharp and precise, whether they are printed on a PostScript printer, saved in PDF format, or imported into a vector drawing program; in other words, they're resolution-independent.

Creating a shape layer involves drawing a vector path, just as you would in an illustration program.

To create a shape layer:

1. Choose a layer on the Layers palette. The new shape layer will be created above this layer. *Note:* If the layer you choose has a vector mask, the shape will become part of the vector mask. To prevent this from happening, make sure the vector mask thumbnail is deselected.

2. Choose a Foreground color for the shape's color fill. (You'll learn how to fill a shape with a gradient or pattern later.)

3. Choose a shape tool on the Toolbox (U or Shift-U) **2**. Once any shape tool is selected, you can switch to a different shape tool by clicking one of the six shape tool buttons on the options bar **3**.

Effects on a clipping path

Apply **layer effects** (Inner Glow, Bevel, etc.) to a shape layer or to a layer that has a vector mask to enhance edges, add a shadow, etc. If you apply the Stroke effect or any of the Overlay effects to stroke or fill the vector mask, you'll be able to modify the stroke or fill at any time.

1 A star **shape** with a solid color fill

2 The **shape** tools

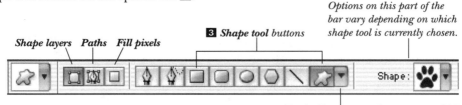

Shape layers *Paths* *Fill pixels*

3 *Shape tool buttons*

Options on this part of the bar vary depending on which shape tool is currently chosen.

Shape :

*For the **Geometry options**, see page 308.*

Create Shape Layer

Photoshop versus ImageReady

	PHOTOSHOP	IMAGEREADY
Pen tools	**yes**	no
Polygon tool	**yes**	no
Custom Shape tool	**yes**	no
Create and edit shape layers	**yes**	no
Create and edit vector masks	**yes**	no
Edit shapes	**yes**	transform or move, but not edit

1 *A shape is created using the Custom Shape tool.*

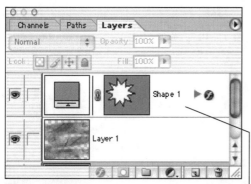

2 *The shape layer appears on the Layers palette. It has an adjustment layer thumbnail and a vector mask thumbnail.*

4. On the shape tool options bar:

If you're using the Rounded Rectangle tool, choose a Radius value; for the Polygon tool, choose a number of Sides; for the Line tool, choose a Weight; or for the Custom Shape tool, choose a shape from the picker.
and
Click the Shape layers (first) button. 🔲 (If this button isn't available, it means an existing vector mask is selected; deselect the mask thumbnail.)

5. Drag in the image window to draw the shape. While dragging, hold down Alt/ Option to draw from the shape's center. Shift-drag to constrain a rectangle to a square, an ellipse to a circle, or a line to a multiple of 45°. *Note:* In Windows, the draw-from-center function (Alt-dragging) may not work for the Custom Shape tool.

6. When the mouse is released, the shape will display **1**. A new Shape 1 layer will be listed on the Layers palette. It will have an adjustment layer thumbnail that controls its fill content and a vector mask thumbnail that controls its contour and location **2**.

TIP Choose Layer Style, Mode, Opacity, and Fill settings for the new layer.

TIP When the Custom Shape tool is chosen, you can right-click/Ctrl-click the image to quickly open the Custom Shape picker.

The link option 7.0!

If the link button next to the Style thumbnail **3** on the Shape Tool options bar is dark (selected), style and color changes will apply to the **current** shape layer. If the link button is light (not selected), style and color changes will apply to a **new** shape layer you create.

3 *Options on the Shape Tool options bar*

The shape tools can be used to create a temporary work path.

To create a work path using a shape tool:

1. Follow steps 1–4 starting on page 304.

2. Click the Paths button on the options bar ❶.

3. Drag in the image window to create the path shape ❷. Alt-drag/Option-drag to draw from the center. Shift-drag to constrain a rectangle to a square, an ellipse to a circle, or a line to a multiple of 45°.

The new work path shape will be listed on the Paths palette ❸. To learn more about work paths, see page 284.

Beware! Next time you use a shape tool with the Paths button chosen again, the existing work path will be replaced! To save the work path so it can't be replaced, double-click Work Path on the Paths palette, then click OK.

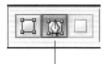

❶ *Click the **Paths** button on the options bar.*

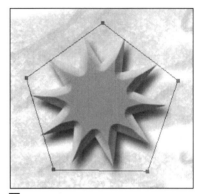

❷ *A pentagonal **work path** is drawn.*

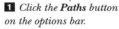

❸ *The **Work Path** appears on the Paths palette.*

1 *Click the **Fill pixels** button on the options bar.*

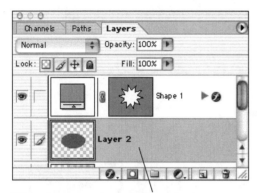

2 *On the Layers palette, the **Fill pixels** shape displays as a normal rasterized layer—not as a shape layer.*

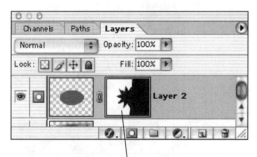

3 *You can use a shape tool with the **Fill pixels** button clicked to create a geometric area within an existing layer mask.*

The shape tools can also be used as a quick drawing tool to create a geometric pixel area on a layer. This is a quick way to produce a precise pixel shape without having to use a vector mask.

To create a geometric, rasterized pixel area:

1. Choose an image layer or create a new layer. A pixel shape cannot be created on a vector layer (shape or type layer).

2. Choose a Foreground color.

3. Choose a shape tool (U or Shift-U). Once a shape tool is chosen, you can then click a different shape tool button on the options bar.

4. On the options bar:
Click the "Fill pixels" button ☐ **1**.
and
If you're using the Rounded Rectangle tool, choose a Radius value; for the Polygon tool, choose a number of Sides; for the Line tool, choose a Weight; or for the Custom Shape tool, choose a shape from the picker.
and
Choose Layer Style, Mode, Opacity, and Fill settings.

5. Drag across the image window to create the shape. A pixel area will be created **2**. Use brushes, editing tools, filters—whatever—to modify the pixels.

TIP To create a geometric pixel area within a layer mask, click an existing layer mask thumbnail on the Layers palette, choose a shape tool, click the "Fill pixels" button on the options bar, then drag in the image window **3**.

You can customize each shape tool so it will behave a certain way each time you use it.

To choose geometric options for a shape tool:

1. Choose a shape tool (U or Shift-U). Once the tool is chosen, you can click a different shape tool button on the options bar.

2. Click the Geometry Options arrowhead on the options bar **1**.

3. Options on the pop-up palette will vary depending on which tool is chosen. For the Ellipse tool, for example, you can click Unconstrained, Circle, Fixed Size, or Proportional. For Fixed Size or Proportional, enter W and H values. Check From Center to have the tool draw from the center.

4. If you chose the Custom Shape tool, click the Custom Shape arrowhead or thumbnail **2**, then click a shape on the picker. You can use the picker menu to load in other libraries.

5. To close the pop-up palette or picker, click the arrowhead again or click outside it.

Since a shape layer contains vector data, you can modify a shape's vector mask at any time, and its crisp edge will stay crisp.

To reposition a shape layer's vector mask:

1. Choose the Path Selection tool (A or Shift-A).

2. Click a shape in the image window.
   or
   Click a shape layer on the Layers palette.

3. Drag the vector mask in the image window **3**. The vector mask thumbnail will update to reflect the new position **4**.

TIP If you click a vector mask thumbnail on the Layers palette (or position the cursor over it with the mouse button up), the vector mask will become highlighted in the image window (this won't cause the path itself to become selected).

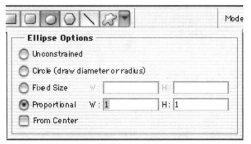

1 *Each **shape** tool has its own **pop-up options** palette.*

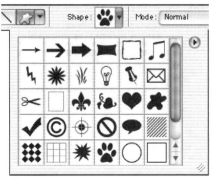

2 *These are the default choices on the **Custom shape** tool **picker**. Other libraries are available.*

3 *The **vector mask** is **dragged** in the image window.*

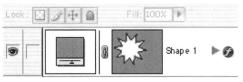

4 *The shape's vector mask thumbnail updates to reflect the shape's new position. Compare with **2** on page 307.*

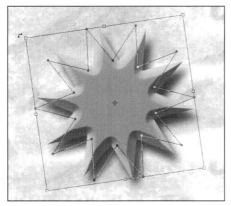

1 *Use the **Path Selection** tool (Show Bounding Box option checked) or the **Free Transform** command to display the bounding box handles on a shape layer's vector mask, then drag a handle to transform it.*

2 *Use the **Direct Selection** tool to drag an anchor point on the vector mask for a shape layer.*

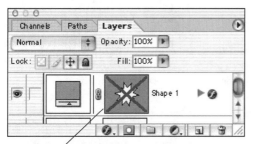

3 *This vector mask is temporarily **hidden**.*

To transform a shape layer:

1. Choose the Path Selection tool (A or Shift-A).

2. Click a shape in the image window.
or
Click a shape layer on the Layers palette.

3. Click the highlighted shape to display its anchor points (and its bounding box, too, if Show Bounding Box is checked on the options bar) **1**.

4. Follow the instructions on pages 138–142 to transform the shape.

To modify the contour of an existing shape layer:

1. Choose the Direct Selection tool (A or Shift -A).

2. Click a shape in the image window.
or
Click a shape layer name on the Layers palette.

3. Click the edge of the highlighted shape to display its anchor points **2**.

4. Follow the instructions on pages 292–293 to reshape the path.

To deactivate a shape layer's vector mask:

Shift-click the vector mask thumbnail for the shape layer on the Layers palette. An "X" will appear over the thumbnail **3** and the entire layer's fill content will display.

(Shift-click the vector mask thumbnail again to remove the "X" and restore the masking effect.)

Edit Shape Layer; Deactivate Vector Mask

To paste a path object from Illustrator into Photoshop as a shape layer:

1. In Illustrator, copy a vector object.

2. In Photoshop, choose Edit > Paste. In the Paste dialog box, click Shape Layer, then click OK **1**. The shape layer will be filled with the current Foreground color, but it won't have a stroke. You have pasted the vector mask outline from the shape layer.

To use the pathfinder options to add or subtract shapes from each other:

1. Create a shape layer.

2. Leave the vector mask for the new shape layer selected.

3. Make sure a shape tool is chosen.

4. Click a pathfinder button on the options bar **2**.

5. Drag partially across the existing shape. A new shape path will be created that either extends or subtracts from the existing shape **3**.

TIP To reverse what a single vector mask shape clips and reveals, select the mask with the Path Selection tool, then on the options bar, click the "Subtract from shape area" button **4**. Click the "Add to shape area" button **5** to restore the original clipping setup.

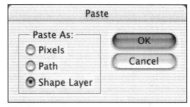

1 *Click **Shape Layer** in the **Paste** dialog box.*

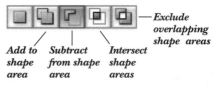

Exclude overlapping shape areas

Add to shape area   *Subtract from shape area*   *Intersect shape areas*

2 *Click a **pathfinder** button. We chose "Subtract from shape area."*

3 *The new shape path **subtracts** (cuts out) from the existing shape area.*

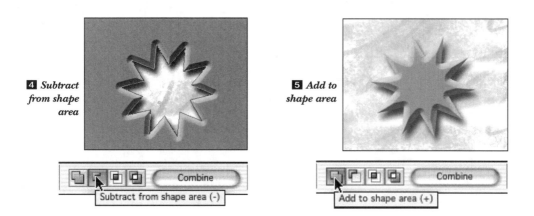

4 *Subtract from shape area*

Subtract from shape area (-)

5 *Add to shape area*

Add to shape area (+)

Quick switcheroo

To change the fill contents of a selected shape to a Gradient or Pattern fill, or to change the command in a selected adjustment layer (e.g., Hue/Saturation to Levels), choose from the Layer > **Change Layer Contents** submenu.

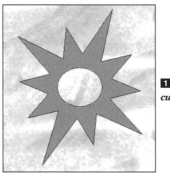

1 *Create a custom shape.*

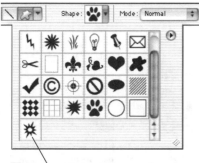

2 *The new shape appears on the Custom Shape picker.*

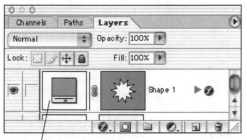

3 *The Shape layer thumbnail*

If you have altered the contour of a preset shape or pasted in a shape from Illustrator, you can then add that new shape to the custom shape picker so you can use it again.

To add a shape to the custom shape picker:

1. Create a custom shape **1**.
or
Create a new shape layer from a pasted Illustrator object.

2. Click the shape layer name on the Layers palette.

3. Choose Edit > Define Custom Shape, enter a Name, then click OK. The new custom shape will appear at the bottom of the custom shape picker **2**, and it will stay on the picker even if you exit/quit and relaunch Photoshop. It will be removed from the picker, however, if you load in a replacement library or restore the default custom shape library to the picker.

The fill contents of a shape layer can be changed at any time.

To change the fill contents of a shape layer:

1. Double-click the shape layer thumbnail on the Layers palette (it has a slider icon) **3**.
or
Choose a shape layer, then choose Layer > Layer Contents Options.

2. Choose a new color from the Color Picker, then click OK.

Custom Shape Picker; Layer Fill Contents

311

Before you can perform pixel edits on a shape layer (e.g., apply brush strokes or a filter) or change a shape's vector mask into a (pixel) layer mask, the shape layer has to be rasterized.

To rasterize a shape layer:

1. Choose a shape layer 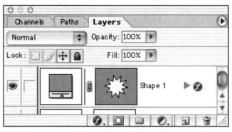.

2. From the Layer > Rasterize submenu, choose:

Shape to convert the shape layer into a filled pixel shape on a transparent layer, without a vector mask. Painting and editing can now occur on the layer **2**.

Fill Content to convert the shape layer's fill content into a pixel area clipped by the existing vector mask. Painting and editing can now occur on the layer **3**.

Vector Mask to convert the vector mask into a pixel-based layer mask in the exact same shape and position as the vector mask. The fill content is still an editable solid color fill. The layer mask can be repositioned within the layer **4**.

Layer produces the same results as the Shape option listed above **5**.

Rasterize Shape Layer — 7.0!

1 *The original shape layer on the Layers palette*

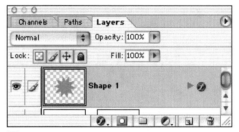

2 *The Rasterize > **Shape** command removed the clipping path.*

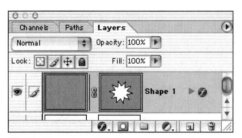

3 *The Rasterize > **Fill Content** command converted the adjustable fill into a normal pixel area.*

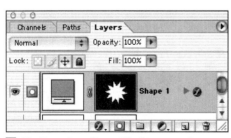

4 *The Rasterize > **Vector Mask** command converted the vector mask into a layer mask.*

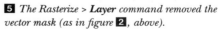

5 *The Rasterize > **Layer** command removed the vector mask (as in figure **2**, above).*

How will it look?

In Photoshop, you can create editable type, which consists of pixels in the same resolution as the overall image. Photoshop and ImageReady use a typeface's vector outlines when resizing editable type and when outputting to PDF or EPS, or to a PostScript printer. The result is type output that is sharp and resolution-independent.

Vector

1 *This is sharp, **editable**, vector type.*

Pixels

2 *This type was **rasterized**, and then **filters** and **layer effects** were applied to it.*

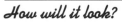

3 *Click the palette button* [icon] *on the options bar to show/hide the **Character/Paragraph** palettes.*

IN THIS CHAPTER you'll learn how to create, transform, move, and warp an editable type layer; change its character and paragraph attributes; rasterize a type layer into pixels; screen back type or screen back an image behind type; fill type with imagery using Paste Into or a clipping group of layers; create fading type; create and use a type selection; add type to a spot color channel; create a type mask for an adjustment layer; find and replace text; and check spelling.

7.0!

Creating type

Different kinds of type

When type is created in Photoshop using the Horizontal or Vertical Type tool **1**, it appears instantly in the image window, and a new layer is created automatically for it. What's more, it's fully **editable**. Not only can you change its attributes (e.g., font, style, point size, color, kerning, tracking, leading, alignment, and baseline shift), you can also transform it, apply layer effects to it, change its blending mode, or change its opacity.

What can't be done to an editable type layer? You can't apply filters or paint strokes to it or fill it with a gradient or a pattern. In order to apply those kinds of effects, you have to **rasterize** the type layer into pixels (Layer > Rasterize > Type) **2**. But you can't have your cake and eat it, too. Once type is rasterized, its typographic attributes (e.g., font, style) can't be changed.

Attributes are chosen for type using the Character palette **3**, the Paragraph palette, and the options bar **4**.

(Continued on the following page)

Editable vs. Rasterized Type

4 *The **options bar** for the **Type** tool*

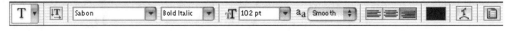

Using the Horizontal or Vertical Type Mask tool, you can create a **selection** in the shape of characters on any layer. You can then convert the type selection into a layer mask (see page 266), save it as an alpha channel, or save it as a shape layer for later use (see page 304).

Since editable type (as opposed to type that is created as a selection on a layer) automatically appears on its own layer, it can be edited, moved, transformed, restacked, or otherwise modified without affecting any other layer. You can be very casual about where you position editable type initially, and about which typographic attributes you choose for it, since it's so easy to edit afterward.

Note: Type that's created in a Bitmap, Indexed Color, or Multichannel image will appear on the Background, not on a layer, and it can't be edited.

To create an editable type layer:

1. Choose the Horizontal Type tool or Vertical Type tool (T or Shift-T) **1**. *7.0!*

2. To create point type, click to define an insertion point (see the sidebar).
or
To create paragraph type, drag a marquee to define the boundaries of the bounding box for the text to fit into.

3. From the options bar, do any of the following:

Choose a **font** family **2**.

Choose a font **style**.

Choose or enter a **size** (.10 to 1296 pt.).

Choose an **Anti-aliasing** method **3**: *7.0!* Sharp (sharpest), Crisp (somewhat sharp), Strong (heavier), or Smooth (smoothest). Photoshop will smooth the edges of the type by introducing partially transparent pixels along its edges. With anti-aliasing off (None), type will have jagged edges (**1**–**4**, next page).

Click an **Alignment** button to align point type relative to its original insertion point, or to align paragraph type to the

Point or paragraph

If you click in the image window with the Horizontal or Vertical Type tool, and then type your characters, you will create **point** type. This kind of type will keep on going, disappearing off the edge of the image, until you type a return. Use this method if you want to control hyphenation and line breaks manually in just a few lines of text.

If you drag in the image window with the Horizontal or Vertical Type tool to define an area for type to fit into before typing your characters, you will create **paragraph** type. Paragraph type is designed for larger text blocks. From the Paragraph palette menu, you can choose between two algorithms for paragraph type—**Adobe Single-line Composer** and **Adobe Every-line Composer**—that control how Photoshop flows type to the next line when the type reaches the edge of the text bounding box. The differences between these two algorithms are subtle.

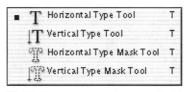

1 *The first two **type** tools create editable type; the second two create a type selection.*

Font family   *Font style*   *Type size*

2 *The left side of the **Horizontal Type** tool options bar*

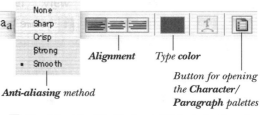

Alignment   *Type color*

Anti-aliasing method   *Button for opening the **Character/Paragraph** palettes*

3 *The right side of the **Horizontal Type** tool options bar*

1 *Anti-aliased* **None**

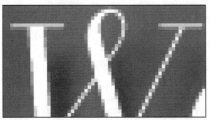

2 *Anti-aliased* **Crisp**

3 *Anti-aliased* **Strong**

4 *Anti-aliased* **Smooth**

5 *The* **Alignment** *buttons control where paragraph type is positioned within its bounding box (or where point type is positioned relative to the insertion point).*

left edge, right edge, or center of its bounding box **5**.

Choose a **color** for the type by clicking the swatch, then choosing a color from the Color Picker (or from the Swatches palette or Colors palette).

If the Character and Paragraph palettes aren't already open, click the palettes button, 🗐 then adjust any of the settings on either palette (you'll learn about these palettes throughout this chapter). **7.0!**

4. Type the text into the image window.

5. Press Enter on the keypad or click the ✔ on the options bar to accept the new text. (To cancel it, press Esc or click the ⊘ button.)

TIP Each time type is created using the Horizontal or Vertical Type tool, a new layer is created **6**. If you tend to create type by trial and error, and the layers start to overpopulate, you can periodically delete any layers you don't need.

Create a preset!

After styling your type, click the Type tool icon at the far left side of the options bar, then click the **Create new tool preset** button 🗐 to save the current type settings to a tool preset. This is like creating a style sheet. You can then choose this tool preset from the **Tool Preset picker**, which opens when you click the Type tool icon on the Type tool options bar, or from the **Tool Presets palette**. **7.0!**

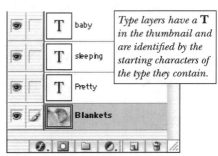

> *Type layers have a* **T** *in the thumbnail and are identified by the starting characters of the type they contain.*

6 *For the most flexibility, place individual words or characters on separate layers—then they can be moved around independently.*

Editing text

To edit text, you need to select it. You can select a single character, a word, or all the characters on the same type layer. You can also select the bounding box for a whole block of text.

To select all or some characters on a type layer:

Choose the Horizontal Type tool **T** or Vertical Type tool ⏐**T** (T or Shift-T), click in the type to create an insertion point, then drag across one or more characters to select them **1**. Or double-click a word to select the whole word; or double-click a word, then drag to select multiple words; or triple-click in a line of text to select the whole line.

or

With any tool selected, double-click the "T" icon for the type layer on the Layers palette. All the text on that layer will become selected, and the appropriate type tool will become selected automatically.

Note: After performing the text edits, to take the text tool out of edit mode and commit to the editing changes, click the ✔ on the options bar, or press Enter on the keypad, or click any other tool, or click a different layer.

(To cancel your editing changes before committing to them, click the ⊘ on the options bar or press Esc.)

TIP To apply layer effects to a type layer (or to edit an existing effect), double-click the layer on the Layers palette (not the layer name). This opens the Layer Style dialog box.

TIP If you want to see the bounding box for a block of text, choose the Move tool (V), click the type layer on the Layers palette, and check Show Bounding Box on the options bar.

7.0!

Selecting type with a type tool

Select **text string**	Drag. Or click at beginning of the text string, then Shift-click at the end.
Select **word**	Double-click
Select **line**	Triple-click
Select **paragraph**	Quadruple-click
Select **all**	Double-click the thumbnail on the Layers palette; or press Ctrl-A/Cmd-A; or quintuple-click the text.

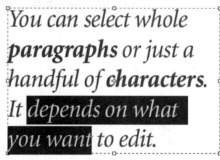

1 *Drag across the characters you want to **select**.*

Back and forth

■ To convert paragraph type to point type, click the type layer in the Layers palette, then choose Layer > Type > **Convert to Point Text**. A carriage return will be added at the end of every line of type except the last line.

■ When point type is converted to paragraph type, any characters that overflow the type bounding box are deleted. To avoid losing any text, click the type layer, then choose Layer > Type > **Convert to Paragraph Text**. Next, choose a type tool, click on the converted text, then resize the box by dragging one of its handles (if the handles are hidden, enlarge the document window first).

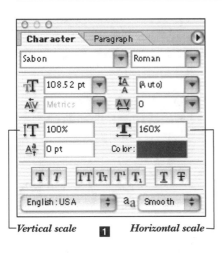

Vertical scale **1** *Horizontal scale*

stretch *Horizontal scale 50%*

stretch *Horizontal scale 100% (normal)*

stretch *Horizontal scale 200%*

stretch *Vertical scale 300%*

2 *Type can be scaled horizontally, vertically, or uniformly.*

Type can be resized interactively. That way, you can see how it's going to look immediately on your screen.

3 *Shift-drag a corner handle to resize type proportionally—and interactively.*

Use the Horizontal scale or Vertical scale commands (discussed below) only if you want to distort your characters (stretch or shorten them). To scale your characters uniformly, one option is to change the point size using the Character palette or the options bar. A second option is to Shift-drag a corner handle (see the second set of instructions on this page).

To scale type by entering a value:

1. On the Layers palette, click the layer that contains the type you want to scale.

2. To open the Character palette, choose the Horizontal Type tool T or Vertical Type tool T (T or Shift-T), then click the button on the options bar (or choose Window > Character).

3. *Optional:* Select the characters or words you want to scale with the Horizontal or Vertical Type tool. If you want all the characters in the layer to be scaled, you don't need to select anything.

4. Change the Vertical and/or Horizontal scale percentage on the Character palette (0–1000%) **1**–**2**.

To scale type by dragging:

1. Click the type layer on the Layers palette.

2. Choose the Move tool (V) and check Show Bounding Box on the options bar.
or
Choose Edit > Free Transform (Ctrl-T/Cmd-T).

3. Drag a corner handle to scale the height and width simultaneously, or drag a side handle to scale just the height or width.
or
Shift-drag a corner handle to preserve the proportions of the type as you scale it **3**.

4. To commit to the scale change, click the ✓ on the options bar or double-click the text block. (To cancel the scale change before committing to it, click the ⊘ on the options bar or press Esc.)

Scale Type

317

To adjust the spacing between (kern) two characters:

1. On the Layers palette, click a type layer.

2. If the Character palette isn't open, click the 🔲 button on the options bar.

3. Choose the Horizontal or Vertical Type tool, then click to create an insertion point between two characters.

4. Choose Metrics from the Kerning pop-up menu to apply the font's built-in kerning (this may be called Auto Kern in other applications). It's important to do this first, before applying kerning manually.

5. Choose a value from the Kerning pop-up menu or enter a value in the field (-1000 to 1000) **1**–**2**. Use a negative value to move the characters closer together or a positive value to spread them apart.
or
Press Alt/Option and the left or right arrow key.

TIP If you press Alt/Option with the left or right arrow with the Move tool chosen, you'll create copies of the type layer instead of kerning or tracking!

To adjust the spacing for (track) a series of characters:

1. On the Layers palette, click a type layer.

2. *Optional:* Choose the Horizontal or Vertical Type tool, then select the text you want to apply tracking to. Don't do this if you want to apply tracking to all the type on the layer.

3. If the Character palette isn't open, click the 🔲 button on the options bar.

4. Choose a value from the Tracking pop-up menu or enter a value in the field (-1000 to 1000) **3**–**4**. Use a negative value to move the characters closer together or a positive value to spread them apart.
or
If you selected type, Press Alt/Option and the left or right arrow key.

TIP If you're creating type for the Web, don't track your letters too close together—they'll be hard to read.

1 *Kerning*

Kern
Kern

2 *Use a negative **kerning** value (-100, in this case) to tighten the **spacing between** characters.*

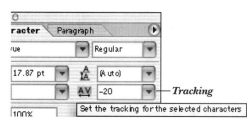

— *Tracking*

3 *The **Character** palette has some features that aren't found on the options bar.*

TRACKING TIPS

Tracking can help or hinder readability, depending on how high the tracking values are. Try not to overdo it!

4 *We like to spread out **little bits** of text, as in the headline in this illustration— but not whole paragraphs.*

Kern; Track

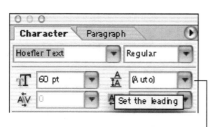

1 *The **Leading** area on the **Character** palette*

It will be well, however, always to bear in mind, that cake of every sort is to be partaken of as a luxury, not eaten for a full meal. Those who attend evening parties several times a week, can hardly take too small a quantity of the sweet and rich preparations. Many a young lady loses her appetite bloom and health by indulgence in these tempting but pernicious delicacies; and dyspeptic complaints frequently are aggravated, if not originated, by the absurd fashion of making our evening circles places for eating and drinking, rather than social and mental enjoyment. They manage these things better in Paris.   *—Sara Josepha Hale, 1841*

It will be well, however, always to bear in mind, that cake of every sort is to be partaken of as a luxury, not eaten for a full meal. Those who attend evening parties several times a week, can hardly take too small a quantity of the sweet and rich preparations. Many a young lady loses her appetite bloom and health by indulgence in these tempting but pernicious delicacies; and dyspeptic complaints frequently are aggravated, if not originated, by the absurd fashion of making our evening circles places for eating and drinking, rather than social and mental enjoyment. They manage these things better in Paris.   *—Sara Josepha Hale, 1841*

2 *The type in both paragraphs illustrated above has the same point size, but different **leading**. Leading affects both the overall look of a page and the readability of the text.*

Leading is the space that separates each line of text from the one above it. Each character can have its own leading value; the highest value in a line controls that line. Consequently, if you apply different leading values to different lines of paragraph text, and then edit the text in some way that causes it to reflow, the spacing between lines may change as a result.

We can't guarantee that your readers will find your writing interesting, but if you use an adequate amount of leading between the lines, at least it won't be a strain to read. So let the type eat up a bit more space on the page—at least your readers won't become weary before they've gleaned your pearls of wisdom!

P.S. If you're going to create a bulky amount of paragraph type, you'll probably want to do it in a layout or Web design program rather than in Photoshop.

To adjust leading in horizontal type:

1. On the Layers palette, click a type layer.

2. *Optional:* Using the Horizontal Type tool, highlight the line or lines of text that you want to apply leading values to. To apply leading to point type, select the whole line. If you don't highlight text, the whole layer will be affected.

3. Choose or enter a Leading value on the Character palette **1**–**2**.

TIP Auto leading is calculated as a percentage of the font size. The ratio is set in the Justification dialog box, which is opened from the Paragraph palette menu. The default value is 120% of the font size. The Auto leading amount for 30pt. type, for example, would be 36pt.

TIP To adjust the vertical spacing between characters in vertical type, highlight the characters you want to adjust, then change the Tracking value on the Character palette.

To shift selected characters above or below the normal baseline:

1. On the Layers palette, click the layer that contains the type you want to shift.

2. Choose the Horizontal or Vertical Type tool (T or Shift-T), then select the characters you want to shift. Otherwise, all the characters on the layer will be shifted.

3. On the Character palette, enter a Baseline shift value **1**. Use a positive value to shift characters above the normal baseline, or a negative value to shift characters below the baseline **2**.

To style type using the Character palette:

1. Select the type to be modified, or click a type layer to modify the whole layer.

2. Click a style button on the Character palette (use tool tips to identify them) or choose from the Character palette menu **3**:

Faux Bold to simulate the bold style or **Faux Italic** to simulate the italic style. Faux Bold isn't available for warped text.

All Caps or **Small Caps**. Small Caps only affects lowercase characters.

Superscript to shrink the type and raise above the baseline, or **Subscript** to shrink the type and lower it below the baseline.

Underline and/or **Strikethrough**.

Discretionary Ligatures or **Old Style** numerals (only for OpenType font character sets that contain the selected characters). Discretionary Ligatures are for ligatures that aren't in regular use.

No Break to have Photoshop keep the selected characters on a single line, whenever possible.

Fractional Widths to have Photoshop use fractions of pixels for type spacing for optimal appearance. Unchecking this option may improve readability for online applications that use small type. This setting applies to the entire layer.

Ersatz

If you're using a font for which no actual bold (or italic) font is installed on your system and you turn on the **Faux Bold** (or **Faux Italic**) option, Photoshop whips up an ersatz bold (or italic) version of that font for you. Type purists (ourselves included) will notice that the faux style doesn't quite match the grace and shape of the authentic font.

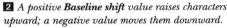

Baseline shift — **1**

+20 pts

0 pts

Normal baseline

−20 pts

2 *A positive **Baseline shift** value raises characters upward; a negative value moves them downward.*

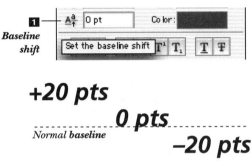

Style buttons   **3** *Character palette menu*

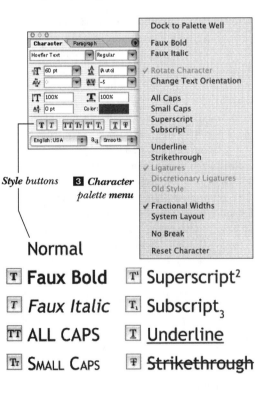

Normal

T **Faux Bold**

T *Faux Italic*

TT ALL CAPS

Tr SMALL CAPS

T Superscript[2]

T Subscript[3]

T Underline

T ~~Strikethrough~~

System Layout to view text through the text handling of the operating system, **7.0!** which may be useful if you're designing dialog boxes or menus.

You can change the orientation of existing horizontal type to vertical, or vice versa.

To change type orientation:

1. On the Layers palette, click a type layer **1**.

2. Choose a type tool, then click the **7.0!** Change "Text orientation" button on the options bar. **T**
or
Choose Change Text Orientation from **7.0!** the Character palette menu.
or
Choose Layer > Type > Horizontal or Vertical **2**.

You may need to reposition the type after applying either command.

TIP To rotate vertical type a different way, double-click its layer thumbnail (and highlight just the characters you want to rotate, if you don't want to rotate them all), then choose Rotate Character from the Character palette menu to check or uncheck the command **3**. This command isn't available for horizontal type.

1 *The original **vertical** type*

2 *The same type after clicking the **Change text orientation** button on the options bar*

3 *The original vertical type (figure **1**) after choosing the **Rotate Character** command on the Character palette menu.*

Type Orientation

Paragraph settings

If you create text as paragraph type rather than point type, Photoshop offers you a variety of formatting options. When you forgo the manual control you have with point text, you get a pretty sophisticated automatic layout tool in exchange.

The Paragraph palette includes settings for justification and alignment as well as for indents and paragraph spacing. The palette menu allows you to fine tune those options.

To set paragraph alignment and justification (horizontal type):

1. On the Layers palette, click a type layer.

2. If you want to modify all the paragraphs in the layer, don't select any text.
   or
   To modify one or more paragraphs, choose the Horizontal Type tool T (T or Shift-T), then click in one paragraph or select a series of consecutive paragraphs.

3. If the Paragraph palette isn't open, click the ▣ button on the options bar, then click the Paragraph tab.

4. Click an alignment and/or justification button at the top of the palette ▮:

   The buttons in the first group—**Left align text, Center text,** and **Right align text**—align type to one edge of the text bounding box ▮.

   The buttons in the second group—**Justify last left, Justify last centered,** and **Justify last right**—justify the type, forcing all but the last line to fill the space between the margins ▮.

   The last button, **Justify all,** forces *all* the lines to fill the space, even the last line.

5. Check Hyphenate at the bottom of the palette to enable automatic hyphenation. Be sure to check this option for justified text to help eliminate any large, unsightly gaps between words.

TIP To change the alignment and/or justification for vertical type, the procedure is the same as above, except the buttons have different labels.

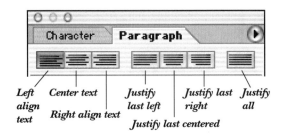

▮ *The alignment and justification buttons at the top of the Paragraph palette, for horizontal type*

Left align text · Center text · Right align text · Justify last left · Justify last centered · Justify last right · Justify all

---

Left align text

Whoever you are holding me now in hand
Whoever you are holding me now in hand,
Without one thing all will be useless,
I give you fair warning before you attempt me further,
I am not what you supposed, but far different…

Center text

Whoever you are holding me now in hand
Whoever you are holding me now in hand,
Without one thing all will be useless,
I give you fair warning before you attempt me further,
I am not what you supposed, but far different…

Right align text

Whoever you are holding me now in hand
Whoever you are holding me now in hand,
Without one thing all will be useless,
I give you fair warning before you attempt me further,
I am not what you supposed, but far different…
Walt Whitman

▮ *Paragraph alignment options*

Justify last left

Civilization is the encouragement of differences. Civilization thus becomes a synonym of democracy. Force, violence, pressure, or compulsion with a view to conformity, is both uncivilized and undemocratic. —*Mohandas Gandhi*

Justify last centered

Civilization is the encouragement of differences. Civilization thus becomes a synonym of democracy. Force, violence, pressure, or compulsion with a view to conformity, is both uncivilized and undemocratic. —*Mohandas Gandhi*

Justify last right

Civilization is the encouragement of differences. Civilization thus becomes a synonym of democracy. Force, violence, pressure, or compulsion with a view to conformity, is both uncivilized and undemocratic. —*Mohandas Gandhi*

Justify all

Civilization is the encouragement of differences. Civilization thus becomes a synonym of democracy. Force, violence, pressure, or compulsion with a view to conformity, is both uncivilized and   undemocratic.   —*Mohandas*

▮ *Paragraph justification options*

Good values

To enter a value in a non-default unit on the Paragraph palette, type the unit after the value: **in** for inches, **pt** for points, **mm** for millimeters, **cm** for centimeters, **px** for pixels, or **pica** for picas. The value will be converted automatically to the unit currently chosen in Edit (Photoshop, in OS X) > Preferences > Units & Rulers > Units: **Type**.

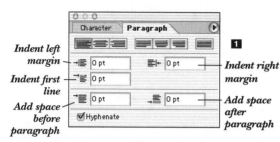

Indent left margin — Indent first line — Add space before paragraph — Indent right margin — Add space after paragraph

Civilization is the encouragement of differences. Civilization thus becomes a synonym of democracy. Force, violence, pressure, or compulsion with a view to conformity, is both uncivilized and undemocratic. —*Mohandas Gandhi*

2 *Indents of 0 (zero)*

Civilization is the encourage-ment of differences. Civilization thus becomes a synonym of democracy. Force, violence, pressure, or compulsion with a view to conformity, is both uncivilized and undemocratic. —*Mohandas Gandhi*

3 *Indented 2 picas **right** and **left***

Civilization is the encouragement of differences. Civilization thus becomes a synonym of democracy. Force, violence, pressure, or compulsion with a view to conformity, is both uncivilized and undemocratic. —*Mohandas Gandhi*

4 *Indent 16 pt. **first line***

Civilization is the encouragement of differences.

Civilization thus becomes a synonym of democracy.

Force, violence, pressure, or compulsion with a view to conformity, is both uncivilized and undemocratic.

5 *Add space before paragraph*

The paragraph indent and space-between-paragraph controls let you shape your paragraphs for improved readability.

To adjust paragraph indents and spacing (horizontal type):

1. On the Layers palette, click the type layer you want to modify.

2. If you want to modify all the paragraphs in the layer, don't select any text.
or
To modify one or more paragraphs, choose the Horizontal Type tool T (T or Shift-T), then click in one paragraph or select a series of consecutive paragraphs.

3. If the Paragraph palette isn't open, click the button on the options bar, then click the Paragraph tab.

4. Change the **Indent left margin, Indent right margin 1**–**3**, or **Indent first line** value **4**. Use an Indent first line value to make text more readable if you don't have room to add space between paragraphs. Don't apply an Indent first line value above zero *and* add space between paragraphs—that would look unprofessional. Use a combination of left and right indentation values to make a pull quote or bulleted list stand out.
and/or
Enter **Add space before paragraph 5** and **Add space after paragraph** values.

TIP To change the alignment and/or justification for vertical type, the procedure is the same as above, except the fields have different labels.

TIP When a type tool and a type layer containing paragraph type are chosen, the paragraph's bounding box is visible. You can reshape the box by moving any of its handles. Or to reshape the text box and also allow the type to be scaled horizontally and/or vertically, Ctrl-drag/Cmd-drag any handle (this works like a temporary Move tool).

Paragraph Indents and Spacing

These are some of the settings that can make the difference between okay-looking type and professional-looking type.

To fine-tune paragraph settings:

From the Paragraph palette menu, choose any of the following:

Roman Hanging Punctuation to have Photoshop move punctuation marks that fall at the ends of lines outside the type bounding box.

Justification and **Hyphenation** to specify the limits within which the Photoshop algorithms can operate as they adjust text to optimize its appearance **1**–**2**. (In the Justification dialog box, you can also set the Auto Leading value as a percentage of the type size.)

Enter a Glyph Scaling value above the default 100% in the Justification dialog box to allow Photoshop to adjust the widths of characters (glyphs) in a line in order to optimize how the text fits inside the bounding box.

Adobe Single-line Composer 3 or **Adobe Every-line Composer 4**, the method Photoshop uses to evaluate potential word breaks (hyphenation) in a paragraph, factoring in letter and word spacing values, in an attempt to minimize hyphenation. The Adobe Single-line Composer does this line by line; the Adobe Every-line Composer does it by evaluating the appearance of each paragraph as a whole. Every-line Composer can change word breaks at the beginning of a paragraph in order to create more visually appealing word breaks toward the end of the paragraph. We like Every-line Composer!

Reset Paragraph to reset the paragraph menu options to their default settings.

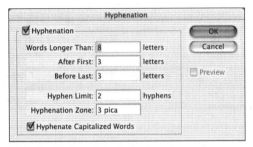

Justification				
	Minimum	Desired	Maximum	
Word Spacing:	80%	100%	133%	
Letter Spacing:	0%	0%	0%	
Glyph Scaling:	100%	100%	100%	
Auto Leading:	120%			

1 *In the **Justification** dialog box, choose **Minimum**, **Desired**, and **Maximum** values for Photoshop to adhere to when adjusting line widths in justified text.*

Hyphenation	
☑ Hyphenation	
Words Longer Than: 8	letters
After First: 3	letters
Before Last: 3	letters
Hyphen Limit: 2	hyphens
Hyphenation Zone: 3 pica	
☑ Hyphenate Capitalized Words	

2 *In the **Hyphenation** dialog box, choose settings for breaks created in paragraph type.*

Civilization is the encouragement of differences. Civilization thus becomes a synonym of democracy. Force, violence, pressure, or compulsion with a view to conformity, is both uncivilized and undemocratic.

—Mohandas Gandhi

3 *Adobe Single-line Composer goes through paragraphs line by line as it hyphenates words, and adjusts the spacing between them.*

Civilization is the encouragement of differences. Civilization thus becomes a synonym of democracy. Force, violence, pressure, or compulsion with a view to conformity, is both uncivilized and undemocratic.

—Mohandas Gandhi

4 *Every-line Composer considers the paragraph as a whole as it strives to optimize the paragraph's appearance.*

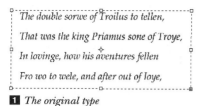

> The double sorwe of Troilus to tellen,
>
> That was the king Priamus sone of Troye,
>
> In lovinge, how his aventures fellen
>
> Fro wo to wele, and after out of Ioye,

1 *The original type*

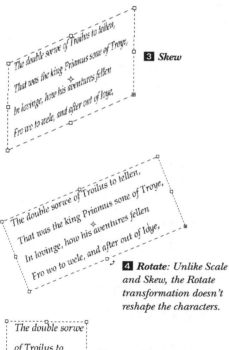

2 *A **Scale** transformation changes the shape of the bounding box and **distorts** the type itself (also true for Skew). The type remains editable.*

3 *Skew*

4 *Rotate: Unlike Scale and Skew, the Rotate transformation doesn't reshape the characters.*

> The double sorwe
> of Troilus to
> tellen,
> That was the king
> Priamus sone of
> Troye,

5 *The Horizontal Type tool was used to transform the paragraph type **bounding box**. The characters don't change in shape or scale.*

Special effects with type

The Transform commands, which we discuss in the first set of instructions below, reshape both the type and its bounding box. You can move, scale, rotate, and skew editable type. For rasterized type, you can do all of the above, plus apply perspective and distort. You can only transform a whole type block—not individual characters.

Another way to transform a block of point or paragraph type is to choose the Move tool (V), choose a type layer on the Layers palette, check Show Bounding Box on the options bar, then move any of the handles on the type's bounding box using the same techniques as for Free Transform.

And finally, a block of point or paragraph type can also be transformed by choosing the type layer on the Layers palette, then choosing Edit > Free Transform. Move the handles to transform the type. This method works with any tool selected (except a pen or shape tool, or the Path Selection tool).

To transform a type bounding box and the type inside it:

Follow the instructions for Free Transform on pages 138–139.

or

On the Layers palette, double-click the type layer thumbnail for paragraph type, then hold down Ctrl/Cmd and use the shortcuts for Free Transform (see page 140) **1**–**4**.

Follow these instructions if you want to modify the overall shape of a block of type without distorting the characters inside it.

To transform a type bounding box, but not the type:

1. On the Layers palette, double-click the type layer thumbnail for paragraph type.

2. Position the cursor over a handle, pause, then drag to scale the bounding box. The type will reflow **5**.

or

(Continued on the following page)

Position the cursor outside one of the corners of the box (curved, double-arrow pointer), then drag to rotate the box
or
Ctrl-drag/Cmd-drag in the box to move the whole type block.

3. To accept the changes, press Enter on the keypad or click the ✔ on the options bar. (To cancel, press Esc or click the ◯ on the options bar.)

Photoshop has a whole set of preset Warp Type transform functions that curve the bounding box and distort the type within it. Warped type remains editable.

To warp type on an editable layer:

1. On the Layers palette, click the text layer you want to warp.

2. To open the Warp Text dialog box **1**:
Choose Layer > Type > Warp Text.
or
Choose the Horizontal or Vertical Type tool (T or Shift-T), then click the Warp Text button 𝕴 on the options bar.

3. Choose from the Style pop-up menu.

4. Click Horizontal or Vertical as the basic orientation for the distortion.

5. Move the Bend, Horizontal Distortion, and Vertical Distortion sliders.

6. Click OK. The layer thumbnail will change to show that the text is warped **2**–**3**.

TIP To scale or reshape warped type to make it fit into a specific area of a composition, choose the warped type layer, choose the Move tool (Show Bounding Box checked), then reshape the bounding box. Pause, if necessary, to let the type redraw.

1 The **Warp Text** dialog box

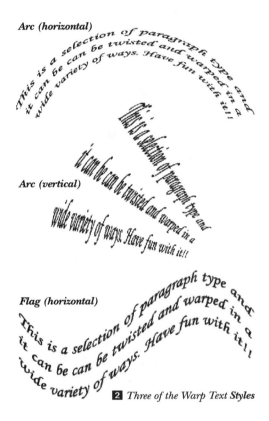

Arc (horizontal)

Arc (vertical)

Flag (horizontal)

2 *Three of the Warp Text Styles*

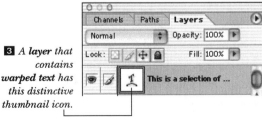

3 *A layer that contains* **warped text** *has this distinctive thumbnail icon.*

Warp Type

Missing fonts 7.0!

If a font is missing (not available or installed) when you open a file that contains editable type, an alert box will display , and an alert triangle will appear on the thumbnail of the offending layer on the Layers palette . If you then try to edit a layer in which that font is used, another alert dialog box will appear. Either open the required font suitcase or choose to have font substitution occur for each affected layer.

1 *The missing fonts alert dialog box*

2 *The missing fonts alert triangle on the Layers palette*

*Filled with a **pattern**, Difference mode*

*Filled with a **pattern** and the **Fresco** filter applied*

*Filled with a **pattern** and a gradient*

*Filled with a **pattern** and the **Palette Knife** filter applied*

3 *Various modifications made to **rasterized type***

To move a type layer:
Method 1
1. Choose the Move tool.

2. Right-click/Control-click the type in the image window and choose the name of the layer you want to move.
or
On the Layers palette, click the name of the layer you want to move.

3. Drag the type in the image window.
or
Press an arrow key.

Method 2
1. Double-click the type layer thumbnail (the "T").

2. Ctrl-drag/Cmd-drag the type in the image window.

To rework type shapes using a filter, a tool (such as the Brush, Blur, Eraser, or Smudge tool), or the Transform > Distort or Perspective command, you must first convert the type into pixels, a process that's called rasterization **3**. Remember, though: Once type is converted to pixels, even though it remains on its own layer, its typographic attributes can't be changed.

To rasterize type into pixels:
1. On the Layers palette, choose the layer you want to rasterize. If you want to preserve the original, editable layer for later use, duplicate it and then rasterize the duplicate.

2. Choose Layer > Rasterize > Type. The ways in which rasterized type can be dressed up are almost limitless—just use your imagination. Here's just one little idea: Turn on "Lock transparent pixels" on the Layers palette, fill the rasterized type with a pattern, apply a filter to it, turn off "Lock transparent pixels," then use the Smudge tool to smudge the edges of the type shapes.

(Continued on the following page)

Move Type; Rasterize Type

To paint on rasterized type, choose the Brush tool and a Foreground color, turn on "Lock transparent pixels" for the type layer, then draw brushstrokes in the image window. To paint behind the type, do it on the layer directly below the type layer **1**.

TIP If you apply the Color, Gradient, or Pattern Overlay effect, choose a blending Mode that allows the paint strokes to show through.

TIP An editable type object that you drag-and-drop, copy and paste, or Place from Adobe Illustrator into Photoshop will be rasterized into pixels automatically; it won't remain as editable type.

Printing dark text on top of a picture can be tricky. The picture has to be light enough to allow the text to be readable, yet visible enough to "read" as an image.

To screen back an image behind type:

1. Choose the background image on the Layers palette. (In our example, we lightened the background behind a Drop Shadow layer effect.)

2. Choose Layer > New Adjustment Layer > Levels, then click OK.
   or
   Choose Levels from the "Create new fill or adjustment layer" ⬤, pop-up menu at the bottom of the Layers palette.

3. Check Preview.

4. Move the gray Input slider a little to the left.
   and
   Move the black Output slider a little to the right.

5. Click OK **2**–**3**.

TIP To further adjust levels, try a different blending mode (e.g., Screen or Lighten) or opacity for the Levels adjustment layer.

TIP To have the adjustment layer only affect the layer immediately below it, Alt-click/ Option-click the line between the two layers on the Layers palette.

Rasterize without rasterizing

To make an editable type layer look painterly without rasterizing it into pixels, make the type layer the base layer in a **clipping group** (see page 271), and then draw brush strokes on the layer directly above the type layer. An advantage of using this method is that you can repaint, reposition, or delete the strokes without affecting the type layer.

1 *We painted on the rasterized type and on the layer below it.*

2 *After applying the **Levels** command to an adjustment layer over an image Background (Input Levels 0, .95, and 255, and Output Levels 92 and 255)*

3 *After filling the adjustment layer with a black-to-white **gradient** (upper-right to lower-left corners) to mask out the Levels effect in the upper-right corner*

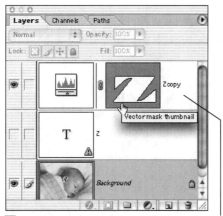

■ *A vector mask with a **Levels adjustment layer***

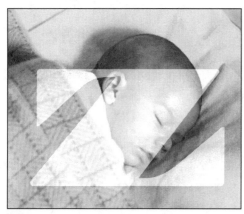

② *Screened back type*

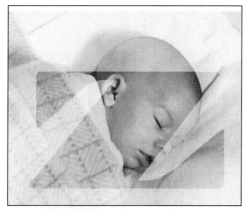

③ *A screened back image with type*

In these instructions, instead of screening back the image, as in the instructions on the previous page, you will be screening back the type itself to allow the image to be visible within it.

To screen back type:

1. Create a type layer.

2. Duplicate the type layer by dragging it over the "Create new layer" button ■ at the bottom of the Layers palette. Hide the original type layer (keep it for future type edits).

3. With the duplicate layer chosen, choose Layer > Type > Convert to Shape. The type layer will be converted into a shape layer with a vector mask. The original type shapes will be preserved, but their typographic attributes will no longer be editable.

4. Choose Layer > Change Layer Content > Levels **■**. The clipping effect won't be visible until you perform step 5.

5. Move the gray Input (midtones) slider to the left to lighten the midtones in the type, then pause to preview. You can also move the Input highlights slider.
and
Move the Output shadows slider to the right to reduce the contrast in the type.

6. Click OK **②**. Click back on the background image layer.

TIP Change the blending mode for the adjustment layer to restore some of the color to the background (try Overlay, Color Burn, or Hard Light mode). Lower the layer's opacity to lessen the Levels effect. You can also apply layer effects to the adjustment layer.

TIP To screen back an image with type, follow steps 1–4 above. For step 5, adjust the sliders to darken the type, remove any opacity or blending mode changes, then create an adjustment layer to lighten the imagery below the type layer **③**.

Screen Back Type

To fill type with imagery using Paste Into:

1. Create a type layer. It can be editable, converted to shape, or rasterized to pixels.

2. Activate a layer in the same file or in another file that contains the imagery you want to fill the type with.

3. Choose Select > All or create a selection.

4. Choose Edit > Copy (Ctrl-C/Cmd-C).

5. Activate the image that contains the type layer, click that type layer, then Ctrl-click/Cmd-click the type layer name.

6. Choose Edit > Paste Into (Ctrl-Shift-V/Cmd-Shift-V) –❷. A new layer with a layer mask will be created automatically, and the pasted image will be revealed through the mask character shapes.

7. *Optional:* With the layer thumbnail for the new layer selected on the Layers palette (not the mask thumbnail), choose the Move tool (V),⊕ then drag to move the pasted image within the type shapes. Now click in the space between the layer thumbnail and the layer mask thumbnail to link the mask to the layer image. The position of the image inside the mask can't be changed while they remain linked.

   Dragging with the Move tool now would move both the mask shape and the image inside it and expose the type layer underneath. To move the type layer and the pasted image layer in unison, after linking the layer mask to the image thumbnail, link the pasted image layer to the type layer.

TIP To fill type with imagery using a layer mask, see page 269; using a vector mask, see page 302.

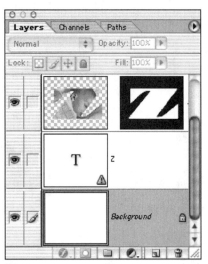

❶ *Type filled with an image using* **Paste Into**

❷ *The second layer is the original type layer; the topmost layer was created after pasting into the type selection.*

Letting go

To **release** a layer from a clipping group, **Alt-click/Option-click** again on the line between an indented layer and the base layer below it.

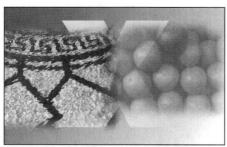

1 *The separate layers before being joined in a clipping group*

2 *The layers pulled apart so you can see their stacking order*

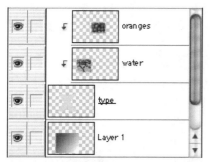

3 *The Layers palette after **Alt-clicking/Option-clicking** the lines above the type layer: The type layer (the underlined name) is the **base** layer of the clipping group.*

To fill type with imagery using a clipping group of layers:

1. Create type using the Horizontal or Vertical Type tool. It can be editable, converted to shape, or rasterized.

2. Move the type layer on the Layers palette just below the layer or layers that are used to fill the type **1**–**2**.

3. Alt-click/Option-click the line between the type layer name and the layer directly above it. The overlying layer will be indented with a down arrow to the left of the thumbnail and the base (bottommost) layer of the clipping group will be underlined. Only pixels that overlap the letter shapes will be visible **3**–**4**.

4. *Optional:* Click the type layer and use the Move tool (V) to reposition the letters in the image window.

5. *Optional:* Alt-click/Option-click the lines between other layers that are directly above the clipping group to add them to the group.

6. *Optional:* Change the mode or opacity for any layer in the clipping group. By default, the blending mode of the base (underlined) layer affects the way the clipping group blends with layers below the whole group. Double-click next to the base layer name. Then in Layer Style, choose Blending Options and uncheck Advanced Blending: Blend Clipped Layers as Group to prevent the base layer from affecting the blending of indented layers with layers below the group.

4 *Type filled with imagery using a **clipping group***

To create fading type:

1. Create type, and leave the type layer active. It can be editable or rasterized.

2. Click the "Add a mask" button ◨ at the bottom of the Layers palette. A layer mask thumbnail will appear next to the layer name **1**.

3. Choose the Gradient tool (G or Shift-G). ▭

4. On the options bar: Click the Gradient picker arrowhead, then click the Foreground to Background swatch in the gradient picker; click the Linear gradient button; choose Mode: Normal; and choose Opacity: 100%.

5. Drag in the image window from top to bottom or left to right, at least halfway across the type. The type layer mask will fill with a white-to-black gradient. Type will be hidden where black is present in the layer mask **2**.

TIP Click the type layer thumbnail or next to the layer name to modify the type or the layer; click the layer mask thumbnail to modify the layer mask. (Read more about layer masks in Chapter 14.)

Layer effects can be applied to editable type layers. (Read more about layer effects on page 244.)

To apply layer effects to semi-transparent type:

1. Create type on an editable type layer.

2. Double-click next to the type layer name.

3. In Layer Style, click one or more of the layer effect names on the left side of the dialog box (e.g., Drop Shadow, Inner Shadow, Inner Glow, or Bevel & Emboss), and choose settings for each effect **3**–**5**. Apply the Satin effect to darken the contents of a type layer; use Color Overlay or Gradient Overlay to apply a tint; use Pattern Overlay to fill with a pattern.

4. Click Blending Options on the top left side of the Layer Style dialog box. For

1 *Layer mask thumbnail*

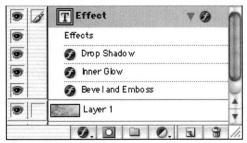

2 *Fading type*

3 *The type layer shapes were used to create the mask for the* **Paste Into** *layer.*

4 *A combination of* **layer effects** *applied to* **type**

5 *More* **layer effects** *applied to* **type**

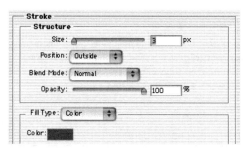

1 *Apply a* **Stroke** *to editable or rasterized type via the* **Layer Style** *dialog box.*

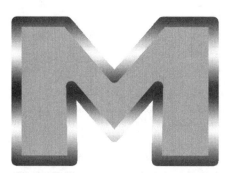

2 *A layer effect* **Stroke** *(Fill Type: Gradient) applied to editable type*

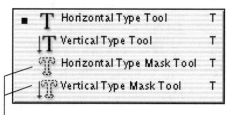

3 *The two* **type mask tools**

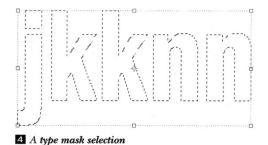

4 *A* **type mask selection**

Advanced Blending, drag the Fill Opacity slider to 0%. The fill opacity can also be adjusted on the Layers palette.

5. Click OK.

TIP To reposition the type with its effect, choose the type layer, choose the Move tool, then drag in the image window.

TIP To modify a layer effect, double-click the *f* icon—the Layer Style dialog box will open.

To stroke a type layer:

1. Click a type layer on the Layers palette.

2. From the "Add layer style" pop-up menu at the bottom of the Layer palette, *f*, choose Stroke.

3. Choose a stroke Size, Position (Outside, Inside, or Center), Blend Mode, Opacity, Fill Type, and Color **1**–**2**.

4. Click OK.

The Type Mask tools create a selection in the shape of type characters. You might want to do this for a variety of reasons: to copy layer imagery in the shape of letters; to mask (limit) an adjustment layer's effect to a type selection; or to add a layer mask using type characters for the mask shapes (Reveal Selection or Hide Selection).

To create a type selection:

1. Activate the layer that you want the type selection to appear on (preferably not a type layer).

2. Choose the Horizontal or Vertical Type Mask tool (T or Shift-T) **3**.

3. Click in the image window where you want the selection to appear. A Quick Mask will display temporarily.

4. Create and style the type **4**.

5. Click the ✓ on the options bar to accept the selection.

TIP Save a type selection to a new channel (click the Save selection as channel

(Continued on the following page)

Stroke Type; Type Selection

button 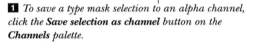 at the bottom of the Channels palette) **1**. It can then be viewed on the Channels palette and loaded onto any layer or layer mask at any time.

Note: Editable text can extend outside the image area, and it can be moved back within the image area at any time. But once a type mask selection is saved and deselected, any characters that extend outside the image area will be lost. If you want to reposition a type mask, do it before you deselect it.

To move a type selection:

1. Choose the Rectangular Marquee tool
 [ ] (M or Shift-M)—not the Move tool!

2. Click the New selection button ▣ on the options bar.

3. Drag from inside the selection in the image window.
or
Press an arrow key. Hold down Shift and press an arrow key to move the type selection 10 screen pixels at a time.

TIP *Beware!* If you drag a type selection using the Move tool, you'll cut away and move pixels inside the letter shapes from the active layer **2**.

TIP To deselect the selection, choose Select > Deselect (Ctrl-D/Cmd-D).

TIP To copy pixels from within a type selection, first position the type selection over the desired pixels. Then choose Edit > Copy to copy pixels only from the active layer, or choose Edit > Copy Merged to copy pixels from all visible layers below the selection.

TIP To paste imagery into a type selection **3**, select and copy an area of pixels from another layer or another image, create a type selection on the destination image, then choose Edit > Paste Into. The type selection will be deselected and a new layer will be created.

Line 'em up

To align or distribute multiple type layers, link them together (click in the second column on the Layers palette), then choose from the Layer > **Align Linked** or Layer > **Distribute Linked** submenu.

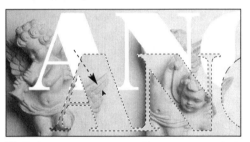

1 *To save a type mask selection to an alpha channel, click the **Save selection as channel** button on the Channels palette.*

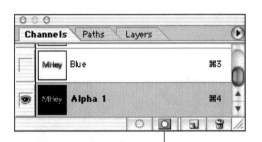

2 *When you use the **Move** tool to move a type selection, the **pixels** in the selection move with the type outline.*

3 *Imagery pasted into a **type selection***

Move Type Selection

Don't lose your pixels

To deselect a selection, be sure to use Select > **Deselect** (Ctrl-D/Cmd-D). Don't press Delete or choose Edit > Clear—those commands will remove pixels from inside the selection!

1 *Type in a spot channel*

2 *A type mask selection in a spot channel displays on the image in the current **Ink Characteristics: Color** (see **3**, below).*

3 *You can change the **Solidity** value to view an onscreen-only simulation of a spot color ink tint. The Solidity value has no effect on actual print output.*

To create type in a spot channel:

1. Create an editable type layer so you'll be able to modify it later on.

2. Follow steps 1–6 on page 207 to create a new spot channel.

3. Choose the type layer, then Ctrl-click/Cmd-click the type layer name or thumbnail to select only the visible parts of the layer (the character shapes).

4. Hide the type layer (click the eye icon).

5. On the Channels palette, choose the spot color channel name, and make sure its eye icon is showing.

6. Choose Edit > Fill, choose Use: Black, Normal mode, choose an Opacity value that will match the tint (density) value for the spot color ink, then click OK. The selection will fill with the spot channel color at 100%.

7. Choose Select > Deselect **1**–**3**.

TIP To move the type in the spot color channel, choose that channel, choose the Move tool (V), then drag in the image window.

TIP To adjust the tint in a spot channel, see page 208.

You can't actually edit type in a spot channel. Instead, you have to remove the existing shapes from the channel and then add the revised text shapes back to it.

To edit type in a spot channel:

1. On the Channels palette, choose the spot channel that contains the type.

2. Choose black as the Foreground color.

3. Choose the Rectangular Marquee tool, [ ] marquee the type, then press Backspace/Delete to delete the type from the channel.

4. Choose Select > Deselect.

5. Double-click the original type layer thumbnail on the Layers palette, edit the type, then click ✔ on the options bar.

6. Follow steps 3–7 from the preceding set of instructions on this page to add the revised type to the spot color channel.

To create a type mask for an adjustment layer:

1. Choose the Horizontal Type Mask tool ⊤ or Vertical Type Mask tool (T or Shift-T), then click in the image window where you want the type to appear.

2. Choose type attributes, enter characters, then click the ✔ on the options bar. Leave the type selected.

3. Activate the layer above which you want the new adjustment layer to appear.

4. Choose an adjust command from the "Create new fill or adjustment layer" pop-up menu ●, at the bottom of the Layers palette **1**. Choose adjustment options, then click OK. The type character shapes will be used as a mask for the adjustment layer. Only pixels directly below the character shapes will be affected by the adjustment **2**.

TIP You can also use an existing type layer to create a selection. First hide the type layer. Then Ctrl-click/Cmd-click the type layer thumbnail to select the type on the Layers palette. Finally, perform step 4, above.

TIP Alt-click/Option-click the layer mask thumbnail (thumbnail on the right) to display just the mask. Alt-click/Option-click it again to restore the full image.

TIP With the adjustment layer selected, choose Image > Adjustments > Invert (Ctrl-I/Cmd-I) to swap the black and white areas in the adjustment layer mask.

TIP Use the Move tool with its Auto Select Layer option unchecked to reposition a mask on a selected adjustment layer.

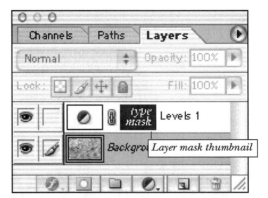

1 *The **type mask selection** functions as a **mask** for the **adjustment layer**.*

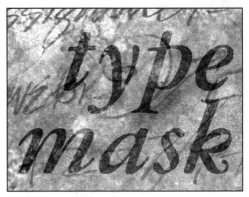

2 *Only pixels **below** the character shapes are affected by the **adjustment layer**.*

Word processing

In Photoshop 7 or later, you can find and replace text, and you can check the spelling of your text on all visible type layers.

To find and replace text: 7.0!

1. *Optional:* Click with the Horizontal or Vertical Type tool to create an insertion point from which to start your search. If you don't do this, the search will begin from the most recently created object.

2. Choose Edit > Find and Replace Text.
   or
   Choose the Horizontal or Vertical Type tool, then right-click/Ctrl-click in the image window and choose Find and Replace Text from the context menu.

3. Enter a search word or phrase in the Find What field 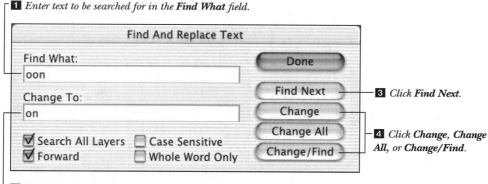.

4. Enter a replacement word or phrase in the Change To field **2**.

5. *Do any of these optional steps:*
   Check **Search All Layers** to find text on any type layer, not just the currently active layer.

   Check **Case Sensitive** to find only those instances that exactly match the upper-case/lowercase configuration of the Find

What text. If this option is unchecked, case will be ignored as a criterion in the search.

Check **Forward** to search from the current cursor position to the end of the text. Leave this option unchecked to search backward from the current cursor position. If Search All Layers is checked, the cursor position is irrelevant.

Check **Whole Word Only** to find the Find What text only if it appears as a complete word—not as part of a larger word (e.g., "for" but not "forward").

6. Click Find Next to search for the first instance of the Find What text after the current cursor position **3**.

7. Click **Change** to replace only the current instance of the Find What text.
   or
   Click **Change All** to replace all instances of the Find What text at once **4**.
   or
   Click **Change/Find** to replace the current instance of the Find What text and search for the next instance.

8. Click Done.

1 *Enter text to be searched for in the **Find What** field.*

Find And Replace Text

Find What:
oon

Change To:
on

☑ Search All Layers   ☐ Case Sensitive
☑ Forward   ☐ Whole Word Only

Done

Find Next ——— **3** *Click **Find Next**.*

Change

Change All ——— **4** *Click **Change**, **Change**

Change/Find ——— *All**, or **Change/Find**.*

2 *Enter replacement text in the **Change To** field.*

Check spelling in Spanish?

Use the **Language** pop-up menu **1** on the Character palette to choose which dictionary Photoshop will use.

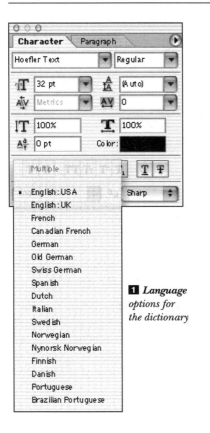

1 *Language options for the dictionary*

The Check Spelling command checks **7.0!** spelling on a single type layer or in an entire document using a built-in dictionary, to which you can add entries. As far as we know, you can't edit the dictionary afterward.

To check spelling:

1. Choose Edit > Check Spelling.
   or
   Choose the Horizontal or Vertical Type tool (T or Shift-T), then right-click/ Ctrl-click and choose Check Spelling Text from the context menu. A type layer doesn't have to be selected.

   The first word the dictionary doesn't recognize will appear in the Not in Dictionary field. The dictionary's best guess for a replacement word will appear in the Change To field, and other possible replacements will be listed in the Suggestions window.

2. *Optional:* Check Check All Layers to have Photoshop search through every type layer in the document, not just the current layer.

3. If the Change To word is incorrect, but the correct word appears on the Suggestions list, click that word. It will appear, highlighted, in the Change To field. If the correct word doesn't appear on the Suggestions list, type it in the Change To field.

4. Choose one of the following options:

   Ignore to ignore the current instance of the word.

   Ignore All to ignore every instance of the word and to continue checking other words.

   Change to change the current instance of the word.

   Change All to change every instance of the word.

   Add to add the unrecognized word to the dictionary, and leave the word in the image unchanged.

5. Click Done.

*The **Check Spelling** dialog box*

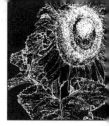

FILTERS 18

PHOTOSHOP'S FILTERS are used to produce myriad special effects, from slight sharpening to wild distortion. For example, you could apply the Sharpen or Blur filter for subtle retouching; apply the Lighting Effects filter to apply illumination; apply one or more of the filters on the Artistic, Brush Strokes, Sketch, or Texture submenu to make your image look hand-rendered; or for a very dramatic change, apply one of the filters on the Stylize or Distort submenu.

This chapter has three components: techniques for applying filters; an illustrated compendium of all the Photoshop filters; and lastly, a handful of step-by-step exercises that utilize filters, including the new Pattern Maker.

Filters are grouped into 13 submenu categories under the Filter menu **1**. Third-party filters appear on their own submenus. (To install third-party filters, see Adobe Photoshop online Help.)

Filter	
Last Filter	⌘F
Extract...	⌥⌘X
Liquify...	⇧⌘X
Pattern Maker...	⌥⇧⌘X
Artistic ▸	Colored Pencil...
Blur ▸	Cutout...
Brush Strokes ▸	Dry Brush...
Distort ▸	Film Grain...
Noise ▸	Fresco...
Pixelate ▸	Neon Glow...
Render ▸	Paint Daubs...
Sharpen ▸	Palette Knife...
Sketch ▸	Plastic Wrap...
Stylize ▸	Poster Edges...
Texture ▸	Rough Pastels...
Video ▸	Smudge Stick...
Other ▸	Sponge...
	Underpainting...
Digimarc ▸	Watercolor...

1 *Filters are grouped into submenu categories under the* **Filter** *menu.*

Filter basics

How filters are applied

A filter can be applied to a whole **layer** or to a **selection** on a layer. For a soft transition between the filtered and nonfiltered areas, **feather** the selection before applying a filter.

Some filters are applied in one step (select it from a submenu). Other filters are applied via a dialog box in which one or more variables are specified. Choose Filter > **Last Filter** [last filter name] **(Ctrl-F/Cmd-F)** to reapply the last-used filter using the same settings. Choose a filter from its submenu to choose different settings. To open the dialog box for the last-used filter with its last-used settings displayed, press **Ctrl-Alt-F/ Cmd-Option-F**.

(Continued on the following page)

The **Groucho** *filter*

All the filters are available for an image in RGB Color or Multichannel mode; not all filters are available for an image in CMYK, Grayscale, or Lab Color mode, or for an image that has 16 bits per channel. None of the filters are available for an image in Bitmap or Indexed Color mode.

Using a filter dialog box

Most filter dialog boxes have a **preview** window 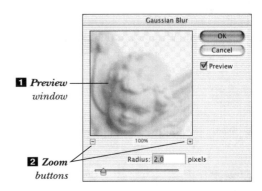. Drag in the preview window to move the image inside it. With some filter dialog boxes open, the pointer becomes a square when it's passed over the image window, in which case you can click to preview that area of the image. (Check the Preview box, if there is one, to preview the effect in the dialog box and the image window.)

TIP Option/Alt drag a slider in a filter dialog box to see an instantaneous rendering of that slider's setting as it's moved.

7.0!

Click the + button to zoom in on the image in the preview window, or click the – button to zoom out 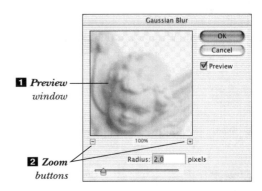. A line will blink on and off below the preview percentage while a filter is rendering in the preview window.

Lessening a filter's overall effect

The **Fade** command can be used to lessen the effect of: a filter, the Extract or Liquify command, an Image > Adjustments command, or any paint, eraser, or editing tool stroke. After applying a filter, choose Edit > Fade [   ]... (Ctrl-Shift-F/Cmd-Shift-F), adjust the Opacity, choose a blending Mode, then click OK .

To lessen a filter's effect with the option to **test** different **blending modes**, do the following:

1. Duplicate the layer that you're going to apply the filter to.

2. Apply the filter to the duplicate layer.

3. On the Layers palette:

   Move the Opacity or Fill slider to the left to lessen (fade) the effect of the filter.
   and
   Choose a different blending mode (**1**–**2**, next page).

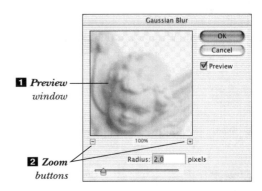

1 *Preview window*

2 *Zoom buttons*

Gaussian Blur
Radius: 2.0 pixels

3 *Filter > Texture >* ***Mosaic Tiles*** *applied to an image*

4 *Use the* ***Fade*** *command to lessen the effect of the most recent edit.*

Fade
Opacity: 75 %
Mode: Normal

5 *After using the* ***Fade*** *command in* ***Overlay*** *mode to lessen the filter effect on the overall image*

1 *The original image*

2 *After applying the **Find Edges** filter to a duplicate of the original layer, lowering the **opacity** of the duplicate layer, and choosing Hard Light **blending mode** (also try Overlay, Color Dodge, or Difference)*

3 *After applying the **Poster Edges** filter to an image and then using the **History Brush** tool to restore the angel's face and tummy to its original state*

Because the filter was applied to a copy of the original layer, later on you can change the blending mode or opacity of the filter effect layer to blend it differently with the original layer, or create a layer mask for the duplicate layer to hide or change the filter effect, or discard the filter layer entirely. When the image is finalized, merge the duplicate layer with the original layer.

Another way to soften a filter's effect is to modify pixels in only one of an image's color components. To do this, choose a layer, click a **channel** color name on the Channels palette, apply a filter (Add Noise is a nice one to experiment with), then click the top channel on the palette (Ctrl-~/Cmd-~) to redisplay the composite image.

And finally, you can selectively reduce a filter effect using the **History Brush**. Set the History Brush icon to a prior state on the History palette, and then draw strokes on the image **3**.

Restricting the area a filter affects

Create a **selection** first on a layer to have a filter affect only pixels within the selection. To create a soft-edged transition between the filtered and nonfiltered areas, **feather** the selection before applying the filter.

You can also use a **layer mask** to limit the effect of a filter. The edge between the white and black areas of a layer mask can be soft, hard, or painterly, depending on the type of brush strokes you use to paint the black areas of the mask. By choosing Layer > Add Layer Mask > Reveal Selection when a selection is active, and then applying a filter to the mask, the filter effect will be visible where the black and white areas of the layer mask meet (try Brush Strokes > Spatter; Pixelate > Pointillize; Stylize > Wind; or Distort > ZigZag or Ripple).

Another option is to create a black-to-white **gradient** in the layer mask and then apply a filter to the layer image (not to the layer mask). The filter will apply fully to the

(Continued on the following page)

Filter Techniques

image where the mask is white and fade to nil in areas where the mask is black **1**–**3**.

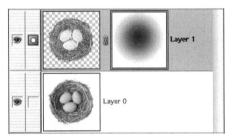

Making filter effects look less artificial

Apply **more than one** filter—the effect will look less canned. If the imagery you're creating lends itself to experimentation, try concocting your own formulas. And test different variables in a filter dialog box. If you come up with a sequence that you'd like to reuse, save it in an action. And remember, if you get carried away and apply too many filters, you can always revert to an earlier state or snapshot using the History palette.

Maximizing a filter's effect

Pumping up a layer's **brightness** and **contrast** values before applying a filter can help intensify the filter's effect (choose Image > Adjust > Levels, move the black Input slider to the right and the white Input slider slightly to the left, then click OK).

To **recolor** a layer after applying a filter that strips color (e.g., the Charcoal filter), use Image > Adjustments > Hue/Saturation (check Colorize).

TIP The Sketch filters (with the exception of Water Paper) reduce a layer's colors to just white and the current Foreground color, so choose a Foreground color before using any of those filters.

Texture mapping using a filter

And finally, in lieu of choosing a preset pattern in some filter dialog boxes (e.g., Conté Crayon, Glass, Lighting Effects, Rough Pastels, or Texturizer) for the filter to apply as a texture, you can load in **another image** to use as the **pattern** for the texture. Lights and darks from the image you load in will be used to create peaks and valleys in the texture. The image you're using for the texture mapping must be saved in the Photoshop file format. In a filter dialog box that contains a Texture pop-up menu with a Load Texture option, choose that option, locate a color or grayscale image file in the Photoshop (.psd) format, then click OK.

1 *A* **radial gradient** *in the* **layer mask**...

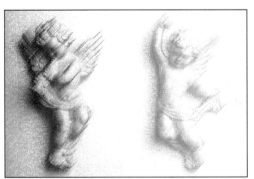

2 *...is diminishing the* **Stamp** *filter effect in the center of the nest.*

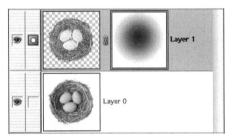

3 *The* **Rough Pastels** *filter is applied to the whole layer, but a* **linear gradient** *in the* **layer mask** *is diminishing the filter's impact on the* **right** *side.*

All the filters illustrated

Artistic filters

Original image

Colored Pencil

Cutout

Dry Brush

Film Grain

Fresco

Neon Glow

Paint Daubs

Palette Knife

Artistic Filters

Artistic filters

Original image

Plastic Wrap

Poster Edges

Rough Pastels

Smudge Stick

Sponge

Watercolor

Underpainting

Blur filters

Original image

Blur More

Gaussian Blur

Motion Blur

Radial Blur

Smart Blur (Normal)

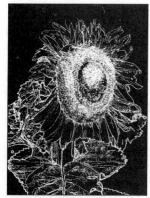

Smart Blur (Edges Only)

Smart Blur (Overlay Edge)

Blur Filters

Brush Strokes filters

Original image

Accented Edges

Angled Strokes

Crosshatch

Dark Strokes

Ink Outlines

Spatter

Sprayed Strokes

Sumi-e

Brush Strokes Filters

Distort filters

Original image

Diffuse Glow

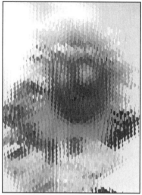

Displace

Glass

Ocean Ripple

Pinch

Polar Coordinates

Ripple

Shear

Distort Filters

Distort filters

Spherize

Twirl

Wave (Type: Square)

Wave (Type: Sine)

ZigZag

Noise filters

Original image

Add Noise

Median

Pixelate filters

Original image

Color Halftone

Crystallize

Facet

Fragment

Mezzotint (Short Strokes)

Mezzotint (Medium Dots)

Mosaic

Pointillize

Pixelate Filters

Render filters

Original image

Clouds

Difference Clouds

Lens Flare

For the Lighting Effects filter, see pages 360–362.

Sharpen filters

Sharpen Edges

Sharpen More

Unsharp Mask

Render Filters; Sharpen Filters

Sketch filters

Original image

Bas Relief

Chalk & Charcoal

Charcoal

Chrome

Conté Crayon

Graphic Pen

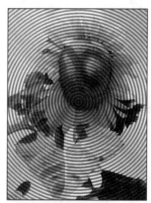

Halftone Pattern (Circle)

Halftone Pattern (Dot)

Sketch Filters

Sketch filters

Original image

Note Paper

Photocopy

Plaster

Reticulation

Stamp

Torn Edges

Water Paper

Stylize filters

Original image

Diffuse

Emboss

Extrude

Find Edges

Glowing Edges

Solarize

Tiles

Tiles, then Fade (Overlay mode)

Stylize filters

Original image

Trace Contour

Wind

Texture filters

Craquelure

Grain (Horizontal)

Mosaic Tiles

Patchwork

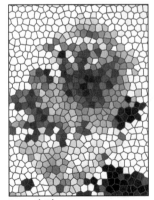

Stained Glass

Texturizer

Added canvas pixels

Selected area

1

PHOTO: PAUL PETROFF

2 *A wrinkled edge produced using the **Ripple** filter*

A few filter exercises

Try applying the Ripple, Twirl, or ZigZag filter to a target layer with a white border to produce a warped paper texture.

To create a wrinkled edge:

1. Choose white as the Background color.

2. Use Image > Canvas Size to add a border (use a one-layer image).

3. Choose the Rectangular Marquee tool (M or Shift-M).

4. Enter 8 in the Feather field on the Rectangular Marquee tool options bar.

5. Drag a selection marquee across approximately three-quarters of the image (not including the border area).

6. Choose Select > Inverse (Ctrl-Shift-I/Cmd-Shift-I). The active selection will now include the added canvas area and part of the image **1**.

7. Apply Filter > Distort > Ripple **2**, Ocean Ripple, Twirl, or Brush Strokes > Spatter, or a combination thereof. Move the preview in the filter dialog box to bring the edge of the image into the preview window.

Take the easy way out:

Use one of the "canned" frame effects from a third-party supplier, such as PhotoFrame from Extensis **3**–**4**. You can apply more than one frame to the same image.

Artistic Edges and Frames

3 *A **Camera** edge from **PhotoFrame***

4 *A **Watercolor** edge from **PhotoFrame***

In these instructions, you'll add a black or gray texture to a layer mask via a filter. Black areas in the layer mask will hide pixels in the layer, revealing imagery from the layer below it.

To apply a texture using a layer mask:

1. With an image open, create a new layer, and fill the new layer with white.

2. Create a layer mask for the new layer by clicking the "Add layer mask" button on the Layers palette, and leave the layer mask thumbnail active.

3. Apply Filter > Noise > Add Noise to the layer mask.

4. Apply another filter or series of filters to the layer mask **1**–**2**. Try a Texture filter (Craquelure, Grain, Mosaic Tiles, Patchwork, or Texturizer). Or try Artistic > Dry Brush (small brush size), Palette Knife (small stroke size), Plastic Wrap (use Levels to increase contrast), Sponge, or Watercolor.

5. *Do any of the following optional steps:*

To intensify a filter's effect, apply the Distort > Twirl or Ripple, or Stylize > Wind filter.

To fade a filter effect, use Edit > Fade (filter name).

Adjust the opacity of the layer that has the layer mask; change blending modes (try Overlay, Soft Light, or Hue).

To limit texture blending to some image channels, double-click the new layer. In the Layer Style dialog box, click Blending Options, and in the Advanced Blending area, uncheck any channels you don't want to blend with the underlying image. You can also change the blending mode and opacity in this dialog box.

1 *A **filter** is applied to the **layer mask**.*

2 *A filter applied via a **layer mask***

3 *The original image*

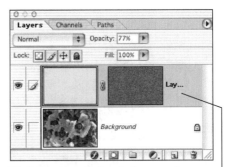

4 *The final image*

1 *The original image*

2 *Theirs*

3 *Ours*

Turn a photograph into a painting or a drawing:

1. Open an image, right-click/Ctrl-click and choose Duplicate Layer from the context menu, then click OK.

2. Choose Filter > Stylize > Find Edges.

3. With the duplicate layer active, click the Add layer mask button. 🔲

4. Paint with black at below 100% opacity on the layer mask to reveal parts of the layer below (**3**–**4**, previous page).

5. *Optional:* Lower the opacity of the duplicate layer.

6. *Optional:* For a dramatic effect of colors on a dark background, click the layer thumbnail, then choose Image > Adjustments > Invert (Ctrl-I/Cmd-I).

TIP To produce a magic marker drawing, apply Filter > Stylize > Trace Contour, then apply Filter > Other > Minimum (Radius of 1 or 2) in lieu of step 2.

We've come up with a way to turn a photograph into a watercolor using the Median Noise and Minimum filters. Compare it to Photoshop's Watercolor filter. Here's an example of a way to apply a combination of filters to the same image.

Our watercolor filter:

1. Duplicate the layer that you want to turn into a watercolor.

2. With the duplicate layer active, choose Filter > Noise > Median.

3. Move the Radius slider to a number between 2 and 8, then click OK.

4. Choose Filter > Other > Minimum.

5. Move the Radius slider to 1, 2, or 3, then click OK **1**–**3**.

6. *Optional:* Apply Filter > Sharpen > Sharpen More.

(sidebar) **Find Edges; Our Watercolor Filter**

In the following instructions, the Mosaic filter is applied using progressive values to a series of rectangular selections, so the mosaic tiles gradually enlarge as the effect travels across the image. (Using a gradient in a layer mask instead would gradually fade the Mosaic effect without changing the size of the mosaic tiles **1**.)

To apply the Mosaic filter using graduated values:

1. Choose a layer.

2. Choose the Rectangular Marquee tool (M or Shift-M).

3. Marquee about one-quarter or one-fifth of the layer, where you want the mosaic tiles to begin.

4. Choose Filter > Pixelate > Mosaic.

5. Enter 6 in the Cell Size field **2**, then click OK.

6. With the selection still active and the Rectangular Marquee tool still chosen, start dragging the marquee, then Shift-drag it to the next adjacent quadrant **3**.

7. Repeat steps 4–6 until you've applied the filter to the whole image, entering 12, then 24, then 30 in the Cell Size field. Or to create larger pixel blocks, enter higher numbers—such as 8, 16, 28, and 34—in the Cell Size field.

8. Deselect (Ctrl-D/Cmd-D) **4**.

1 *This is the **Mosaic** filter applied using a **gradient** in a **layer mask**.*

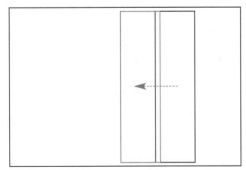

2 *Enter a number in the **Cell Size** field in the **Mosaic** dialog box. Enter progressively higher numbers each time you repeat step 5.*

3 *Apply the Mosaic filter to a rectangular selection, move the marquee, then reapply the filter, and so on.*

4 *A **graduated mosaic***

1 *Select an object.*

2 *Copy the selection to a new layer.*

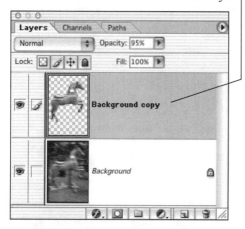

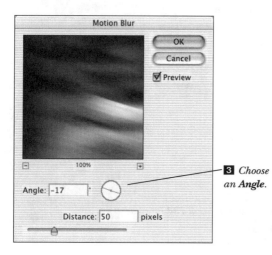

3 *Choose an Angle.*

To create an illusion of motion, you will select an object that you want to remain stationary, copy it to a new layer, and then apply the Motion Blur filter to the original background.

To motion blur part of an image:

1. Select the imagery that you want to remain stationary **1**.

2. Choose Select > Feather (Ctrl-Alt-D/ Cmd-Option-D).

3. Enter 5 in the Feather Radius field, then click OK.

4. Use the Ctrl-J/Cmd-J shortcut to copy the selected imagery to a new layer **2**.

5. Choose the original layer that contains the background imagery.

6. Choose Filter > Blur > Motion Blur.

7. Choose or enter an Angle between –360 and 360 **3**. (We used –17 for our image.) *and*
   Choose a Distance (1–999) for the amount of blur. (We entered 50 for our image.)

8. Click OK **4**.

4 *The completed **Motion Blur***

Motion Blur Part of an Image

The Lighting Effects filter produces a tremendous variety of lighting effects. You can place up to 16 light sources in your image, and you can assign a different color, intensity, and angle to each source.

Note: For optimal use of this filter, allocate a minimum of 50MB of RAM to Photoshop.

To cast a light on an image:

1. Make sure your image is in RGB Color mode .

2. Choose a layer. *Optional:* Select an area on the layer to limit the filter's effect.

3. Choose Filter > Render > Lighting Effects.

4. From the Style pop-up menu, choose Default or a preset lighting effect 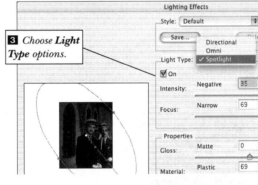.

5. For Light Type 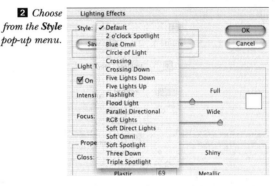:

Check **On** to preview the lighting effect in the dialog box.

Choose from the **Light Type** pop-up menu. Choose Spotlight to produce a narrow, elliptical, cone-shaped beam.

Move the **Intensity** slider to adjust the brightness of the light. Full Intensity creates the brightest light . Negative creates a black light effect.

For the Spotlight Light Type, you can move the **Focus** slider to adjust the size of the beam of light that fills the ellipse shape (**5** a–b, next page). The spotlight's highest intensity falls where the radius touches the edge of the ellipse.

To change the **color** of the light, click the color swatch, then choose a color from the Color Picker.

6. Do any of the following in the preview window:

Drag the center point to move the entire light.

1 *The original RGB image*

2 *Choose from the Style pop-up menu.*

3 *Choose Light Type options.*

4 *The Default style spotlight ellipse at Full Intensity*

5a *The Default spotlight ellipse with a* **Wide Focus***: The light is strongest at the sides of the ellipse.*

5b *The Default spotlight ellipse with a* **Narrow Focus**

6 *The Default spotlight ellipse after dragging the* **end** *and* **side points** *inward to narrow the light beam*

7a *The spotlight ellipse* **rotated** *to the left by dragging a side point*

7b *The spotlight ellipse after dragging the* **radius** *inward to make the light beam more round*

Drag either endpoint toward the center point to make the light more intense **6**.

For an ellipse, drag either side point to change the direction of the light, or to widen or narrow it **7 a–b**.

7. Move the Properties sliders to adjust the surrounding light conditions on the active layer:

Gloss controls the amount of surface reflectance on the lighted surfaces.

Material controls which parts of the image reflect the light source color— Plastic (the light source color is like a glare) or Metallic (the object surface glows).

Exposure lightens or darkens the whole layer **8 a–b**.

Ambience controls the balance between the light source and the overall light in the image **9 a–b**. Move this slider in small increments.

Click the Properties color swatch to choose a different **color** from the Color Picker for the ambient light around the spotlight.

8. *Do any of these optional steps:*

To add the current settings to the Style pop-up menu, click **Save**, enter a name, then click OK.

(Continued on the following page)

8a *The spotlight ellipse with the* **Exposure** **Property** *set to* **Over**

8b *The spotlight ellipse with the* **Exposure** **Property** *set to* **Under**

9a *The spotlight ellipse with a* **Positive** **Ambience Property**

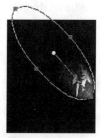

9b *The spotlight ellipse with a* **Negative** **Ambience Property**

Lighting Effects Filter

To **add** another light source, drag the lightbulb icon into the preview window .

To **delete** a light source, drag its center point over the trash icon. One light source must remain.

To **duplicate** a light source, Alt-drag/Option-drag its center point.

9. Click OK.

Note: The last-used settings of the Lighting Effects filter will remain in the dialog box until you change them or exit/quit Photoshop. To restore the default settings, choose Default from the Style menu. To remove the currently selected style from the pop-up menu, Click Delete, then click Delete again.

TIP To create a textured lighting effect, choose an existing alpha channel that contains a texture from the Texture Channel pop-up menu, and move the Height slider to adjust the height of the texture. This works best with the Spotlight Light Type.

TIP An Omni light creates a circular light source **2**. Drag an edge point to adjust its size.

TIP Shift-drag the side points on an ellipse to resize the ellipse, but keep its angle constant. Ctrl-drag/Cmd-drag the angle line to change the angle or direction of the ellipse, but keep its size constant.

TIP To create a pin spot, choose Light Type: Spotlight, move the Intensity slider to about 55, move the Focus slider to about 30, and drag the side points of the ellipse inward to narrow the ellipse. To cast light on a different part of the image, move the whole ellipse by dragging its center point.

TIP If the background of an image was darkened too much from a previous application of the Lighting Effects filter, apply the filter again to shine an additional light into the dark area to recover some detail. Move the Properties: Exposure and Ambience sliders a little to the right.

1 *Dragging a* **new light source** *onto the preview box*

2 *The default* **Omni** *light is spherical, like a flashlight shining perpendicular to the image.*

Lighting effects by example

To produce **3**, we used a Spotlight with a wide Focus, rotated and reshaped the ellipse, moved the Exposure Property slider slightly toward Over to brighten the light source, and moved the Ambience Property slider slightly to the left to darken the background of the image. Then we Alt-dragged/Option-dragged the ellipse to duplicate the light and illuminate the face on the right. And finally, we created a new, low-intensity light to illuminate the background **4**.

3 *The* **final** *image*

4 *These three ellipses show the light source positions that were used to produce the image above.*

Lighting Effects Filter

1 *Click a **layer** to use for the **pattern tile** (or select an area of a layer and choose Edit > Copy).*

Pattern Maker 7.0!

The Pattern Maker filter allows you to generate multiple patterns from imagery on a layer or imagery that has been copied to the Clipboard. Instead of utilizing the imagery exactly, though, Photoshop jumbles pixels slightly in order to create an assortment of different pattern tiles. You can use this feature simply to fill a layer with a pattern once, or you can save your favorite pattern tiles as a pattern preset to use with any tool or command that uses pattern presets, such as Pattern Overlay in Layer Style, the Healing Brush tool, the Pattern Stamp tool, or the Fill command.

The sample to be used for a tile can range from an area just a few pixels square to a whole layer. If the tile is smaller than the layer it's generated from, it will be repeated in a grid formation. If the tile is the same size as the current layer, just one tile will be used to fill the whole layer.

Note: The Pattern Maker filter can only be used on 8-bit images in RGB Color, CMYK Color, Lab Color, and Grayscale image modes.

To generate a pattern:

1. Click the layer that contains the imagery to be used for the pattern **1**. Since this layer will be replaced by the pattern, we suggest you duplicate it, and then click the original or the duplicate layer.
or
To generate a pattern in a new layer or file, select the area of imagery you want to use for the pattern, and choose Edit > Copy. Then add a layer, or create a new file, that has the dimensions you want the final image to have (don't Paste).

Note: If you create a non-rectangular selection, the filter will automatically square it off using the bounding box for the selected area.

2. Choose Filter > Pattern Maker. You can resize the dialog box by dragging the lower-right corner.

(Continued on the following page)

Pattern Maker

3. To generate a pattern in the current layer, choose the Rectangular marquee tool in the dialog box, ▢ then marquee the area you want to use as the pattern **1**. You can drag the selection marquee to a different spot.

or

To generate a pattern in a new layer or file based on whatever selection is on the Clipboard, check Use Clipboard as Sample (don't worry if the preview window is blank).

4. To specify the dimensions of tiles in the generated pattern **2**:

Enter or choose a Width value and a Height value.

or

Click Use Image Size to have the tile size match the current image size. This option creates a pattern using one large tile instead of multiple tiles.

5. From the Offset pop-up menu, choose the direction in which tiles will be offset in the generated pattern (None, Horizontal, or Vertical), then enter or choose an offset Amount (0–99%). The tiles will be offset from each other by a percentage of the tile's dimensions in the chosen direction.

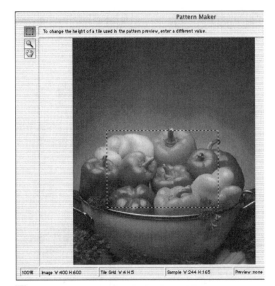

1 *In the **Pattern Maker** dialog box, either marquee the area to be used for the tile using the **Rectangular marquee** tool, or click **Use Clipboard** to create a tile based on the current contents of the Clipboard.*

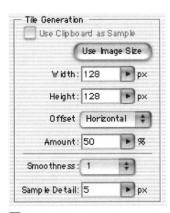

2 *In the **Tile Generation** area of the **Pattern Maker** dialog box, you can specify dimensions for the tile.*

Pattern Maker

Using the preview

Do any of the following in the Pattern Maker dialog box:

■ To magnify the preview, choose the **zoom** tool (Z) 🔍 in the dialog box, then click the preview image. To zoom out, Alt-click/Option-click the preview image. The zoom level will be listed in the lower-left corner of the dialog box.

■ To move the pattern in the preview window, choose the **hand** tool (H) ✋ in the dialog box or hold down Spacebar, then drag in the preview window. To move the pattern, the zoom level must be 100% or higher.

■ If you're curious to know where the nonprinting tile boundaries are, check Preview: **Tile Boundaries**. To choose a different color for the boundaries to make them contrast better with the imagery, click the color swatch, then choose a color from the Color Picker.

1 *Click* **Generate** *to have the filter generate a pattern using the tile. Click* **Generate Again** *to create more tile variations.*

6. Click Generate (Ctrl-G/Cmd-G). The tiled pattern will display in the preview area **1**. See the sidebar.

> **TIP** If the tile takes time to process, a Progress bar will appear. You can press Esc to cancel the generation in midstream.

7. Click Generate Again to have additional randomized patterns be generated using the same options, or change any of the options, such as the Width and/or Height, then click Generate Again.

> **TIP** To switch between the original image and the generated pattern in the preview window, choose Original or Generated from the Show pop-up menu in the Preview area on the right side of the dialog box.

To use a different part of the image for the pattern, choose Show: Original in the Preview area, move or redraw the sample marquee, then click Generate Again.

8. Once the pattern preview is to your liking, the next step is to delete any tiles you don't want and save any tiles that you may want to use later. For this, see the instructions on the following page.

> **TIP** The default Smoothness and Sample Detail settings work well for most samples, and increasing these values will cause the pattern to generate more slowly, so we don't recommend changing them unless you need to. However, if the pixels in the sample lack contrast, Photoshop may oversharpen the edges when it generates the pattern. Raise the Smoothness to reduce the prominence of edges within the tiles; raise the Sample Detail value to produce a more abstract pattern, with more deviation from the original imagery.

> **TIP** If the current layer's transparent pixels are locked, the pattern will only replace nontransparent pixels.

Pattern Maker

7.0! Using the Tile History section of the Pattern Maker dialog box, you can navigate through the patterns that have been generated, delete any pattern tiles you don't need, and save any tile as a pattern preset for future use.

To navigate through tiles:

Click the First Tile button, Previous Tile button, Next Tile button, or Last Tile button **1**.

or

Highlight the current tile number, type the number of the tile you want to view, then press Enter/Return.

TIP With Tile History: Update Pattern Preview checked, the full pattern will regenerate in the preview area. With this option unchecked, the tiles will only preview in the thumbnail, but you'll be able to zip through them more quickly.

7.0! When you delete a tile from the Tile History, its preview is discarded too.

To delete a tile:

1. Use the navigation buttons to locate the tile you want to delete.

2. Click the Delete Tile from History (trash) button.

7.0! When a tile is saved as a preset pattern, it becomes a swatch on the current pattern picker and is available for any command or tool that that picker is accessed from.

Note: When a tile is saved as a preset pattern, only that single tile is saved—not the full, generated pattern.

To save a tile as a preset pattern:

1. Use the navigation buttons to locate the tile you want to save.

2. Click the Saves Preset Pattern button. 💾

3. Type a Name for the preset **2**, then click OK. To create and manage preset libraries, use the Preset Manager (see page 404).

Note: The tile will be saved to the pattern picker—even if you click Cancel in the Pattern Maker dialog box.

Saves Preset Pattern — First Tile — Previous Tile — Next Tile — Last Tile

1 *Use the **Preview** buttons to **navigate** through the tile variations.*

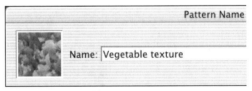

2 *Type a name for the preset in the **Pattern Name** dialog box.*

Pattern Maker

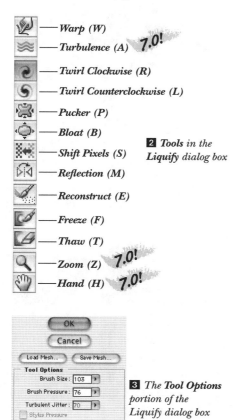

1 *The* **Liquify** *dialog box, after applying the* **Twirl Clockwise** *tool to an image*

— *Warp (W)*

— *Turbulence (A)* **7.0!**

— *Twirl Clockwise (R)*

— *Twirl Counterclockwise (L)*

— *Pucker (P)*

— *Bloat (B)*

— *Shift Pixels (S)*   **2** *Tools in the*

— *Reflection (M)*   *Liquify dialog box*

— *Reconstruct (E)*

— *Freeze (F)*

— *Thaw (T)*

— *Zoom (Z)* **7.0!**

— *Hand (H)* **7.0!**

3 *The* **Tool Options** *portion of the Liquify dialog box*

THE **LIQUIFY COMMAND** lets you twist, warp, stretch, and otherwise distort all or part of an image layer. Like the Extract command, Liquify gives you a full-size preview right in the dialog box **1**. You apply the distortion (or reconstruction) with a Liquify tool **2**, whose size and pressure are adjustable (like the brushes in the rest of Photoshop), and you can also use the brush to freeze parts of the image to protect them from distortion, as you would use a mask. You can undo the havoc you have wrought, partially or completely, with the Reconstruct tool. The edits become permanent when you click OK.

Note: This command works only on 8-bit images in RGB Color, CMYK Color, Lab Color, and Grayscale image modes.

To distort an image using the Liquify command:

1. Choose a layer or select part of an image layer. We suggest you work on a duplicate layer. You could also make a snapshot of the original image using the History palette. Liquify will not work on an editable type or shape layer.

2. Choose Filter > Liquify (Ctrl-Shift-X/ Cmd–Shift-X). The dialog box is resizable. **7.0!** If you created a rectangular selection, only the selected portion will appear in the dialog box. If the selection is non-rectangular, or is feathered, and View Options: Frozen Areas is checked, the unselected part of the layer will be masked. This is akin to using the Freeze tool, as discussed in step 4.

3. In the Tool Options area **3**:

Enter or choose a Brush Size (1–600 pixels), and choose a Brush Pressure (1–100%) for the rate at which distortion

(Continued on the following page)

Liquify Command

will be applied. These settings apply to all the Liquify tools!

If you're using a graphics tablet, check Stylus Pressure to have the brush pressure be controlled by the stylus.

4. *Optional:* To apply a mask to protect areas of the image from distortion, choose the **Freeze** tool (F), then paint on the image. The higher the Brush Pressure, the stronger the freeze effect. Drag again over the same spot to intensify.

> **TIP** You can choose a different overlay color for the frozen area from the View Options: Freeze Color pop-up menu. The default color is red.

5. *Optional:* To remove protection from the frozen areas, choose the **Thaw** tool (T), then paint on the preview image.

6. Do any of the following optional steps:

   To thaw all frozen areas and freeze all unfrozen areas, click Freeze Area: **Invert**.

   To thaw the entire image (make it all editable again), click **Thaw All**.

   To hide the mask created by the Freeze tool, uncheck View Options: **Frozen Areas**.

   Note: Even though frozen pixels won't be distorted by the Liquify tools, those tools can distort non-frozen areas using distortion patterns from the frozen imagery.

7. Choose any of these Liquify tools (type the shortcut to switch to the desired tool) and paint on the image in the dialog box:

   The **Warp** tool (W) pushes pixels in the direction you drag the brush **1**.

   The **Turbulence** tool (A) jumbles pixels, creating a crumbly effect **2**. Adjust the Tool Options: Turbulence Jitter value to control the tightness of the effect.

   The **Twirl Clockwise** (R) and **Twirl Counterclockwise** (L) tools rotate pixels as long as you hold down the mouse button or drag. The higher the Brush Pressure, the faster the rotation (see **1** on the previous page).

3 *After applying the **Pucker** tool: The brush was held stationary at the top of the tree.*

1 *After applying the **Warp** tool: The arrow shows the direction of the brush stroke.*

2 *After applying the **Turbulence** tool: The arrow shows the direction of the brush stroke.*

1 *We used the **Reflection** tool to pick up pixels from the right side of the stroke.*

2 *Here we Alt-dragged/Option-dragged downward with the **Reflection** tool. The tool picked up pixels from the start of the stroke.*

The **Pucker** (P) and **Bloat** (B) tools push pixels toward or away from the center of the brush as long as you hold down the mouse button or drag (**3**, previous page). The higher the Brush Pressure, the more quickly the pixels move.

The **Shift Pixels** tool (S) moves pixels at right angles from the direction the brush is moved. By default, the pixels move to the left of the brush. Alt-drag/ Option-drag to move pixels to the right of the brush.

The **Reflection** tool (M) copies pixels from the area to the right of your brush and applies a mirror image of them to the area the brush passes over **1**–**2**. The tool picks up pixels on the right side of an upward stroke, or the left side of a downward stroke. Alt-drag/Option-drag to copy pixels from the opposite side of the brush.

TIP Before using the Reflection tool, freeze the area you're going to reflect.

To have only the currently active layer display in the preview window, uncheck **Backdrop**. Or to have all or only one of the currently visible layers display, check Backdrop, choose the desired layer (or All Layers) from the pop-up menu, and choose an opacity for that layer for its display in the preview window. Whether this option is on or off, the Liquify command affects only the active layer.

To change the **Zoom** level of the preview image in the dialog box, choose the Zoom tool (Z), then click or drag in the preview window. Alt/Option-click to zoom out. Or choose a preset zoom level from the pop-up menu at the bottom left of the dialog box.

To move the image in the preview window, choose the **Hand** tool (H), then drag. Or to access this tool without selecting it, spacebar-drag instead.

(Continued on the following page)

8. To partially or completely undo the Liquify changes, read about the Reconstruction controls on page 371.

9. Click OK.

TIP To have the freeze mask conform to a selection, before choosing the Liquify command, create a selection, save it as an alpha channel, deselect, choose Image > Liquify, then choose that alpha channel from the Freeze Area: Channel pop-up menu. (To reverse the frozen and unfrozen areas in the image, click Invert.)

To help you gauge the extent of your Liquify command edits, you can superimpose a mesh over the image. The mesh gridlines display the same pattern of distortion as the image itself. The mesh comes in handy if portions of your image lack a clear pattern, and it's especially useful when using the Reconstruct tool. You can adjust the size and color of the mesh.

To display the mesh using View Options controls:

1. In the Liquify dialog box, check View Options: Mesh **1**. A regularly-spaced set of gridlines now covers the image **2**.

2. Do any of the following optional steps:

Choose a different size for the mesh from the Mesh Size pop-up menu.

Choose a different color for the mesh from the Mesh Color pop-up menu.

If the mesh is visible and you want to hide the image, uncheck View Options: Image. This will enable you to see the distortion pattern in the mesh more clearly.

TIP In Photoshop 7 or later, you can save your meshes and then apply them to other images. In the Liquify dialog box, click Save Mesh, type a name for the mesh, choose a location for it, then click Save. To load in a mesh, click Load Mesh.

1 *The default **View Options** in the **Liquify** dialog box*

2 *The palm tree modified using the **Warp** tool: Both the **image** and the **mesh** are visible.*

1 *The **Reconstruction** controls in the **Liquify** dialog box*

After you've applied distortion to your image, you can use the Reconstruction controls **1**, together with the Reconstruct tool, to undo some or all of the distortion, or to extend the distortion into other areas of the image.

TIP You can apply the Undo command via the Ctrl-Z/Cmd-Z shortcut while using the liquify or reconstruction controls.

To remove all distortion from the preview image:

In the Liquify dialog box, click Revert in the Reconstruction area. The preview image (including any frozen areas) will return to the state it was in when you originally opened the Liquify dialog box. (Don't confuse the Revert button with the Revert brush mode, which is discussed next.)

To return all unfrozen areas to their initial state:

1. In the Liquify dialog box, choose Mode: Revert from the pop-up menu in the Reconstruction area.

2. Click the Reconstruct button. The unfrozen parts of the preview image will return to the state were in when you opened the Liquify dialog box; the frozen areas won't change.

To return individual unfrozen areas to their initial state:

1. In the Liquify dialog box, choose Mode: Revert from the pop-up menu in the Reconstruction area.

2. Choose the Reconstruct tool (E), then click and hold on, or drag over, the areas you want to restore. The restoration happens more quickly at the center of the brush cursor.

To learn about the other Reconstruction modes, see the following page.

Liquify Reconstruction

Perhaps as part of your use of the Liquify command you have frozen an area or areas to which you have applied distortion. Using the Reconstruct tool, you can then extend the distortion from the frozen areas into unfrozen areas in interesting ways. You can also use this tool to sample a distortion pattern from one part of the image and apply it to another part of the image.

To extend distortions from frozen areas into unfrozen areas:

1. In the Liquify dialog box, use the Freeze tool (F) to freeze one or more areas that have already been distorted. In this case, the borders of the image will act as if they are frozen, too. You could try reconstructing an area between two frozen areas.

2. In the Reconstruction area, choose a reconstruction Mode (other than Revert) from the pop-up menu ◼.

3. Choose the Reconstruct tool (E), then click and hold the mouse, or drag, on the image preview to restore unfrozen areas. Restoration occurs more quickly at the brush's center. The distortion, if any, will be sampled from the starting point.
   or
   Click the Reconstruct button to reconstruct all the unfrozen areas. Your edits will be undone in reverse order, like a movie playing backwards. To stop the process in midstream, press Spacebar.

   Note: Pressing Esc in Windows or Esc or Cmd-period in the Mac OS won't stop the reconstruction process, even though the Adobe online help says it does.

TIP To undo all of your distortion and tool settings changes without closing the dialog box, Alt-click/Option-click Reset.

The Reconstruction modes

The Rigid, Stiff, Smooth, and Loose Modes extend the distortion from frozen areas into unfrozen areas, each in their own fashion. What results is part distortion and part restoration. **Smooth** and **Loose** produce additional distortion, with a gradual transition between the frozen and non-frozen areas; **Rigid** and **Stiff** also produce additional distortion, but with a sharper transition between the frozen and non-frozen areas. When you extend distortions, click on, or drag once or twice over, the unfrozen areas.

The three choices at the bottom of the Mode pop-up menu allow you to copy various characteristics of the distortion at a specific point to other, unfrozen parts of the image. **Displace** copies the displacement of the starting point to another point, moving it from one part of the image to another. **Amplitwist** copies the displacement, rotation, and scaling from the starting point to other parts of the image. **Affine** copies all aspects of the distortion from the starting point to reconstructed areas, including displacement, rotation, horizontal scaling, vertical scaling, and skew.

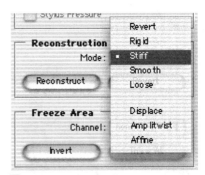

◼ *The Reconstruction Mode pop-up menu in the Liquify dialog box*

AUTOMATE 20

*An **included** command has a black check mark; an excluded command doesn't.*

*An **action***

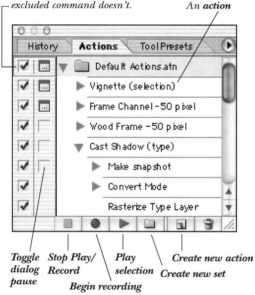

Toggle dialog pause — Stop Play/Record — Begin recording — Play selection — Create new action / Create new set

1 *With the **Actions** palette in **list** (edit) mode, you can exclude a command, toggle a dialog box pause on or off, rearrange the order of commands, record additional commands, rerecord a command, delete a command, or save actions and/or sets to an actions file. This is the default (start-up) mode.*

2 *This is the **Actions** palette in **button mode**. To turn Button mode on or off, choose Button Mode from the Actions palette menu. The button colors and function keys chosen in the Action Options dialog box are displayed here.*

AN **ACTION IS A** recorded sequence of menu commands, tool operations, or other image-editing functions that can be played back on a single file, a group of files, or a folder full (batch) of files. Actions are especially useful for producing consistent editing results on multiple images. For example, you could use an action to apply a series of Adjustment submenu commands or a sequence of filters. You could also save a sequence of concise steps into an action to prepare multiple images for print output, or to convert multiple images to a different file format or image mode.

An action can be anything from a simple keyboard shortcut to an incredibly complex series of commands that trigger still other actions, or that process a whole batch of images. Actions can help you save seconds or hours of work time, depending on how you use them. Start by recording a few simple actions. You'll be programming more complex processes and boosting your productivity in no time.

Actions can be created in Photoshop or ImageReady. The Actions palette is used to record, play back, edit, delete, save, and load actions **1**–**2**. Each action can be assigned its own keyboard shortcut for quick access. Actions can also be triggered via droplets—small applications created from actions. Dragging a file or folder full of files onto a droplet icon activates the action.

TIP Make a snapshot of an image before running an action on it. That way, you can quickly revert, if necessary, to the pre-action state of the image without having to undo any action steps.

TIP With the Action Palette in list (edit) mode, Alt-click/Option-click a right-pointing triangle to reveal (or hide) all the steps in an action (or reveal an action and all the steps within a set).

Actions

Actions

Actions are saved in sets on the Actions palette. Sets are a convenient way of organizing task-related actions.

To create a new actions set:

1. Click the "Create new set" button ▢ at the bottom of the Actions palette.

2. Type a Name for the set **1**, then click OK.

As you create an action, the commands you use are recorded. When you're finished recording, the commands will appear as a list in indented (nested) format on the Actions palette.

Note: Some operations, such as Brush tool strokes, can't be recorded.

To record an action:

1. Open an image or create a new one. Just to be safe, experiment by recording and playing back the action on a copy of the file.

2. Click the "Create new action" button ▣ at the bottom of the Actions palette, or choose New action from the Actions palette menu.

3. Enter a name for the action **2**.

4. *Optional:* Assign a keyboard shortcut Function Key and/or display Color to the action. The color you choose will be displayed only in button mode.

5. Click Record.

6. Execute the commands that you want to record as you would normally apply them to any image. When you enter values in a dialog box and then click OK, those settings will be recorded (unless you click Cancel).

7. Click the Stop button ▣ or press Esc to stop recording.

8. The action will now be listed on the Actions palette. Click the downward-pointing triangle (with the palette in list mode) to collapse the action's list.

1 *Enter a **Name** for the new set.*

2 *Enter a **Name** for the new action.*

Recordable features 7.0!

The following tools and palettes **can** be used when recording an action:

TOOLS

Marquee, Move, all the Lasso tools, Magic Wand, Crop, Slice, Magic Eraser, Gradient, Paint Bucket, Type, Shape, Notes, Eyedropper, Color Sampler

PALETTES

Color, Swatches, Styles, Layers, Channels, Paths, History, Actions

The following **can't** be used when recording an action: Brush, Pencil, Dodge, Burn, Sponge, Blur, Sharpen tools, tool options, view commands, and window commands

It's all relative

The recording of any position-related operation (using a selection tool, or the Slice, Gradient, Magic Wand, Path, or Notes tool) is based on the current ruler units. The units can be **actual** (e.g., inches or picas) or **relative** (e.g., percent). An action that is recorded when an actual measurement unit is chosen can't be played back on an image that is smaller than the original that was used for recording, whereas an action recorded when a relative unit is chosen will work in any other relative space and on an image of any dimensions. To change the units, go to Edit (Photoshop, in OS X) > Preferences > Units & Rulers, then choose a unit, or choose "percent" from the Units: Rulers pop-up menu.

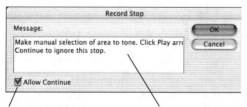

*Check **Allow Continue** to create a Continue button which the person replaying the action can press to bypass the stop command and resume playback.*

1 *Enter a **message** in the **Record Stop** dialog box to guide the user during playback.*

TIP Alt-click/Option-click the "Create new action" button to automatically create a new action (default name of Action 1) without using a dialog box. Alt-click/Option-click the "Create new set" button to automatically create a new set (default name of Set 1).

TIP To rename an action, double-click its name (press Enter/Return when done).

TIP Include the Save command in an action with caution. When using the Save As command, be sure not to change the file name. You may want to make the action pause at the Save dialog box to prevent existing files from being overwritten (see below). To delete a Save or any other command from an action, see page 382.

You can insert a variety of commands into an action. For example, you can insert a stop into an action that will interrupt the playback, at which point you can manually perform a non-recordable operation, such as drawing brushstrokes or spotting dust specs. When the manual operation is finished, you resume the playback by clicking the Play button again. A stop can also be used to allow an informative alert message to display at the pause.

To insert a stop in an action:

1. As you're creating an action, pause at the point at which you want the stop to appear. For an existing action, click the command name after which you want the stop to appear.

2. Choose Insert Stop from the Actions palette menu.

3. Type an instructional or alert message for the person who's going to replay the action **1**. It's a good idea to specify in your stop message that after performing a manual step, the user should click the Play button on the Actions palette to resume the playback.

(Continued on the following page)

Insert Stop

4. *Optional:* Check Allow Continue to include a Continue button in the stop alert box 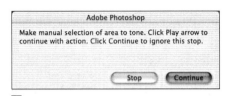. This allows the user to choose to continue the action without performing any manual tasks. *Note:* If Allow Continue isn't checked, you will still be able to click Stop at that point in the action playback and then click the Play button on the palette to resume the action playback.

5. Click OK.

6. The stop will be inserted below the command you highlighted in step 1 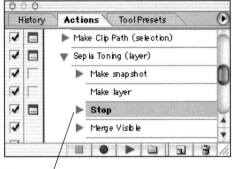.

TIP If an action is replayed while the Actions palette is in button mode, the Play button won't be accessible for resuming the playback after a stop. Click the action name again (the Play button will be red) to resume the playback instead. Choose list mode for the palette when you're using stops.

The Insert Menu Item provides a method for including many nonrecordable commands into an action. You can also use Insert Menu Item if you want your user to have some control over an action. An action that contains a menu item will pause at that command, and the relevant dialog box will open.

To insert a menu item in an action:

1. In an existing action, click the command name after which you want the menu item to be inserted.

2. Choose Insert Menu Item from the Actions palette menu 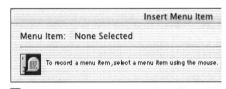.

3. Choose the command from the menu bar. The Insert Menu Item dialog box will tell you which command you've chosen 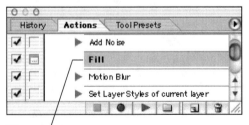.

4. Click OK. The item will now appear in your action . Modal control is disabled for that command.

1 *The **Continue** button lets the user continue an action without performing manual tasks.*

2 *A **Stop** command*

3 *When **Insert Menu Item** has been chosen, the dialog box tells you to choose a menu item.*

4 *The menu item **Fill** has been chosen.*

5 *The inserted menu item*

Insert Menu Item

A path also can be inserted into an action, just as if you copied and pasted it from another document or application. Because the path is saved in the action, you can place it in as many files as you want. After the path is placed, your action can transform and/or manipulate the path as you wish.

Note: Adding paths to your actions requires significant memory. To increase the memory allotted to Photoshop, see page 395.

To insert a path in an action:

1. Create the path you want to use in an action (see pages 284–288), and leave the work path name selected on the Paths palette.

2. Start recording the action, and pause at the point in your action at which you want the path to be inserted. Or for an existing action, click the command name after which you want the path to be inserted.

3. Choose Insert Path from the Actions palette menu. The command "Set Work Path" will be added to the action ◼.

4. Choose Save Path from the Paths palette menu, then click OK to accept the default name.

5. Finish recording your action, including any transformations of the path.

TIP If percent is the current ruler unit, the action will draw the path in proportion to the size of the playback document. For example, if you create a path, insert that path into an action using an 8.5″ x 11″ document, and then play the action back in a document half that size, the path will be drawn at 50% of its original size.

◼ *The **work path** you created appears in the action, along with a list of the path's anchor points and related attributes.*

Insert Path

To exclude or include a command from playback:

1. Make sure the Actions palette is in list—not button—mode. (In button mode, you can only execute an entire action, and any previously excluded commands won't play back.)

2. On the Actions palette, click the right-pointing triangle next to an action name to expand the list, if it isn't already expanded.

3. Click in the leftmost column to remove the check mark and exclude that command from playback . (Click in the same spot again to restore the check mark and include the command.)

1 *The "Vignette" action is expanded on the Actions palette, and the Feather step is **unchecked** to **exclude** it from playback.*

To play back an action on an image:

1. Open the image that you want to play back the action on.

2. Choose list mode for the Actions palette (uncheck button mode).

3. Click an action name on the palette.

4. Click the Play button on the palette.
or
Create a droplet from the desired action, then drag files onto the droplet icon (to make your own droplets, see page 381).

Playback options

Four options for playback control are available in the Playback Options dialog box, which is accessible via the Actions palette menu when the palette is in list mode.

Accelerated: The fastest option.

Step by Step: When this option is chosen, the action's list expands on the Actions palette. Each step applies to the image as the commands on the action list highlight and execute.

Pause for [   ] seconds: This option works like Step by Step, but with an additional user-defined pause inserted at each step.

Pause for Audio Annotation: This option allows the pausing of the playback until the audio annotation has completed.

More playback options

■ To play an action starting from a specific command within the action, click that command name, then click the Play button or choose Play from the Actions palette menu.

■ To play one command in a multi-command action, click the command name, then Ctrl-click/Cmd-click the Play button or Ctrl/Cmd double-click the command.

The ability to replay an action using the Batch command is one of the most powerful features of actions.

Note: For efficient batching, organize your files and folders ahead of time. Make sure all your source files are in the same folder—and make sure the destination folder exists!

To replay an action on a batch of images:

1. Make sure all the files to be batch processed are located in the same folder.

2. Choose File > Automate > Batch.

3. Choose a set from the Set pop-up menu and choose an action from the Action pop-up menu ■.

4. Choose Source: Folder.
 and
 Click Choose, locate the folder that contains the files to be processed, then click Choose.

5. Choose Destination: None to have the files stay open after processing; or choose Save and Close to have the files save over their originals; or choose Folder to have the files save to a new folder (click Choose to specify the destination folder).

6. *Optional:* If you chose Folder for the previous steps and checked Override Action "Save As" Commands, the images will save to the folder designated in step 5 during playback only when a Save command occurs in the action.

7. Click OK. The batch processing will begin.

TIP For efficient memory management, before batching, go to Edit (Photoshop, in OS X) > Preferences > General, and set the History States to 1. You can even include the setting and resetting of the history states as part of the action itself!

■ *In the* **Batch** *dialog box, choose the action you want to* **Play***, locate the files you want to process (the* **Source***), and specify where you want the processed files to be saved (the* **Destination***).*

If Folder is chosen as the Destination for batch files, there are many options for the resulting file names. For example, the files can be named sequentially using serial numbers or letters so they don't replace each other in the new folder. There are also options for ensuring that the file names are compatible with various operating systems.

To choose batch naming options:

1. Create a folder for saving the processed files.

2. Choose File > Automate > Batch.

3. Choose Destination: Folder.

4. Choose options from the pop-up menus in the File Naming area **1**, or simply type in any text you want to include in the name.

5. Make sure the Example name exhibits the naming convention that you chose.

6. Check any of the boxes for file name Compatibility: Windows, Mac OS, or Unix.

Note: The files being processed by the Batch command are always saved in their original format. To force them to save to another format, when creating the action, record the Save As command (leave the name alone, but choose the desired format), then record the Close command. When choosing batch settings, be sure to check the Override Action "Save As" Commands option.

7. *Optional:* By default, Photoshop will stop the batch process when it encounters an error message. You can choose to have the Batch play through and just keep track of the error messages in a text file by choosing Log Errors to File from the Errors menu. If this option is chosen and errors are encountered, a message will appear after processing. In order to see the logged error messages, click Save As and name the error log file before running the batch.

1 *In the **Batch** dialog box, choose **File Naming** options.*

Back and forth

To make a droplet that was created in Windows useable on Mac OS (Mac OS-ready), drag the droplet onto the Photoshop 7 **application** icon. To make a Mac-made droplet useable on Windows, add the extension **.exe** at the end of the droplet name.

Note: References to file names and paths within an action aren't supported between operating systems.

An action can be turned into its own little "mini" application, called a droplet. The droplet can sit out on the desktop or in a folder waiting to be triggered. If you drag a file or a folder full of files onto the droplet icon, the droplet will cause the file to be processed automatically.

Because a droplet is like a standalone "action," it can be given to other users or used on other computers. Photoshop 7 will launch in order to let the droplet do its work, just in case the program isn't open when any graphic files are dragged onto the droplet icon.

To create a droplet from an action:

1. Choose File > Automate > Create Droplet.

2. Click Choose, choose the location where you want to save the droplet **1**, enter a name in the Save As field, then click Save.

3. Choose a set from the Set pop-up menu and choose an action from the Action pop-up menu.

4. Check any Play options you want to be included in the droplet.

5. Choose Destination options (see steps 4 through 6 on page 380).

6. Click OK to have Photoshop create the droplet **2**.

TIP In ImageReady, you can create a droplet simply by dragging an action to the Desktop.

1 *In the* **Create Droplet** *dialog box, choose a location for saving the droplet.*

2 *A* **droplet** *icon*

Droplets

Note: A command that's available only under certain conditions (e.g., the Feather command requires an active selection) can't be added to an action unless you also set up or add in that condition.

To add commands to an action:

1. On the Actions palette, click the right-pointing triangle next to an action name to expand the list, if it's not already expanded, then click the command name after which you want the new command to appear.

2. Click the "Begin recording" button. ⬤

3. Perform the steps to record the command(s) that you want to add.

4. Click the Stop button ■ to stop recording.

TIP To copy a command from one action to another, expand both action lists, then Alt-drag/Option-drag the command you want to copy from one list to the other. If you don't hold down Alt/Option while dragging, you'll cut the command from the original action. Be careful if you copy any Save commands—they may contain info that's specific to the original action.

Beware! To save the current list of actions as a set for later use, follow the instructions on page 385 *before* clearing any items from the Actions palette.

To delete a command from an action:

1. Click the name of the command that you want to delete. Shift-click to highlight additional commands, if desired.

2. Click the Delete button 🗑 at the bottom of the Actions palette, then click OK.
or
Drag the command to the Delete button.

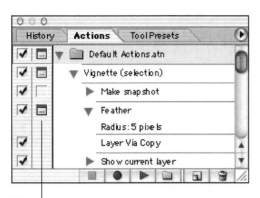

1 *The **dialog box** icon*

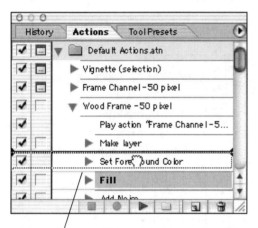

2 *The Fill command being **moved upward** on the list*

A modal control is a pause in an action. A modal control can be turned on for any command that uses a dialog box or tool that requires pressing Enter/Return to apply the effect. If you encounter a modal control upon playing back an action, you can either enter different settings in the dialog box or click OK to proceed with the settings that were originally recorded for the action.

To activate/deactivate a modal control in an action:

1. Make sure the Actions palette is in list mode (not button mode).

2. On the Actions palette, click the right-pointing triangle (list toggle button) next to the action name to expand the list, if it's not already expanded.

3. Click in the second column from the left to display the dialog box icon **1**. (Click again in the same spot if you want to remove the modal control.) The action will pause and display this command's dialog box when the modal control is encountered, at which point you can enter new values, or accept the existing values, or cancel. The playback will resume after you close the dialog box.

TIP You can also click the dialog box icon next to an action name to turn on/off all the dialog boxes in that action.

Beware! Changing the order of commands in an action may cause a different overall effect to occur in any images it's played back on.

To change the order of commands:

1. On the Actions palette, click the right-pointing triangle next to an action name to expand the list, if it's not already expanded.

2. Drag a command upward or downward on the list **2**.

To rerecord an entire action using different dialog box settings:

1. Click the name of the action that you want to revise.

2. Choose Record Again from the Actions palette menu. The action will play back, stopping at any command that uses a dialog box.

3. When each dialog box opens, enter new settings, if desired, then click OK. When the dialog box closes, the rerecording will continue.

4. To stop the rerecording, click Cancel in a dialog box or click the Stop button ■ at the bottom of the Actions palette.

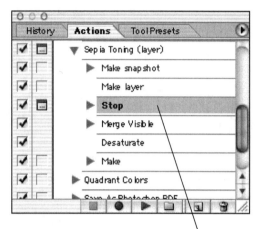

1 *Double-click the command you want to rerecord.*

To rerecord a single command in an action:

1. On the Actions palette, double-click the command you want to rerecord **1**.

2. Enter new settings.

3. Click OK. Click Cancel to have any revisions be disregarded.

If you want to experiment with an action or add to it without messing around with the original, work on a duplicate.

To duplicate an action:

Click an action, then choose Duplicate from the Actions palette menu.
or
Drag an action over the "Create new action" button at the bottom of the Actions palette **2**.

TIP To duplicate a command in an action, click the command name, then choose Duplicate from the palette menu. Or drag the command over the "Create new action" button at the bottom of the Actions palette.

To delete an entire action:

1. Click the action you want to delete.

2. Click the Delete button 🗑 at the bottom of the Actions palette, then click OK.
or
Alt-click/Option-click the Delete button.

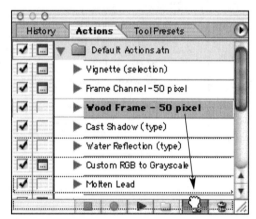

2 *To duplicate an action, drag the action name over the Create new action button.*

Where are actions stored?

In Windows, the actions that are visible on the Actions palette list are stored in the **Actions Palette.psp** file in \Windows\Application Data\ Adobe\Photoshop\7.0\Adobe Photoshop 7.0 Settings.

In the Mac OS, they're stored in the **Actions Palette** file in Users > [User Name] > Library > Preferences > Adobe Photoshop 7 Settings. They live there until they're replaced or the file is trashed. To keep a set from being inadvertently removed, save it as a separate file!

For easy access, save your Actions Sets in Applications > Adobe Photoshop 7 > Presets > **Photoshop Actions**. Then they will appear at the bottom of the Actions palette menu.

To save a **text** version of an actions set, hold down Ctrl-Alt/Cmd-Option while choosing Save Actions. This file can't be imported back into Photoshop.

Actions and AppleScript

Mac OS: An action can be controlled from another scriptable application, such as AppleScript. AppleScript is a relatively easy scripting language to learn. A scriptable application such as InDesign, Filemaker Pro, QuarkXPress, or Hypercard lets you drive actions externally using the AppleScript do-script command.

Actions are stored automatically in actions sets (a set can contain one or more actions). Follow these instructions to save an actions set to a separate file for use on another computer or as a backup to prevent accidental or inadvertent loss.

To save an actions set to a file:

1. Click the actions set you want to save.

2. Choose Save Actions from the Actions palette menu.

3. Type a Name for the actions set file.

4. Choose a location in which to save the actions set file.

5. Click Save. The new file will be regarded as one set, regardless of the number of actions it contains.

TIP If you Alt-drag/Option-drag an action into another actions set, it will copy automatically.

To load an additional actions set onto the Actions palette:

1. Click the set name that you want the loaded set to appear below.

2. Choose Load Actions from the Actions palette menu.

3. Locate and highlight the actions set file you want to append, then click Load.
   or
   Choose an actions set name from the bottom of the palette menu.

To replace the current actions set with a different actions set:

1. Choose Replace Actions from the Actions palette menu.

2. Locate and click the actions set file that you want to replace the existing sets with.

3. Click Load.

You can make an action run within another action.

Beware! The action that will be added to another action will run through all of its commands, and thus will affect the currently open image. So, make sure that you perform this recording on a duplicate image!

To run one action in another action:

1. Open a file.

2. On the Actions palette, click the right-pointing triangle (list toggle button) next to the action name to expand the list, if it's not already expanded, then select the command after which you want the added action to appear **1**.

3. Click the "Begin recording" button. ●

4. Click the action to be added **2**.

5. Click the Play button ▶ to record it into the other action (you can't double-click the action). The added action will run through its commands. The new command on the actions list will have this name: "Play action [action name] of set [set name]."

6. Click the Stop button ■ when the added action is finished playing.

TIP An action can include multiple actions, but careful planning is essential. An action may have been moved or modified or may be unavailable the next time you call upon it. Spend some time organizing your actions and sets, and back up often.

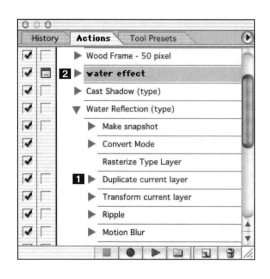

Run One Action in Another Action

File	
New...	⌘N
Open...	⌘O
Browse...	⇧⌘O
Open Recent	▶
Close	⌘W
Close All	⌥⌘W
Save	⌘S
Save As...	⇧⌘S
Save for Web...	⌥⇧⌘S
Revert	
Place...	
Import	▶
Export	▶
Workgroup	▶
Automate	▶
File Info...	
Page Setup...	⇧⌘P
Print with Preview...	⌘P
Print...	⌥⌘P
Print One Copy	⌥⇧⌘P
Jump To	▶

Automate ▶
Batch...
Create Droplet...
Conditional Mode Change...
Contact Sheet II...
Fit Image...
Multi-Page PDF to PSD...
Picture Package...
Web Photo Gallery...

1 *The* ***Automate*** *commands under the File menu*

Other automate commands

In addition to the Batch and Create Droplet commands on the Automate submenu, there are six other commands that work like actions on steroids: Conditional Mode Change, Contact Sheet II, Fit Image, Multi-Page PDF to PSD, Picture Package, and Web Photo Gallery **1**. These commands combine many complex command sequences into one dialog box setting. Adobe will more than likely offer more of these pumped-up actions in the future, and surely third-party developers will supply even more. It's a computer doing what a computer does best.

By adding this command to an action, you can ensure that all the files being processed will have the desired image mode.

To perform a conditional image mode change:

1. Choose File > Automate > Conditional Mode Change.

2. Choose the source file image mode that you want to convert **2**.

3. Choose the desired image mode from the Target Mode: Mode drop-down menu. If the image mode of the processed file doesn't match any of the chosen Source Modes, an alert dialog box will appear (click OK) **3**.

4. Click OK.

5. Respond to any mode change prompts that may display.

Conditional Mode Change

Source Mode
☑ Bitmap   ☑ RGB Color
☑ Grayscale   ☐ CMYK Color
☑ Duotone   ☑ Lab Color
☑ Indexed Color ☑ Multichannel

(All) (None)

(OK)
(Cancel)

Target Mode
Mode: [CMYK Color ▼]

2 *Choose* ***Source Mode*** *and* ***Target Mode*** *options in the* ***Conditional Mode Change*** *dialog box.*

⚠ Mode of the document does not match any selected Source Modes.

(OK)

3 *This alert dialog box will appear if the image mode of the processed file doesn't match any of the chosen Source Modes.*

A contact sheet is an arrangement of image thumbnails on a page, all with the same size bounding box—with or without file name captions.

To create a contact sheet:

1. Move all the images you want to appear on the contact sheet or sheets into one folder, or nest them in subdirectories/subfolders of that folder. Also make sure all the files you want to appear on a contact sheet or sheets are saved in a format that Photoshop can read. And finally, make sure none of those files are open.

2. Choose File > Automate > Contact Sheet II.

3. Click Choose, locate the folder that contains the images for the contact sheet, then click "Select [folder name]." **1**

Optional: Check Include All Subdirectories/Subfolders if you want to include images in any subdirectories/subfolders inside the designated folder—not just files on the top level of the source directory/folder.

4. Choose a measurement unit from the Document: Width and Height pop-up menus, then enter a Width and Height for the contact sheet.

Optional: Check Flatten All Layers to have all images (and captions, if chosen) appear on a single layer. Uncheck this option to have each image and caption appear on its own layer.

5. Choose a Resolution for the sheet.

6. Choose a Mode for the contact sheet.

7. In the Thumbnails area of the dialog box, choose a Place option to specify the direction in which the images are to be arranged: in horizontal or vertical rows. *and* Enter the number of Columns and Rows to appear on the contact sheet.

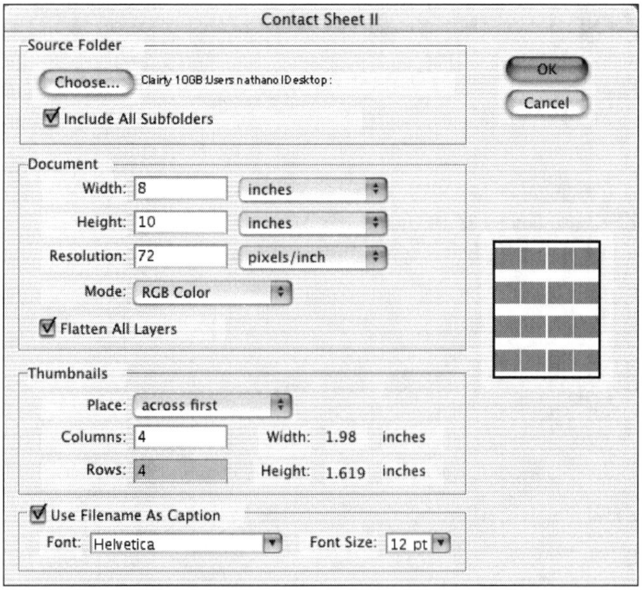

1 *In the Contact Sheet II dialog box, locate the images to be put on a contact sheet and choose layout options for the sheet.*

Contact Sheet (sidebar)

1 *A contact sheet with filename captions*

Fit Image

Fit Image
Constrain Within
Width: [576] pixels
Height: [720] pixels
OK
Cancel

2 *Enter the desired dimensions in the **Fit Image** dialog box.*

The contact sheet layout will preview on the right side of the dialog box.

8. *Optional:* Check Use Filename As Caption to have a caption with the file's name appear under each thumbnail. If you choose this option, also choose a Font and Font Size for the captions.

9. Click OK **1**. Save the contact sheet file when you're finished.

Note: Be forewarned, the Fit Image command changes an image's dimensions via resampling (by adding or deleting pixels). The image resolution will remain constant.

To fit an image to width and/or height dimensions:

1. Open a file.

2. Choose File > Automate > Fit Image.

3. Enter the desired Constrain Within: Width and Height dimensions **2**.

The smaller of the numbers will be used for the fit. For example, say your source image is 210 x 237 and you enter 275 in the Height field and 1500 in the Width field. The image will be fit to the 275 dimension at the original aspect ratio (with a long dimension of 310).

4. Click OK.

Fit Image

A multi-page Acrobat PDF file can be imported into Photoshop. See pages 68 and 70 to learn more about PDF. (.psd is the extension for the Photoshop file format.)

To convert a multi-page PDF to Photoshop format:

1. Choose File > Automate > Multi-Page PDF to PSD.

2. Under Source PDF, click Choose, then locate and select the PDF file you want to convert ▮.

3. Click a Page Range: All or click From and enter a page range. It's a good idea to be familiar with the source file, because you won't see a preview of the PDF file.

4. In the Output Options area, enter a Resolution. For a PDF that contains type, for print output, enter a minimum Resolution of 250 ppi so the type will rasterize well. For Web output, 72 ppi is sufficient for a PDF.

5. Choose a Mode (you can change the image mode later in Photoshop).

   Checking Anti-aliased slightly softens the edges of type characters, but it also makes them slightly thinner.

6. Under Destination, leave the Base Name as is or enter a new name for the converted file. The name will be followed by 0001.psd, 0002.psd, and so on, to identify the source pages.

7. Click Choose, then locate and click a destination folder for the converted files.

   Optional: Check Suppress Warnings to prevent any warnings from appearing during the conversion.

8. Click OK. Image windows will quickly display and close on screen while the conversion process is happening. When it's completed, all the converted files will be located in the folder you designated in the previous step, and they can be opened and edited like any other Photoshop files.

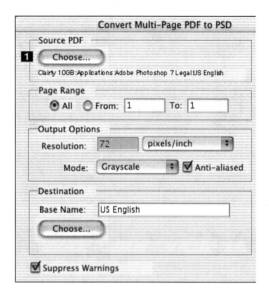

PDF to PSD

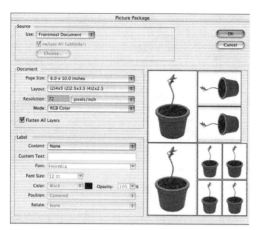

1 *Choose **Source**, **Document**, and **Label** options in the **Picture Package** dialog box.*

2 *This is the (2) 4 x 5 & (2) 2.5 x 3.5 & (4) 2 x 2.5 **Picture Package Layout**. Many other layout options are available. To create your own custom layouts, see "Customizing picture package layouts" in Adobe Photoshop online Help.*

The Picture Package plug-in arranges multiple sizes of one image on the same sheet, like the layouts produced by traditional photo studios. You can choose from a variety of preset sizes and configurations.

To create a picture package:

1. Choose File > Automate > Picture Package.

2. For Source, click Choose **1**, locate the image you want to use, then click Choose.
or
Choose Use: Frontmost Document to use the currently open, active image.

3. In the Document area, choose a Layout option for the size (in inches) of the images that will appear on the page. The layout will preview in the dialog box.
and
Choose a Resolution.
and
Choose a color Mode.

Optional: Check Flatten All Layers to have all images (and labels, if chosen) appear on one layer. Uncheck to have each image and label appear on a separate layer.

4. In the Label area, if you want each file to be labeled, choose a Content type: Custom Text, Filename, Copyright, Caption, Credit, or Title. For Custom Text, type the desired label in the Custom Text field. The last four will be extracted from information found in File > File Info.
and
Choose a Font, Font Size, Color, and Opacity for the labels.
and
Choose a Position for each label, relative to the image.
and
Choose a Rotate option or leave it on the default setting of None.

5. Click OK. Sit by idly while the command processes **2**. (Press Esc, if need be, to stop the command during processing.)

6. Save the new file in the desired format.

Picture Package

391

Using the Web Photo Gallery command, you can export multiple images directly as a Web site—Photoshop does all the work for you! You'll get, automatically: a gallery homepage with its index.htm file, which can be opened in any Web browser for previewing the photo gallery; individual JPEG image pages inside an images sub-folder; HTML page files inside a pages sub-folder; and JPEG thumbnail images inside a thumbnails subfolder.

Note: When you're ready to upload your Web gallery to a server, ask your Internet service provider (ISP) which file and folder naming conventions to use, and also ask them for uploading instructions.

To create a Web gallery:

1. Make sure the images you want to use for the gallery are contained or nested in one folder.

2. Choose File > Automate > Web Photo Gallery.

3. Choose a layout style for the website from the Styles menu (a teeny sample of the style will appear in the dialog box).

4. *Optional:* Enter an Email address to serve as a contact address for the gallery.

5. Choose an Extension for the HTML file: .htm or .html.

6. Choose Options pop-up menu settings for text information, image size, resolution, fonts used, file naming conventions, and link colors:

Choose **Banner**, then enter the information you want to appear on every page of the gallery 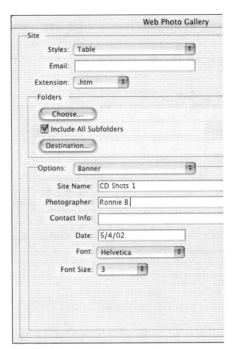. Type the Site Name, Photographer, and Date, and choose a Font and Font Size for the banner text.

Choose **Large Images**, then choose quality, size, and border settings for the images to be used on every gallery page . The size of the border around each image is measured in pixels. If you check Resize Images, Photoshop will resize the source images for placement on individual

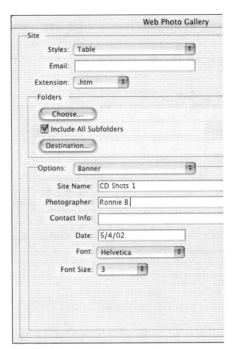

1 *With **Banner** chosen on the Options pop-up menu in the **Web Photo Gallery** dialog box*

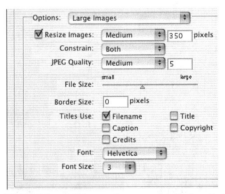

2 *With **Large Images** chosen on the Options pop-up menu in the **Web Photo Gallery** dialog box*

7.0!

7.0!

1 *With **Thumbnails** chosen on the Options pop-up menu in the **Web Photo Gallery** dialog box*

2 *With **Custom Colors** chosen on the Options pop-up menu in the **Web Photo Gallery** dialog box*

3 *With **Security** chosen on the Options pop-up menu in the **Web Photo Gallery** dialog box*

image pages for you; with this option unchecked, Photoshop will leave the source image size alone.

If you checked Resize Images, choose a rough size from the Resize Images pop-up menu or enter a specific size, in pixels, and choose a JPEG Quality (0–12). The higher the JPEG Quality, the larger the file size. You can also move the slider.

Check any Titles Use options (extracted from the File > File Info dialog box). Choose Font and Font Size settings.

Choose **Thumbnails** to set options for pictures on the home page of the web gallery **1**. Choose the thumbnail image Size, and choose thumbnail layout settings (Columns, Rows, and Border Size fields). Check Titles Use options (extracted from the File > File Info dialog box), and choose Font and Font Size settings.

Choose **Custom Colors** to choose colors for Background, Banner Text, and Links spaces **2**. Click a color swatch to change it via the Color Picker (remember to use Web-safe colors, if possible).

Choose **Security** to display text over your images as an anti-theft measure **3**. Choose a type of Content: Custom Text, Filename, Copyright, Caption, Credit, or Title. For Custom Text, type the desired text in the Custom Text field. The last four are extracted automatically from information found in File > File Info.
and
Choose a Font, Font Size, Color, and Opacity for the text.
and
Choose a Position for the text, relative to the image.
and
Choose a Rotate option or leave it on the default setting of None.

7. Click Choose, locate the folder that contains the images you want to use, then click Choose.

(Continued on the following page)

Web Photo Gallery

Optional: Check Include All Subdirectories/Subfolders if you want to include images in any subdirectories/subfolders inside the designated folder—not just files on the top level of the source directory/folder.

8. Click Destination, locate the folder that you want to save the resulting HTML files in, then click Choose.

9. Click OK. Photoshop will create the following files: at least one home page named index, HTML files for the other pages of the site (all with the extension chosen in step 5), and JPEG files for the images and thumbnails.

TIP Keep all the gallery files and folders within one folder in order to preserve the links.

TIP If you click a thumbnail or caption in a Web browser, an enlarged view of that image will appear. You may also get navigation arrows to enable the viewer to navigate to the previous picture, next picture, or home page **1**.

TIP If a Web Photo Gallery style uses navigation arrows, the arrow images will save as individual files in the "Images" folder in your chosen destination folder, under the names home.gif, previous.gif, and next.gif. You can open any of these images in ImageReady and edit them, or replace them with your own images. If you edit the image, choose File > Save Optimized, and save with the same name, to the same location. Answer yes to any alert dialog boxes that appear.

TIP For more information about this feature, see "Customizing and creating web photo gallery styles" in Adobe Photoshop online Help.

1 *This is the finished **Web Photo Gallery** homepage. Clicking a thumbnail image or name here on the homepage links you to an enlarged image view page, complete with navigation arrows.*

PREFERENCES 21

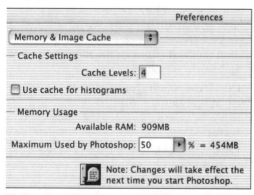

1 *To access the Preferences dialog box quickly, press* ***Ctrl-K/Cmd-K***. *To get to a different pane, use the shortcut illustrated on the pop-up menu (in the Mac OS, press Cmd + the number; in Windows, press Ctrl + the number), or click* ***Next*** *or* ***Prev*** *on the right side of the dialog box.*

2 *The* ***Memory & Image Cache*** *Preferences in the Mac OS*

PREFERENCES ARE settings that apply to the application as a whole, such as which ruler units are used, or if channels display in color. Most preference changes take effect immediately; a few take effect upon re-launching (we've noted those exceptions). All are saved when you exit/quit Photoshop.

To access the General Preferences dialog box the fast-and-easy way, press Ctrl-K/Cmd-K. From there, you can cycle through the various panes using the shortcuts listed on the pop-up menu **1**. You can also use the Edit (Photoshop, in OS X) > Preferences submenu to access the preferences dialog boxes.

In addition to the Preferences, the Preset Manager is also covered in this chapter.

To reset all the preferences to their default values:
Hold down Ctrl-Alt-Shift (Win)/Cmd-Option-Shift (Mac OS) at Startup. Click Yes to delete the Photoshop settings file. Do the same thing at startup for ImageReady.

Memory & Image Cache Preferences
The image cache is designed to help speed up screen redraw when you're editing or color adjusting high-resolution images. Low-resolution versions of the image are saved in individual cache buffers and are used to update the on-screen image. The higher the **Cache Levels** value (1–8), the more buffers are used, and the speedier the redraw **2**.

Check **Use cache for histograms** for faster, but slightly less accurate, histogram display in the Levels and Histogram dialog boxes.

Specify the maximum percentage of RAM to be used by Photoshop in the **Maximum Used by Photoshop** field.

395

General Preferences

Choose the Adobe **Color Picker** to access the application's own Color Picker. If you're trying to mix a color in Photoshop to match a color in a browser, use the Windows or Apple Color Picker.

Choose an **Interpolation** option for reinterpretation of an image as a result of resampling or transforming. Bicubic is slowest, but highest quality. Nearest Neighbor (Faster) is fastest, but poorest quality.

Choose a keyboard shortcut for Redo from the **Redo Key** pop-up menu.

Enter the maximum number of **History States** that can be listed on the History palette at a time (1–100).

From the **Print Keys** pop-up menu, choose which keyboard shortcuts you want to use to invoke the Print and Print with Preview commands.

Check **Export Clipboard** to have the current Clipboard contents stay on the Clipboard when you exit/quit Photoshop.

Check **Show Tool Tips** to see an on-screen display of the name of the tool or icon currently under the pointer.

Uncheck **Keyboard Zoom Resizes Windows** to prevent the illustration window from resizing when the view size is changed via the Ctrl/Cmd- + (plus) or Ctrl/Cmd- - (minus) shortcut.

Check **Auto-update open documents** to have documents save automatically when jumping between Photoshop and ImageReady. Documents update after jumping, whether this option is on or off.

Check **Show Asian Text Options** to show and set options for Chinese, Japanese, and Korean type on the Character and Paragraph palettes.

Mac OS only: Check **Use System Shortcut Keys** to have the operating system's shortcuts override any conflicting Photoshop shortcuts.

Check **Beep When Done** to have a beep sound when any command that takes time to process (has a progress bar) is finished processing.

With **Dynamic Color Sliders** checked, colors above the sliders on the Color palette will update as the sliders are moved. Turn this option off to speed performance.

With **Save Palette Locations** checked, palettes that are open when you exit/quit Photoshop will appear in their same location when you re-launch.

With **Show Font Names in English** checked, font names on the Font pop-up menu will display in English, regardless of the native language.

With **Use Shift Key for Tool Switch** checked, hidden tools can be accessed using Shift and the letter assigned to them (e.g., press Shift-R to cycle through the Blur, Sharpen, and Smudge tools).

Check **Use Smart Quotes** to have typographically-correct curly quotation marks be inserted automatically when text is created.

Click **Reset All Warning Dialogs** to re-enable all warning prompt messages that have been disabled by choosing the Don't Show Again option in individual message dialog boxes.

General Preferences *in the Mac OS*

General Preferences *in Windows*

File Handling Preferences

Choose **Image Previews**: Never Save to save files without previews, or choose Always Save to save files with the specified previews, or choose Ask When Saving to assign previews for each individual file when it's saved for the first time.

Mac OS: Click Icon to display a thumbnail of the image in its file icon on the desktop. Click Full Size to include a 72-ppi PICT preview for applications that require this option in order to import a non-EPS file. Click Macintosh Thumbnail and/or Windows Thumbnail to have a thumbnail of an image display when its name is highlighted in the Open dialog box.

Mac OS: Choose **Append File Extension**: Always or Ask When Saving to have a three-letter abbreviation of the file format (e.g., .tif for TIFF) be included when a Macintosh file is saved. This is helpful when converting files for Windows, and essential when saving files for the Web.

Win and Mac: Choose/check **Use Lower Case** to have the extension appear in lowercase characters.

Check **File Compatibility**: Ask Before Saving Layered TIFF Files to have the TIFF Options dialog box open when an image that contains multiple layers is saved as a TIFF. **7.0!**

Check **Always Maximize Compability for Photoshop (PSD) Files** to maximize file compatibility with previous versions of Photoshop and other programs (e.g., a rasterized version of each layer is saved for programs that don't support vector data). This option produces larger file sizes and causes files to save more slowly.

Check **Enable Workgroup Functionality** if **7.0!** you're sharing files with others via a WebDAV (Web Distributed Authoring and Versioning) server. Such servers use a check-out, check-in file system to ensure that only one person works on a file at a time. Use the Check Out from Server and Update from Server pop-up menus to specify how files are checked out and updated from the server.

In the **Recent file list contains [   ] files** field, enter the maximum number of files that can be listed on the File > Open Recent submenu (0–30).

Display & Cursors Preferences

Check **Color Channels in Color** to have individual RGB or CMYK channels display in color on the Channels palette in the image window. Otherwise, channels will display as grayscale.

Check **Use Diffusion Dither**, when using a monitor set to 8-bit color, to have Photoshop use a dithering method to improve color simulation.

Check **Use Pixel Doubling** to speed up preview redraws by having a low-resolution preview display first. This doesn't affect actual pixels—it affects only redraw.

For the **Painting Cursors** (Eraser, Pencil, Brush, Clone Stamp, Pattern Stamp, Smudge, Blur, Sharpen, Dodge, Burn, Sponge, Healing Brush, Patch, and Paint Bucket tools) click Standard to have the cursor be an icon of the tool being used,

or click Precise to have it be a crosshair icon, or click Brush Size to have it be a round icon the exact size of the brush tip (up to 999 pixels).

For the non-painting tools (Marquee, Lasso, Polygon Lasso, Magnetic Lasso, Magic Wand, Crop, Eyedropper, Pen, Magnetic Pen, Measure, and Color Sampler), click **Other Cursors**: Standard or Precise.

TIP Depending on the current Preferences setting, depressing the Caps Lock key will turn Standard cursors to Precise, Precise to Brush Size, or Brush Size to Precise.

Standard cursor   ***Precise*** cursor   ***Brush Size*** cursor

Display & Cursors Preferences

Preferences

Display & Cursors ⇕

Display
☑ Color Channels in Color
☐ Use Diffusion Dither
☐ Use Pixel Doubling

OK
Cancel
Prev
Next

Painting Cursors
○ Standard
○ Precise
⦿ Brush Size

Other Cursors
⦿ Standard
○ Precise

Transparency & Gamut Preferences

A checkerboard grid is used to represent transparent areas on a layer (areas that don't contain pixels). You can choose a different **Grid Size**.

Change the **Grid Colors** for the transparency checkerboard by choosing Light, Medium, Dark, Red, Orange, Green, Blue, or Purple. Or choose Custom, then choose a color from the Color Picker.

Check **Use video alpha (requires hardware support)** if you use a 32-bit video card that

allows chroma keying for video editing. You will be able to see through certain parts of the video image.

To change the color used to mark out-of-gamut colors on an image when View > **Gamut Warning** is on, click the Color square, then choose a color from the Color Picker. You can lower the Opacity of the Gamut Warning color to make it easier to see the image color underneath.

Grid Size: Large; Grid Colors: Medium

Units & Rulers Preferences

Choose a unit of measure from the Units: **Rulers** pop-up menu for the horizontal and vertical rulers that display in the image window. (Choose View > Rulers to display the rulers.)

Choose the same or a different unit for **Type** from the Type pop-up menu.

Note: If you change the measurement units for the Info palette **1**, the ruler units will also change in this dialog box, and vice versa.

TIP You can also change ruler units by right-clicking/Ctrl-clicking either ruler in the image window and choosing a unit from the context menu. Or to open the Units & Rulers Preferences dialog box quickly, double-click either ruler.

Enter **Column Size** Width and Gutter values to help the Image Size and Canvas Size commands fit images for the appropriate column width in a layout program.

You can enter **New Document Preset Resolutions** in the Print Resolution and Screen Resolution fields. The default settings are 300 ppi for print and 72 ppi for on-screen display.

For **Point/Pica Size**, click PostScript (the default) to have Photoshop use the newfangled method for calculating the points-to-inch ratio, or click Traditional to use the pre-desktop publishing ratio.

Units symbols	
Pixels	**px**
Inches	**in** or **"**
Centimeters	**cm**
Millimeters	**mm**
Points	**pt**
Picas	**p**
Percent	**%**

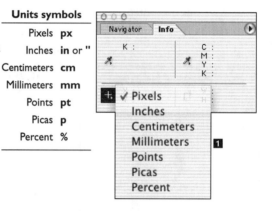

Guides, Grid & Slices Preferences

Note: Changes in this dialog box preview immediately in the image window.

Choose a preset color for the removable ruler **Guides** from the Color pop-up menu. Or click the color square to choose a color from the Color Picker. Choose Lines or Dashed Lines for the Guides Style.

Choose a preset color for the non-printing **Grid** from the Color pop-up menu. Or click the color square to choose a color from the Color Picker. Choose Lines, Dashed Lines, or Dots for the Grid Style.

To have grid lines appear at specific unit-of-measure intervals, choose a unit of measurement from the drop-down menu, then enter a new value in the **Gridline every** field. If you choose percent from the drop-down menu, grid lines will appear at those percentage intervals, starting from the left edge of the image.

For the grid lines between the thicker grid line increments chosen in the Gridline every field, enter a number in the **Subdivisions** field.

7.0! Choose a preset **Line Color** for the lines that are used to mark slices.

7.0! Check **Show Slice Numbers** to have a slice number display in the upper-left corner of every slice.

A ***guide*** *line pulled down from the horizontal ruler*

A ***grid*** *line*

A *grid **subdivision***

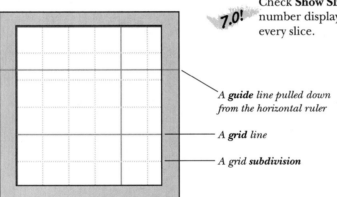

Preferences

Guides, Grid & Slices

Guides
- Color: ▓ Light Blue
- Style: Lines

Grid
- Color: Custom
- Style: Lines
- Gridline every: 1   inches
- Subdivisions: 4

Slices
- Line Color: ▓ Light Blue
- ☑ Show Slice Numbers

OK
Cancel
Prev
Next

Plug-ins & Scratch Disks Preferences

Note: For changes made in this dialog box to take effect, you must exit/quit and relaunch Photoshop.

Click **Additional Plug-Ins Folder**, then click Choose if you need to relocate or use another plug-ins folder. Photoshop needs to know where to find this folder in order to access third-party plug-ins. *Note:* Photoshop's internal Plug-Ins module shouldn't be moved out of the Photoshop folder unless you have a specific reason for doing so. Moving it could inhibit access to filters, the Import-Export and Effects commands, and some file formats under the save commands.

Some third-party plug-ins installed for earlier versions of Photoshop may need the pre-version 7 serial number in order to run properly. Enter this number in the **Legacy Photoshop Serial Number** field. *7.0!*

The **First** (and optional Second, Third, or Fourth) **Scratch Disk** is used when available RAM is insufficient for processing or storage. Choose an available hard drive from the First pop-up menu. Startup is the default.

As an optional step, choose an alternative **Second, Third,** or **Fourth** hard drive to be used as extra work space when necessary. If you have only one hard drive, of course you'll have only one scratch disk.

TIP *Mac OS:* Hold down Cmd-Option to have the Plug-Ins folder dialog box open when Photoshop is launched. If you continue to hold down these keys, the Scratch Disk Preferences dialog box will open.

Windows: Hold down Ctrl-Alt to have the Scratch Disks Preferences dialog box (not the Plug-Ins Preferences) open when Photoshop is launched.

TIP If your scratch disk is a removable cartridge, removing the cartridge while Photoshop is running may cause the program to crash.

Dialog box showing:
Preferences
Plug-Ins & Scratch Disks
Additional Plug-Ins Folder
\<None\>   Choose...
Legacy Photoshop Serial Number:
Scratch Disks
First: Startup
Second: Macintosh HD
Third: None
Fourth: None
Note: Scratch disks will remain in use until you quit Photoshop.
OK Cancel Prev Next

Plug-ins & Scratch Disks Preferences

No doubt you've already become acquainted with many of the pickers, such as the brush and gradient pickers. The Swatches palette also functions as a picker. Each picker item is called a **preset**, and each collection of presets is called a **library**. The Preset Manager is used to organize, append, replace, and reset which items are loaded onto each of the pickers; those same changes can also be made in the individual pickers. Changes made to a picker will be reflected in the Preset Manager, and vice versa.

To use the Preset Manager:

1. Choose Edit > Preset Manager.
or
With any palette or picker pop-up palette open (e.g., brush picker, gradient picker), choose Preset Manager from the palette menu (Peter Piper picked...).

7.0!

2. *Optional:* Click the arrowhead in the circle ⊙ at the top of the dialog box and choose a different view for the Preset Manager: Text Only, Small Thumbnail, Large Thumbnail, Small List, or Large List. For Brushes, you can also choose Stroke Thumbnail to see a sample of the brush stroke alongside the brush thumbnail.

7.0!

3. Choose a category of presets from the Preset Type pop-up menu **1**.

4. *Do any of the following:*

Click the arrowhead in the circle and choose a library name from the bottom of the menu. Click Append to add that library to the current library, or click OK to replace the current library with the new one.

Click Load, then locate a library to append to the current library.

Click or Shift-click the presets you want to delete, then click Delete. The default presets can be deleted, and they can be restored at any time.

5. Click Done. The edited picker will update.

TIP Preset libraries can be shared among Photoshop users.

Directions to the library

Each preset library type has its own file extension and default folder, which is located in the Adobe Photoshop 7 > **Presets** folder.

The **default preset** libraries are not listed on the picker menu or the Preset Manager menu. In Mac OS X, these libraries are stored separately for each user and are located in Users/your user name/Library/Preferences/Adobe Photoshop 7.0 Settings under their respective file names. For pre–OS X Macs, they are in System Folder > Preferences > Adobe Photoshop 7.0 Settings. In Windows, the libraries are located in Windows/Application Data/Adobe Photoshop/7.0/Adobe Photoshop 7.0 Settings.

7.0!

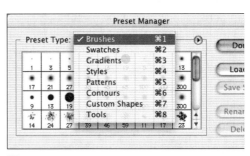

1 *Choose a category from the **Preset Type** pop-up menu in the **Preset Manager**.*

Preset Manager

A preset by any other name

To rename a preset, double-click the preset **thumbnail** in the Preset Manager, then change the name in the dialog box that opens. Or if the Preset Manager is in Text Only view or a List view, double-click the preset **name**, then change it. You can also select multiple presets, then click **Rename**. In this case, each name dialog box will open automatically in succession.

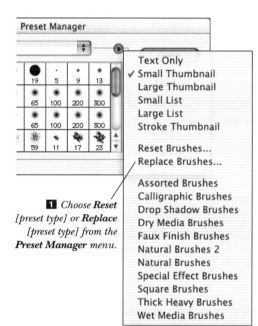

1 *Choose* ***Reset*** *[preset type] or* ***Replace*** *[preset type] from the* ***Preset Manager*** *menu.*

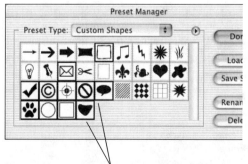

2 *Shift-click the presets you want to save in a* ***subset***.

To reset or replace a preset:

1. Choose Edit > Preset Manager, or choose Preset Manager from any picker or palette menu. **7.0!**

2. From the Preset Type pop-up menu, choose the preset type you want to reset or replace.

3. *Optional:* Any unsaved presets on the list will be deleted, so we recommend saving the current library before proceeding (see the next set of instructions).

4. From the Preset Manager menu **1**:

   Choose **Reset** [preset type] to restore the default library for the chosen type, then click Append to append the default presets to the current library, or click OK to replace the current library with the default preset (click Cancel if you change your mind).
   or
   Choose **Replace** [preset type], locate a library to replace the current library with, then click Load.

The Preset Manager can also be used for copying a subset of selected presets from a currently open library into a new library.

To save a subset of items in their own library:

1. Choose Edit > Preset Manager, or choose Preset Manager from any picker or palette menu. **7.0!**

2. From the Preset Type pop-up menu, choose the preset type you want to save as a subset.

3. Shift-click the presets you want to save in a subset **2**.

4. Click Save Set, leave the location as the default preset folder, then enter a name for the new library in the Save As field.

5. Click Save, then click Done.

TIP You can select multiple presets in the Preset Manager, but you can select only one preset in an actual picker.

Preset Manager

If you define a new brush, pattern, or custom shape via the Edit menu, add a new swatch to the Swatches palette, add a new style to the Styles palette, create a new gradient in the Gradient Editor dialog box, or create a new contour in any Contour picker, that new preset item will display on the appropriate tool's picker on the options bar. The new item will also display for the chosen Preset Type in the Preset Manager.

The new item will be saved in the Adobe Photoshop Preferences file temporarily, and it will display in the picker even after you exit/quit and relaunch Photoshop—as long as you don't open another library in the same category (e.g., another brush library), or reset the picker, or reset the picker category in the Preset Manager. If you do any of those things, the new item will be discarded. Ah—but here's how you can save it.

To save an item in a new preset library from a palette or picker:

1. Create a new item for the current options bar or dialog box picker.

2. From a palette menu or picker menu, choose Save [preset type].

3. Enter a name, leave the default extension and location as is, then click Save.

Note: In order for a newly-created library name to appear on the palette or picker menu and on the Preset Type pop-up menu in the Preset Manager **1**, you must exit/quit and relaunch Photoshop.

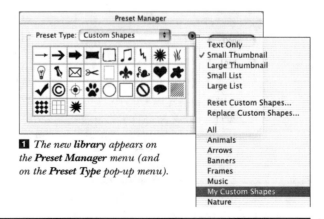

1 *The new* **library** *appears on the* **Preset Manager** *menu (and on the* **Preset Type** *pop-up menu).*

PRINT 22

Resolution of output devices

Hewlett Packard LaserJet	600 or 1200 dpi
Hewlett Packard InkJet	1200 x 600, 2400 x 1200 dpi
IRIS SmartJet	600 dpi (looks like 1600 dpi)
Canon Color Laser/Fiery	600 x 600 dpi
Epson Stylus Color/Photo ink-jet	2880 x 720 dpi
Linotronic imagesetter	1200–4000 dpi

100%		Doc: 502K/OK

Press and hold on the **status** *bar in the lower-left corner of the application window (Win)/image window (Mac) to display the* **page preview**—*a thumbnail of the image relative to the paper size.*

Width: 504 pixels
Height: 340 pixels
Channels: 3 (RGB Color)
Resolution: 72 pixels/inch

Alt-press/Option-press and hold on the status bar to display **file information.**

AN **IMAGE CAN** be printed from Photoshop to a laser printer, to a color printer (e.g., ink-jet, dye sublimation), or to an imagesetter. A Photoshop image can also be imported into and then printed from a drawing application, such as FreeHand or Illustrator; a layout application, such as QuarkXPress or InDesign; or a multimedia application, such as Director or After Effects. Your file can also be prepared for viewing online. (For online output, see the next chapter.)

This chapter contains instructions for setting options for printing from Photoshop, applying trapping, preparing an image for other applications, saving a file in the EPS, DCS, TIFF, BMP, or PICT format, creating a duotone, and creating a percentage tint of a Pantone color. The last part of the chapter is devoted to color reproduction basics. (To print a spot color channel, see page 209.)

Printing from Photoshop

Getting a good print from an image, especially a color image, is more art than science. It is not accomplished simply by twiddling Photoshop's dials and knobs alone, but requires a thorough understanding of the settings available on your printing device, as well as the color management software built into your computer's operating system. Here, we can provide only the basics for printing from Photoshop. You'll also need to refer to the program's manual, which contains a wealth of specialized technical information, as well as the documentation for your printer. If you're preparing images for output by a service bureau, be sure to consult the experts there before setting up your image for printing.

(Continued on the following page)

Print

7.0!

The organization of printing commands has changed significantly in Photoshop 7. All printing parameters determined by your printer, print drivers, or operating system are now taken care of in the Page Setup and Print dialog boxes.

■ To choose Photoshop-specific options, including color management options, use the Print with Preview command. This is where you'll be taken if you use our old friend, the shortcut **Ctrl-P/Cmd-P**.

■ The basic **Print** command is linked to Ctrl-Alt-P/Cmd-Option-P.

■ Even more direct is the **Print One Copy** command (Ctrl-Alt-Shift-P/Cmd-Option-Shift-P).

Note: Only the currently visible layers and channels will print.

The first step, whatever the kind of print job, is to tell Photoshop what type of printer and paper size you're using.

To choose a paper size and orientation:

1. Choose File > Page Setup (Ctrl-Shift-P/ Cmd-Shift-P).

2. From the Paper Size pop-up menu, choose the paper size you want the file to print on **1**.

3. Click one of the Orientation buttons to have Photoshop print the image parallel to the length or width of the paper.

4. *Windows:* From the Source pop-up menu, choose the tray that holds the paper you want to print on **2**. Click the Printer button to choose printer-specific options.

5. *Mac OS:* To reduce or enlarge the printed image, enter a Scale value. *Note:* It's probably safer to change the Scale in the Print dialog box, because there you can preview the results.

Choose the desired printer from the Format for pop-up menu, then use the Settings menu to switch to other panels for printer-specific options.

6. Click OK.

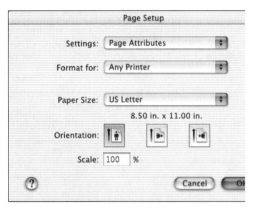

1 *The **Page Setup** dialog box in **Mac OS X***

2 *The **Page Setup** dialog box in **Windows***

Page Setup *(sidebar tab)*

Resolution overkill?

If your image resolution is greater than two and a half times the screen frequency (which is way higher than you need) you'll get a warning prompt when you send the image to print. If this occurs, copy the file using File > Save As with As a Copy checked, then lower the image resolution using Image > **Image Size**.

In Photoshop 7, the simple Print command takes you directly to the Print dialog box defined in your printer's driver, bypassing all Photoshop-specific options.

Note: Only currently visible layers and channels will print.

To print using the basic Print command:

1. Choose File > Print (Ctrl-Alt-P/ Cmd-Option-P). The default Print dialog box for your printer opens **1**–**2**.

2. Choose the number of copies to be printed.

3. Choose the printer-specific options that are appropriate for your document.

4. Click OK/Print.

1 *The* **Print** *dialog box for a* **color**, *non-PostScript, ink-jet printer in* **Mac OS X**, *showing the Print Settings panel*

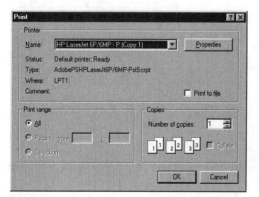

2 *The* **Print** *dialog box for a* **black-and-white** *PostScript printer in* **Windows**

Print

Note: Only the currently visible layers and channels will print.

Pressing Ctrl-P/Cmd-P (the Print with Preview command) takes you to the redesigned Print dialog box. Formerly known as the Print Options dialog box, it combines into one location numerous options which used to be scattered among several dialog boxes.

To print using the Print with Preview command:

1. Choose File > Print with Preview (Ctrl-P/ Cmd-P) **1**.

2. Check Center Image to position your image in the center of the page, or uncheck Center Image and enter new top and left values to move the image on the page.

3. Change the Scaled Print Size: Scale percentage or enter specific Height and Width values to reduce or enlarge the image for printing purposes only. *Note:* The Scale, Height and Width options are linked; changing any one option will cause the other two to change.

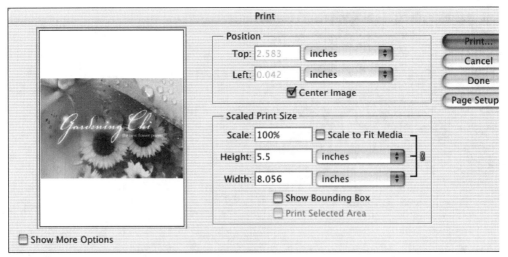

1 *The **Print** dialog box, showing a print **preview** of the file*

Print with Preview (side margin)

Quick print

If you're in a hurry, and if you've already configured your print options to your liking, you can skip all print-related dialog boxes by using File > **Print One Copy** (Ctrl-Alt-Shift-P/Cmd-Option-Shift-P).

4. Check Scale to Fit Media to have the image be adjusted to fit on the paper size chosen in File > Page Setup.

5. Check Show Bounding Box to have a box be placed around your image to show the image boundary. Pull a handle or side of the box to scale your image for printing purposes only. You can also drag the box to change the image's position on the printed page, if Center Image isn't checked.

6. If a rectangular selection is currently active in the image, check Print Selected Area to print only that selected portion.

7. Check Show More Options to display Color Management and Output settings (discussed on the following pages).

8. When you have finished choosing options, do one of the following:

Click the Print button to access your printer's Print dialog box (see page 409) and initiate the printing process proper. *or*

Click Done to close the dialog box, saving the Print settings for this docment. *or*

Click the Page Setup button, to bring up the Page Setup dialog box, if you haven't done so already (see page 408).

(If you click Cancel to close the dialog box, you'll lose all changes you've made to these settings.)

9. Pressing Alt/Option changes the functions of these buttons:

Print becomes Print One Copy. The document will print immediately, without presenting the printer's Print dialog box first.

Cancel becomes Reset. All settings in the dialog box will be returned to their default values.

Done becomes Remember. The settings will be saved for the open document, but the dialog box won't close.

Print with Preview

To print using color management:

1. Choose File > Print with Preview (Ctrl-P/ Cmd-P).

2. Check Show More Options and choose Color Management from the pop-up menu (**1**, next page):

3. Choose your **Source Space**. We recommend that you select the Document option, which uses the color profile of your image (for the specifics of color management, see Chapter 2). It will probably say U.S. Web Coated or Untagged CMYK, unless you've selected a different CMYK color space in the Color Settings dialog box. The Proof Setup option uses the color profile of your proof that you chose in View > Proof Setup > Custom.

4. From the Print Space: **Profile** pop-up menu:

   Choose Same As Source to print using the Source Space profile. There will be no color conversion during the printing process.
   or
   If you're using a PostScript Level 2 or higher printer (Level 3 if your image is in CMYK mode), consider choosing PostScript Color Management if you can't find your printer's profile in the list of Profiles. This option will send all of the file's color information along with the Source Space profile to the printer; the printer (rather than Photoshop) will manage the color conversion process.

   TIP The only way to determine which is the best Print Space setting is to run multiple test prints. Try the various color space settings and decide which space gives you the best print results.

5. Choose Relative Colormetric for the rendering **Intent**, if that pop-up menu is available. As noted in Chapter 2, Intent determines how the color conversion will render when sent to any Print profile other than Same as Source.

6. Check **Use Black Point Compensation** if printing the image in RGB mode, but consult your print shop before checking it for a CMYK image that will be printed on a device with a different profile.

TIP To print an individual layer or channel, make that the sole visible layer or channel before choosing File > Print.

TIP Our service bureau advises us to not choose Lab color for the image mode or for the profile from the Print Space Profile menu. The reasons: Very few people calibrate their monitors or edit images in Lab color mode. Also, our service bureau claims that printouts sent to both dye sublimation and IRIS printers show banding and color shifts when sent as Lab color mode. When sent as CMYK color mode, the printouts produced better results. Ask your service bureau or print shop for their opinion.

(Continued on the following page)

Print with Preview: Color Management

1 *When **Show More Options** is checked in the Print dialog box, the **Color Management** pane (and the Output pane) becomes available.*

7. Check Show More Options, choose **Output** from the pop-up menu, then **1**:

To print a colored background around the image, click **Background**, then choose a color.

To print a black border around an image, click **Border**, choose a measurement unit, then enter a Width (0–10 pts).

Bleed prints crop marks inside the image at a specified distance (Width) from the edge of the image (0–9.01 pts).

Click the **Screen** button to change the halftone screen settings, including the dot shape. This brings up the Halftone Screens dialog box (see page 417).

Clicking **Transfer** opens the Transfer Functions dialog box, which allows you to compensate for a mis-calibrated imagesetter by adjusting dot gain values.

Interpolation reduces jaggies when outputting to some PostScript Level 2 (or higher) printers.

Calibration Bars creates a grayscale and/or color calibration strip outside the image area.

Registration Marks creates marks that a print shop uses to align color separations.

Corner Crop Marks and **Center Crop Marks** create short little lines that a print shop uses to trim the final printed page.

Caption prints the text that was entered into the File > File Info box, outside the image area.

Labels prints the image's title and the names of its channels.

1 *When **Show More Options** is checked in the **Print** dialog box, the **Output** options become available.*

For film output, ask your print shop whether you should check **Negative** and/or **Emulsion Down**.

Check **Include Vector Data** to have Photoshop print the edges of vector objects (type and shapes) at the printer's full resolution.

Choose an **Encoding** method from the pop-up menu, if you're using a PostScript printer. Binary is the default option. JPEG encoding (available only on PostScript Level 2 or higher printers) compresses image files and speeds up the transfer of data to the printer, but results in lower image quality. If you run into problems with your print spooler or printer driver, use ASCII encoding. This option doubles the size of print files, slowing down the printing process correspondingly. In general, you should use Binary encoding in the Mac OS, and ASCII in Windows.

8. Click Print, or for the other buttons, see step 8 on page 411.

step 8 on page 411.

The Print with Preview output options

Calibration bar →

Caption → image w/ print options

Photoshop's Trap command slightly overlaps solid color areas in an image to help prevent gaps that may occur due to plate misregistration or paper shift. Trapping is necessary only when two distinct, adjacent color areas share less than two of the four process colors. You don't need to trap a continuous-tone or photographic image.

Note: Photoshop's Trap command flattens all layers and it uses only the spread technique, unlike other applications which may also use the choke method. Consult with your press shop before using this command, and apply it to a copy of your image; store your original image without traps.

To apply trapping:

1. Open the image to which you want to apply trapping **1**, and make sure it's in CMYK Color mode.

2. Choose Image > Trap.

3. If a prompt appears, click OK.

4. Enter the Width that your press shop recommends **2**.

5. Click OK.

Desktop ink-jet printers

When printing to a desktop ink-jet printer, leave your image in RGB mode. Even though such printers do print using CMYK inks (some use a six-color process), their drivers expect to receive RGB data and then perform the conversion to CMYK internally. Usually, the printer driver installation program installs a set of profiles for the printer, for printing on different kinds of paper. When the time comes to print, go to File > Print with Preview (Ctrl-P/Cmd-P), check Show More Options, and choose Color Management from the pop-up menu. In the Print Space pane of the dialog box, choose the profile for your printer and type of paper from the Profile pop-up menu.

1 *Open the image to which you want to apply trapping.*

2 *Choose a **Trap Width**.*

Color separation basics

Convert the image to CMYK Color mode, then choose File > Print with Preview. Check Show More Options, then choose Color Management from the pop-up menu. Under Source Space, choose Document. It should say U.S. Web Coated (SWOP) v2, unless you've chosen a different option in your Color Settings dialog box. Under Print Space, choose Separations for the Profile, then click Print.

TIP In the Output panel of the Print with Preview dialog box, check the Calibration Bars, Registration Marks, Corner Crop Marks, Center Crop Marks, or Labels options. Some of these options may not be available on a non-PostScript printer.

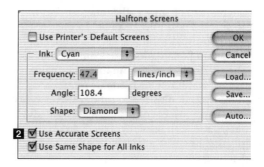

1 *The EPS Options dialog box in Windows*

Note: Before printing your file, save your image at the resolution that your prepress house says is appropriate for the color printer or imagesetter you're going to use.

To prepare a file for an IRIS or dye sublimation printer, or an imagesetter:

1. To print on a PostScript Level 2 (or higher) printer, choose File > Print with Preview (Ctrl-P/Cmd-P), click Screen, uncheck Use Printer's Default Screens, check Use Accurate Screens, click OK, and then click Done or Print. Be sure to choose Image > Mode > CMYK Color before saving as EPS.

2. Choose File > Save As and check the As a Copy option (Ctrl-Shift-S/ Cmd-Option-S).

3. Choose a location in which to save the file.

4. Choose Format: Photoshop EPS, then click Save.

5. Choose a Preview option **1**, and choose Encoding: Binary.

6. If you've changed the screen settings in the Halftone Screens dialog box (as per your service bureau's instructions), then check Include Halftone Screen.

7. Click OK.

Screens

For a PostScript Level 2 (or higher) printer, click **Screens** in the Print Preview dialog box, uncheck Use Printer's Default Screens, then check **Use Accurate Screens 2**, but don't change the Ink angles. The Halftone Screens options will take effect if you print from Photoshop, or save the file in the EPS or DCS 2 format and then print to a PostScript printer.

Preparing files for other applications

Photoshop to QuarkXPress

To color-separate a Photoshop image in QuarkXPress, you can convert it to CMYK Color mode before importing it into QuarkXPress. Different imagesetters require different formats, so ask your prepress house whether to save your image in the TIFF (see pages 424–425) or EPS file format (see pages 421–422) or in either of the two DCS formats (see page 423). QuarkXPress can also convert an RGB TIFF into a CMYK TIFF. Ask your prepress house which program to use for the conversion.

Photoshop to InDesign

InDesign can separate Photoshop PDFs (RGB or CMYK), and it can import PSD files directly. It can also read any ICC profile embedded in a Photoshop file.

Photoshop to After Effects

You can import a layered Photoshop image into Adobe After Effects 5.x and position it in the Time Layout window to create animated effects over time for Video or QuickTime output. A layered Photoshop file can be imported as an After Effects composition file; individual layers and groups will remain intact.

Alternatively, a layered Photoshop image can be imported and merged into After Effects as a pre-composited image. To keep the Photoshop layers, adjustment layers, layer effects, blending modes, and alpha channels intact when you import the image, in After Effects use File > Import > File. In the Import File dialog box, select a layered Photoshop file, then choose Composition from the Import As pop-up menu. Editable type layers will render correctly in After Effects (you don't need to render them first). Layer masks and vector masks will also import into, and render correctly in, After Effects. Some, but not all layer effects can be imported.

Keeping a background transparent

To import a Photoshop image into a drawing or page layout application and maintain its transparent background, save the image with a **vector mask** (see page 298).

Check your preferences

Before saving a file for use in another application, find out if the target application requires the **Always Maximize Backwards Compatibility for Photoshop (PSD) Files** option 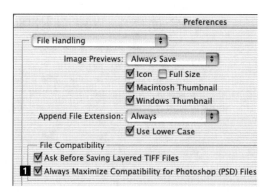 to be checked in Photoshop's File Handling Preferences in order to open a Photoshop format file. This option saves a composited image for preview along with the layered version for applications that don't support layers. It also saves a rasterized copy of any vector art for those applications that don't support vector data. Note that checking this option will result in lengthier saving times and larger file sizes. Some applications also require the **Image Previews** options to be checked. For a Web file, however, uncheck Image Previews to save a few extra bytes of storage size and speed up the transfer time.

A Photoshop clipping group will import into After Effects as a composition. As such, it can be placed and manipulated as a unit. If you double-click a clipping group composition in the After Effects Project window, the separate layers of the clipping group will display in the Time Layout window.

Photoshop to Illustrator

Compatibility between Photoshop 7 and Illustrator 10 has been greatly maximized. If you drag-and-drop a Photoshop selection or layer into Illustrator, the image will appear on the Layers palette in Illustrator as a group containing a generic clipping path and the image. Any opacity, blending modes, masking, or clipping of the image will be ignored.

You can use the Path Selection tool to drag-and-drop a path or vector mask from Photoshop into Illustrator. Or you can use Photoshop's File > Export > Paths to Illustrator command to export a saved path, then open the saved path file in Illustrator. In either case, the path will become an editable vector object in Illustrator, with no fill or stroke.

If you copy and paste a layer from Photoshop into Illustrator, any layer mask or vector mask will be ignored.

If you place a Photoshop image with the Link option checked in Illustator's Place dialog box, it will appear on the Layers palette as one image sublayer. The image will be properly masked but certain blending modes may produce strange effects.

If you embed a Photoshop image as you place it (uncheck the Link option), or open the image in Illustrator, you can choose whether layers will be converted into objects or flattened into one layer. If you opt to convert Photoshop layers into objects, each object will appear on its own nested layer within an image sublayer. The Background will also be a separate, opaque layer. It can be deleted or modified in Illustrator. All transparency values and blending modes

(Continued on the following page)

Photoshop to Illustrator

will be preserved and listed as editable appearances in Illustrator. Layer masks will become opacity masks, vector masks will become clipping paths, and shape layers will become vector objects. Any Paths palette clipping path that was saved with the Photoshop file will remain in effect. Each separate layer will have a bounding box the size of the original Photoshop image.

If you opt to flatten Photoshop layers into one image layer, all transparency, blending modes, and layer mask effects will be preserved visually, but they won't be editable in Illustrator. Any Paths palette clipping path in the Photoshop file will remain in effect.

The resolution of any Photoshop TIFF, EPS, or PSD image that's opened or placed in Illustrator will remain intact, but the Photoshop image will take on the color mode of the Illustrator file. Illustrator raster filters, raster effects, and certain vector effects can be applied to the imported image.

Photoshop to CorelDRAW 10

Save the file as EPS, TIFF, JPEG, BMP, or PSD (Photoshop format), and in RGB Color or CMYK Color mode. In CorelDRAW, use File > Import to place the file into a CorelDRAW file. Alternatively, you could drag-and-drop a layer or copy-and-paste a layer or a selection from Photoshop into a CorelDRAW window. Note, however, that all vector data, such as shapes or type, is turned into bitmaps. CorelDRAW 10 can read a layered Photoshop image, with each layer becoming a separate object. You can use the Export Paths to Illustrator command to export a Photoshop path to a file, and then open that file in CorelDRAW.

Once it's imported into CorelDRAW, the bitmap image can be moved around; you can perform some bitmap edits on it; you can apply a filter to it; you can convert it to a different color mode or change its color depth; and you can resample it by changing its image size and/or resolution.

Photoshop to a film recorder

Color transparencies, also called chromes, are widely used as a source for high-quality images in the publishing industry. A Photoshop file can be output to a film recorder to produce a chrome. Though the output settings for each film recorder may vary, to output to any film recorder, the pixel count for the height and width of the image file must conform to the pixel count the film recorder requires for each line it images.

If the image originates as a scan, the pixel count should be taken into consideration when setting the scan's resolution, dimensions, and file storage size.

For example, let's say you need to produce a 4 × 5-inch chrome on a Solitaire film recorder. Your service bureau advises you that to output on the Solitaire, you have the choice of a 4K image at 4096 pixels x 3276 pixels, for a resolution of 819 dpi; an 8K image at 8192 pixels x 6553 pixels, for a resolution of 1638 dpi; or a 16K image at 16,384 pixels x 13,107 pixels, for a resolution of 3276 dpi. (Other film recorders may require different resolutions.) Choose File > New, enter the desired dimensions and resolution, and choose RGB Color Mode. Click OK to produce the image entirely within Photoshop, or note the resolution and dimensions and ask your prepress shop to match those values when they scan your image.

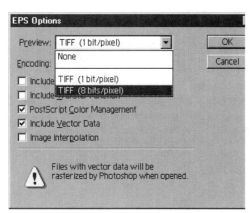

1 *Choose a **TIFF** preview option from the **Preview** pop-up menu in the **EPS Options** dialog box.*

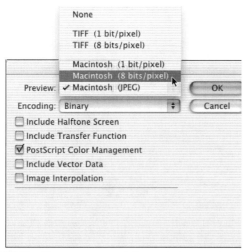

2 *The **EPS** format is available for an image in any image mode except Multichannel. Layers are flattened and alpha channels and spot channels are discarded when you save a file in this format.*

The EPS format is a good choice for importing a Photoshop image into an illustration program or into a page layout program (e.g., QuarkXPress, PageMaker, or InDesign). Printing an EPS file requires a PostScript or PostScript-emulation printer.

To save an image as an EPS:

1. If the image is going to be color-separated by another application, choose Image > Mode > CMYK Color.

2. Choose File > Save As (Ctrl-Shift-S/ Cmd-Shift-S).

3. Enter a name and choose a location in which to save the file.

4. Choose Format: Photoshop EPS.

5. *Optional:* Check Embed Color Profile to have Photoshop embed a color profile that tags the image with your working color space. Or you can check Use Proof Setup to have a "soft proof" be included with your file (an onscreen preview of how your image will look when it's printed on a certain type of printer). For more on color management, see Chapter 2.

Click Save. Note that any layers will be flattened. The EPS Options dialog box opens.

6. From the Preview pop-up menu, choose a 1-bit/pixel option to save the file with a black and white preview, or choose an 8-bits/pixel option to save the file with a grayscale or color preview (Win) **1**/ (Mac) **2**.

Mac OS: Choose either TIFF preview option if you're planning to open the file in a Windows application.

7. For most purposes, you should choose Encoding: Binary, as Binary encoded files are smaller and process more quickly than ASCII files. However, for some applications, PostScript clone printers, or printing utilities that can't handle Binary files, you'll have to choose

(Continued on the following page)

Save as EPS

ASCII. JPEG is the fastest encoding method, but it causes some data loss. A JPEG file can print only on a PostScript Level 2 or higher printer.

8. If you've changed the frequency, angle, or dot shape settings in the Halftone Screens dialog box, then check Include Halftone Screen.

9. The PostScript Color Management Option will convert the file's color data to the printer's color space. Don't choose this option if you're going to import the file into another color managed application—unpredictable color shifts may occur!

10. If you have vector elements on your page (shapes or type), check Include Vector Data. Note that saved vector data in EPS files is available to other applications, but when you reopen the file in Photoshop, the vector data will be rasterized.

11. Check Image Interpolation if the image is low resolution and you want it to be anti-aliased.

12. Click OK.

Multichannel

You can save a **Multichannel mode** image in the **Photoshop DCS 2.0** format as a single file or multiple files. The DCS 2.0 format preserves channels. A Multichannel image can't be saved as a Photoshop EPS for composite (single-page) printing. Converting an image to Multichannel mode flattens all layers and converts the channels to spot color channels.

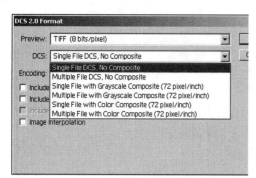

1 *Choose a **DCS** option in the **DCS 2.0 Format** dialog box (Windows).*

2 *Choose a **DCS** option in the **DCS 2.0 Format** dialog box (Mac OS).*

The DCS formats are relatives of the EPS format. The DCS 1.0 (Desktop Color Separation) format pre-separates the image in Photoshop, and it produces five related files, one for each CMYK channel and one for the combined, composite CMYK channel. The newer DCS 2.0 format preserves any spot color channels along with the color channels, and also offers the option to save the combined channels into one file or as multiple files. A DCS file can be printed only on a PostScript printer.

To save an image as a DCS 2.0:

1. Choose Image > Mode > CMYK Color, choose File > Save As (Ctrl-Shift-S/ Cmd-Shift-S), enter a name, choose a location in which to save the file, then choose Format: Photoshop DCS 2.0.

Optional: Check Embed Color Profile or Use Proof Setup. For details see step 5 on page 421.

2. Click Save. The DCS 2.0 Format dialog box opens.

3. From the Preview pop-up menu, choose a 1 bit/pixel option to save the file with a black and white preview or choose an 8 bits/pixel option to save the file with a grayscale or color preview.

4. Choose a DCS option: Single File (all the separations together in one file) or Multiple File (one file for each separation), and with No Composite, a Grayscale Composite, or a Color Composite preview **1** (Win)/**2** (Mac OS).

5. Choose an Encoding option: Binary, ASCII, or JPEG (with compression).

6. Leave both Include Halftone Screen and Include Transfer Function unchecked. Let your prepress shop choose settings for these options.

7. Check Include Vector Data if you have any vector graphics (shapes or type).

8. Check Image Interpolation if the image is low-resolution and you want it to be anti-aliased.

9. Click OK.

Save as DSC 2.0

A TIFF file can be imported by most applications, including QuarkXPress, PageMaker, and InDesign. Color profiles are recognized by, and color management options are available for, this format. QuarkXPress, PageMaker and InDesign can color-separate a CMYK TIFF.

Check the Layers option to preserve the layers in your file. You can also choose to save any spot color channels, alpha channels, or annotations in your file.

Beware! Currently, few image or layout programs can work with a layered TIFF. Those that don't will flatten a TIFF on import!

To save an image as a TIFF:

1. Choose Image > Mode > CMYK Color, choose File > Save As (Ctrl-Shift-S/Cmd-Shift-S), enter a name, and choose a location for the file **1**.

2. Choose Format: TIFF.

3. *Optional:* Not all programs can import a TIFF with an alpha channel. If your target application doesn't do so, uncheck Alpha Channels to discard any alpha channels.

4. *Optional:* Check Embed Color Profile to have Photoshop include the current embedded color profile in the TIFF file. For more on color management, see Chapter 2.

5. Click Save. The TIFF Options dialog box opens.

6. Choose an Image Compression method **2**. All compression methods reduce a file's storage size. However, some programs can't open a TIFF that's saved with JPEG or ZIP compression. In this case, the non-lossy LZW compression method is recommended. For a layered TIFF, choose a Layer Compression method.

7.0!

Note: If you're ultimately going to color-separate your file, service bureaus recommend using no compression at all.

7. Choose IBM PC or Macintosh for the platform the file will be exported to.

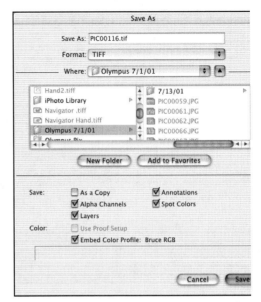

1 *The Save As dialog box in the Mac OS*

2 *The TIFF Options dialog box in the Mac OS*

Save as TIFF

1 *In the* **BMP Options** *dialog box, choose a* **File Format** *and a color* **Depth**.

2 *In the* **PICT File Options** *dialog box (Mac OS only), choose a* **Resolution** *(color depth, actually) and a* **Compression** *level.*

8. Check Save Image Pyramid to create a file that contains multiple resolutions of your image. Photoshop doesn't currently offer options for opening image pyramids; Adobe InDesign does.

Check Save Transparency if your file contains transparency.

9. Click OK.

Note: Photoshop can't save transparent areas (Transparency) without also saving Layers, so be sure to check both options.

A BMP or PICT file can be opened or placed as a bitmap image in Adobe Illustrator. Both of these file types can also be imported into most multimedia applications. Only the Macintosh version of Photoshop can save a PICT file, and the image can't be in CMYK Color mode.

To save an RGB image as a BMP or PICT:

1. Choose File > Save As.

2. Enter a name and choose a location in which to save the file. Check Alpha Channels to save any alpha channels in the file.

3. *Windows:* Choose Format: BMP, then click Save.

Mac OS: Choose Format: PICT File or BMP, then click Save.

4. For a BMP file, click a File Format option and a Depth option **1**. To choose a different encoding method (useful primarily to game developers), click the Advanced Modes button.

or

For a PICT file, click a Resolution option **2**. (For an image in Grayscale mode, check 2, 4, or 8 bits/pixel.) Then choose a Compression setting. The JPEG compression options are available only for an image that has a 32-bit resolution. The lower the quality setting, the greater the compression.

5. Click OK.

Producing duotones

Only about 50 shades of an ink color can be printed from one plate, so print shops are sometimes asked to print a grayscale image using two or more plates instead of one, adding midtones or highlights to extend an image's tonal range. The additional plates can be gray or a color tint. You can convert an image to Duotone mode in Photoshop to create a duotone (two plates), tritone (three plates), or quadtone (four plates).

Note: Duotone printing is tricky, so be sure to ask your print shop for advice. A duotone effect can't be proofed on a PostScript color printer, though; only a press proof is reliable. If you're a novice at duotones, try using one of the duotone (or tritone or quadtone) curves presets provided by Photoshop. You can load them in to use as is or adapt them for your own needs (click Load in the Duotone Options box, then open Adobe Photoshop 7 > Presets > Duotones).

To produce a duotone:

1. Choose Image > Mode > Grayscale. An image with good contrast will work best.

2. Choose Image > Mode > Duotone. The Duotone Options dialog box opens.

3. Check Preview to see your color and curves changes immediately.

4. Choose Type: Duotone **1**.

5. Click the Ink 2 color square. (Ink 1 will be the darkest ink; the highest ink number should be the lightest ink.) The Custom Colors dialog box opens.

6. To choose a matching system color, like a Pantone color, choose from the Book pop-up menu, then type a color number or click a swatch. Subtle colors tend to look better in a duotone than bright colors.
   or
   To choose a process color, click Picker, then enter C, M, Y, and K percentages.

7. Click OK.

Threes and fours

Printing a **tritone** (three inks) or a **quadtone** (four inks) requires specifying the order in which the inks will print on press. Ask your print shop for advice!

Back to square one

The Duotone dialog box opens with the last-used settings. If you change the duotone Type and then want to restore the last-used settings, hold down Alt/Option and click **Reset**.

Click a **curve** to modify it. Click a **color square** to choose a color. Don't change the spot color name.

1 *In the **Duotone Options** dialog box, choose Type: **Duotone**, then click the **Ink 2** color square.*

Duotone

Nice curves

Reshaping the duotone curve for an ink color affects how that color is distributed among an image's highlights, midtones, and shadows. With the curve shape shown in the screenshot on the previous page, Ink 2 will tint the image's midtones. To produce a pleasing duotone, try to distribute Ink 1 and Ink 2 in different tonal ranges.

Here's an example. Use black as Ink 1 in the shadow areas, somewhat in the midtones, and a little bit in the highlights. Then use an Ink 2 color in the remaining tonal ranges—more in the midtones and light areas and less in the darks.

The image's **highlights**   *The image's* **midtones**   *The image's* **shadows**

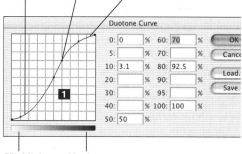

Highlights   *Shadows*

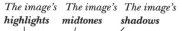

2 *This is the **Duotone Curve** dialog box for a monotone print. The 100% value has been lowered to the desired PANTONE tint percentage.*

8. For a process color, enter a name next to the color square. For a custom color, leave the name as is.

9. Click the Ink 2 curve.

10. Click to create data points or drag existing points in the graph in the Duotone Curve dialog box **1**. To produce a pleasing duotone, the Ink 1 curve should be different from the Ink 2 curve.

11. Click OK.

12. Click the Ink 1 curve, then repeat steps 10 and 11.

13. *Optional:* Click Save to save the current settings to use with other images.

14. Click OK to close the dialog box.

15. Save the file in the EPS format.

TIP To reduce black ink in the highlights, for the black ink (Ink 1) curve, enter 10 in the 0% field. To reduce color in the shadows, for the color ink (Ink 2) curve, enter 85 in the 100% field.

Here's a low-budget—but effective—way to expand the tonal range of a grayscale image. It's printed as a monotone (using one plate).

To print a grayscale image using a Pantone tint:

1. Open a grayscale image.

2. Choose Image > Mode > Duotone.

3. Choose Monotone from the Type pop-up menu.

4. Click the Ink 1 color square, then click Custom, choose the desired Pantone color, then click OK.

5. In the Duotone Options dialog box, click on the Ink 1 curve.

6. In the 100% field, enter the desired tint percentage value **2**. Leave the 0% field at 0 and all other fields blank, then click OK.

7. Click OK to close the dialog box.

8. Save the file in EPS format.

Print Grayscale using Pantone Tint

Color reproduction basics

A computer monitor displays additive colors by projecting red, green, and blue (RGB) light, whereas an offset press prints subtractive colors using CMYK or spot color inks. Obtaining good CMYK color reproduction on an offset press is a real art. The output image will resemble the onscreen image only if the monitor is carefully calibrated for that output device. *Note:* In this section, we're discussing offset press output. For online imaging issues, see the next chapter!

Photoshop determines how to convert an RGB image to CMYK mode and how to display a CMYK mode preview based on the current settings in the Color Settings dialog boxes. Some of these dialogs are discussed on the following pages.

These are the major steps in color separation:

■ Choose Color Settings

■ Obtain a color proof using those settings

■ Match the onscreen preview to the proof

To enter custom CMYK settings:

1. Choose Edit (Photoshop, in OS X) > Color Settings (Ctrl-Shift-K/Cmd-Shift-K).

2. From the Working Spaces: CMYK pop-up menu, choose one of the default U.S. prepress defaults that matches your chosen press and paper type (unless you're printing your file in Japan or Europe).

3. If you want control over the various CMYK settings, then choose Custom CMYK from the CMYK menu. Name your setting **1** and choose or enter the Ink Options for the offset press, such as the Ink Colors and Dot Gain. Ask your print shop about these settings.

   Other characteristics of the offset press are entered in the Separation Options area, but since these settings are particular to each press, you must ask your print shop for this information. In short, the Separation Type tells Photoshop about the type of press used: Does the press use the GCR (gray component replacement) or UCR (undercolor removal)

Ask your print shop at the outset

As we said a second ago, color-separation is an art. Start by asking your print shop the following questions so you'll be able to choose the correct scan resolution and settings in the Custom CMYK dialog box:

What lines-per-inch setting is going to be used on the press for my job? This will help you choose the appropriate scanning resolution.

What is the dot gain for my choice of paper stock on that press? Allowances for dot gain can be made using the Custom CMYK dialog box.

Which printing method will be used on press—UCR or GCR? GCR produces better color printing and is the default choice in the Custom CMYK dialog box. (GCR stands for Gray Component Replacement, UCR stands for Undercolor Removal.)

What is the total ink limit and the black ink limit for the press? These values can also be adjusted in the Custom CMYK dialog box.

Note: Change the dot gain, GCR or UCR method, and ink limits before you convert your image from RGB Color mode to CMYK Color mode. If you change any of these values after conversion, you must convert the image back to RGB Color mode, readjust the values, then reconvert to CMYK Color mode.

In which file format should the file be saved? Ask the print shop what file format it needs.

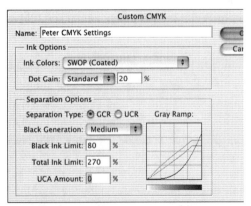

1 *In this screenshot of the **Custom CMYK** dialog box, the **Black Ink Limit** and the **Total Ink Limit** values have been changed as per a print shop's recommendations. The graph maps the current values.*

Total readout

To display total ink coverage percentages on the Info palette for the pixels currently under the pointer, choose **Total Ink** from the pop-up menu next to the leftmost eyedropper on the palette **1**. This readout is based on the current CMYK settings.

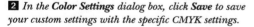

2 *In the Color Settings dialog box, click Save to save your custom settings with the specific CMYK settings.*

Another option

To save your custom CMYK settings as just a profile, not as a full color setting, from the CMYK pop-up menu in the Working Spaces area of the Color Settings dialog box, choose **Save CMYK**. Leave the name, extension, and file location as is, then click Save. The new profile can now be accessed by choosing Load from the same CMYK pop-up menu.

method, and how does the print shop handle black ink?

The Black Generation amount controls how much black ink is used when the RGB components of light are translated into CMY inks. Black is substituted for a percentage of CMY inks to prevent inks from becoming muddy when they're mixed together. How much black is substituted is determined by the Black Generation amount.

Finally, each press shop uses its own amount of ink coverage on each separation plate. Some shops use less than 100% maximum ink coverage for each plate. Ask your press shop for its Total Ink Limit percentage settings.

Continue with the following steps.

Instead of reentering this information every time you need to do an RGB-to-CMYK conversion, you can save your Custom CMYK settings, and all other settings, as a preset.

To save a Color Setting preset incorporating your custom CMYK settings:

1. Once you've entered your CMYK settings in the Custom CMYK dialog box, enter a name, then click OK.

2. Set the other Working Spaces options, click Save **2**, name the file, leave the default location of the Settings folder as is, then click Save again.

3. Enter any notes in the Color Settings Comment dialog box and click OK twice. The next time you output in that particular press situation, open the Color Settings dialog box, and from the Settings pop-up menu, choose the preset you just saved for that press. *Note:* These settings affect the conversion from RGB Color mode to CMYK Color mode. If you subsequently readjust any settings in the Custom CMYK dialog box, you'll have to reconvert your image from RGB to CMYK again using the new settings. Always keep a copy of your image in RGB Color mode for reconverting.

CMYK Settings as Preset

The Proof Colors and Proof Setup commands provide a way to soft-proof an image by using the custom CMYK profile you set up in the previous steps, or by using the color profile for output devices available in your system. Soft proofs provide a fairly accurate preview of how an image will look when printed to that specific output device.

To create a custom proof setup:

1. Choose View > Proof Setup > Custom.

2. From the Profile pop-up menu, choose the custom CMYK profile you created on the previous pages **1**. If Color Settings has been set to the custom CMYK profile (as explained on the previous pages), then the profile should be the current Working CMYK space on the list. Otherwise, look near the bottom of the menu list to locate your custom CMYK profile.

3. Choose an Intent. Ask your print shop for advice on this. See page 46 for more on Intents.

4. Click the Save button, and enter a name. Leave the location and extension as is. Click Save, then click OK.

5. Choose View > Proof Colors (Ctrl-Y/ Cmd-Y) to verify that the soft proofing feature is on (it should now have a check mark). The saved proofing profile will be listed at the bottom of View > Proof Setup submenu.

TIP When Proof Colors is on (checked), the name of the proofing profile being used will be listed on the document's title bar.

TIP Proof Colors needs to be turned on for each image that's opened. The onscreen soft proof of each RGB Color mode image will now reflect the profile chosen on the Proof Setup submenu (in this case, the custom CMYK settings profile), but the actual image information will be changed only if the image is converted to CMYK Color mode using the current Color Settings.

File compression

To reduce the storage size of an image, use a compression program, such as WinZip or PKZip (Win) or Stuffit (Mac). Compression using this kind of software is non-lossy, which means the compression doesn't cause data loss.

If you don't have compression software, choose File > Save As, and choose TIFF from the Format pop-up menu. If you want to save the file without alpha channels, also uncheck Alpha Channels. Click Save. Check the LZW or Zip Compression option in the TIFF Options dialog box. LZW and Zip compression are non-lossy. Not all applications will import an LZW or Zip TIFF, though. And some applications will import an LZW or Zip TIFF only if it doesn't contain any alpha channels.

If you're saving an image for print output, we don't recommend using the JPEG file format, because JPEG compression is lossy, and additional image data is lost with each compression. The data loss may not be noticeable on screen, but it may be quite noticeable on high-resolution output. JPEG is more suitable for Web output.

1 *Choose View > **Proof Setup** > **Custom** to open this dialog box.*

Desaturate another way

You can use Image > Adjustments > **Hue/Saturation** on a layer instead of the Sponge tool to correct out-of-gamut colors in individual color categories. Move the Saturation slider to the left to desaturate.

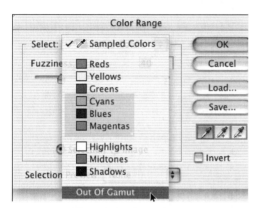

1 *Choose Select:* ***Out Of Gamut*** *in the* ***Color Range*** *dialog box.*

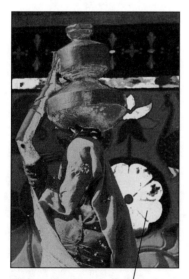

2 *For illustration purposes,* ***out-of-gamut*** *colors in this image are shown in white instead of the usual gray.*

If you convert an image to CMYK Color mode, its colors are automatically forced into printable gamut. In certain cases, however, you may want to see which areas are out-of-gamut (non-printable) in RGB Color mode first, and then change some of them manually. Use the steps below to display out-of-gamut colors and bring them into printable gamut.

Note: CMYK color equivalents are generated based on the current CMYK settings in the Color Settings dialog box, so adjust those settings first (see page 428).

To correct out-of-gamut colors:

1. Open your RGB Color image.

2. Choose View > Gamut Warning.

3. *Optional:* To select and restrict color changes to only the out-of-gamut areas, choose Select > Color Range, choose Select: Out Of Gamut **1**, then click OK.

4. Choose the Sponge tool (O or Shift-O).

5. On the Sponge tool options bar, choose Desaturate from the Mode pop-up menu, choose a Flow percentage, and choose a tip from the Brush picker.

6. Choose a layer.

7. Drag across the gray, out-of-gamut areas **2**. As they become desaturated, they'll redisplay in color. Don't desaturate colors too much, though, or they'll become dull.

TIP To preview the image in CMYK, choose View > Gamut Warning again to uncheck the command. Next, make make sure Working CMYK is chosen on the View > Proof Setup submenu. This should reflect your CMYK settings in the Color Settings dialog box. Finally, choose View > Proof Colors.

TIP When the pointer is over an out-of-gamut pixel, exclamation points will appear next to the CMYK readout on the Info palette.

Correct Out-of-Gamut Colors

Color correction: a first glance

Such a complex topic as color correction is beyond the scope of this QuickStart Guide. It involves using many commands, including Levels, Curves, Color Balance, and Unsharp Mask. You can get some assistance from the resources listed in the sidebar at right. Just by way of introduction, though, these are the basic steps in the color correction process:

■ Calibrate your monitor.

■ Scan or acquire a PhotoCD image into Photoshop, or open an image from a digital camera.

■ Limit tonal values to determine where the darkest shadow and lightest highlight areas are in the image, and then limit the highest and lowest tonal values to the range that your print shop specifies. (Areas outside this range won't print well.)

■ Color balance to correct any undesirable color cast in the image. You can correct the overall color balance or the neutral gray component of the image.

■ Unsharp Mask to resharpen the image.

■ Print a CMYK proof, and then analyze the proof with color-reading instruments to determine the exact color characteristics of the output.

■ Readjust the Photoshop image, then print and analyze another proof.

For onscreen output, do all your color correction in RGB Color mode. Proof it by viewing it on other monitors or through different Web browsers.

For print output, if you're working with a CMYK scan, do all your correction in CMYK Color mode. For an image that's going to be color separated, Adobe recommends working in RGB Color mode, and then converting the image to CMYK Color mode using the proper Color Settings options.

TIP Use adjustment layers for your color adjustments so you'll be able to easily readjust the image on a non-flattened copy of the image later on.

Continue your studies

From Peachpit Press:

Real World Adobe Photoshop 7
by David Blatner and Bruce Fraser

Real World Scanning and Halftones, *2nd Ed.*
by David Blatner, Glenn Fleishman, and Steve Roth

Proof it

To fine-tune your settings, it's a good idea to print a CMYK proof. Use the CMYK test image called Olé No Moire (Testpict.tif for Windows) that Photoshop provides for this purpose. It's on the Photoshop 7 Installation CD, in Goodies > Calibration. Before opening it, however, choose Edit > Color Settings, and for Profile Mismatches, check Ask When Opening. Open the image. If the Missing Profile alert box opens, click Leave as is (don't color manage), then click OK. As the accompanying ReadMe document tells you, don't bother using this procedure with most desktop color printers. They're actually RGB output devices, and won't be affected by any changes you make to your CMYK settings.

WEB/IMAGEREADY 23

PEACHPIT PRESS
Quality How-to Computer Books

About
News
Books
Features
Resources
Order
Find

Welcome!

Academic Resources

Press Releases

User Groups

Contact Peachpit

Request a Catalog

On Site Construction
Creating your own Web site doesn't have to be hard, especially if you have Jeff Carlson and Glenn Fleishman's Real World Adobe GoLive 6 book to refer to while you're building it. While Jeff and Glenn cover advanced topics like mastering JavaScript and creating database-driven, dynamically served sites, they also realize that you have to start somewhere. In this week's features section, Jeff and Glenn discuss two approaches to building sites with Adobe GoLive 6, give you the nine-step quick and dirty guide to creating a starter site, and load you up with lots of useful tips.

WWB author chats
Please join Peachpit Press and World Without Borders on **Wednesday, July 3**, at 6 p.m. PDT/9 p.m. EDT as we welcome **Michael Rubin**, author of **Beginner's Final Cut Pro: Learn to Edit Digital Video**.

To join in, just point your Java-enabled browser to the **World Without Borders community**. For a complete schedule of upcoming chats, visit the **News** page.

Hot off the press!

The Little iMac Book, Third Edition
You just bought an iMac. Now what? Turn it off and flip open the latest edition of Robin Williams's best-selling title for a friendly tour of iMac features old and new.

Pro Tools 5 for Macintosh and Windows: Visual QuickStart Guide
Record, edit, and mix your own music using Pro Tools, the industry standard tool for editing digital audio. Step-by-step, this handy how-to guide shows you the way.

The Little iDVD Book
You don't have to be a Hollywood hotshot to make your own DVDs, Bob LeVitus tells you everything you need to know in this one little book.

Pay a visit to the Peachpit Press Web site:
http://www.peachpit.com.

THIS CHAPTER covers the preparation of Photoshop images for the World Wide Web (online) using **ImageReady**, Photoshop's sister application that's designed specifically for preparing images for the Web.

The basics

When you're preparing graphics to be viewed online (as opposed to print), issues of storage and transmission of data are especially important. All of these issues come into play during **optimization,** the process by which a file is saved within specific format, storage size, and color parameters. The overall goal for each image is to preserve its quality, but compress it enough to make it download quickly on the Web. You want to reduce the file size just until the image quality reaches its reduction limit (starts to degrade). Keep this goal in mind as you choose optimization settings.

While you can optimize your images using Photoshop's File > Save for Web command (a one-stop optimize dialog box), we recommend using ImageReady instead because its optimization controls and options, as they say in computer parlance, are more "robust."

Before you plunge into ImageReady, though, you need to familiarize yourself with some general concepts, such as file formats, image compression, and color depth—all of which impact how successfully images download on the Web. Then, once the groundwork is laid, you'll follow step-by-step instructions for optimizing your images.

(Continued on the following page)

Introduction

You'll be jumping back and forth between ImageReady and Photoshop for the instructions in this chapter. If Photoshop is already launched, and you want to go to ImageReady (or go back to Photoshop from ImageReady), click the **Jump to** button at the bottom of the Toolbox **1** or press **Ctrl-Shift-M/Cmd-Shift-M**.

ImageReady's Optimize palette is illustrated below, with two different file formats chosen (GIF and JPEG) **2**–**3**.

Why not use Photoshop?

Many of ImageReady's file optimization features have counterparts in Photoshop's File > **Save for Web** dialog box (e.g., Original, Optimized, 2-Up, and 4-Up preview tabs at the top of the main window; a Color Table palette; and format, matte, quality, and other options). Photoshop also has a Preview menu and a Preview in (browser) button. So once you learn how to use ImageReady, you can either stick with that program (as we do), or you can use the Save for Web dialog box, which is illustrated on page 502.

Photoshop's **Save a Copy** command can also be used to save copies of a file in the GIF, JPEG, or PNG format, but ImageReady has more options for saving files in these formats because of all of its optimization variables and preview features.

1 The **Jump to ImageReady/Photoshop** button

2 *ImageReady's* **Optimize** *palette, with* **GIF** *chosen as the format: GIF is recommended for images containing sharp-edged elements, such as flat-color areas, line art, and text. The PNG-8 format is similar to GIF and uses the same Optimize palette options.*

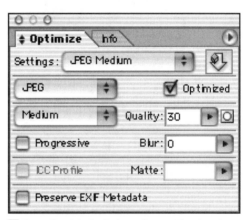

3 *ImageReady's* **Optimize** *palette, with* **JPEG** *chosen as the format: This format is good for continuous-tone, photographic images.*

Introduction (side tab)

Golden rules for Web output

- Let the content of the image—whether it be flat colors or continuous tones—determine which file **format** you choose.

- Use an image as **low** in **pixel size** as is practical, balancing the file size with image quality.

- For flat-color images, choose colors using the Web color sliders and the **Web Safe** color ramp on the Color palette, and Web-shift any existing flat-color areas.

- Try to **reduce** the number of colors in the image's Color Table.

- View your Web image through a Web **browser** on computers other than your own, so you can see how quickly it actually downloads and how good (or bad) it looks.

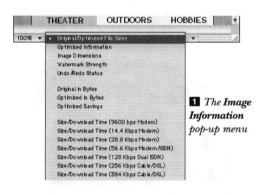

1 *The Image Information pop-up menu*

2 *With **Original/Optimized File Sizes** chosen from ImageReady's **Image Information** pop-up menu, you can view the size readouts for a file.*

The basic formula for outputting an image for online viewing may seem straightforward: Design the image in Photoshop (RGB Color mode), save it, Jump to ImageReady, then optimize the file for Web output. But how do you know if you've been successful? If the image downloads quickly in the browser and looks okay, you chose the right optimization settings for it. If the image looks overly dithered (grainy), was subject to unexpected color substitutions, or takes too long to view on the Web page, it's not outputting well.

Four important issues you'll need to address for online output are covered in this section: The pixel size of the image, the color palette, the color depth, and last but not least, the file format (GIF, JPEG, or PNG).

Image size

Your first task is to calculate the appropriate image size, but it's not hard to figure out. Normally, you'll be designing images for an 800-by-600-pixel viewing area, the most common monitor size, and for a 56 Kbps modem, the most common modem speed. The Web browser window will display within these parameters, so your maximum image size will occupy only a portion of the browser window—about 10 inches wide (740 pixels) by 7.5 inches high (550 pixels). The image resolution needs to be just a mere 72 ppi.

To determine the file storage size of an image, don't rely on Photoshop's Document Sizes reading on the image window status bar. Instead, Jump to ImageReady (click the bottom of the Photoshop Toolbox), click the Optimized tab, make sure **Original/Optimized File Sizes** is chosen from the Image Information pop-up menu at the bottom of the main window **1**, and note the file size information **2**. Saving a file in the GIF, JPEG, or PNG file format reduces its storage size significantly because these formats have built-in compression schemes. We'll discuss these formats in depth soon.

(Continued on the following page)

Compression

If you know the exact file size of the compressed image, you can then calculate how long it will take to transmit over the Web. Better still, choose Size/Download Time from ImageReady's Image Information pop-up menu at the bottom of the image window, for various modem speeds, and look at the readouts **1**. Just by way of example, a 50K file traveling on a 56 Kbps modem will take about 9 seconds to download.

The degree to which the GIF, JPEG, or PNG file format compresses depends on how compressible the image is **2**–**3**. Both the GIF and JPEG formats cause a small reduction in image quality, but it's worth the size-reduction tradeoff because your image will download faster on the Web. ImageReady offers weighted optimization, which helps finesse that tradeoff by letting you selectively compress different areas of an image (see page 447).

A document with a solid background color and a few solid-color shapes will compress a great deal (expect a file size in the range of 20 to 50K). A large document (over 100K) with many color areas, textures, or patterns (e.g., an Add Noise texture covering most of the image) won't compress nearly as much.

Continuous-tone, photographic images may compress less than flat-color images when saved in the GIF format. If you posterize a continuous-tone image down to somewhere between four and eight levels, the resulting GIF file size will be similar to that of a flat-color image, but you will have lost the continuous color transitions in the bargain. So JPEG is the best format choice for a photographic-type image.

To summarize, if an image has to be large (say, 500-by-400 pixels or larger), it should ideally contain only a handful of large, flat-color shapes. For an image that has intricate shapes and colors, try to restrict its size to only a portion of the Web browser window. Another option is to divide it into slices (much more about that later!).

Browser window layer

Take a screen shot of your browser window, open the file in Photoshop, and paste it into a document as your bottommost layer. Now you can design your layout for that specific browser window's dimensions.

1 *Choose a **Size/Download Time** from ImageReady's **Image Information** pop-up menu.*

2 *A **20K GIF**, from a **5-level posterized** image…*

3 *…as compared with a **120K GIF**, from a **continuous-tone** image*

*GIF is a suitable optimization format for this image because it contains **flat colors**.*

*GIF is also a good format choice for this **hybrid** image, which contains both sharp-edged elements (the type) and continuous-tone elements (the ducky).*

TIP Patterned imagery that completely fills the background of a browser window is usually created using a tiling method in a Web-page creation program, or using HTML code, but ImageReady can also be used to create the code for, and generate, background tiling (see pages 499–501).

GIF

GIF is an 8-bit file format, which means a GIF image can contain a maximum of 256 colors. This format is a good choice for images that contain flat-color areas and shapes with well-defined edges, such as type.

To save an image in the GIF format, and to see how it will actually look when it's viewed via the browser, you can either use File > Save for Web in Photoshop or optimize and save it in ImageReady (see page 443).

Your color choices for a GIF image should be based on what a Web browser palette can realistically display. Most browser palettes are 8-bit, which means they can display only 256 colors. Colors that aren't on the palette are simulated by dithering, a display technique that intermixes color pixels to simulate other colors.

To prevent unexpected dithering, one approach is to optimize your image using ImageReady's Web palette. Another option is to Web Snap most of the image colors in ImageReady, and manually Web-shift any critical areas of flat color, where color substitutions would be particularly noticeable. A third option is to use the weighted optimization feature to fine-tune dithering and color reduction. You'll learn these methods in this chapter.

TIP If you want to apply a gradient fill to a large area of an image, and you're going to use the GIF format, create a top-to-bottom gradient. A top-to-bottom gradients will produce a smaller file size than a left-to-right or diagonal gradient.

(Continued on the following page)

GIF

Color depth

An image's color depth is the amount of color information available for each of its pixels. If you lower an image's color depth, you will reduce the actual number of colors it contains. That, in turn, will reduce its file size and speed up its download time on the Web. Color reduction may produce dithered (grainy) edges and duller colors, but you'll get the reduction in file size that you need.

You can reduce the number of colors in an 8-bit image to fewer than the 256 colors it originally contained by using Photoshop's Save for Web dialog box or ImageReady's Optimize palette. Both features provide options that will give you the opportunity to preview how your image will look with fewer available colors.

TIP To evaluate its color quality, preview your image at 100% view.

JPEG

The JPEG format is a better choice than GIF for preserving color fidelity if your image is continuous-tone (contains gradations of color or is photographic) and your viewers have 24-bit monitors, which have the capacity to display millions of colors.

A JPEG plus: It can take a 24-bit image and make it as small as the GIF format can make an 8-bit image.

JPEG has some shortcomings. First, a JPEG file has to be decompressed when it's downloaded for viewing on a Web page, which takes time.

Second, JPEG is not a good choice for flat-color images or type because its compression methods tend to produce artifacts along the well-defined edges of these kinds of images.

And third, not all Web users have 24-bit monitors. A JPEG image will be dithered on an 8-bit monitor, though dithering in a continuous-tone image will be less noticeable than in an image that contains flat colors. You can lower your monitor's setting to

Color depth

Number of colors	Bit depth
256	8
128	7
64	6
32	5
16	4
8	3
4	2
2	1

*JPEG optimization is suitable for this **continuous-tone** image.*

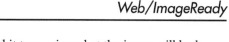

*JPEG isn't a great choice for optimizing **sharp-edged** imagery. Note the artifacts around the type.*

*The word "duck" looks crisper in this **GIF**.*

8-bit to preview what the image will look like in an 8-bit setting, or simply use View > Preview > Browser Dither in ImageReady. If it doesn't contain type or objects with sharp edges, the JPEG image will probably survive the conversion to 8-bit.

JPEG format files can also be optimized as Progressive JPEG, which is supported by both the Netscape Navigator and Internet Explorer browsers (versions 4 and up). A Progressive JPEG displays in increasing detail as it downloads onto a Web page.

If you choose JPEG as your output format, you can experiment in ImageReady or in Photoshop's Save for Web dialog box by optimizing an image, then using the 4–Up option to preview several versions of the image in varying degrees of compression. Decide which degree of compression is acceptable by weighing the file size versus diminished image quality. In ImageReady, you can save the optimized file separately, and leave the original file intact to preserve it for potential future revision.

Each time an image is optimized using the JPEG format, some image data is lost. The greater the degree of compression, the greater the data loss. To prevent such data loss, first edit and save your image in Photoshop. Next, Jump to ImageReady; perform further edits, if desired, optimize the file, and finally, use File > Save Optimized to output the file in the JPEG format. Don't panic —we'll break it down into steps for you!

PNG-8 and PNG-24

The two PNG formats, PNG-8 and PNG-24, can save partially transparent pixels (e.g., soft, feathered edges) using a method called alpha transparency. With alpha transparency, a pixel can have any one of 256 levels of opacity, from totally transparent to totally opaque. The PNG-8 format is limited to a maximum of 256 colors in the optimized image and is similar to the GIF format. The PNG-24 format allows for millions

(Continued on the following page)

PNG-8; PNG-24

of colors in the optimized image and is more similar to the JPEG format. The compression method used by both PNG formats is lossless, meaning it doesn't cause data loss.

Are there any drawbacks to using PNG? For one thing, animation can't be done in the PNG format (animation *can* be done in the GIF format), and PNG-24 files have larger file sizes than (aren't compressed as much as) equivalent JPEGs. More importantly, PNG is just now supported directly by the two major Web browsers: Internet Explorer versions 4.0 and later directly support PNG, as does Netscape Navigator 6 and later.

Dithering

Dithering is the intermixing of two palette colors to create the impression of a third color. It's used to make images that contain a limited number of colors (256 or fewer) appear to have a greater range of colors and shades. Dithering is usually applied to continuous-tone images to increase their tonal range, but—argh, life is full of compromises —it can also make them look grainy.

Dithering usually doesn't produce aesthetically pleasing results in flat-color images. This is because the browser palette will dither pixels to re-create any color that the palette doesn't contain. You're better off creating flat colors in Photoshop or Image-Ready using the Web Color sliders and the Web Safe color ramp on the Color palette. Existing flat-color areas should also be selected and Web-shifted to bring them into the Web-safe gamut.

Continuous-tone imagery, on the other hand, is in a way already dithered. Some continuous-tone imagery looks fine on a Web page with no dithering and 256 colors. The fewer the colors the palette of a non-dithered continuous-tone image contains, the more banding will occur in its color transitions. You'll choose a Dither value for whichever file format you choose in ImageReady or in Photoshop's Save for Web dialog box. Raising the Dither value will

*A closeup of an image with a **small** amount of **dithering***

*The same image with a **lot** of **dithering***

Halos nobody wants

Here's a way to prevent halos when copying anti-aliased objects to other programs. Ctrl-click/Cmd-click a layer name in Photoshop to select an object on its layer without its anti-aliased edge, then zoom in (at least 200% view) so you can see the object's edge clearly. Use Select > Modify > **Contract** to contract the selection by 1 or 2 pixels in order to remove the anti-aliased edge **1**–**2**, copy the object selection, and then paste it into your other program.

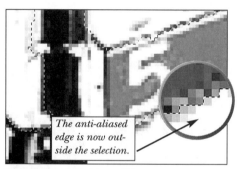

The anti-aliased edge is now outside the selection.

1 *After using the Magic Wand tool to select the white background around the signpost, and then inversing the selection, some of the original anti-aliased edge remained. Select > Modify > **Contract** (by 1 pixel) was then used to shrink the selection inward.*

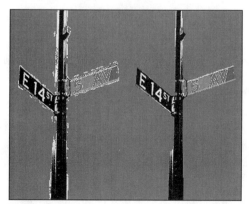

2 *These two pixel images were pasted into another program. The object on the left was copied without contracting the selection in Photoshop. The object on the right was copied after contracting the selection in Photoshop in order to remove its halo.*

make color transitions look more seamless, but will also cause the image to look more grainy. You can decide which of these two evils appears lesser to your eye.

One more consideration: Dithering adds noise and additional colors to the file, so compression is less effective when dithering is turned on than when it's off. So, with dithering enabled, you may not be able to achieve your desired degree of file compression. As is the case with most Web output, you'll have to strike an acceptable balance between aesthetics and file size. (Dithering is discussed further on page 453.)

Anti-aliasing

Anti-aliasing blends the edges of an object with its background by adding pixels with progressively less opacity along the object's edges. When imagery is composited or montaged in Photoshop, anti-aliasing helps to smooth the transitions between shapes. With anti-aliasing off, the edges of an object will look sharp because its edge pixels won't be blended with the background color.

If you create a selection using a tool with anti-aliasing on, though, a fringe of pixels may be picked up in the selection from the background of the original image. If you copy and paste this type of shape onto a flat-color background, the fringe may become painfully visible. To prevent this from happening, before creating your selection, uncheck Anti-aliased on the options bar for your marquee, lasso, or Magic Wand tool.

You can also use the Matte option on ImageReady's Optimize palette to control how partially transparent pixels (the kind of pixels that are created by anti-aliasing) are treated in GIFs and JPEGs. Both Photoshop and ImageReady also provide options for controlling the amount of anti-aliasing on type. These options can be chosen in, and will transfer correctly between, the two programs. The new matting and anti-aliasing controls both help to eliminate unwanted halos.

Anti-aliasing

441

The ImageReady Toolbox

If Photoshop is launched, and you want to go to ImageReady (or vice versa), click the **Jump to** button at the bottom of the Toolbox or press **Ctrl-Shift-M/Cmd-Shift-M**.

The ImageReady Toolbox **1** looks similar to Photoshop's, but it contains a few extra Web-related tools for creating image maps, viewing image maps, viewing slices, previewing rollovers and animation effects, and switching to a Web browser.

Like Photoshop, ImageReady has a context-sensitive tool options bar, which changes depending on which tool is currently chosen **2**–**3**. Drag the bar's left edge to move it anywhere on the desktop. To collapse/expand the bar, double-click the left edge **4**.

1 *The ImageReady Toolbox*

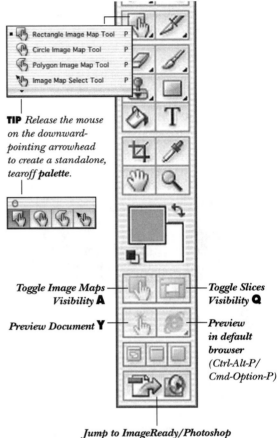

TIP *Release the mouse on the downward-pointing arrowhead to create a standalone, tearoff **palette**.*

Toggle Image Maps Visibility **A**

Preview Document **Y**

Toggle Slices Visibility **Q**

Preview in default browser (Ctrl-Alt-P/ Cmd-Option-P)

Jump to ImageReady/Photoshop (Ctrl-Shift-M/Cmd-Shift-M)

2 *The options bar with the **Rectangle shape** tool chosen*

3 *The options bar with the **Type** tool chosen*

4 *Double-click the left edge of the options bar to collapse/expand the whole bar.*

Four GIF color-reduction methods

Note: ImageReady tool tips calls this pop-up menu "color reduction algorithms" (huh?).

Perceptual

Generates a color table based on the colors currently in the image, with particular attention paid to how people actually perceive colors.

Selective

Generates a color table based on the colors currently in the image. The Selective option favors preserving flat colors and Web-safe colors. This table's strength is in preserving overall color integrity.

Adaptive

Generates a color table based on the part of the color spectrum that represents most of the colors in the image. This choice produces a slightly larger optimized file.

TIP If you switch among the Perceptual, Selective, or Adaptive options, most of the Web-safe colors that are currently on the Color Table palette will be preserved.

Web

Generates a color table by shifting image colors to colors that are available in the standard Web-safe palette. (The Web-safe palette contains only the 216 colors that the Windows and Mac OS browser palettes have in common.) This choice produces the least number of colors, and thus the smallest file size, but not necessarily the best image quality.

To optimize an image in the GIF or PNG-8 format:

1. If you're working in Photoshop 7, save your file, then click the Jump to button at the bottom of the Toolbox (Ctrl-Shift-M/Cmd-Shift-M). ImageReady will launch, if it isn't already open, and the image will open in that application.
or
In ImageReady, choose File > Open, locate an image, then click Open.

2. Click the 2-Up tab at the top of the image window to display both the original and optimized previews of the image simultaneously **1**.

3. Display the full Optimize palette (Window > Optimize) **2**.

4. Choose a named, preset combination of optimize settings from the Settings pop-up menu. Leave the preset as is, and save your file.
or
Follow the remaining steps to choose custom optimization settings.

5. Choose GIF or PNG-8 from the optimized file format pop-up menu.

6. Choose a color **reduction** method (algorithm) from the next pop-up menu (see the sidebar at left).

(Continued on the following page)

(Continued on the following page)

Optimize as GIF or PNG-8

1 *2-Up view in ImageReady*

2 *ImageReady's Optimize palette*

The GIF and PNG-8 formats permit a maximum of only 256 colors.

Perceptual, Selective, **1** and Adaptive render the optimized image using colors from the original image.

Web shifts all the image colors to Web-safe colors **2**. This is not generally the best choice if the image contains continuous-tone areas, blends, or gradients.

Custom optimizes image color based on a palette you have previously saved in Photoshop or ImageReady.

Mac OS and Windows optimize image color based on the Standard palette for each particular operating system.

7. From the next pop-up menu, choose a **Dither** method: No Dither, Diffusion, Pattern, or Noise. Dithering simulates image colors for 8-bit display (you won't be able to see this on the palette), and it increases a file's size. Diffusion produces the most subtle results, with the least increase in file size.

   Also choose a Dither percentage **3**–**4**. A high Dither value will produce more color simulation and a larger file size. To modify dithering using a channel, see page 447.

8. Choose the maximum number of **Colors** to be generated in the color table by choosing a standard setting from the drop-down menu or by entering an exact number in the field. For the Web, Mac, and Windows palettes, this field defaults to Auto. Auto sets the number of colors in the color table automatically to either the number of colors used in the image or to 256, whichever is lower. You can choose or enter a Colors number to override the Auto setting.

9. Check **Transparency** to have ImageReady preserve any transparent pixels in the image (areas on a layer where the checkerboard pattern shows). The GIF format doesn't allow for partially transparent pixels; the PNG-8 format does

1 *The **Selective** palette produces a **smoother** optimization.*

2 *The **Web** palette produces a **dithered** optimization.*

3 *Selective palette with a **high Dither** value*

4 *The **Web** palette with a **high Dither** value produces, as one would expect, a lot of **dithering**.*

Optimize as GIF or PNG-8

Fading away redux

Another way to have your GIF or JPEG image fade into a flat-color background is to create two layers in your Photoshop or ImageReady document: a lower layer that contains a flat color filled with the Web-safe color that will be used on the Web page, and an upper layer that contains the image element with a soft edge or an effect such as Drop Shadow or Outer Glow.

1 *A GIF image with* **Transparency** *checked and* **Matte** *set to* **a color,** *resulting in a thin line of color along the edge of each shape*

2 *A GIF image with* **Transparency** *checked and* **Matte** *set to* **None:** *There's a hard edge along each shape.*

 3 *To apply transparency dithering, check* **Transparency,** *then choose from the* **Transparency Dither** *pop-up menu.*

(see the sidebar). Transparency permits the creation of nonrectangular image borders. With Transparency unchecked, transparent pixels will be filled with the current Matte color.

10. To control how partially transparent pixels along the edge of an image blend with the background of a Web page (as on the edges of anti-aliased elements), choose a **Matte** option. Set the Matte color to the color of the Web page background, if you happen to know what that color is **1**. Any soft-edged effect (such as a Drop Shadow) on top of transparent areas will fill with the current Matte color. If the backgound color is unknown, set Matte to None, which will result in a hard, jagged edge **2**.

Another option is to choose Matte: None, check Transparency, then choose one of three options from the **Transparency Dither** pop-up menu **3**. These effects will look the same on any background. Diffusion Transparency Dither applies a random pattern to partially transparent pixels and diffuses it across adjacent pixels. This is often the least noticeable of the three dither patterns, and the only one that lets you set the dithering amount. Pattern Transparency Dither applies a halftone pattern to the partially transparent pixels. Noise Transparency Dither applies a pattern similar to Diffusion Transparency Dither, but it doesn't affect adjacent pixels. All four Transparency Dither options eliminate halo effects along the edge of an image when it's displayed on the Web.

11. Check **Interlaced** to have the GIF or PNG image display in successively greater detail as it downloads on the Web page. This option causes the file size to increase slightly.

12. Choose or enter a **Web Snap** percentage to establish the range of colors that will automatically snap to their Web-safe equivalents. The higher the Web Snap,

(Continued on the following page)

the fewer the number of colors in the image and the smaller the file size, but also the more dithered or posterized the image will become .

13. *Optional:* For a GIF only, you can adjust the **Lossy** value to further reduce the file size of the optimized image. As the name "Lossy" implies, some image data will be discarded, but the slight reduction in image quality may be justified by the savings in file size. (To modify lossiness using a channel, see page 447.)

14. Save the file (see pages 456–457).

TIP To save a current (Unnamed) set of palette options, choose Save Settings from the palette menu. Enter a name (Windows: Use the .irs extension), locate and open the Adobe Photoshop 7 > Presets > Optimize Settings folder (the default), then click Save. Your saved set will display on the Settings pop-up menu in ImageReady and in the Save for Web dialog box in Photoshop.

ImageReady's master palettes offer a way to ensure that every image in a group uses an identical palette, and can help you save storage space.

To create a master palette for optimized images in ImageReady:

1. In ImageReady, choose Image > Master Palette > Clear Master Palette.

2. Open an image whose colors you want to use in building a master palette.

3. Choose Image > Master Palette > Add to Master Palette .

4. Repeat steps 2 and 3 to add the colors of any other images to the master palette.

5. Once you've added all the desired images, choose Image > Master Palette > Build Master Palette.

6. Finally, choose Image > Master Palette > Save Master Palette.

7. Type a name for the palette, then click Save. The palette can now be applied to other images.

How to treat a hybrid

For a hybrid image that contains both flat-color areas or type and photographic imagery, the best choice for optimization may be the GIF format using the Perceptual, Selective, or Adaptive palette (not the Web palette). This combination will strike a good balance between keeping the flat-color areas Web safe and rendering the continuous-tone areas pretty well.

1 *The **Selective** palette with a **high Web Snap** value produces **posterization**.*

2 *Choose Image > Master Palette > **Add to Master Palette** to add the colors from the currently open image to a master palette.*

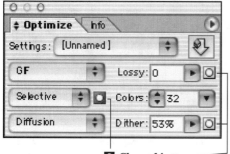

1 *Enter a **Name** in the **Save Selection** dialog box.*

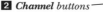

2 *Channel buttons*

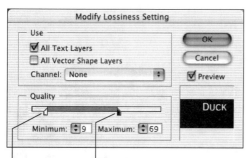

Minimum slider   Maximum slider

3 *You can favor text or vector shapes without first creating a separate channel.*

To apply a master palette to an image:

1. Open an image within ImageReady.

2. From the Color reduction algorithm pop-up menu on the Optimize palette, choose the master palette that you saved.

Weighted optimization lets you set maximum and minimum quality limits for compressing GIF, PNG, and JPEG images. By creating and saving a selection channel, the maximum limits will be applied to the channel's white areas (the area inside the original selection), and minimum limits will be applied to the black areas (areas outside the selection). Color reduction and dithering limits can be set for GIFs and PNG-8s, lossy value limits for GIFs, and overall quality limits for JPEGs.

To use weighted optimization:

1. Create an alpha channel by selecting an area in the image and choosing Select > Save Selection. Leave the Channel pop-up menu set to New **1**, enter a name in the Name field, then click OK. Then, on the Optimize palette, click a channel button next to the color reduction pop-up menu or the Lossy or Dither field for a GIF or PNG **2**, or next to the Quality field for a JPEG.

or

To optimize GIF text or vector shapes without first creating a specific channel, just click the Lossy channel button on the Optimize palette.

2. In the Modify Lossiness Setting dialog box **3**, check All Text Layers and/or All Vector Shape Layers. For all other areas, choose your selection's channel from the Channel pop-up menu. Also set the Minimum and Maximum limits for the image quality using the sliders, arrows, or text fields. These settings will control how much optimization is applied to the black or white parts of the channel.

3. Click OK.

Apply Master Palette; Weighted Optimization

To use the ImageReady previews:

Click the 4-Up tab on the main window to see an original view and three previews simultaneously. ImageReady will use the current Optimize palette settings to generate the first preview (on the upper right), and then automatically generate ("autopopulate") the two other previews as variations on the current optimization settings. You can click on any preview and change the Optimize palette settings for just that preview.

The Optimized preview(s) will update every time a value or setting is changed on the Optimize palette. To stop the preview from updating, click the Stop button on the main window progress bar **1**. A halted preview button (triangle with an exclamation point) will display in the lower-right corner of any halted preview **2**. If you change a setting on the Optimize palette or click the alert triangle, the preview will update automatically.

TIP The Save Optimized command saves the image using the currently chosen Optimized palette settings.

Jump To

Leave both Photoshop and ImageReady open so you can quickly make changes to the same open file in either program. To jump back and forth, choose from the File > **Jump To** submenu, or click the **Jump to** button on the toolbox, or press **Ctrl-Shift-M/ Cmd-Shift-M**.

The two programs are in sync: The same file can be open in both programs, and changes made to the file in one program will automatically be reflected in the other **3**. If you start working on an image in Image-Ready, jump to Photoshop to perform some edits, then jump back to ImageReady, the Photoshop edits will be identified on the History palette in ImageReady as a single history state named **Update From Photoshop**. Photoshop's History palette will list an **Update from ImageReady** history state when a change is made in ImageReady. You can click an earlier state at any time to undo an edit made in the other program.

Revert is a state

The **Revert** command is now recorded as a **state** on the History palette in Photoshop and ImageReady, and it won't wipe out the existing states. This means you can undo a Revert.

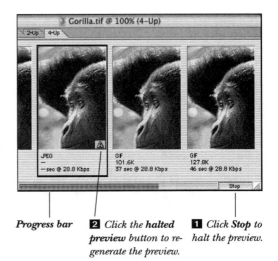

Progress bar   **2** *Click the **halted**   **1** *Click **Stop** to*
preview button to re-   halt the preview.
generate the preview.

3 *This **Update** progress bar will appear if you open a file in ImageReady, edit it in Photoshop, and then Jump back to ImageReady. Regardless of whether you check or uncheck **Auto-Update Files** in General Preferences in ImageReady or **Auto-update open documents** in Photoshop, files will automatically update in both programs.*

ImageReady Previews; Jump To

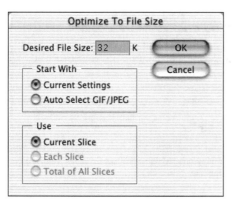

1 *Using the Optimize To File Size dialog box, you can have ImageReady make the optimization calculations for you.*

2 *Click the Droplet icon on the Optimize palette, or drag it to the Desktop.*

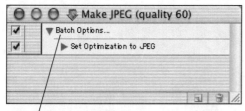

3 *A droplet icon on a Mac OS Desktop*

4 *Double-click Batch Options to open the Batch Options dialog box.*

Why not let ImageReady make all the decisions for you? All you need to decide is how large you want the optimized image to be.

To quick-optimize:

1. *Optional:* Click a slice to optimize just that area of the image.

2. Choose Optimize to File Size from the Optimize palette menu.

3. Enter a Desired File Size value for the final optimized file size **1**.

4. Click Start With: Current Settings to use the current settings on the palette.
or
Click Auto Select GIF/JPEG to let ImageReady pick the optimize method.

5. Click Use: Current Slice. Or click Each Slice or Total of All Slices, if available.

6. Click OK. Presto—ImageReady will choose all the Optimize palette settings for you and generate an optimized file based on your designated file size.

A droplet is a tiny but powerful application that holds and applies the Optimize palette settings that were in effect when the droplet was created.

To create and apply a droplet:

1. Click the Droplet icon on the Optimize palette **2**, ⬇ choose a location in which to save it, then click Save.
or
Drag the Droplet icon from the Optimize palette to the Desktop.

2. To optimize a file or a whole folder of files using the Optimize palette settings in the droplet, drag the file or folder icon over the droplet icon on the Desktop. An optimized version of the file(s) will be saved in the same location as the droplet.

Note: ImageReady and/or Photoshop must be launched for a droplet to work!

TIP You can double-click the droplet **3**, then double-click the Batch Options command **4** to open the Batch Options dialog box.

Quick-Optimize; Droplets

JPEG is the format of choice for optimizing continuous-tone imagery (photographs, paintings, gradients, or blends) for display on the Web. If you optimize to this format, the file's 24-bit color depth will be preserved, and these colors will be seen and enjoyed by any Web viewer whose monitor is set to millions of colors (24-bit depth). Keep in mind, however, that JPEGs are optimized using a compression method that is lossy, which means it causes image data to be eliminated.

The PNG-24 format is similar to JPEG, except that PNG allows for multiple levels of transparency along edges and employs a lossless method of compression. PNG-24 files are larger than equivalent JPEGs.

To optimize an image in the JPEG or PNG-24 format:

1. If you're working in Photoshop, save your file, then click the Jump to button at the bottom of the Toolbox. ImageReady will launch, if it isn't already open.
or
In ImageReady, choose File > Open, locate the image, then click Open.

2. Click the 2-Up tab at the top of the main window to display the original and optimized previews of the image simultaneously.

3. Display the full Optimize palette (Window > Optimize) **1**.

4. From the **Settings** pop-up menu, choose JPEG High **2**, JPEG Low, JPEG Medium, or PNG-24. Leave this preset setting as is, then save your file.
or
Follow the remaining steps to choose custom settings.

5. Choose JPEG as the format from the next pop-up menu.

6. From the next pop-up menu, choose Low, Medium, High, or Maximum as the compression quality for the optimized image (**1**–**2**, next page).
or

JPEGs and Web-safe colors

JPEG compression adds compression artifacts to an image. Because of this, Web-safe colors in a JPEG image are rendered un-Web-safe after compression, but this is acceptable because the JPEG format is usually used to optimize continuous-tone images, and on these type of images, browser dither isn't objectionable. Don't try to match a color area in a JPEG file to a color area in a GIF file, or on the background of a Web page, though, because the JPEG color will shift and dither when the image is compressed.

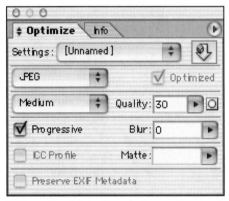

1 *ImageReady's **Optimize** palette, with **JPEG** chosen*

2 *A **JPEG** optimized with **High** Quality*

Optimize as JPEG or PNG-24

Check your profiles

An embedded profile will slightly increase a file's size. As of this writing, Internet Explorer for Mac versions 4.01 and later support profiles. On the Mac, ColorSync makes sure the browser and the operating system know the viewer's monitor profile. This helps to ensure consistent color between the monitor and JPEG files. As color management support and profile automation improve, embedded profiles will become standard. Windows has a bit of catching up to do in this area. For the moment, use your own judgment.

1 *A JPEG optimized with* **Medium** *Quality*

2 *A JPEG optimized with* **Low** *Quality: Note how pixelated the image has become.*

Move the **Quality** pop-up slider to an exact level of compression. Watch the adjacent compression pop-up menu setting change as you change the Quality value. (To vary the compression using a selection channel, see page 447.)

Always remember, the lower the compression, the higher the quality—and the larger the file size.

7. Check **Progressive** to have the optimized image display on the Web page in successively greater detail.

8. Increase the **Blur** value to lessen the visibility of JPEG artifacts that arise from the JPEG compression method, and also to reduce the file size. Be careful not to over-blur the image, though, or your details will soften too much. The Blur setting can be lowered later to reclaim some of the diminished sharpness.

9. *Optional:* Check ICC Profile to embed an ICC Profile in the optimized image. To utilize this option, the original image must have had a profile embedded into it in Photoshop. See the sidebar on this page.

10. Choose a **Matte** color to be used for areas of transparency in the original image. If you choose "None," transparent areas will appear as white.

Note: The JPEG format doesn't support transparency. To have the Matte color simulate transparency, use the same solid color as the background of the Web page, if that color is known.

11. *Optional:* Check Optimized to produce the smallest file size. Check Preserve EXIF Metadata if you imported the file from a digital camera and want camera settings, caption, and keyword information to be saved with the file.

12. Save the file (see pages 456–457).

TIP To save the current settings as a named preset, see page 446.

Optimize as JPEG or PNG-24

Let's say you have an image that you're going to optimize in the GIF format using the Perceptual, Selective, or Adaptive palette, but the image contains flat-color areas that aren't Web-safe. Before outputting that image online, you can make the flat-color areas Web-safe yourself.

To make flat-color areas Web-safe:

1. Open the image in ImageReady, and optimize it in the GIF format.

2. Choose the Eyedropper tool (I).

3. Click on a flat-color area to be made Web-safe **1**.

4. Open the Color Table palette. The color you just clicked on will now be the highlighted swatch **2**.

5. Click the "Shift colors to Web palette" button at the bottom of the palette. A diamond with a diagonal line will display on the selected swatch to signify that the color was shifted to its Web-safe equivalent.

6. *Optional:* Click the "Lock color" button to have the currently selected swatch be preserved even if the number of colors in the GIF palette is reduced.

TIP Shift-click with the Eyedropper tool on other areas in the image to select more than one color, then Web-shift all the selected colors at once. Or use the Magic Wand tool or a lasso or marquee tool to create a selection or selections in the image, choose the Select All From Selection command from the Color Table palette menu, then click the "Shift colors to Web palette" button at the bottom of the Color Table palette.

TIP To assign transparency to a particular color in the Color Table, click the "Map to Transparent" button. To unassign the color, click the button again.

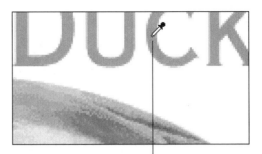

1 *Click on a flat-color area with the Eyedropper tool.*

A **diamond** *signifies that that swatch was made Web-safe via the Optimize palette.*

A **small square** *signifies that a swatch is* **locked**.

A diamond with a **diagonal line** *signifies that that swatch was made Web-safe via the Shift colors to Web palette button.*

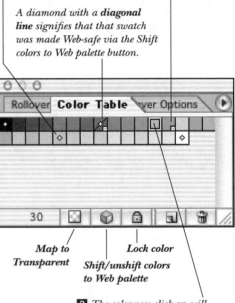

Map to Transparent

Lock color

Shift/unshift colors to Web palette

2 *The color you click on will become the highlighted swatch on the Color Table palette in ImageReady.*

7.0!

1 *An image optimized as a JPEG in ImageReady with* **Browser Dither** *turned off*

2 *This is the same image optimized as a JPEG, but with Preview >* **Browser Dither** *turned on. The image's millions of colors are reduced to the browser's 8-bit color palette (and the Web viewer's 8-bit monitor).*

Using various preview methods in ImageReady, you can get a pretty reliable idea of how optimized images will look when they're viewed online. This will help you choose appropriate settings as you optimize your images.

Fewer than than 10 percent of Web viewers use 8-bit monitors, which display a maximum of 256 colors. Macintosh and Windows browsers, on the other hand, use a color palette of 216 colors. Dithering is used to re-create any colors in an image that are not on the browser palette.

To preview potential browser dither in an optimized image:

1. Open the image in ImageReady, and show at least one optimized preview in the main window.

2. Right-click/Ctrl-click and choose Display Preview > Browser Dither; or choose View > Preview > Browser Dither; or press Ctrl-Shift-Y/Cmd-Shift-Y) **1**–**2**.

Controlling dithering

When you use ImageReady to optimize an image, the application applies dithering to simulate colors that were in the original image but which won't appear on the color palette of the optimized image. You can control the amount of this type of dithering via the Dither option on the Optimize palette. If you raise the Dither value, colors in the optimized image will more closely match colors in the original—but with the drawback of a slightly larger file size.

The Web Snap value on the Optimize palette also affects the amount of browser dither in an image. The higher the Web Snap value, the less the optimized image will be dithered, and the smaller its file size will be. If the Browser Dither option is on, the more closely colors in the optimized image will match colors in the browser's 8-bit palette, and the less dramatically the optimized image will change. Some degree of dithering is acceptable in continuous-tone imagery, though, and it's more pleasing than the color banding that a high Web Snap value can cause.

Since the Windows operating system uses a higher gamma value than the Macintosh operating system, an image will appear darker on Windows than on a Mac. When you create Web graphics for cross-platform use, it's important to preview and adjust your image for both platforms.

To preview Windows and Mac gamma values:

With an optimized preview showing in ImageReady, choose View > Preview > Standard Macintosh Color to simulate the Mac gamma value, or Standard Windows Color to simulate the Windows gamma value.

Choose View > Preview > Uncompensated Color to preview the image without gamma compensation. Choose Use Embedded Color Profile to match the ImageReady preview (based on the monitor RGB) with the profile assigned to, or embedded in, the image in Photoshop. This option will be grayed out if the image lacks a profile.

TIP Press Ctrl-Alt-Y/Cmd-Option-Y to cycle through the first three Preview submenu options *Note:* When using this shortcut, it's hard to tell which preview is showing.

You can compensate for differences between operating systems for an individual file.

To change the gamma for an optimized file:

1. With an image with an optimized preview showing in ImageReady, choose Image > Adjustments > Gamma.

2. Click Windows to Macintosh to change the gamma to the Mac gamma value. The image will look darker on a Mac **1**–**2**.
   or
   Click Macintosh to Windows to change the gamma to the Windows gamma value. The image will look lighter on a Mac **3**.

3. Click OK.

TIP You can also use the slider to manually choose a gamma value in between the button choices, or to set a gamma value for another platform. The gamma setting

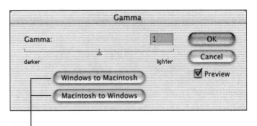

1 *Click either of these buttons in the **Gamma** dialog box to preview the other platform's gamma values.*

2 *An image after clicking the **Windows to Macintosh** button: The lower gamma value has caused the image to look darker.*

3 *The same image after clicking the **Macintosh to Windows** button. Here the image looks lighter.*

Keep the code

There are two methods for copying source code from ImageReady into an HTML-editing program. One, you can drag through the source code that's displayed at the bottom of the browser window to select it **3**, and then copy and paste it into the HTML-editing or Web-page creation program. Or, two, in ImageReady, you could choose Edit > Copy HTML Code > For All Slices for the current file, and then paste the source code into an HTML-editing or Web-page creation program.

1 *Click this button to* **preview** *your optimized image in a* **browser**.

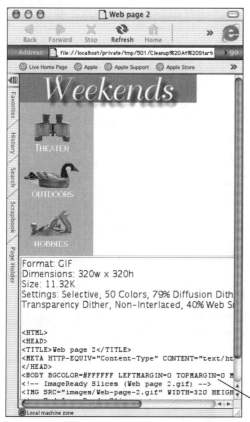

2 *An image being viewed in Microsoft's* **Internet Explorer**

is a relative setting, meaning if you set a value, close the dialog box, then reopen the dialog box, the setting will be back at 1.

For a more definitive simulation of online viewing for an optimized image, use ImageReady's Preview in Browser feature. You can choose from any of the browsers that are currently installed in your system.

Note: This preview feature won't test the actual download time for an image over an actual Web connection, and it will display a preview for your monitor type only—not for any other monitor type. Nevertheless, it's still very useful.

To preview an optimized image in a browser on your system:

1. With an optimized image opened in ImageReady, click the Preview in Default Browser button on the Toolbox **1**, or press this button and choose a browser from the submenu.

2. The browser will launch and the image will load into the browser window **2**. Any GIF animations or rollovers created in ImageReady will also be preview-able.

3. Exit/quit out of the browser, if desired, then click back on any ImageReady palette or window to switch back to ImageReady.

Note: Be sure to preview your final files by actually uploading them to the Web. Do this on both computer platforms, and ideally, on a spectrum of monitor types.

TIP If your monitor's color depth setting is higher than 8-bit, and you want to see how an image will look in an 8-bit browser, set your system to 256 colors first, then launch your browser. We've seen only minor differences between this method and choosing View > Preview > Browser Dither (in ImageReady).

3 *The* **HTML source code** *from ImageReady*

To save a file in ImageReady:

1. Make sure you're in ImageReady and the file you want to save is open, then choose File > Save (Ctrl-S/Cmd-S).

2. Enter a file name and leave the file extension for the Photoshop format (.psd) as is. Choose a location, then click Save. The saved file won't contain optimization settings.

Follow these instructions to save a file as an optimized file according to the settings currently chosen on the Optimize palette.

To save an optimized file in ImageReady:

1. Choose File > Save Optimized (Ctrl-Alt-S/Cmd-Option-S).

2. To control how the file will be saved, choose one of the following from the **Format** pop-up menu 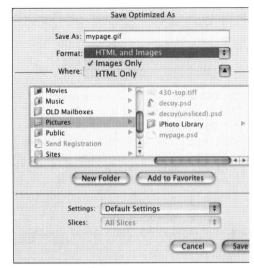:

HTML and Images to create an HTML file and save the image slices in a separate folder of files.

Images Only to save just the image slices.

HTML Only to create an HTML file without saving the image files. A separate HTML file will automatically be assigned the .htm or .html extension, and it will be saved in the same location as the optimized file.

3. *Optional:* To choose additional options, choose Other from the Settings pop-up menu. The **Output Settings** dialog box opens.

To choose HTML preferences for formatting and coding, choose **HTML** from the second pop-up menu **2**. Use these options to establish consistency between the HTML in ImageReady and that of other HTML-editing applications. Check Include GoLive 5 (or Earlier) Code if you want your HTML or JavaScript to be editable from within Adobe GoLive.

Click OK now, or follow the next step before clicking OK.

1 *Choose from the **Format** pop-up menu in the **Save Optimized As** dialog box.*

2 *The **Output Settings** dialog box, with custom settings chosen in the **HTML** pane*

1 *Choose options for saving files in the **Saving Files** pane of the **Output Settings** dialog box.*

4. Choose **Saving Files** from the second pop-up menu, then choose File Naming conventions for any autogenerated files, such as slices and rollover frames, to be saved with the optimized file and used in the HTML page **1**. Consult with your HTML specialist before making changes in these fields. If the naming convention seems confusing, leave the default settings as is.

Check any platform Filename Compatibility options.

Check any Optimized Files options. Enter the name of the folder you want to save the autogenerated files in.

5. Click OK to exit the Output Settings dialog box.

6. Type a file name, choose a location, then click Save.

TIP Use the Save As or Save Optimized As command to save a version of a file under a different name.

TIP To attach a URL or an Alt tag to an image, use the Slice palette (see page 473).

TIP You can also open the Output Settings dialog box by choosing from the File > Output Settings submenu.

To update an existing HTML file:

If you have modified an optimized file, and you want to update the HTML file that's associated with it, choose File > Update HTML, locate the HTML file for that image, then click Open. Click Replace, if an alert box appears. Click OK when the update is finished. Any HTML code generated for the optimized file will be updated, even if the code was already copied and pasted into a larger HTML file, or that larger file contains tables from other image files.

Update HTML File

Using the File Info dialog box, you can modify the browser window page title for, or embed copyright information into, an HTML file.

To change a Web page title or embed copyright information:

1. With the image open in ImageReady, choose File > File Info (Ctrl-Shift-K/ Cmd-Shift-K).

2. Change the page title in the Caption field **1**. The page title is the text that displays on the title bar of the browser window (the text between the HTML <TITLE> tags). The default title is the title of the current file for the image. *and/or*
Enter information in the Copyright field to embed pertinent copyright information into the HTML file.

3. Click OK.

Color matching between applications

If you try to mix a color in Photoshop using the same RGB values as a color used in another application, you probably won't be able to achieve an exact match because other applications use either the Windows Color Picker or Apple Color Picker (depending on the platform) to determine each R, G, and B component color value, whereas Photoshop, by default, uses its own color picker.

If you use the Windows or Apple color picker instead, the colors you mix using the RGB sliders on the Color palette in Photoshop will match colors used in other applications. To switch pickers, choose Edit (Photoshop, in OS X) > Preferences > General, choose Color Picker: Windows/Apple, then click OK. Remember to reset this preference to the Photoshop color picker when you're done.

1 *Use the* **File Info** *dialog box to modify the page title for your HTML file for display in the browser window, and/or to embed copyright information into your HTML file.*

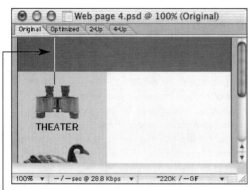

1 *Click with the **Type** tool to create an insertion point, then start typing.*

2 *The type is entered.*

As in Photoshop, type in ImageReady is entered directly on the image, and it can be styled using the options bar, the Character palette, or the Paragraph palette. To learn how to create type in ImageReady, read Chapter 17, "Type."

Furthermore, in ImageReady, as in Photoshop, type automatically appears on its own layer and remains editable until or unless you rasterize its layer. You can apply any layer effect or style to editable type and it will remain editable. When type is optimized in ImageReady, whether it's rasterized or not, it becomes bitmapped, like the overall image.

Some significant differences should be noted, though: Unlike type in Photoshop, type in ImageReady can't be created as a selection, converted to a work path, or converted to shapes.

To enter type in ImageReady:

1. Make sure the Original view is chosen for the image in the main window.

2. Choose the Type tool (T or Shift-T). T

Optional: On the options bar, click the Text orientation button ⊥ to switch the type's orientation.

3. Click in the image window where you want the type to start. A flashing insertion marker will appear **1**.

4. Create point or paragraph type (see pages 314–315) **2**.

Tips for creating online type

■ All type layer attributes and anti-aliasing options are preserved for editable or rasterized type when jumping a file between Photoshop and ImageReady.

■ Type in Photoshop or ImageReady can be anti-aliased. Since anti-aliasing works by adding colors to type edges, it also adds colors to a file's Color Table and slightly increases its storage size.

(Continued on the following page)

Type in ImageReady

Some people think small type should be anti-aliased if it's being created for on-screen output, but we think small type looks better aliased. Use ImageReady's preview features to decide for yourself.

■ To help make online type more legible, choose a larger point size for it than you would choose for print output.

Note: The same type size on a Web page will display differently on a Mac screen than on a Windows screen due to the ppi resolution difference between Mac OS and Windows monitors (72 for the former, 96 for the latter). Be sure to test your page(s) on both platforms.

■ You can toggle the Faux Bold or Faux Italic style on or off via ImageReady's Character palette menu. These type styles are designed for use with font families that lack a true bold or italic style. You'll also find an Underline option there for producing the Web convention of under-lined text links (these aren't the actual links, though!).

■ Remember to make your type colors Web-safe to prevent dithering. To make a color Web-safe in ImageReady, choose the Eyedropper tool, click on a type character in an optimized preview, then Web-shift the color using the Color Table palette (see page 452).

To make a non-Web-safe color Web-safe in Photoshop 7, double-click the T thumbnail on the type layer, then click the Color swatch on the options bar or the Character palette. In the Color Picker, either click the non-Web color alert icon 🔲 to have Photoshop substitute the closest Web-safe equivalent or check Only Web Colors, then click OK.

Mixed optimization

Hybrid images, which contain both continuous-tone imagery and flat-color areas (such as type), pose a special challenge **1**. You can use the slicing feature in Photoshop or ImageReady to frame off different areas of a hybrid image, and then apply a different optimization to each area. To facilitate slicing for mixed optimization, whenever possible, position type so it doesn't overlap any continuous-tone areas. Optimize type slices as GIF and continuous-tone areas as JPEG. (For more information about slicing, see pages 461–473.)

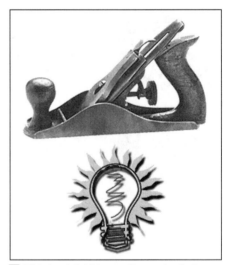

1 *This is a hybrid image: It contains both* **continuous-tone** *imagery and* **flat**-*color areas.*

Behind the scenes

In HTML, a table can be used as a grid system to control the layout of graphics and text on a Web page. Table cells can be coded to display separate images and data or portions of a large, sliced graphic. Frames function like separate windows within the larger browser window. A frame can display an HTML graphic, page, or site independently from the other frames on the same Web page. To learn more about HTML tables and frames, see:

Designing Web Graphics 3: *How to Prepare Images and Media for the Web* (New Riders Publishing) or ***Creative HTML Design 2:*** *A Hands-on Web Design Tutorial* (Pearson Education), both by Lynda Weinman

HTML 4 for the World Wide Web: *Visual QuickStart Guide (4th edition)* by Elizabeth Castro (Peachpit Press)

HTML & XHTML: *The Definitive Guide* by Chuck Musciano and Bill Kennedy (O'Reilly & Associates)

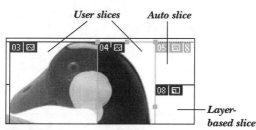

User slices   Auto slice

Layer-based slice

1 *All **three** types of **slices** can be combined in the same image. Every document starts out with a default auto slice that is the size of the entire image. It has a light gray label and is numbered "01."*

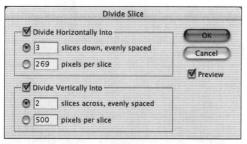

2 *Use the **Divide Slice** dialog box to divide an image into slices using a command, rather than manually.*

Slicing

Slicing is a process by which an image is divided into distinct **zones**. One purpose for slicing an image (especially a large one) is to enable it to download faster. A group of small slices will download more quickly than the whole, large image will. The browser assembles the slices into the overall image in sequence using HTML tables and frames.

There are three types of slices **1**:

- ■ Slices created using the **Slice** tool are called **user slices** (this page, and next).

- ■ **Layer-based slices** (page 463) resize automatically to include all visible pixels within the currently selected layer.

- ■ Whatever's left of the image after you've created user slices and/or layer-based slices, ImageReady will divide into **auto slices**. Auto slices have gray labels.

Slices can be created, selected, edited, and displayed in Photoshop or ImageReady, but we prefer to use ImageReady, since it offers more options for slicing. To show the Slice palette in ImageReady, choose Window > Slice or click the Palette toggle button on the Slice Select tool options bar. In Photoshop, click Slice Options on the Slice Select tool options bar to view the Slice Options dialog box.

To slice an image using a command:

1. In an image that contains just the default single slice, choose Slices (or right-click/Ctrl-click) > Promote to User Slice, then choose Slices > Divide Slice. Check Preview.

2. Check Divide Horizontally Into to create horizontal slices **2**, then enter the desired number of slices in the "slices down, evenly spaced" field, or enter the desired number of "pixels per slice" for the height of each horizontal slice. *and/or* Check Divide Vertically Into to create vertical slices, then enter the desired number of slices in the "slices across,

(Continued on the following page)

evenly spaced" field or enter the desired number of "pixels per slice" for the width of each vertical slice.

3. Click OK . A label will appear in the upper-left corner of each slice, bearing that slice number. Numbering begins at "01" and proceeds from left to right, and top to bottom.

TIP After the Divide command is used, all the slices will be selected. To highlight only one slice, choose the Slice Select tool, 〃 then click on that slice zone.

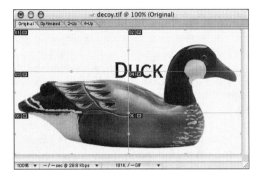

1 *An image divided into **six slices***

Using the Slice tool, you can control manually where the slice divisions occur. You can resize, reposition, or restack a user slice—but not an auto slice.

To slice an image manually:

1. Choose the Slice tool (K or Shift-K). 〃

2. Drag diagonally across part of the image to define the first slice **2**–**3**. A label with a number will appear in the upper-left corner of the slice zone, and a thin highlight (frame) with resizing handles will appear around the new slice. ImageReady will divide the rest of the image into auto slices.

3. *Optional:* Draw additional user slices with the Slice tool. Each new slice will be assigned a label and a number, and ImageReady will continue to redivide and renumber the rest of the image into auto slices as it sees fit.

2 *Drag to create a **slice** using the **Slice** tool.*

3 *A **new slice** is created.*

4. *Optional:* To divide a slice into smaller user slices, choose the Slice Select tool (K or Shift-K), 〃 click a user slice or auto slice to highlight it, choose Slices > Divide Slice, then click OK. Each new slice will be assigned its own number.

TIP A selected slice will display normally; a nonselected slice will be dimmed. In ImageReady, to adjust how light or dark a slice looks when it's highlighted, choose a different User Slices and/or Auto Slices percentage in the Color Adjustments area of Edit (ImageReady, in OS X) > Preferences > Slices **4**.

4 *A section of the **Slices Preferences** dialog box*

Manual Slicing

Plot your slices

To plot your slice areas before creating them, display the rulers (Ctrl-R/Cmd-R); drag guides from the rulers, releasing them where you want the slice borders to occur; then choose Slices > **Create Slices from Guides**. *Beware!* This command deletes all previous slices. Also, since guides always extend from edge to edge, you will be able to produce a checkerboard of similarly sized slices, but not a more irregular arrangement. You can resize the resulting slices by dragging handles on the slice border, or combine two or more selected slices by choosing Slices > Combine Slices, but this may be more laborious than using the Slice tool.

The borders between layer-based slices automatically update whenever you transform, move, or add layer effects to that layer. Layer-based slices are especially useful when creating rollovers that contain effects (such as a Drop Shadow) that could enlarge the layer.

To create a layer-based slice:

Choose a layer on the Layers palette, then choose Layer > New Layer Based Slice. Simple as that.

To convert an auto slice or a layer-based slice into a user slice:

1. Choose the Slice Select tool (K or Shift-K). ➤

2. Click the slice you want to convert.

3. Choose Slices > Promote to User Slice.

TIP For an auto slice, you can right-click/ Ctrl-click and choose Promote to User Slice.

To delete slices:

1. Choose the Slice Select tool (K or Shift-K). ➤

2. To delete one slice, click on it; to delete multiple slices, Shift-click all the slices you want to delete. Then choose Delete Slice(s) from the Slices menu or the Slice palette menu, or press Backspace/ Delete.
   or
   To delete all the slices in an image, choose Slices > Delete All.

Layer-Based Slices; Delete Slices

If you make a user slice smaller, ImageReady will automatically generate and renumber the surrounding auto slices to fill in the exposed gaps.

If a slice is enlarged, it may obscure slices behind it. You can manually remove any of the hidden slices. Don't worry, though—when you save an optimized file, any overlapping slice frames or table cells are eliminated. To see what's hiding behind a slice, you can use any of the buttons for restacking slices on the Slice Select tool options bar to assist you.

To resize user slices:

1. Choose the Slice Select tool. Slice borders will automatically display.

2. Click the user slice you want to resize.

3. Drag a side handle to resize the slice along one axis or drag a corner handle to resize along two axes **2**–**3**.

Hide/show slice borders and labels

In ImageReady, click the **Slice Visibility** button on the Toolbox **1** (or press "Q") to toggle between hiding and showing slices. In ImageReady or Photoshop, hide or show slices using View > **Show** > **Slices**.

Hide slices

1 *The Slice Visibility button on the Toolbox*

2 *To resize a user slice, drag a handle using the Slice Select tool.*

3 *The auto slices around the resized slice will reconfigure automatically.*

Join forces

To combine multiple auto slices or user slices into one larger slice, select two or more slices, then choose Slices > **Combine Slices**. The resulting single user slice will have the dimensions of the smallest rectangle that could surround all the selected slices.

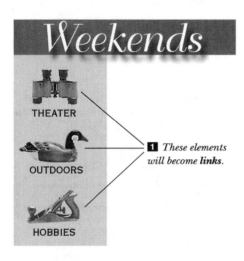

1 *These elements will become **links**.*

2 *A **slice** is created for each element that will become a **link**.*

You can attach a URL link to a slice on a Web page. When that slice is clicked on by a Web viewer, the viewer is taken automatically to the Web page that's associated with that URL address. Slices with links are usually created over prominent or conspicuous graphic elements (buttons, words, or icons) so the viewer can identify them easily.

In ImageReady, you can create multiple slices in a single image, and you can assign a different URL address to each slice. Using slices to define all the links in an image eliminates the need to create, align, or resize multiple image layers.

To slice an image into multiple links:

1. Open or create an image that contains imagery that you want to use as links. Commonly used link elements include buttons, thumbnails, or icons **1**. A series of links arranged in a column or row is called a "navigation bar."

2. Choose the Slice tool (K or Shift-K). 🖊

3. Drag diagonally to create a slice over each individual portion of the image that you want to become a link **2**.

4. Choose the Slice Select tool (K or Shift-K). 🖊

5. Click on a slice. The selected slice will display as a thumbnail on the Slice palette. (Choose Window > Slice if the palette isn't displayed.)

6. Enter the destination Web address in the URL field **3**.

7. *Optional:* The Target info tells the browser which HTML frame to load the link contents into and which existing HTML frames to preserve. The Target field becomes available when information

(Continued on the following page)

Slice into Multiple Links

Animation	Image Map	‡ Slice		
	Type:	Image		BG: None
THEATER	Name:	Web page 4_03		
03 — GIF	URL:	http://www.cityfun.com/weekends/theater		
	Target:			

3 *Enter the destination Web address in the **URL** field.*

is entered into the URL field. Press Tab to move to this area of the palette, then choose one of the following from the drop-down menu: _blank to have a new browser window open for the link contents; _self to have the new link contents load into the HTML frame for the current slice; _parent to have the new link contents replace the current HTML frames; and _top to have the new link contents load into the entire browser window (this is similar to the _parent option).

8. Repeat steps 5–7 for any other slices you want to designate as links.

TIP If the image has only one slice (the default auto slice for the image), you can attach a link address to the entire image via the URL field on the Slice palette.

Overlapping slices are displayed and numbered based on the order in which they were created. You can rearrange the stacking order of user slices and layer-based slices at any time.

To change the stacking position of a slice:

1. Choose the Slice Select tool (K or Shift-K), 🔪 then click the slice whose stacking order you want to change **1**.

2. Click a stacking order button on the options bar (unavailable stacking options will be dimmed) **2**–**3**.

By aligning user slices along a common edge or distributing them evenly along the same axis, you can create smaller HTML files that will download more quickly. You can't align or distribute layer-based slices, because their position is tied to their layers.

To align user slices along a common edge:

1. Choose the Slice Select tool, 🔪 then Shift-click the slices you want to align.

2. Click one of the six alignment buttons in the options bar **4**. The slices will align—not the imagery inside them!

1 *Slice #13 is behind other slices.*

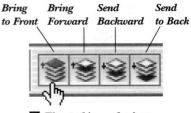
2 *The **stacking order** buttons on the **Slice Select** tool options bar*

3 *Slice #13 has become slice #06, and is now in **front** of the slices around it.*

4 *To align multiple slices, click an **alignment** button on the **Slice Select** tool options bar.*

1 *Click a **distribution** button on the **Slice Select** tool options bar.*

2 *This image, because it contains overlapping elements, is a good candidate for coding as an **image map** using the Layer Options palette.*

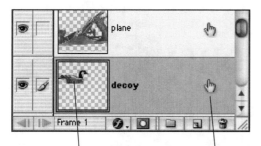

3 ***Pixel areas** (not transparent areas) will become **hotspots** for the **image map**.*

4 *After the **URL** address is entered on the Image Map palette, a **hand** icon appears near the layer name, indicating the presence of a link.*

5 *Choose a **Shape** and enter the **URL** address on the **Image Map** palette.*

To evenly distribute user slices along a common axis:

1. Choose the Slice Select tool (K or Shift-K), ☞ then Shift-click the slices you want to distribute.

2. Click one of the six distribution buttons on the options bar **1**.

An image map is an image that contains designated hotspots, each with its own URL link **2**. Use this method if your hotspot shape is nonrectangular, or if you'd rather use a single image file instead of the multiple files that slices would require.

ImageReady lets you create layer-based or tool-based image maps. A layer-based map, which includes any nontransparent pixel areas in a layer, is automatically updated whenever you edit that layer. Tool-based maps can be aligned to a common edge or distributed along a common axis. You can also duplicate a tool-based map's dimensions and settings. It's easy to change a layer-based map to a tool-based one.

To create a layer-based image map:

1. On the Layers palette, choose a layer that contains transparent areas **3**.

2. Choose Layer > New Layer Based Image Map Area. A rectangular image map will surround the layer's nontransparent areas.

3. From the Shape pop-up menu on the Image Map palette, choose a shape for the hotspot (Rectangle, Circle, or Polygon) **5**.

4. Enter a URL address (including the "http://" prefix). A hand icon will appear to the right of the layer name on the Layers palette **4**.

5. *Optional:* The Target info tells which HTML frame to load the link contents into and which existing HTML frames to preserve. The Target field becomes available once a URL is entered.

(Continued on the following page)

6. *Optional:* In the Alt field, enter the word or words you want displayed if the user's Web browser doesn't display images (see page 473).

7. Repeat steps 1–6 for any other layers.

TIP You can change an image map's shape by choosing the Image Map Select tool (P or Shift-P), 🖑 clicking the image map, then choosing from the Shape pop-up menu on the Image Map palette.

TIP When using a Polygon, you can adjust how tightly the image map follows the image's outline using the Quality field or slider.

To create a tool-based image map:

1. Choose the Rectangle Image Map, 🖑 Circle Image Map, 🖑 or Polygon Image Map 🖑 tool (P or Shift-P).

2. Draw a rectangle or circle over an area in the image window. (Shift-drag to create a square. Alt-drag/Option-drag to draw a rectangle or circle from its center.)
or
Create a straight-sided polygon by clicking on a starting point, then clicking for each subsequent corner until you surround the area. Double-click anywhere, and the shape will close automatically **2**.

3. Enter a URL address (including the "http://" prefix) on the Image Map palette.

4. *Optional:* The Image Map palette's Target field identifies into which HTML frame the link contents will be loaded and which existing HTML frames will be preserved (see page 466). The Target field becomes available once you enter a URL.

5. *Optional:* In the Image Map palette's Alt field, enter the word or words you want displayed if the user's Web browser doesn't display images.

6. Repeat steps 1–5 for any other image maps you want to create.

Sidebar (right column):

Client or server?

ImageReady codes an image map in HTML either as **client-side** or **server-side**. To choose between these two options, choose File > Output Settings > Image Maps, then click an option in the Type area **1**.

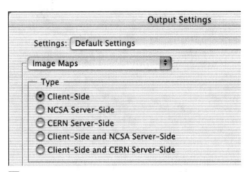

1 *Click a Type option in the Output Settings dialog box.*

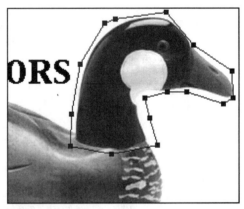

2 *Double-click to have a shape close automatically.*

Margin (left side): **Tool-Based Image Map**

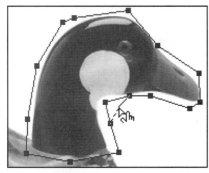

1 *You can enter exact dimensions for an* **image map** *on the options bar.*

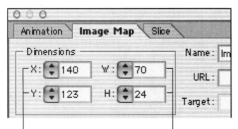

2 *Image map* **location**   *Image map* **dimensions**

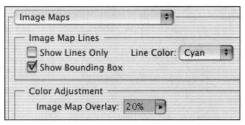

3 *You can* **resize** *an image map* **manually.**

4 *The* **Image map visibility** *button on the Toolbox*

TIP To specify the exact dimensions of a rectangle or circle before you draw it, check Fixed Size on the options bar, then enter Width and Height values **1**.

TIP To precisely reposition a rectangle or circle after you draw it, change the X and Y values on the Image Map palette. To resize the image map, change the W and H values **2**, or choose the Image Map Select tool, then drag any of the handles on the image map **3**.

To change an image map from layer based to tool based:

1. Choose the Image Map Select tool (P or Shift-P), then click the layer-based image map you want to convert.

2. From the Image Map palette menu, choose Promote Layer Based Image Map Area.

To hide/show image maps:

To toggle between the hide and show settings, click the "Image Map visibility" button on the Toolbox **4** or press "A".
or
Choose View > Show > Image Maps.

TIP You can change the display characteristics for image maps (such as whether the line and/or the bounding box are visible) in Edit (ImageReady menu, in OS X) > Preferences > Image Maps **5**.

5 *The* **Image Maps Preferences** *pane in ImageReady*

Layer to Tool-Based Image Map; Hide/Show

To select an image map:

1. Make sure the image maps are visible and choose the Image Map Select tool (P or Shift-P). 🖑

2. Click an image map in the image window (Shift-click to select more than one image map, if desired).

To delete an image map:

Select an image map, then press Backspace/Delete.

or

From the Image Map palette menu, choose Delete Image Map Area.

By aligning tool-based image maps along a common edge or distributing them evenly along the same axis, it's possible to create smaller HTML files that will download more quickly. You can't align or distribute layer-based image maps because their position is tied to their layers.

To align tool-based image maps along a common edge:

1. Choose the Image Map Select tool (P or Shift-P), 🖑 then Shift-click the image maps you want to align.

2. Click one of the six alignment icons on the options bar.

To evenly distribute tool-based image maps along a common axis:

1. Choose the Image Map Select tool (P or Shift-P), 🖑 then Shift-click the image maps you want to distribute.

2. Click one of the six distribution buttons on the options bar **1**.

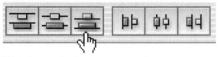

1 *Select multiple image maps, then click a* **distribution** *button on the* **Image Map Select** *tool options bar.*

Select, Delete, Align, Distribute Image Maps

1 *The continuous-tone element (the plane) in this **hybrid** image should be optimized as a **JPEG**; the vector element (lightbulb) should be optimized as a **GIF**.*

2 *Drag the **Droplet** icon from the **Optimize** palette over any unselected slice.*

If the image you're working with is a hybrid, meaning it contains both sharp-edged elements (e.g., type or linework) and continuous-tone areas, try to draw a slice around each of those areas. Then you can optimize each slice separately using settings that are appropriate for that type of imagery **1**.

To optimize an individual slice:

1. Choose the Slice Select tool (K or Shift-K).

2. Click a slice.

3. Choose Optimize palette settings. Use the GIF format to optimize sharp-edged areas; use the JPEG format to optimize continuous-tone areas.

TIP If you select two or more slices that have different Optimize palette settings, the palette will display only the settings that are shared by the selected slices. If you change any of the available settings, however, the new settings will apply to all the currently selected slices.

TIP If you later decide you want to optimize all the slices the same way, choose the Slice Select tool, choose Select > All Slices, then choose settings on the Optimize palette. If you choose Select > Deselect Slices, the Optimize palette will go blank.

This technique for copying optimization settings is speedy and efficient.

To copy optimization settings from one slice to another:

1. Choose the Slice Select tool (K or Shift-K).

2. Click a slice that has the desired optimization settings.

3. Drag the droplet icon from the Optimize palette over any unselected slice. The current palette settings will be applied to that slice **2**.

When user slices are linked, they automatically share the same optimization settings. Linked slices that are optimized in the GIF format also share the same Color Table and dither pattern, which helps to disguise any edge seams.

To link slices:

1. Choose the Slice Select tool (K or Shift-K).

2. Click a slice, then Shift-click one or more additional slices **1**.

3. Right-click/Ctrl-click and choose Link Slice, or choose Slices > Link Slices. The linked slices will now have their own label color **2**.

TIP To add a slice to an already linked set, select the slice you want to add, plus all the slices in the set, then choose Slices > Link Slices.

1 *Three slices are **selected**.*

To unlink slices:

To unlink one slice, click on it with the Slice Select tool (K or Shift-K), then right-click/Ctrl-click and choose Unlink Slice, or choose Slices > Unlink Slice.
or
To unlink a set of slices, click one of the slices in the set with the Slice Select tool, then right-click/Ctrl-click and choose Unlink Set, or choose Slices > Unlink Set.
or
To unlink all the slices in an image, then right-click/Ctrl-click and choose Unlink All, or choose Slices > Unlink All.

Note: Auto slices created by ImageReady are already linked. If you unlink an auto slice, it will become a user slice.

2 *The **linked** slices share the same label color.*

Older, nongraphic Web browsers (or any browser for which the Show Pictures preference is turned off) will display text but no Web graphics. In order to display an image as a generic icon with text for browsers that can't or won't display graphics, Web designers attach a unique HTML Alt tag to each graphic. Then, if the image displays in the browser only as the Alt tag text, any attached URL links will still link the viewer to the designated site. Alt tags also help visually impaired people use text browsers that "speak" the link. Here's how to attach an Alt tag to a slice in ImageReady.

To attach an Alt tag to a slice or to an entire image:

1. Show the Slice palette. If the expanded palette isn't displayed, keep double-clicking the palette tab until the full palette displays.

2. *Optional:* Click a slice using the Slice Select tool (K or Shift-K).

3. In the Alt field on the Slice palette, enter the word or words that you want to substitute for the image **1**.

1 *In the **Alt** field on the **Slice** palette, enter the word or words that you want to substitute for the image.*

Rollovers

Now that you understand something about slices, you're ready to create another kind of hotspot: a **rollover**. A rollover is a screen event that occurs when the mouse is moved over or clicks on an area of a Web page that has a built-in modification. Rollovers are like the voice of a Web page, causing a visual change in the dynamic parts of a page, and they make Web pages more entertaining. Three basic types of rollovers can be created:

- A **change** in an image area (e.g., a color changes, a layer effect appears)

- The **substitution** of one image for another

- Text or a **secondary** graphic that appears in another area of the browser window (when the mouse is over a button, keyword, or icon)

To create a rollover, first you need to divide the image into slices. (So go back and read the slice section first—no cheating!) In ImageReady, rollovers are created using the Rollovers palette, and by displaying and hiding layers on the Layers palette. That's all a rollover really does—it turns the layers that contain visual changes on or off, as per your built-in instructions. (To create a rollover using a layer effect, see page 477. To create a secondary rollover, see page 481.)

To create a rollover for a slice:

1. Select a layer, choose the Slice tool (K or Shift-K), ✎ then marquee the area to be used for the rollover.

2. If the imagery you want to use for the rollover is not already on its own layer, choose Select > Create Selection from Slice, then choose Layer > New > Layer via Copy (Ctrl-J/Cmd-J).
   or
   If the imagery in the slice is already on a separate layer, duplicate that layer now via the Layers palette.

3. Leave both the new layer and its associated slice selected.

Three basic rollovers

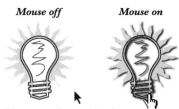

Mouse off   *Mouse on*

The image **changes** *(in this case, a Drop Shadow layer effect appears).*

Mouse off

Mouse on

A **new image** *is substituted for the current image.*

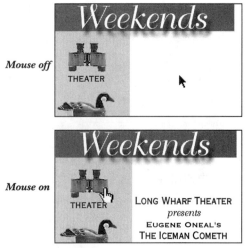

Mouse off

Mouse on

Secondary *text (or an image) appears in another area of the image.*

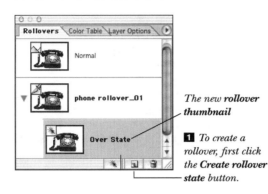

*The new **rollover thumbnail***

1 *To create a rollover, first click the **Create rollover state** button.*

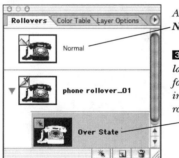

2 *To change a rollover state, double-click its thumbnail, then choose an option in the **Rollover State Options** dialog box.*

*An image in the **Normal** rollover state*

3 *A duplicate layer was inverted for the same image in the **Over** rollover state.*

4 *When the **Over** thumbnail is chosen, the **inverted** layer becomes **visible** and the **normal** layer is **hidden**.*

4. Click the Rollovers tab to display the *7.0!* Rollovers palette. The currently selected slice will appear as a thumbnail on the palette.

5. Click the "Create rollover state" button ◼ at the bottom of the Rollovers palette **1**. A rollover state will appear as a new thumbnail on the palette.

6. *Optional:* ImageReady automatically assigns a rollover state to thumbnails in this default sequence: Over, Down, Click. If you want to override this default sequence, double-click the new rollover *7.0!* thumbnail, and in the Rollover State Options dialog box, choose the rollover state that you want to be the initiator (triggering event) for the rollover you'll create in the remaining steps **2**.

Over: The mouse must be over the slice area, but not pressed down.

Down: The mouse button must be down when it's over the slice. Some Web designers like to have a special graphic display for the mouse button down.

Click: The mouse must be clicked (button pressed and released) when it's over the slice. A click will cause the browser to attempt to link to any URL that's attached to the slice.

Click OK.

7. Modify the imagery on the separate or duplicate layer (that was created in step 2) to make it look different from the original layer. Suggestions: Invert the layer's color or luminosity (Image > Adjustments > Invert) **3**; apply a texture or distort filter to the layer; change the layer's hue or saturation (see also the sidebar on the next page); or paste in new imagery. The imagery on the original layer won't change.

8. On the Layers palette, leave the duplicate layer showing and hide the original layer from which the duplicate was created **4**. The new rollover state

(Continued on the following page)

Create a Rollover

Create a Rollover

should still be selected on the Rollovers palette. Then select the Normal state on the Rollovers palette, hide the duplicate layer, and show the original layer on the Layers palette.

9. Click back and forth between the Normal and rollover thumbnails on the Rollovers palette, and compare them in the main window. The Rollovers palette tracks which layers are visible or hidden, as well as other changes on the Layers palette, as each rollover thumbnail is selected. Make sure the correct layers are visible or hidden for each Rollover state.

For a more realistic preview, you can click the Preview in Default Browser button on the Toolbox. Or try Image-Ready's preview function (see page 480). Roll the mouse over or click where the rollover is to see the effect.

Beware! Always take note of which thumbnail is currently selected on the Rollovers palette as you modify a layer. Each thumbnail should have, and produce, a different look. Rollover effects created via painting, filters, transformations, or substitute imagery require separate layers for each state. In order to display each rollover state, you'll need to hide or show the different layers.

TIP Choose Palette Options from the Rollovers palette menu to choose a Thumbnail Size for the Rollovers palette.

TIP To create a rollover in which supplemental imagery is added to an existing image, create new imagery on a duplicate or additional layer, making sure to match the size and location of the imagery on the original layer –. In this case, the original layer should always remain visible.

7.0!

TIP To display an image's animations, slices, and image maps on the Rollovers palette, choose Palette Options from the palette menu, check "Include Slices and Image Maps" and check "Include Animation Frames," then click OK.

More rollover ideas

Here are some further suggestions for modifying a **duplicate** layer (step 7 on page 475):

To produce a rollover in which imagery enlarges and contracts, scale the duplicate layer up a bit using Edit > Transform > Scale, or use Filter > Blur > Radial Blur to stretch the shape **1**–**2**, or use Filter > Distort > Pinch (with a negative Amount) to bulge it out **3**.

To make a button or image area look like it's flipping, use Edit > Transform > Flip Horizontal or Flip Vertical (see the ducky on page 474).

1 *The **original** button*

2 *After applying the **Radial Blur** filter*

Since this button changes sizes for a rollover, it is a good choice for a layer-based slice. The slice will resize based on the largest area of imagery on the layer.

3 *After applying the **Pinch** filter to the original image (negative Amount)*

4 *An image in the **Normal** rollover state*

5 *In the **Over** rollover state, a layer with a hand-drawn glow effect has become visible below the bulb layer.*

1 *The image in the Normal rollover state*

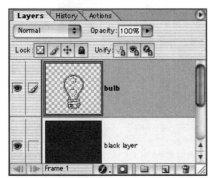

2 *Choose a layer that contains some transparent areas.*

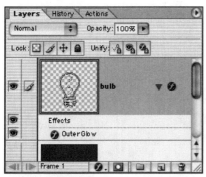

3 *The image in the Over rollover state: An Outer Glow effect that was added to the layer becomes visible on the Layers palette...*

4 *...and on the image.*

A great advantage to using layer effects to produce a rollover is that you don't have to duplicate a layer to achieve a visible change between rollover states because different layer effects can be applied to (or turned off for) the same layer for each rollover state.

To create a rollover using a layer effect:

1. Choose the Slice Select tool, 𝕊 then click a slice.

2. Click the "Create rollover state" button 🔳 at the bottom of the Rollovers palette.

3. Double-click the new rollover thumbnail and choose a rollover state.

4. Display the Layer Options palette.

5. Choose a layer that has transparent areas **1**–**2**.

6. Choose and apply an effect from the "Add layer style" pop-up menu at the bottom of the Layers palette. 🔘 Try Inner Shadow to recolor the inner edges of the layer image or Outer Glow to recolor the area behind the layer imagery.

7. The Layer Options palette will now show options for the layer effect you just chose. To intensify an effect, increase the Size, Distance, Depth, or Intensity. If you're using the Bevel and Emboss effect to make a button look convex, click the opposite option on the Effects palette (e.g., Up versus Down) to reverse the lighting direction and make the rollover version look concave (see page 495). Try the Color Fill effect at a low opacity to apply a tint and enhance a concave effect.

8. Preview the rollover (instructions on page 480).

TIP ImageReady's Styles palette contains predefined layer effects or combinations of effects that you can use (see page 497).

TIP A layer effect will only be visible on the Layers palette **3** (and on the image **4**) when the rollover state thumbnail that it's assigned to is selected.

TIP To remove an effect, see page 496.

7.0!

The Create layer-based rollover button automatically makes the current layer a layer-based slice and creates a new rollover state using that slice. *Note:* The only way you can produce changes between rollover states when producing a rollover this way is by using layer effects.

To create a layer-based rollover:

1. Choose a layer (not the Background).

2. Click the "Create layer-based rollover" button ✹ at the bottom of the Rollovers palette. An icon that indicates the slice is layer-based ➷ will display next to the layer name on the Rollovers palette, and an icon indicating that the layer contains a layer-based slice ✐ will appear for the layer on the Layers palette.

7.0!

Normally, changes made to the active layer affect only the current rollover state or animation frame. ImageReady 7's new Match command and Unify buttons, however, let you control whether changes will be applied in the active layer's position, visibility, style, or a combination thereof, to the image's other states or frames. The Match command lets you control which frames the changes are applied to, while the Unify buttons apply them to all the states or frames. Both features are major time-savers when you need to unify a variety of layer-based effects across a rollover or animation. These features replace the Animation palette's Match Layer Across Frames command.

Beware! Any preexisting layer style effects are deleted when the Match command is chosen.

To use the Match command to apply attributes from the current layer:

1. Choose a state on the Rollovers palette **1**, and the layer you want to change on the Layers palette **2**. Add effects to the layer or change its visibility.

2. Choose Layer > Match or choose Match from the Layers palette menu (Ctrl-M/Cmd-M).

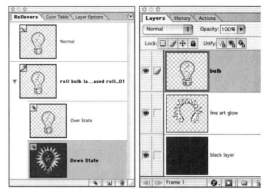

1 *Choose a rollover **state**…* **2** *…then choose the **layer** to be changed. We want a glow effect and the black layer to appear (match up) on all our states.*

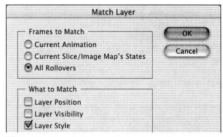

3 *In the **Match Layer** dialog box, choose which frames and characteristics you want matched.*

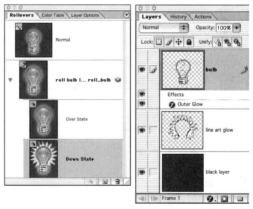

4 *We applied a glow layer style to the Down state, then used Match to apply the layer style to other states. We next selected the "black layer" and used Match again to apply layer visibility to other states. We didn't make the "line art glow" layer visible in the other states.*

Layer-Based Rollover; Match

Layer position *Layer visibility* *Layer style*

1 *The **Unify** buttons on ImageReady's **Layers** palette*

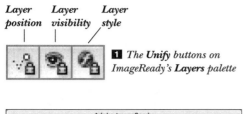

2 *This alert box will appear, asking if you want to match an attribute from the current layer.*

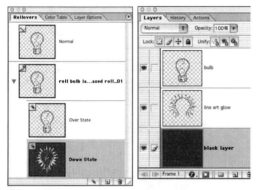

3 *To unify what's visible in one state with all the rollover states, we chose the Down state from the **Rollovers** palette and the "black layer" from the **Layers** palette.*

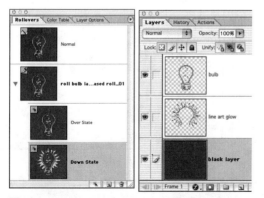

4 *After clicking the **Unify: Layer visibility** button for the selected "black layer" on the Layers palette, that layer became visible in all the rollover states.*

3. Click which frames you want matched, check what you want matched (layer position, visibility, style), then click OK (**3**, previous page).

4. The changes will automatically be applied to all the other rollover states or animation frames (**4**, previous page).

TIP If you make further changes to the original layer, reapply the Match command to reapply the new changes to the other states or frames.

Beware! Any preexisting layer style effects are deleted when the Unify command is chosen.

To use the Unify buttons to apply changes from the active layer: 7.0!

1. Click the state you want to use on the Rollovers palette and the layer you want to change on the Layers palette.

2. Click one, two, or all three of the Unify buttons on the Layers palette **1**.

3. Depending on your choice, a dialog box will appear **2**, asking if you want to match the current layer's position, visibility, style, or a combination thereof with the other rollover states and animation frames. Click Match to unify those states or frames with any future changes in the current layer **3**–**4**.

TIP To turn off a Unify command, choose the layer, then click the highlighted button again.

TIP To automatically apply any changes in the Normal state or Frame 1 to all the other states or frames, choose Propagate Frame 1 Changes from the Layers palette menu.

Unify

You can preview a rollover within ImageReady or, if you prefer, stick with the tried-and-true Web browser-based preview. Take ya pick.

To preview a rollover in ImageReady:

1. Click the Preview Document button 🖑 on the Toolbox (Y).

2. Move your cursor over the image within the image window to see the rollover in action. To stop the action, click the Preview Document button again.

To preview a rollover in a Web browser:

1. Save your ImageReady file.

2. Choose a currently installed browser from the File > Preview in submenu.
or
Click the Preview in Default Browser button 🖉 on the Toolbox (Ctrl-Alt-P/Cmd-Option-P).

3. In the browser, roll the mouse over (Over), press the mouse down on (Down), or click on (Click) the area of the image that contains the rollover.

Note: You can verify a URL address of an image map even if you're not currently online. Pass the mouse over the image map area, and the attached URL address will appear at the bottom of the browser window.

Note: You won't be able to preview the Down state in any pre-4.0 browser version of Navigator or Explorer. In these earlier browser versions, the mouse action will open a browser context menu instead.

The slice name matches the slice number (see █ 1, next page).

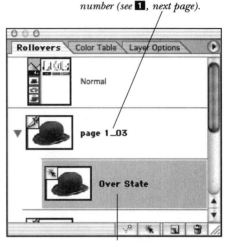

█ 1 *When the **Over** thumbnail is selected...*

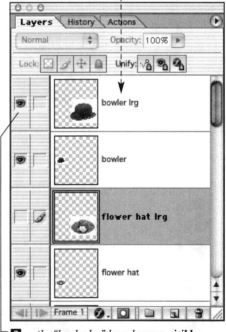

█ 2 *...the "bowler lrg" layer becomes **visible**.*

1 *For this layout, we created a column of small images and then sliced each one of them* **individually**. *A larger version of each slice image was used as a separate* **secondary** *rollover image.*

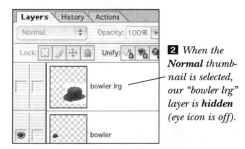

2 *When the* **Normal** *thumbnail is selected, our "bowler lrg" layer is* **hidden** *(eye icon is off).*

3 *In the final layout, the secondary* **rollover image** *is* **hidden** *for the Normal state.*

In a secondary rollover, as the viewer moves the mouse over a keyword, image, or icon, supplementary text or a supplementary image appears. When the viewer moves the mouse away from the keyword or image, the supplementary info disappears. Using secondary rollovers helps to reduce visual clutter because it reduces how much text or how many images initially appear on a Web page.

To create a secondary rollover:

1. Create a new layer, then create the supplementary image or text on that layer.
   or
   Use Copy and Paste or drag-and-drop to create a new layer, then edit the image on that new layer.

2. Choose the Move tool, then drag the layer imagery to the correct location relative to the overall image **1**.

3. Choose the Slice tool (K or Shift-K).

4. Draw a new slice over part of an image to become the Normal rollover state. The slice will appear as a new thumbnail on both the Slice and Rollovers palettes.

5. Click the "Create rollover state" button **⬓** at the bottom of the Rollovers palette. A copy of the current slice will appear as a new thumbnail on the palette.

6. With the new Over state on the Rollovers palette still selected, make the secondary image layer visible on the Layers palette (**1**–**2**, previous page).

7. Click the Normal rollover state thumbnail (or the thumbnail the rollover state is nested in), and make sure the new secondary image layer is hidden for that state **2**–**3**. *Don't* hide the layer that contains the image in the original slice zone the mouse will be rolling over. This layer should be visible for all the states.

To create a button for a Web page:

1. Click the Normal state on the Rollovers palette.

2. Choose a shape tool: Rectangle, Rounded Rectangle, or Ellipse (U or Shift-U).

3. On the shape tool options bar, click the Create New Shape Layer button.

4. Choose a Foreground color, then drag diagonally to draw a shape . The shape will appear on its own layer automatically. Add a text layer, if desired.

5. *Optional:* To quickly apply a predefined rollover effect to the button, display the Styles palette, choose Rollover Buttons from the Styles palette menu, then click Replace when asked if you want to replace the current styles. Click on any of the listed styles, and the Rollovers palette will automatically display all that style's button states and generate the necessary slices . You can also drag a style name or swatch from the Styles palette over the button layer on the Layers palette or over the shape in the main window.

Note: If you apply a predefined layer effect that already has rollover states, a layer-based slice will be applied automatically to your shape. In this case, skip to step 7.

6. Choose the Slice tool, then draw a slice around the new button for the Normal rollover state. The new slice will appear as a thumbnail on both the Slice and Rollovers palettes.

7. Follow steps 3–9, starting on page 474, to create a rollover using the button .

1 *The new* ***shape***

2 *Styles for the button's* ***Normal****,* ***Over****, and* ***Down*** *states are automatically created using a predefined rollover button style from the* ***Styles*** *palette.*

3 *If none of the button styles suits your needs, you can* ***build your own buttons*** *using the Rollovers and Layers palettes.*

GIF animations

In a GIF animation, multiple image frames play back in a user-specified sequence. Animated effects that you can create for a Web page include text or graphics that move, fade in or out, or change in some other way.

To produce an animation in ImageReady, you'll create multiple image frames via the Animation palette. Then you'll modify individual layers via the Layers palette for each frame (each frame has its own unique Layers palette setup). And finally, you'll save the sequence of frames as a single GIF file—ready for online viewing.

In this QuickStart Guide, we provide the instructions for creating two basic animation effects: moving a layer element and fading a layer element in or out. Once you've mastered the basics, you'll be ready to try more complex animation projects.

The Animation palette

The currently selected frame

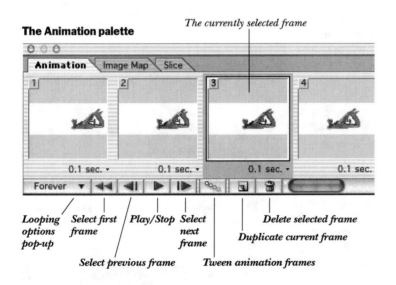

To move layer imagery across an image via animation:

1. Open or create an image that has a Background, and a layer that contains imagery silhouetted on transparency (see pages 108 and 227–231) **1**.

2. Display the Animation palette (click the Animation tab or choose Window > Animation).

3. Choose a layer on the Layers palette.

4. Choose the Move tool and drag the layer element to one side of the main window **2**. The current thumbnail on the Animation palette will update to reflect this new position.

5. Click the "Duplicate current frame" button at the bottom of the Animation palette. **3** The Duplicate frame should now be selected. The layer chosen for step 3 should still be selected.

6. Choose the Move tool (V), then drag the layer element to the opposite side of the main window **3**. The current thumbnail on the Animation palette will update to reflect this change **4**. Leave this layer selected!

7. Click the Tween button on the Animation palette. (Tweening adds frames in between selected frames.)

8. Click Layers: **All Layers** to copy pixels from all layers to the new frames—even layers that weren't modified (**1**, next page). (Also choose this option to record changes that occur simultaneously in two or more layers.) Or click **Selected Layer** to copy pixels from only the currently selected layer to the new frames. All other layers will be hidden.
and
Check which layer **Parameters** the in-between frames will modify: Position, Opacity, and/or Effects (more about layer effects on page 495).
and

Move Layer Imagery Via Animation

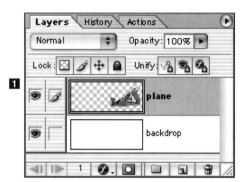

2 *Drag the layer element to one* **side** *of the main window.*

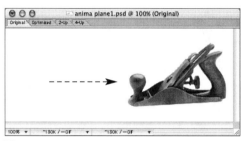

3 *Drag the same layer element to the* **opposite** *side of the main window for the* **duplicate** *animation frame.*

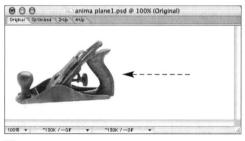

4 *The* **original** *(start) and* **duplicate** *(end) frames*

More animation options

■ Click, then Shift-click, to **select** a range of frames. Drag to **move** one frame or a selected range of frames.

■ To flatten each frame into a layer, choose **Flatten Frames into Layers** from the Animation palette menu. Any preexisting layers will remain.

■ To reverse the frame sequence, choose **Reverse Frames** from the Animation palette menu. This is equivalent to playing the animation backward.

Tween it again

To redo a tween, modify the sequence's start and end frames, Shift-click to select all the frames that were added by the tween, then click the Tween button. You could also delete all the tweened frames and redo the whole tween operation.

From the **Tween with** pop-up menu, choose to add the in-between frames between the currently selected frame and the Previous Frame. (*Note:* If you select two or more frames before opening the Tween dialog box, only the Selection option will be available on this pop-up menu.)
and
Via the **Frames to Add** arrows or field, specify how many frames are to be added in total (1–100). The greater the number of frames, the smoother (less choppy) the animation, but also the larger the file size and the longer its download time.

9. Click OK **2**. Now preview the animation (see page 487).

TIP You can use an editable or rasterized type layer for an animation. You can make type fade in or out or move across the image, or use it in any other layer animation effect.

TIP If you want your animations to download and play back quickly, keep them small in pixel size (approximately 200 by 200 pixels or less).

1 *Use the* **Tween** *command to add* **in-between frames** *to an animation.*

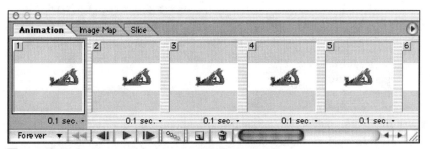

2 *The* **Animation** *palette after* **tweening***. When the animation is played back, the layer element moves smoothly from one side of the main window to the other.*

Move Layer Imagery Via Animation

485

To make imagery fade in or out:

In order to make stationary or moving imagery fade in or out on a Web page, you'll need to adjust the opacity of the imagery instead of, or in addition to, its position. Follow the instructions starting on page 484, but choose an Opacity value (and position, if desired) for the starting layer for step 4 **1**, then choose an Opacity value (and position, if desired) for the ending layer for step 6 **2**. Make sure Opacity is checked in the Tween dialog box (step 8) **3**.

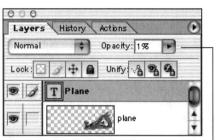

1 *The **Opacity** setting on the Layers palette for the **first** animation frame*

To remove frames from an animation:

To remove one frame from an animation, click the frame, then choose Delete Frame from the Animation palette menu or drag the frame over the palette Delete button (this can be undone).

or

To delete the entire animation except for the first frame, choose Delete Animation from the Animation palette menu, then click Delete.

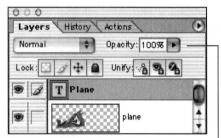

2 *The **Opacity** setting on the Layers palette for the **second** animation frame*

To choose options for animation playback:

Beware! Don't jump to or click on another program or choose Preview in (browser) while an animation is playing. If you do so, the animation will continue to play in the background and will steal processing time from the application you clicked on or jumped to.

Choose a **Looping** option from the pop-up menu in the lower-left corner of the Animation palette to specify whether the animation will play back Once or play back Forever (loop continuously) (**1**, next page). Or choose Other and enter the specific number of playback times for the animation, then click OK. Resist creating an endlessly looping animation—they're tedious to watch, and may turn off your Web viewers.

To specify how long an individual, selected frame will be displayed during playback,

3 *After tweening, the tool **moves** to the left and the word "Plane" **fades in**.*

What you can tween

An animation can include a change in a layer element's **position** (as in the steps on pages 484–485), a change in a layer's **opacity**, or a transition from one layer **effect** to another. Or you can simply tween between a layer effect that's turned **on** and the same effect turned **off**. Since these types of modifications are created via Layers palette options, they don't affect actual layer pixels. (The animation effect discussed on the next page does actually change layer pixels.)

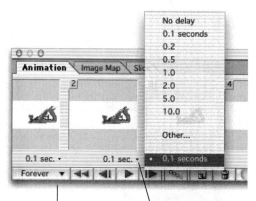

1 *Choose a looping option for the animation (Once or Forever).*

2 *The default frame delay time is No delay (0 seconds). You can choose a different delay time for any individual frame in the animation from the pop-up menu below that frame. A delay time of 0.1 seconds will be slightly slower than the default.*

choose a **delay value** from the Select frame delay time pop-up menu below the frame on the Animation palette **2**. Each frame can have a different delay setting. The "No delay" option is the equivalent of 0 seconds. You can also choose Other, enter a custom delay time (0–240 seconds), then click OK.

The looping and frame delay settings will save with the file and control the animation playback when the Web page is viewed in a browser.

To preview an animation:

1. Click the Original or Optimized tab in the main window.

2. If the first frame isn't selected, click the "Select first frame" button at the bottom of the Animation palette **3**.

3. Click the Play button **4**. The animation will play back at a slower-than-normal pace. (The ImageReady preview is slower than the realistic Preview in [browser]).

4. Click the square Stop button to stop the animation.

5. Save the file, then click the Preview in Default Browser button 🔳 on the Toolbox. Click back in ImageReady when you're finished previewing. If the animation won't play properly in the browser, see page 494.

TIP The Stop button only appears when an animation is playing, the Play button only when the action has stopped. **7.0!**

3 *Select first frame*   **4** *Play/Stop*

Preview an Animation

In these instructions, you'll learn how to make a layer element rock back and forth. This type of animation modifies actual pixels and is copied to all the existing frames. You'll be creating a duplicate layer for each incremental stage (rocking position) of the layer modification.

To create a rocking animation:

1. Open an image, and open the Animation palette.

2. Click the Duplicate current frame button ⬛ at the bottom of the Animation palette **1**. The Duplicate frame will now be selected.

3. Click the Tween button ◦◦◦ on the Animation palette, click Layers: All Layers, enter the desired number of Frames to Add to complete the animation, then click OK.

4. Click the animation frame where you want the rocking effect to start.

5. On the Layers palette, duplicate the layer that is to be animated.

6. On the duplicate layer, edit actual pixels (e.g., rotate the layer slightly, apply brush strokes, make color or tonal adjustments, or perform other modifications) **2**. Hide the original layer so you can see the change. The change will display inside the selected frame on the Animation palette. Reposition the imagery, if necessary.

7. Click the next animation frame (or click the Next frame button ▮▶ at the bottom of the Layers palette). Show the original layer and hide the duplicate, modified layer **3**.

8. Click the next consecutive frame. Show the duplicate, modified layer and hide the original, unmodified layer.

9. Continue to alternately hide, then show, the two layers for the remaining frames in the animation.

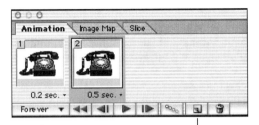

1 *Duplicate current frame*

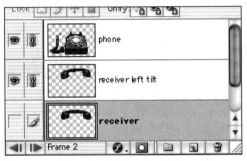

2 *The "receiver left tilt" layer is **visible** and the "receiver" layer is **hidden**. The handle rotates to the left.*

3 *Now the "receiver" layer is **visible** and the "receiver left tilt" layer is **hidden**.*

Create Rocking Animation

Re-editing

If you want to make an additional pixel edit (e.g., another transformation) to the original layer element, make yet another duplicate of that layer, and perform the edit on the new duplicate. Then, for one animation frame, show the original layer and hide the duplicates. For the next animation frame, show the first duplicate layer and hide the original and second duplicate. For the next animation frame, show the second duplicate layer and hide the original and first duplicate, and so on –.

| "Receiver left tilt" shows | "Receiver" shows | "Receiver right tilt" shows |

1 *The **animation sequence***

2 *For the animation sequence pictured above, three layers were used to create three positions for the receiver, and we made each layer visible in the order pictured.*

To edit an animation:

If you go back and change pixels on a layer (e.g., apply paint, adjust the color or luminosity, or perform a transformation), those modifications will be copied automatically to all the animation frames in which that layer is visible.

If you hide or show a layer; change a layer element's position, opacity, or blending mode; or change a layer effect for one frame, those changes won't be copied to any other frames because these types of edits are achieved via the Layers palette and don't actualy change pixels.

To copy changes in a layer's position, visibility, or style, use the new Match command (see pages 478–479) or use the Unify buttons in the Layers palette (see page 479).

Note: The Match command and Unify buttons remove any changes on the currently selected layer that were achieved through tweening. If you can't afford to lose such changes, edit your animation using the method described on the next page instead.

Since some of the Layers palette edits fall into the categories of the Parameters in the Tween dialog box (Position, Opacity, and Effects), you can also change those Parameters manually for individual frames at any time without affecting any other frames.

In these instructions, an animation is expanded by adding all or a part of the same animation in reverse. During playback, the animation will play forward and then backward in a smooth loop.

To make an existing animation reverse itself to the first frame:

1. Click the last frame on the Animation palette.
2. Click the Tween button.
3. Click Layers: All Layers; check all the Parameter boxes; choose Tween with: First Frame; then enter the desired number of Frames to Add.
4. Click OK.

7.0!

Follow these steps if you created an animation effect for a layer and have now decided you want to add another animation effect to a different layer.

To apply a second animation effect to an existing animation:

1. Choose or create the layer that you want to apply the second animation to.

2. On the Animation palette, click the frame where you want the new animation effect to start **1**.

3. For the start of this layer's animation sequence, position the layer imagery exactly where you want it, and adjust its opacity or effect(s), if desired **2**.

4. Click the frame where you want the new animation sequence to end.

5. For the end of this layer's animation sequence, modify the layer element's position or opacity, or remove or adjust any layer effects. Keep the layer selected!

6. If you chose the first and last animation frames for steps 2 and 4, respectively, choose Select All Frames from the Animation palette menu.
or
If you did *not* choose the first and last animation frames for steps 2 and 4, click the frame you chose for step 2, then Shift-click the frame you chose for step 4 to select a range of frames.

7. Click the Tween button on the Animation palette to tween without choosing options.
or
Choose Tween from the Animation palette menu, click Layers: Selected Layer, check the Parameters you've just modified (Position, Opacity, or Effects), then click OK **3**.

The secondary animation effect will develop incrementally within the range of frames you selected in the previous step. Any preexisting layer animation effects will be preserved.

1 *The **starting** frame for the second animation effect*

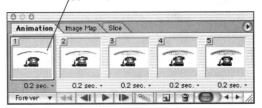

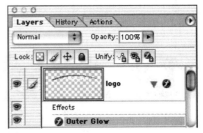

2 *The Invert command was applied to the "logo" layer to make the type white, and an Outer Glow effect was added.*

Outer Glow, 4% Opacity

A tweened frame in the middle

Outer Glow, 100% Opacity

3 *The completed **animation***

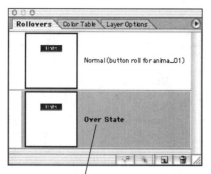

1 Create a **new rollover** thumbnail for a slice. (We unchecked the "Include Slices and Image Maps" option for the Rollovers palette.)

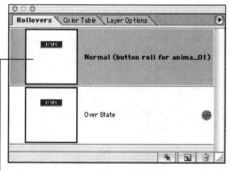

2 Add frames to the animation via the **Animation** palette.

3 When you click the **Normal** rollover thumbnail...

4 ...all the frames except the first frame disappear from the palette.

It's easy to program a secondary rollover so it triggers an animation sequence—and it makes for a lively and entertaining Web page. To achieve this effect, you'll combine the new rollover and animation skills you've acquired.

To make a rollover trigger an animation sequence:

1. On the Rollovers palette, create a new rollover thumbnail for a selected slice in an image, preferably using the Over state (see page 474) **1**.

2. With the new rollover thumbnail selected on the Rollovers palette (not the Normal rollover thumbnail), click on the Animation palette and create frames and events for the animation (see page 484) **2**. Or copy frames and paste frames (using commands from the Animation palette menu) from another animation file.

3. Click the Normal rollover thumbnail **3**. All the frames except the first frame will temporarily disappear from the Animation palette **4**.

4. Save the file and preview it using the Preview in Default Browser button. 🔎

TIP Choose Palette Options from the Rollovers palette menu, check Include Animation Frames, then click OK. On the Rollovers palette, click the arrow next to a rollover state **5**, and animation frame thumbnails for that state will display.

7.0!

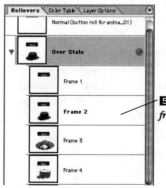

5 Animation frame thumbnails

Rollover Trigger Animation

The Warp Text feature, which lets you apply any of 14 distortions, makes it easy to create text animations.

To create a warped type animation:

1. Open or create an image that has a Background, and a layer with editable type surrounded by transparency.

2. Choose the type layer on the Layers palette **1**.

3. Display the Animation palette, click the first frame, then click the "Duplicate current frame" button.

4. With the Type tool still selected, click the Create Warp button on the Type options bar **2**.

5. In the Warp Text dialog box:

Choose a warp style from the Style pop-up menu **3**.
and
Click Horizontal or Vertical to control the direction of the warp.
and
Use the Bend, Horizontal Distortion, and Vertical Distortion sliders or fields to achieve the desired degree of "warpage." Your adjustments will preview in the image window.

6. Click OK **4**.

7. The current frame in the Animation palette will update to display the warp. With the second frame still selected, click the Tween button on the Animation palette. Click Layers: All Layers, enter the desired number of Frames to Add, then click OK.

8. Choose a delay value for the frames, and click the Play button on the Animation palette to run the animation.

TIP Not all of ImageReady's animation features may be available for warped vertical type.

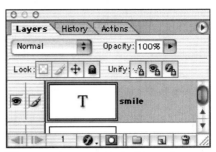

1 *Start with a normal **editable type layer**.*

2 *Click the **Create Warp** button on the **Type** tool options bar.*

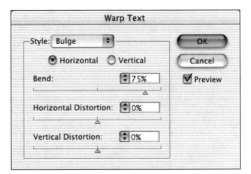

3 *Adjust the **Style** and **Bend** parameters in the **Warp Text** dialog box.*

4 *The finished **warped type animation***

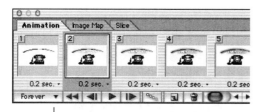

1 *As long as the file stays in the* **Photoshop** *format, each animation element stays on a* **separate layer**.

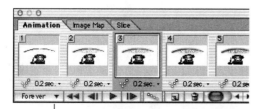

2 *In the Save* **Optimized** *format, the animation frames are unchanged, but now each layer* **matches** *a specific* **frame** *in the animation.*

To remove or adjust warped type:

1. Choose a warped type layer.

2. Choose the Type tool, then click the Create Warp button 🝰 on the Type tool options bar.

3. To remove the warp, from the Style pop-up menu, choose None.
or
To adjust the warp, choose a different Style; or click the opposite orientation button; or adjust the Bend, Horizontal Distortion, or Vertical Distortion settings.

TIP You can also click any frame on the Animation Palette, then click the Create Warp button and adjust the warp for just that frame.

To save a GIF animation:

Use File > **Save** to save an animation as a Photoshop file; the GIF settings currently on the Optimize palette will be stored in the file. Choose the Perceptual, Selective, or Adaptive palette from the Optimize palette, and whichever Dither method you think will help to smooth the transitions between frames. The Save command has no effect on the Layers palette (compare this with the Save Optimized command, which is discussed next) **1**. This is the file to keep for future editing.

When you use File > **Save Optimized** (Ctrl-Alt-S/Cmd-Option-S), the format is automatically set to GIF—not Photoshop. There is one exception to this: If the file contains a rollover that triggers an animation, the format will automatically be set to HTML instead of GIF. The Save Optimized command has a dramatic effect on layers. Instead of preserving the separate layer elements that make up the animation, Save Optimized matches each layer to a specific frame in the animation **2**. Watch what happens on the Layers palette when you reopen the Save Optimized file. Read more about the Save Optimized command on page 456.

To optimize an animation:

1. Choose Optimize Animation from the Animation palette menu.

2. Check Optimize By: Bounding Box to save the initial frame, as well as just the areas that are modified from one frame to the next 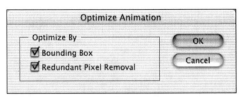. This will reduce the file size, but it also may limit which GIF editors besides ImageReady can edit it.
and/or
Check Redundant Pixel Removal to remove any pixels in an object or a background that don't change, and thus would be repetitive (redundant) when each new frame loads. This also helps to reduce the file size.

Note: Neither option will change the way the animation actually looks—it all happens behind the scenes.

1 *Click either or both **Optimize By** options in the **Optimize Animation** dialog box.*

Ways to slim an animation down

The speed at which an animation plays back in a browser is partially determined by the speed of the Web viewer's CPU, as well as such factors as the browser version and the amount of RAM currently allocated to the browser.

If the animation you've created is too large or unwieldly to be played back in the browser, or if it takes too long to download, here are a couple of remedies: Either lower its file size using the Image > Image Size command, or lower its file size by cropping. Regardless of which method you use, be sure to work on a copy of the file (use File > Save As).

In addition to cropping, you can also reduce a file's size by lowering the number of layers or animation frames it contains, or by lowering the number of colors in its color table. Remember, a smaller file size makes for faster downloading. (Did we say that before?)

Soft-edged effects

Most of the layer effects produce soft-edged shadows and colors. Soft edges don't always optimize well in the GIF format, but GIF is the only format that can be used for animations. Keep this in mind as you create animations, and be sure to preview them using the Preview in Default Browser button. ⚑ Try using the new Transparency Dither options (see page 445).

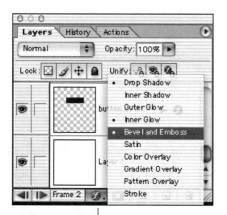

1 *Add layer effect pop-up menu*

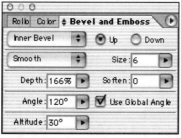

2 *Choose **separate** settings for each **effect**.*

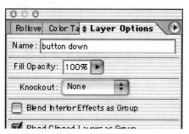

3 *When a layer name is clicked, the **Layer Options** palette displays.*

Layer effects

ImageReady offers the same layer effects as Photoshop (see page 244). While Photoshop controls layer options through the Layer Style dialog box, in ImageReady, they're handled using a contextual Layer Options palette.

Effects work the same way in Photoshop as they do in ImageReady. They're listed below the name of the layer to which they're applied, and they move with that layer. You'll find an expand/collapse arrow on the right side for listing the effects, and a hide/show icon for each effect.

To apply layer effects in ImageReady:

1. Choose a layer.

2. Choose an effect from the Layer > Layer Style submenu.
or
Choose from the "Add layer effect" pop-up menu ⚙ at the bottom of the Layers palette **1**.

3. Choose options for the effect from the Layer Options palette. The Options palette will show different options for each effect **2**.

4. *Optional:* Apply additional effects to the same layer.

5. Click any layer name to bring back the Layer Options palette. See page 260 for information on these features. If the options shown in figure **3** aren't visible on the Layer Options palette, choose Show Options from the palette menu.

TIP You can copy one effect at a time by dragging it to another layer. Or drag a layer's main Effects bar over another layer to copy all the effects under that bar.

TIP Click the up/down arrowhead on the Options palette tab to show more options (e.g., the Contour options) for each effect. Check out the full set of options for Bevel and Emboss!

(Continued on the following page)

TIP To display an applicable context menu for layers or effects, right-click/Ctrl-click a layer name, an effect layer name, or the layer's main Effects bar 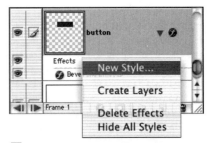.

To remove a layer effect:

To remove one effect, drag it over the "Delete layer" (trash) button on the Layers palette.

or

To remove all the effects under a layer, drag the layer's main Effects bar over the "Delete layer" button **2**.

1 *This **context menu** will open if you right-click/Control-click an **Effects** bar.*

Other layer features in ImageReady

■ Here's an easy way to remember which image edits apply automatically to animation frames and which don't: Changes that are made via the Layers palette don't alter actual pixels and thus **don't** automatically appear on new animation frames or rollover states. These changes include choosing a different blending mode, adjusting a layer's opacity, hiding or showing a layer, applying or adjusting an effect, and moving layer elements. Except for moving layer imagery, modifications made without using the Layers palette **do** apply automatically to animation frames.

■ To help you navigate through frames on the Animation palette, you can use the Current frame number readout, Previous frame button, or Next frame button on the Layers palette **3**.

■ To align image elements (e.g., navigation buttons) on a Web page layout, link those layers, then choose Layer > Align Linked (see page 273).

■ To organize layers and effects, you can create layer sets, which can be shown or hidden as needed (see pages 145 and 136).

■ To protect layers and layer sets, you can use the lock commands in ImageReady (see pages 145 and 147).

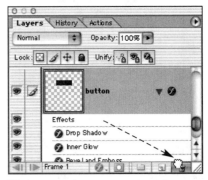

2 *Drag the **Effects** bar over the **Delete** layer button.*

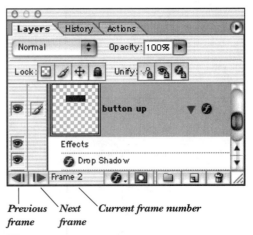

Previous frame   *Next frame*   *Current frame number*

3 *Use these buttons on the **Layers** palette to navigate through frames on the **Animation** palette.*

Remove Layer Effects; Other Layer Features

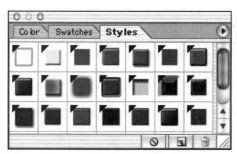

1 *This is the **Small Thumbnail** display mode on the **Styles** palette. Styles that contain **rollovers** have a triangle in the upper-left corner.*

2 *This is the **Large Thumbnail** display mode on the **Styles** palette in ImageReady. (In Large Thumbnail mode in Photoshop, large thumbnails display without the text.)*

3 *After choosing a layer, **click** a swatch or swatch name on the **Styles** palette.*

The Styles palette is a convenient place to store individual effects or combinations of effects. Once saved on the Styles palette, an effect or effects combo can be applied to any layer with a click of the mouse. The same styles are available in both Image-Ready and Photoshop (they're stored in Adobe Photoshop 7 > Presets > Styles).

In ImageReady, choose from three display modes for the Styles palette from the palette menu: Small Thumbnail **1**, Small List, or Large Thumbnail (name and swatch) **2**.

(To save an effect as a style, see the following page.)

To apply a style to a layer:

Choose a layer, then click a style on the Styles palette **3**.
or
Drag a Style name or swatch over any selected or unselected layer on the Layers palette **4**.
or
Drag a Style name or swatch over imagery in the image window.

Note: Normally, when you apply a style to a layer, any currently applied effects are replaced by the effects in the style. But if you hold down Shift as you click or drag a style name, that style's effects will be *added* to any existing effects—not replace them. Effects in the style will *replace* any existing effect with the same name, however (e.g., a Drop Shadow effect in the style will replace a Drop Shadow effect that's already been applied to the layer).

4 *Or drag directly from the **Styles** palette to a layer on the **Layers** palette.*

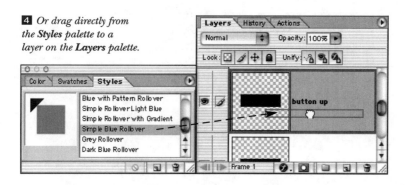

Layer Styles

To preserve a layer effect as a style:

1. In Photoshop or ImageReady, display the Styles palette.

2. Drag one nested effect layer onto the Styles palette.

   or

   To preserve a combination of effects, drag the nested Effects bar from the Layers palette onto the Styles palette **1**.

   Regardless of which method you use, a New Style 1 will be created.

3. With the new style still selected, choose Style Options from the Styles palette menu, rename the style, then click OK **2**.

Rollover styles

Rollover states can be stored in a style, along with layer effects. To do this, create a layer-based slice for an ImageReady layer, then create a rollover for that layer. Drag the layer name or the layer shape over the Styles palette, or select the layer name and choose New Style from the Styles palette menu. Be sure to check Include Rollover States in the Style Options dialog box **2**. Click OK.

Now you can drag the rollover style thumbnail (designated by the triangle in the upper-left corner) from the Styles palette over a layer name or layer shape in the image window to apply that rollover. Or click the thumbnail to apply it to the currently active layer.

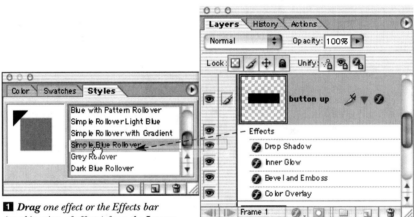

1 *Drag one effect or the Effects bar (combination of effects) from the **Layers** palette to the **Styles** palette...*

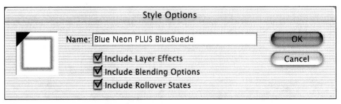

2 *...then **rename** the new style.*

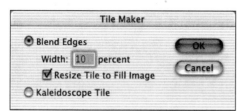

1 *Choose tiling options in the **Tile Maker** dialog box.*

Background tiling

Tiling produces a repetition of the same image in a checkerboard pattern. It's a frequently used method for filling (and decorating) the background of a Web page. Why use tiling rather than one large image for this purpose? First, because a small tile file will download more quickly than a large image will. And second, a tiled image will always fill the viewer's entire browser window—regardless of the window size.

You can use ImageReady to convert an image into an HTML tile file and then attach that HTML tile file as a background to a particular image (see the instructions on the next two pages). The background will display when the file is previewed in a browser. You could also assign a color instead of a tiled image to fill the background of a Web page.

To create a tile for an HTML background:

1. In ImageReady, open an image to be used for the tile. Use a low-contrast image with close color values, if possible, so the imagery and type that download on top of it will be readable.

2. If there are any slices, right-click/Ctrl-click and choose Delete All Slices, or choose Slices > Delete All.

3. *Optional:* Crop the image if you want to use only part of it.

4. Choose Filter > Other > Tile Maker.

5. Click Blend Edges **1** to make each tile edge blend (overlap) with the next tile. Enter a Width percentage (1–20) for the amount of blending (overlap).

6. Check Resize Tile to Fill Image to make the tile size match the current image size. With this option unchecked, the tile will be reduced in size by the current Width amount (e.g., a Width of 10 will reduce the tile size by 10 percent).
   or

(Continued on the following page)

Click Kaleidoscope Tile to have the filter generate an abstract image from the original.

7. Click OK **1**–**2**.

8. Choose File > Save Optimized (Ctrl-Alt-S/Cmd-Option-S), change the default name, choose a location in which to save it, then click Save.

To preview an image as a tiled background:

1. Open an image in ImageReady.

2. Right-click/Ctrl-click and choose Delete All Slices, or choose Slices > Delete All.

3. Choose File > Output Settings > Background.

4. Click View As: Background **3**.

5. Click OK.

6. To preview the background, click the Preview in Default Browser button on the Toolbox, or press the button and choose from the available browsers.

1 *This image was tiled using the **Tile Maker** filter, with Blend Edges, Width 10, and Resize options chosen. The tile edges blend.*

2 *This image was optimized for use as a background image, but the Tile Maker filter **wasn't** used on it, so the tile edges don't blend.*

3 *The **Output Settings** dialog box with the **Background** pane displayed, and View Document As: **Background** chosen*

Take a road more traveled

While ImageReady is capable of producing HTML background tiling, you may find reason to attach a tiled background to your Web page in a Web-page creation program like Adobe GoLive or Macromedia Dreamweaver. Ask your Web programmer or layout specialist which program to use to code background tiling into the overall Web-page code.

Tiling tips

■ An image will be repeated, if necessary, to fit within the dimensions of the browser window. If you don't want the background image to repeat at all, use a large optimized image of around 800-by-800 pixels that contains few colors and shapes.

■ If the file you've chosen for the background image contains an animation, the animation will automatically play back repetitively across the browser page. Visually overwhelming, yes, but maybe just the kind of effect you're looking for.

1 *The **Output Settings** dialog box with the **Background** pane displayed, and View Document As: **Image** chosen.*

To attach an HTML tile file as a background for an image:

1. Open the image.

2. Choose File > Output Settings > Background.

3. Choose Default Settings from the Settings pop-up menu, and click View Document As: Image (if available) **1**.

4. Click Choose, locate the optimized file, then click Open.
and/or
To choose a solid color for the background, choose a color from the BG Color drop-down menu, or if a color swatch is displayed, click the swatch and choose a color from the color picker (check Only Web Colors). This color will display while any imagery is downloading, and through any transparent areas in the main image or tile.

5. Click OK.

6. To preview the background, click the Preview in Default Browser button [image] on the Toolbox, or press the button and choose from the available browsers.

To remove an HTML tile background or solid color from an image:

1. Open the image, then choose File > Output Settings > Background.

2. Delete the file name from the Image field.
or
Choose None from the Color pop-up menu.

3. Click OK.

HTML Background Tiling

To use Photoshop's Save for Web dialog box:

As we mentioned earlier in this chapter, Photoshop's Save for Web dialog box is like ImageReady Lite. ImageReady has all of the same optimizing features as the Save for Web dialog box—and much, much more. If you want to learn more about the Save for Web optimizing features, just use the page numbers in the callouts in the illustration below to direct you to the equivalent information about ImageReady.

TIP The shortcut for opening the Save for Web dialog box is Ctrl-Shift-Alt-S/ Cmd-Option-Shift-S.

TIP Choose Edit Output Settings from the Optimize menu to change the HTML and image output settings (see page 456).

Preview tabs (upper-left corner of the dialog box): See page 448.

Slice Visibility: See page 464.

Preview menu: See pages 453–454.

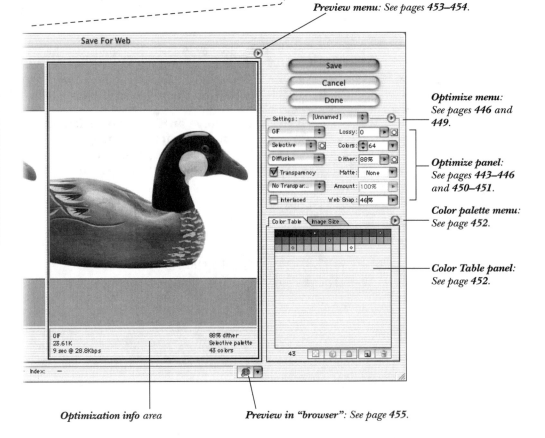

Optimize menu: See pages 446 and 449.

Optimize panel: See pages 443–446 and 450–451.

Color palette menu: See page 452.

Color Table panel: See page 452.

Optimization info area

Preview in "browser": See page 455.

SHORTCUTS **A**

	Windows 98/NT	Mac OS
GENERAL SHORTCUTS		
Show/hide all palettes, including Toolbox	Tab	Tab
Show/hide all but Toolbox	Shift + Tab	Shift + Tab
Undo	Ctrl + Z	Cmd + Z
Accept crop, transform, or any dialog box	Enter	Return or Enter
Toggle Cancel to Reset in dialog box	Alt	Opt
Cancel crop, transform, or any dialog box	Esc or Ctrl + . (period)	Esc or Cmd + . (period)
Accept type tool entry via keyboard	Enter (on numeric keypad)	Enter
Activate button in alert dialog box	First letter of button (e.g., N = No)	First letter of button (e.g., N = No)
Increase value in highlighted field by 1 or .1 (or .01, in Rotate Canvas)	Up Arrow	Up Arrow
Increase value in highlighted field by 10 or 1 (or .1, in Rotate Canvas)	Shift + Up Arrow	Shift + Up Arrow
Decrease value in highlighted field by 1 (or .1)	Down Arrow	Down Arrow
Decrease value in highlighted field by 10 (or 1)	Shift + Down Arrow	Shift + Down Arrow
Adjust angle in 15° increments	Shift + drag in angle wheel	Shift + drag in angle wheel
Cancel out of pop-up slider (mouse button up)	Esc	Esc
Commits edit in pop-up slider (mouse button up)	Enter	Return or Enter
Help	F1	Help
Access Adobe Online	Click on identifier icon on Toolbox	Click on identifier icon on Toolbox
PALETTES		
Show/hide Brushes	F5	F5
Show/hide Color	F6	F6
Show/hide Layers	F7	F7
Show/hide Info	F8	F8
Show/hide Actions	F9	F9
Show Options bar	Double-click tool, or press Enter if tool is selected	Double-click tool, or press Return if tool is selected

	Windows 98/NT	Mac OS
TOOLS		
Choose a tool		
Rectangular Marquee	M	M
Move	V	V
Lasso	L	L
Magic Wand	W	W
Crop	C	C
Slice	K	K
Healing Brush	J	J
Brush	B	B
Clone Stamp	S	S
History Brush	Y	Y
Eraser	E	E
Gradient	G	G
Blur	R	R
Dodge	O	O
Path Selection	A	A
Type	T	T
Pen	P	P
Shape	U	U
Notes	N	N
Eyedropper	I	I
Hand	H	H
Zoom	Z	Z
Cycle through tools		
Marquee tools	Shift + M	Shift + M
Lasso tools	Shift + L	Shift + L
Rubber Stamp tools	Shift + S	Shift + S
Blur, Sharpen, and Smudge tools	Shift + R	Shift + R
Dodge, Burn, and Sponge tools	Shift + O	Shift + O
Pen tools	Shift + P	Shift + P
Type tools	Shift + T	Shift + T
Eyedropper tools	Shift + I	Shift + I
Cycle through above tools	Alt + click in tool slot	Option + click in tool slot

	Windows 98/NT	Mac OS
Toggle tools		
Move tool	Ctrl	Cmd
Hand tool	Spacebar	Spacebar
Zoom Out	Spacebar + - (minus)	Spacebar + - (minus)
Zoom In	Spacebar + + (plus)	Spacebar + + (plus)
Precise cursors	Caps Lock	Caps Lock
Pencil to Eyedropper	Alt	Option
Line to Eyedropper	Alt	Option
Paint Bucket to Eyedropper	Alt	Option
Blur to Sharpen; Sharpen to Blur	Alt	Option
Dodge to Burn; Burn to Dodge	Alt	Option
TOOL BEHAVIOR		
Change brush opacity in 10% increments	Number keys (2 = 20%, 3 = 30%)	Number keys (2 = 20%, 3 = 30%)
Change brush opacity in 1% increments	Number keys (2 + 3 = 23%)	Number keys (2 + 3 = 23%)
Constrain tools		
Constrain to horizontal or vertical axis (Eraser, Brush, Pencil, Blur, Sharpen, Smudge, Dodge, or Burn tool)	Shift + drag	Shift+ drag
Draw, erase, etc. in straight lines (Eraser, Brush, Pencil, Blur, Sharpen, Smudge, Dodge, or Burn tool)	Shift + click	Shift + click
Constrain to 45° axis (Line, Gradients, (or Convert Point tool)	Shift + drag	Shift + drag
Crop tool		
Rotate crop marquee	Drag outside crop marquee	Drag outside crop marquee
Move crop marquee	Drag inside crop marquee	Drag inside crop marquee
Resize crop marquee	Drag crop handles	Drag crop handles
Maintain aspect ratio of crop box	Shift + drag handles	Shift + drag handles
Resize crop from center	Alt + drag handles	Option + drag handles
Constrain crop from center	Alt + Shift + drag handles	Option + Shift + drag handles
Apply crop	Enter	Enter/Return
Slice tool		
Toggle between Slice and Slice Select tool	Ctrl	Cmd
Draw square slice	Shift + drag	Shift + drag
Draw from center outward	Alt + drag	Option + drag

	Windows 98/NT	Mac OS
Draw square slice from center outward	Alt + Shift + drag	Option + Shift + drag
Reposition slice while drawing it	Spacebar + drag	Spacebar + drag

Move tool

Move constrained to 45°	Shift + drag	Shift + drag
Copy selection or layer	Alt + drag	Option + drag
Select layer by name	Right-click	Control + click
Select topmost visible layer	Right-mouse + Alt + click	Control + Option + click
Link with topmost visible layer	Right mouse + Shift + click	Control + Shift + click
Nudge layer or selection 1 pixel	arrow key	arrow key
Nudge layer or selection 10 pixels	Shift + arrow key	Shift + arrow key

Lasso tool

Add to selection	Shift + click, then draw	Shift + click, then draw
Delete from selection	Alt + click, then draw	Option + click, then draw
Intersect with selection	Alt + Shift + click, then draw	Option + Shift + click, then draw
Temporary Polygonal Lasso	Hold down Alt, then click	Hold down Option, then click

Polygonal Lasso tool

Add to selection	Shift + click, then draw	Shift + click, then draw
Delete from selection	Alt + click, then draw	Option + click, then draw
Intersect with selection	Alt + Shift + click, then draw	Option + Shift + click, then draw
Temporary Lasso	Alt + drag	Option + drag
Constrain to 45° while drawing	Shift + drag	Shift + drag

Magnetic Lasso tool

Add to selection	Shift + click, then draw	Shift + click, then draw
Delete from selection	Alt + click, then draw	Option + click, then draw
Intersect with selection	Alt + Shift + click, then draw	Option + Shift + click, then draw
Add point	Single click	Single click
Remove last point	Backspace or Delete	Delete key
Close path	Double-click or Enter	Double-click or Enter or Return
Close path using straight line segment	Alt + double-click	Option + double-click
Cancel operation	Esc	Esc/Cmd + . (Period)
Switch to Lasso	Alt + drag	Option + drag
Switch to Polygonal Lasso	Alt + click	Option + click
Increase width option	] (close bracket)	] (close bracket)
Decrease width option	[(open bracket)	[(open bracket)

	Windows 98/NT	**Mac OS**
Eraser tool		
Erase to History	Alt + drag	Option + drag
Smudge tool		
Smudge using Foreground color	Alt	Option
Burn and Dodge tools		
Set Burn or Dodge to Shadows	Alt + Shift + S	Option + Shift + S
Set Burn or Dodge to Midtones	Alt + Shift + M	Option + Shift + M
Set Burn or Dodge to Highlights	Alt + Shift + H	Option + Shift + H
Sponge tool		
Desaturate setting	Alt + Shift + D	Option + Shift + D
Saturate setting	Alt + Shift + S	Option + Shift + S
Freeform Pen tool (Magnetic option)		
Add point	Single click	Single click
Remove last point	Backspace or Delete	Delete
Close path	Double-click or Enter	Double-click or Enter
Close path using straight line segment	Alt + double-click	Option + double-click
Cancel operation	Esc	Esc
Switch to Freeform Pen	Alt + drag	Option + drag
Switch to Pen	Alt + click	Option + click
Increase magnetic width	] (close bracket)	] (close bracket)
Decrease magnetic width	[(open bracket)	[(open bracket)
Measure tool		
Measure constrained to 45° axis	Shift + drag	Shift + drag
Create protractor	Alt + click + drag end point	Option + click + drag end point
Eyedropper tool		
Choose Background color	Alt + click	Option + click
Toggle to Color Sampler tool	Shift	Shift
Delete sampler	Alt + Shift + click on sampler	Option + Shift + click on sampler
Color Sampler tool		
Delete sampler	Alt + click on sampler	Option + click on sampler
DISPLAY		
Change view size		
Zoom in	Ctrl + Spacebar + click or drag or Ctrl + Alt + + (plus)	Cmd + Spacebar + click or drag or Cmd + + (plus)
Zoom out	Ctrl + Alt + Spacebar + click or Ctrl + Alt + - (minus)	Cmd + Option + Spacebar + click or Cmd + - (minus)

	Windows 98/NT	Mac OS
Zoom to 100%	Double-click Zoom tool	Double-click Zoom tool
Zoom to fit in window	Double-click Hand tool	Double-click Hand tool
Fit on screen	Ctrl + 0	Cmd + 0
Actual pixels	Ctrl + Alt + 0	Cmd + Option + 0
Zoom in without changing window size	Ctrl + + (plus)	Cmd + Option + + (plus)
Zoom out without changing window size	Ctrl + - (minus)	Cmd + Option + - (minus)
Change zoom %, keep zoom field highlighted	Shift + Enter	Shift + Return

Hand tool

Toggle to zoom in	Ctrl	Z
Toggle to zoom out	Alt	Option
Fit image on screen	Double-click tool	Double-click tool

Zoom tool

Zoom out	Alt + click	Option + click
Actual pixels	Double-click tool	Double-click tool

Show/hide

Show/hide Extras	Ctrl + H	Cmd + H
Show/hide Path	Ctrl + Shift + H	Cmd + Shift + H
Show/hide Rulers	Ctrl + R	Cmd + R
Show/hide Guides	Ctrl + ; (semicolon)	Cmd + ; (semicolon)
Show/hide Grid	Ctrl + " (quote)	Cmd + " (quote)

Grid and guides

Snap to Guides	Shift + Ctrl + ; (semicolon)	Shift + Cmd + ; (semicolon)
Lock Guides	Alt + Ctrl + ; (semicolon)	Option + Cmd + ; (semicolon)
Snap to Grid	Shift + Ctrl + " (quote)	Shift + Cmd + " (quote)
Snap guide to ruler	Shift + drag guide	Shift + drag guide
Toggle guide orientation (H/V)	Alt + drag guide	Option + drag guide

Move image in window

Scroll up one screen	Page up	Page up
Scroll up 10 units	Shift + page up	Shift + page up
Scroll down one screen	Page down	Page down
Scroll down 10 units	Shift + page down	Shift + page down
Scroll left one screen	Ctrl + page up	Cmd + page up
Scroll left 10 units	Ctrl + Shift + page up	Cmd + Shift + page up
Scroll right one screen	Ctrl + page down	Cmd + page down

	Windows 98/NT	Mac OS
Scroll right 10 units	Ctrl + Shift + page down	Cmd + Shift + page down
Move view to upper-left corner	Home key	Home key
Move view to lower-right corner	End key	End key

Navigator palette

Scroll viewable area of image	Drag view box	Drag view box
Move view to new portion of image	Click in preview area	Click in preview area
View new portion of image	Ctrl + drag in preview area	Cmd + drag in preview area
Change zoom %, keep zoom field highlighted	Shift-Enter	Shift-Return

Screen modes

Toggle Standard/Full Screen with Menu/Full Screen modes	F	F
Toggle menu when in Full Screen with Menu mode	Shift + F	Shift + F

View

Preview > CMYK	Ctrl + Y	Cmd + Y
Gamut Warning	Ctrl + Shift + Y	Cmd + Shift + Y

FILE MENU

New	Ctrl + N	Cmd + N
New, with last document size settings		Cmd + Option + N
Open	Ctrl + O	Cmd + O
Browse	Ctrl + Shift + O	Cmd + Shift + O
Open As	Ctrl + Alt + O	
Close	Ctrl + W	Cmd + W
Save	Ctrl + S	Cmd + S
Save As	Ctrl + Shift + S	Cmd + Shift + S
Save A Copy	Ctrl + Alt + S	Cmd + Option + S
Save for Web	Ctrl + Alt + Shift + S	Cmd + Option + Shift + S
Revert	F12	F12
Page Setup	Ctrl + Shift + P	Cmd + Shift + P
Print with Preview	Ctrl + P	Cmd + P
Print	Ctrl + Alt + P	Cmd + Option + P
Print One Copy	Ctrl + Alt + Shift + P	Cmd + Option + Shift + P
Exit/Quit	Ctrl + Q	Cmd + Q
Jump to Adobe ImageReady	Ctrl + Shift + M	Cmd + Shift + M

	Windows 98/NT	Mac OS
PREFERENCES		
General	Ctrl + K	Cmd + K
File Handling	Ctrl + 2	Cmd + 2
Display & Cursors	Ctrl + 3	Cmd + 3
Transparency & Gamut	Ctrl + 4	Cmd + 4
Units & Rulers	Ctrl + 5	Cmd + 5
Guides, Grid & Slices	Ctrl + 6	Cmd + 6
Plug-Ins & Scratch Disks	Ctrl + 7	Cmd + 7
Memory & Image Cache	Ctrl + 8	Cmd + 8
CLIPBOARD		
Cut	Ctrl + X	Cmd + X
Copy	Ctrl + C	Cmd + C
Copy Merged	Ctrl + Shift + C	Cmd + Shift + C
Paste	Ctrl + V	Cmd + V
Paste Into	Ctrl + Shift + V	Cmd + Shift + V

BLENDING MODES

Layer blending modes

	Windows 98/NT	Mac OS
Set layer to next blend mode	Shift + + (plus)	Shift + + (plus)
Set layer to previous blend mode	Shift + - (minus)	Shift + - (minus)

Blending modes for brush or layer

	Windows 98/NT	Mac OS
Normal	Alt + Shift + N	Option + Shift + N
Dissolve	Alt + Shift + I	Option + Shift + I
Darken	Alt + Shift + K	Option + Shift + K
Multiply	Alt + Shift + M	Option + Shift + M
Color Burn	Alt + Shift + B	Option + Shift + B
Linear Burn	Alt + Shift + A	Option + Shift + A
Lighten	Alt + Shift + G	Option + Shift + G
Screen	Alt + Shift + S	Option + Shift + S
Color Dodge	Alt + Shift + D	Option + Shift + D
Linear Dodge	Alt + Shift + W	Option + Shift + W
Overlay	Alt + Shift + O	Option + Shift + O
Soft Light	Alt + Shift + F	Option + Shift + F
Hard Light	Alt + Shift + H	Option + Shift + H
Vivid Light	Alt + Shift + V	Option + Shift + V

	Windows 98/NT	Mac OS
Linear Light	Alt + Shift + J	Option + Shift + J
Pin Light	Alt + Shift + Z	Option + Shift + Z
Difference	Alt + Shift + E	Option + Shift + E
Exclusion	Alt + Shift + X	Option + Shift + X
Hue	Alt + Shift + U	Option + Shift + U
Saturation	Alt + Shift + T	Option + Shift + T
Color	Alt + Shift + C	Option + Shift + C
Luminosity	Alt + Shift + Y	Option + Shift + Y
Behind (Brush tool only)	Alt + Shift + Q	Option + Shift + Q

COLOR
Colors

	Windows 98/NT	Mac OS
Swap Foreground/Background colors	X	X
Reset to default colors	D	D

Fill

	Windows 98/NT	Mac OS
Open Fill dialog box	Shift + Backspace	Shift + Delete
Fill with Foreground color	Alt + Delete/Backspace	Option + Delete
Fill with Foreground color, Preserve Transparency on	Shift + Alt + Delete/Backspace	Shift + Option + Delete
Fill with Background color	Ctrl + Delete/Backspace	Cmd + Delete
Fill with Background color, Preserve Transparency on	Shift + Ctrl + Delete/Backspace	Shift + Cmd + Delete
Fill from previous history state	Ctrl + Alt + Backspace	Cmd + Option + Delete

Color palette

	Windows 98/NT	Mac OS
Cycle through color bars	Shift + click on color bar	Shift + click on color bar
Open Color Bar dialog box	Ctrl + click on color bar	Cmd + click on color bar
Choose specific color bar	Right-click on color bar	Control + click on color bar

Swatches palette

	Windows 98/NT	Mac OS
Add Foreground color as a new swatch	Click in empty slot	Click in empty slot
Choose swatch as Foreground color	Click on swatch	Click on swatch
Choose swatch as Background color	Ctrl + click on swatch	Cmd + click on swatch
Delete swatch	Alt + click on swatch	Option + click on swatch

BRUSHES
Brushes palette

	Windows 98/NT	Mac OS
Select first brush	Shift + ,	Shift + ,
Select previous brush	,	,

	Windows 98/NT	Mac OS
Select next brush	. (period)	. (period)
Select last brush	Shift + . (period)	Shift + . (period)
Increase brush size	]	]
Decrease brush size	[	[
Increase brush hardness	Shift +]	Shift +]
Decrease brush hardness	Shift + [	Shift + [
Delete brush	Alt + click	Option + click
Rename brush	Double-click on stroke thumbnail	Double-click on stroke thumbnail

SELECTIONS

All	Ctrl + A	Cmd + A
Deselect	Ctrl + D	Cmd + D
Reselect	Ctrl + Shift + D	Cmd + Shift + D
Inverse	Ctrl + Shift + I	Cmd + Shift + I
Feather	Ctrl + Alt + D	Cmd + Option + D
Nudge selection marquee 1 pixel	Arrow key	Arrow key
Nudge selection marquee 10 pixels	Shift + arrow key	Shift + arrow key

FILTERS

Reapply last filter	Ctrl + F	Cmd + F
Fade last filter	Ctrl + Shift + F	Cmd + Shift + F
Reapply filter with the last settings	Ctrl + Alt + F	Cmd + Option + F

Lighting Effects dialog box

Clone light in preview area	Alt + drag light	Option + drag light
Delete light in preview area	Delete key	Delete key
Adjust light footprint without changing angle	Shift + drag handle	Shift + drag handle
Adjust light angle without changing footprint	Ctrl + drag handle	Cmd + drag handle

LAYERS

Layer menu

New > Layer	Ctrl + Shift + N	Cmd + Shift + N
New Layer without dialog box	Ctrl + Alt + Shift + N	Cmd + Option + Shift + N
Layer via Copy	Ctrl + J	Cmd + J
Layer via Cut	Ctrl + Shift + J	Cmd + Shift + J
Group with previous	Ctrl + G	Cmd + G

	Windows 98/NT	**Mac OS**
Ungroup	Ctrl + Shift + G	Cmd + Shift + G
Merge Down/Linked/Group	Ctrl + E	Cmd + E
Merge Visible	Shift + Ctrl + E	Shift + Cmd + E
Display menu with list of layers in the image at the current pointer location	Ctrl + click	Cmd + click

Layers palette

Show/hide layer	Click in eye column	Click in eye column
Toggle show all layers/show just this layer	Alt + click on eye column	Option + click on eye column
Show/hide multiple layers	Click + drag thru eye column	Click + drag thru eye column
Link layer to current target layer	Click in link column	Click in link column
Turn on/off linking for multiple layers	Click + drag thru link column	Click + drag thru link column
Create new, empty layer	Click Create new layer button	Click Create new layer button
Create new, empty layers with Layer Options dialog box	Alt + click Create new layer button	Option + click Create new layer button
Duplicate layer	Drag layer to Create new layer button	Drag layer to Create new layer button
Delete layer using warning alert	Click Delete current layer button	Click Delete current layer button
Delete layer, bypass warning alert	Alt + click Delete current layer button	Option + click Delete current layer button
Change layer opacity in 10% increments	Number keys (2 = 20%, 3 = 30%)	Number keys (2 = 20%, 3 = 30%)
Change layer opacity in 1% increments	Number keys (2 + 3 = 23%)	Number keys (2 + 3 = 23%)
Toggle last chosen Lock button for target layer on/off	/ (forward slash)	/ (forward slash)
Load layer pixels as selection	Ctrl + click layer thumbnail	Cmd + click layer thumbnail
Add layer pixels to selection	Ctrl + Shift + click layer thumbnail	Cmd + Shift + click layer thumbnail
Subtract layer pixels from selection	Ctrl + Alt + click layer thumbnail	Cmd + Option + click layer thumbnail
Intersect layer pixels with selection	Ctrl + Alt + Shift + click layer thumbnail	Cmd + Option + Shift + click layer thumbnail
Activate top layer	Shift + Alt +]	Shift + Option +]
Activate next layer (up)	Alt +]	Option+]
Activate previous layer (down)	Alt + [	Option + [
Activate bottom layer	Shift + Alt + [	Shift + Option + [
Edit layer style	Double-click layer	Double-click layer

	Windows 98/NT	Mac OS
Layer Effects		
Toggle show/hide effect	Show/hide layer effect eye icon	Show/hide layer effect eye icon
Edit layer effect options	Double-click layer effect name	Double-click layer effect name
Move effect to different layer	Drag effect on Layers palette	Drag effect on Layers palette
In Layer Style dialog box		
Drop Shadow	Ctrl + 1	Cmd + 1
Inner Shadow	Ctrl + 2	Cmd + 2
Outer Glow	Ctrl + 3	Cmd + 3
Inner Glow	Ctrl + 4	Cmd + 4
Bevel and Emboss	Ctrl + 5	Cmd + 5
Satin	Ctrl + 6	Cmd + 6
Color Overlay	Ctrl + 7	Cmd + 7
Gradient Overlay	Ctrl + 8	Cmd + 8
Pattern Overlay	Ctrl + 9	Cmd + 9
Stroke	Ctrl + 0	Cmd + 0
Adjustment layers		
Edit adjustment layer	Double-click adjustment thumbnail	Double-click adjustment thumbnail
Layer masks		
Create layer mask with Reveal All/ Reveal Selection	Click on mask button	Click on mask button
Create layer mask with Hide All/ Hide Selection	Alt + click on mask button	Option + click on mask button
Link/unlink layer and layer mask	Click Lock layer mask icon	Click Lock layer mask icon
Open Layer Mask Options dialog box	Double-click layer mask thumbnail	Double-click layer mask thumbnail
Toggle layer mask on/off	Shift + click layer mask thumbnail	Shift + click layer mask thumbnail
Toggle rubylith mode on/off	\	\
Toggle viewing layer mask/composite	Alt + click layer mask thumbnail	Option + click layer mask thumbnail
Toggle Group/Ungroup with previous	Alt + click line between layers	Option + click line between layers
Merge layers		
Merge down a copy of current layer into layer below	Alt + Merge Down	Option + Merge Down
Merge a copy of all visible layers into current layer	Alt + Merge Visible	Option + Merge Visible
Merge a copy of linked layers into current layer	Alt + Merge Linked	Option + Merge Linked

	Windows 98/NT	**Mac OS**
Arrange layers		
Bring to Front	Ctrl + Shift +]	Cmd + Shift +]
Bring Forward	Ctrl +]	Cmd +]
Send to Back	Ctrl + Shift + [	Cmd + Shift + [
Send Backward	Ctrl + [	Cmd + [
CHANNELS PALETTE		
Target individual channels	Ctrl + [1–9]	Cmd + [1–9]
Target composite channel	Ctrl + ~ (tilde)	Cmd + ~ (tilde)
Show or hide channel	Click in eye column	Click in eye column
Add/remove channel to targeted channels	Shift + click on channel	Shift + click on channel
Create new channel	Click on New Channel button	Click on New Channel button
Create new channel with Channel Options dialog box	Alt + click New Channel button	Option + click New Channel button
Duplicate channel	Drag channel to New Channel button	Drag channel to New Channel button
Delete channel using warning alert	Click Delete Channel button	Click Delete Channel button
Delete channel bypassing warning alert	Alt + click Delete Channel button	Option + click Delete Channel button
Create new spot color channel	Ctrl + click New Channel button	Cmd + click New Channel button
Create new channel from selection	Click on Save Selection button	Click on Save Selection button
Create new channel from selection, with Channel Options dialog box	Alt + click Save Selection button	Option + click Save Selection button
Load channel as selection	Click Load Selection button or Ctrl + click channel thumbnail	Click Load Selection button or Cmd + click channel thumbnail
Add channel to selection	Shift + click Load Selection button or Ctrl + Shift + click channel thumbnail	Shift + click Load Selection button or Cmd + Shift + click channel thumbnail
Subtract channel from selection	Alt + click Load Selection button or Ctrl + Alt + click channel thumbnail	Option + click Load Selection button or Cmd + Option + click channel thumbnail
Intersect channel with selection	Alt + Shift + click Load Selection button or Ctrl + Alt + Shift + click thumbnail	Option + Shift + click Load Selection button or Cmd + Option + Shift + click thumbnail
Edit Channel Options	Double-click alpha channel name	Double-click alpha channel name
QUICK MASK		
Toggle Quick Mask on/off	Q	Q
Invert Quick Mask mode	Alt + click Quick Mask button	Option + click Quick Mask button
Open Quick Mask Options dialog box	Double-click Quick Mask button	Double-click Quick Mask button

	Windows 98/NT	**Mac OS**
PATHS		
Paths palette		
Create new path	Click New Path button	Click New Path button
Create new path, with New Path dialog box	Alt + click New Path button	Option + click New Path button
Duplicate path	Drag path to New Path button	Drag path to New Path button
Delete path using warning alert	Click Delete Path button	Click Delete Path button
Delete path, bypass warning alert	Alt + click Delete Path button	Option + click Delete Path button
Save work path into path item	Drag Work Path onto New Path button	Drag Work Path onto New Path button
Convert selection into work path	Click Make Work Path button	Click Make Work Path button
Convert selection into work path, with Work Path dialog box	Alt + click Make Work Path button	Option + click Make Work Path button
Convert path into selection	Click Load Selection button	Click Load Selection button
Convert path into selection, with Make Selection dialog box	Alt + click Load Selection button	Option + click Load Selection button
Stroke/fill path		
Stroke path with Foreground color	Click Stroke Path button	Click Stroke Path button
Stroke path with Stroke Path dialog box	Alt + click Stroke Path button	Option + click Stroke Path button
Fill path with Foreground color	Click Fill Path button	Click Fill Path button
Fill path using Fill Path dialog box	Alt + click Fill Path button	Option + click Fill Path button
Paths and selections		
Load path as selection	Ctrl + click path thumbnail	Cmd + click path thumbnail
Add path to selection	Ctrl + Shift + click path thumbnail	Cmd + Shift + click path thumbnail
Subtract path from selection	Ctrl + Alt + click path thumbnail	Cmd + Option + click path thumbnail
Intersect path with selection	Ctrl + Alt + Shift + click thumbnail	Cmd + Option + Shift + click thumbnail
HISTORY		
History palette		
Step forward	Shift + Ctrl + Z	Cmd + Shift + Z
Step backward	Alt + Ctrl + Z	Cmd + Option + Z
Duplicate history state (other than current)	Alt + click state	Option + click state
Create new snapshot	Click Create new snapshot button	Click Create new snapshot button
Create new document from state/snapshot	Click Create new document button	Click Create new document button

	Windows 98/NT	**Mac OS**
History brush tool		
Constrain to horizontal or vertical axis	Shift + drag	Shift + drag
Paint straight lines	Shift + click	Shift + click
TRANSFORM		
Free Transform	Ctrl + T	Cmd + T
Transform > Again	Ctrl + Shift + T	Cmd + Shift + T
Free Transform, with duplication	Ctrl + Alt + T	Cmd + Option + T
Transform Again, with duplication	Ctrl + Alt + Shift + T	Cmd + Option + Shift + T
Scale using center point (free transform)	Alt + drag corner handles	Option + drag corner handles
Skew using center point (free transform)	Ctrl + Alt + Shift + drag side handles	Cmd + Option + Shift + drag side handles
ADJUSTMENTS DIALOGS		
Levels	Ctrl + L	Cmd + L
Auto Levels	Ctrl + Shift + L	Cmd + Shift + L
Auto Contrast	Ctrl + Alt + Shift + L	Cmd + Option + Shift + L
Curves	Ctrl + M	Cmd + M
Color Balance	Ctrl + B	Cmd + B
Hue/Saturation	Ctrl + U	Cmd + U
Desaturate	Ctrl + Shift + U	Cmd + Shift + U
Invert	Ctrl + I	Cmd + I
Reopen dialog box		
Levels, with last settings	Ctrl + Alt + L	Cmd + Option + L
Curves, with last settings	Ctrl + Alt + M	Cmd + Option + M
Color Balance, with last settings	Ctrl + Alt + B	Cmd + Option + B
Hue/Saturation, with last settings	Ctrl + Alt + U	Cmd + Option + U
TYPE		
Type tools		
Designate type origin	Click or click + drag	Click or click + drag
Designate type origin while over existing type	Shift + click or click + drag	Shift + click or click + drag
Re-edit existing type	Click on type in image	Click on type in image
Edit Type Options	Double-click type thumbnail	Double-click type thumbnail
Reposition type while typing	Ctrl + drag type in image	Cmd + drag type in image
Zoom in on image	Ctrl + + (plus)	Cmd + + (plus)
Zoom out of image	Ctrl + - (minus)	Cmd + - (minus)

	Windows 98/NT	**Mac OS**
Alignment		
Left (or Top)	Ctrl + Shift + L	Cmd + Shift + L
Center	Ctrl + Shift + C	Cmd + Shift + C
Right (or Bottom)	Ctrl + Shift + R	Cmd + Shift + R
Size		
Increase point size by 2 pts.	Ctrl + Shift + >	Cmd + Shift + >
Increase point size by 10 pts.	Ctrl + Alt + Shift + >	Cmd + Option + Shift + >
Decrease point size by 2 pts.	Ctrl + Shift + <	Cmd + Shift + <
Decrease point size by 10 pts.	Ctrl + Alt + Shift + <	Cmd + Option + Shift + <
Choose 100% Horizontal Scale	Ctrl + Shift + X	Cmd + Shift + X
Choose 100% Vertical Scale	Ctrl + Alt + Shift + X	Cmd + Option + Shift + X
Leading		
Increase leading by 2 pts.	Alt + Down Arrow	Option + Down Arrow
Increase leading by 10 pts.	Ctrl + Alt + Down Arrow	Cmd + Option + Down Arrow
Decrease leading by 2 pts.	Alt + Up Arrow	Option + Up Arrow
Decrease leading by 10 pts.	Ctrl + Alt + Up Arrow	Cmd + Option + Up Arrow
Auto leading	Ctrl + Alt + Shift + A	Cmd + Option + Shift + A
Justification		
Justify paragraph, left align last line	Ctrl + Shift + J	Cmd + Shift + J
Justify paragraph, force last line	Ctrl+ Shift + F	Cmd + Shift + F
Hyphenation		
Toggle paragraph hyphenation on/off	Ctrl + Alt + Shift + H	Cmd + Opt + Shift + H
Toggle single/every-line composer	Ctrl + Alt + Shift + T	Cmd + Opt + Shift + T
Kerning/tracking		
Increase kern/track $^{20}/_{1000}$ em space	Alt + Right Arrow	Option + Right Arrow
Increase kern/track $^{100}/_{1000}$ em space	Ctrl + Alt + Right Arrow	Cmd + Option + Right Arrow
Decrease kern/track $^{20}/_{1000}$ em space	Alt + Left Arrow	Option + Left Arrow
Decrease kern/track $^{100}/_{1000}$ em space	Ctrl + Alt + Left Arrow	Cmd + Option + Left Arrow
Set tracking to 0	Ctrl + Shift + Q	Cmd + Control + Shift + Q
Baseline shift		
Increase baseline shift by 2 pts.	Alt + Shift + Up + Arrow	Option + Shift + Up + Arrow
Increase baseline shift by 10 pts.	Ctrl + Alt + Shift + Up Arrow	Cmd + Option + Shift + Up Arrow
Decrease baseline shift by 2 pts.	Alt + Shift + Down + Arrow	Option + Shift + Down + Arrow
Decrease baseline shift by 10 pts. Arrow	Ctrl + Alt + Shift + Down Arrow	Cmd + Option + Shift + Down

	Windows 98/NT	Mac OS
Move insertion point		
Move to the right one character	Right arrow	Right arrow
Move to the left one character	Left arrow	Left arrow
Move up one line	Up arrow	Up arrow
Move down one line	Down arrow	Down arrow
Move to the right one word	Ctrl + Right Arrow	Cmd + Right Arrow
Move to the left one word	Ctrl + Left Arrow	Cmd + Left Arrow
Select		
Select word	Double-click	Double-click
Select one character to the right	Shift + Right Arrow	Shift + Right Arrow
Select one character to the left	Shift + Left Arrow	Shift + Left Arrow
Select one word to the right	Ctrl + Shift + Right Arrow	Cmd + Shift + Right Arrow
Select one word to the left	Ctrl + Shift + Left Arrow	Cmd + Shift + Left Arrow
Select one line	Triple-click	Triple-click
Select one line above	Shift + Up Arrow	Shift + Up Arrow
Select one line below	Shift + Down Arrow	Shift + Down Arrow
Select one paragraph	Quadruple-click	Quadruple-click
Select all characters	Ctrl + A	Cmd + A
Select characters from insertion point	Shift + click	Shift + click
Horizontal Type Mask and Vertical Type Mask tools		
Add to selection	Shift + click, then draw	Shift + click, then draw
Designate type origin	Click + drag	Click + drag
CURVES DIALOG BOX		
Add color as new point on curve	Ctrl + click in image	Cmd + click in image
Add color as individual points for each curve	Ctrl + Shift + click	Cmd + Shift + click
Move 2 points	Arrow keys	Arrow keys
Move points in multiples of 15	Shift + arrow keys	Shift + arrow keys
Add point	Click in grid	Click in grid
Delete point	Ctrl + click on point	Cmd + click on point
Deselect all points	Ctrl + D	Cmd + D
Toggle grid between fine and coarse	Alt + click in grid	Option + click in grid
Select next control point	Ctrl + Tab	Cmd + Tab
Select previous control point	Ctrl + Shift + Tab	Cmd + Shift + Tab
Select multiple control points	Shift + click	Shift + click

	Windows 98/NT	Mac OS
HUE/SATURATION DIALOG BOX		
Move range to new location	Click in image	Click in image
Add to range	Shift + click/drag in image	Shift + click/drag in image
Subtract from range	Alt + click/drag in image	Option + click/drag in image
Edit master	Ctrl + tilde	Cmd + tilde
Edit individual colors	Ctrl + 1–6	Cmd + 1–6
Slide color spectrum	Ctrl + drag on ramp	Cmd + drag on ramp
GRADIENT EDITOR		
New gradient	Ctrl + N	Cmd + N
Save gradient as map settings	Ctrl + Alt + click Save button	Cmd + Option + click Save button
Noncontiguous selection of gradients in list	Ctrl + click gradient name	Cmd + click gradient name
Contiguous selection of gradients in list	Shift + click gradient name	Shift + click gradient name

©Naomi Shea

Index

Index

©Alan Mazzetti, Repair Ripoffs